A Programmer's
GUIDE TO SOUND

Tim Kientzle

Addison-Wesley Developers Press

An Imprint of Addison Wesley Longman, Inc.
Reading, Massachusetts • Harlow, England • Menlo Park, California
Berkeley, California • Don Mills, Ontario • Sydney
Bonn • Amsterdam • Tokyo • Mexico City

Many of the designations used by manufacturers and sellers to distinguish their products are claimed as trademarks. Where those designations appear in this book, and Addison-Wesley was aware of a trademark claim, the designations have been printed in initial capital letters or all capital letters.

The author and publisher have taken care in preparation of this book, but make no expressed or implied warranty of any kind and assume no responsibility for errors or omissions. No liability is assumed for incidental or consequential damages in connection with or arising out of the use of the information or programs contained herein.

Library of Congress Cataloging-in-Publication Data
Kientzle, Tim.
  A programmer's guide to sound / Tim Kientzle.
    p. cm.
  Includes index.
  ISBN 0-201-41972-6
  1. Electronic digital computers--Programming. 2. Computer sound
processing.   I. Title.
QA76.6.K55 1997
006.5--dc21   97-29920

Sponsoring Editor	Mary Treseler
Project Manager	John Fuller
Production Coordinator	Melissa M. Lima
Cover Design	Dietz Design
Text Design and Composition	Tim Kientzle

Addison-Wesley books are available for bulk purchases by corporations, institutions, and other organizations. For more information please contact the Corporate, Government, and Special Sales Department at (800) 238-9682.

A-W Developers Press is a division of Addison Wesley Longman, Inc.
Find A-W Developers Press on the World Wide Web at:
http://www.aw.com/devpress/

1 2 3 4 5 6 7 8 9 -MA- 01 00 99 98 97
First Printing, September, 1997

TO BETH

Contents

• v •

Part Two   System Specifics

Part Three   Compression

Part Four   *General File Formats*

Part Five   Music File Formats

Part Six   Audio Processing

Part Seven   Appendices

Introduction

Some years ago, I found myself researching a variety of different file formats. For graphics formats such as GIF, I had no trouble finding good, detailed descriptions of the overall format and the bit-by-bit details of the underlying compression. However, I was hard pressed to find comparable information for even the most popular audio formats. Although basic formats are outlined in several places, solid information about the compression methods used is surprisingly hard to find.

I'm clearly not the only person to have encountered this problem. I've seen many audio tools that boast of support for a vast number of file formats but lack support for any compression methods at all.

In the intervening years, I have managed to piece together much of the necessary information and wrote this book to bring it together in a single place. This book documents a variety of common audio file formats and audio compression standards and also discusses many related issues that arise in programming audio on a variety of systems.

Source Code

As a programmer, I'm often frustrated when otherwise excellent books stop just short of giving me the details I need. For that reason, when I write about programming, I include detailed, tested source code. Even if the text description omits some critical detail, you can always look at the source code, which must somehow address that issue. By organizing the book around the source code, I hope to ensure that every detail you need is here.

In many cases, you may be able to use my source code directly in your software project. I encourage you to do so. But please pay attention to the conditions listed at the top of each source file. If you have any questions, please feel free to contact me through the publisher. Even if you don't have questions, I'd like to hear about how you used my code and what your experiences were. If there's enough interest and the publisher is willing, I may update this book to better fit your needs.

About This Book

The software in this book was tested by automatically extracting the source code from the electronic files for the book. The book was produced using noweb, LaTeX 2_ε and dvips typesetting software running on FreeBSD 2.1. The source code was tested under FreeBSD 2.1 with the GNU GCC compiler suite, Windows 95 using Microsoft Visual C++ 5.0, and Mac OS 7.6 using Metrowerks CodeWarrior Gold 11. NuMega's BoundsChecker and ParaSoft's CodeWizard were also used to test the source. The text fonts are Adobe Garamond and Computer Modern Typewriter; headings are in Adobe Helvetica and Monotype Arial. Artwork is from the *Digitart Musicville* collection from Image Club Graphics.

Acknowledgments

Many people have generously contributed to the production of this book: Mary Treseler and the staff at Addison-Wesley patiently endured my seemingly endless revisions and last-minute changes. George Wright, John Miles, Bobby Prince, Gene Turnbow, Tom White, and several others provided thoughtful, honest criticism of my early drafts, which immeasurably improved the end product. Jon Erickson and the staff at *Dr. Dobb's Journal* supported my efforts. Above all, Beth provided invaluable help in organizing, editing, indexing, and endless other tasks.

As always, any errors that remain are my own.

Part One
Basics

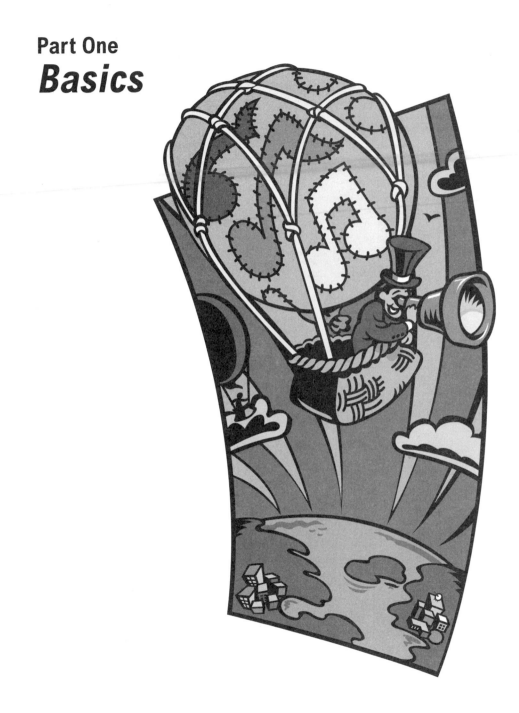

From Hollow Logs to Cyberspace 1

Sound is integral to the way we understand and relate to our world. Throughout our lives, a variety of sounds weave themselves into a rich tapestry, one that we rely on more than we may realize. I've been told that babies, even in the womb, are soothed by the gentle murmuring of their mothers' heartbeats. When a cold or flu dampens our hearing, the world seems farther away and flatter than usual because the sound is different. A still forest glen is carpeted not only with leaves, but also with the many small sounds of insects, birds, and whispering breezes.

This soundscape applies to computer use as much as to any other part of our lives. The clicking of keyboards and mouse buttons, the gentle rasping of CD-ROM drives, the hum of power supply fans, and the distinctive scream of connecting modems are just some of the sounds that texture our computer use.

Now that high-quality synthesized sound is fairly standard on desktop computers, our daily soundscape is gradually extending into the virtual realm. Currently, this capability is used primarily in games and in various network broadcasting systems, but it's finding other uses, as well. For example, spoken help allows the user to focus on the problem on her screen rather than switch back and forth between the problem and the help text. Similarly, some programmers have found that attaching sounds to certain program actions makes their programs easier to debug.

However, storing and delivering sound is more subtle than it might appear because of the interplay of a number of issues.

Storage Space High-quality sound requires either a lot of storage or the mastery of some tricky compression issues.

Speed (Bandwidth) If you use uncompressed sound, you need to ensure that it can be transferred rapidly and reliably, which is especially difficult with network applications. If you use compressed sound, you need to make sure that the processor can uncompress it quickly enough. In practice, it's possible to have too much or too little compression.

Latency (Delay) When you play a sound, there are always delays while you access data on disk, set up sound hardware, establish a network connection, or begin your processing. Even one-hundredth of a second can be objectionable in many applications.

These issues can interact in subtle ways. Suppose you're writing a two-way network conferencing program. Modems have limited bandwidth, so you'll need good compression to maintain high audio quality. However, many audio compression algorithms work with large blocks at a time. If you use one of these algorithms, you need to wait to collect enough sound, then compress and transfer it, which can introduce a lengthy delay. Balancing bandwidth and latency requirements requires care.

What Is Sound?

Technically, sound consists of pressure waves that move through a compressible medium. The precise mechanics vary somewhat according to the material, but the broad principles are the same.[1] Molecules, whether of air, water, or metal, like to keep—on average—equally far apart from all of their neighbors. So whenever the molecules in one area are squeezed closer together than their neighbors, they force themselves back apart, which in turn compresses their neighbors.

Figure 1.1 shows how this works. The dark areas indicate where molecules are squeezed close together (these are areas of high pressure). The lighter areas indicate where molecules are relatively sparse. When the tightly compressed molecules in the first image force themselves apart, they end up compressing their neighbors, who in turn will force apart to compress their neighbors, and so on.

There are several ways to think about this dance. If you follow a single molecule, you'll find that it wiggles back and forth but doesn't move very far. But if you stand back and look at the high pressure as the important entity, you'll see Figure 1.1 as illustrating a moving *pressure wave*.

Natural Sounds

Vibrating objects and pressure waves are the basic components of sound. If you hit a drum, the top of the drum will vibrate. As it moves up, it compresses the air above it,

---

[1]A typical college physics class is divided into several sections, separated by the following statement: "Everything so far in this class is wrong; now we're going to learn how it really works." This applies to acoustics just as well as it does to relativity. This section deliberately takes a rather simplified approach.

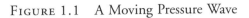

FIGURE 1.1   A Moving Pressure Wave

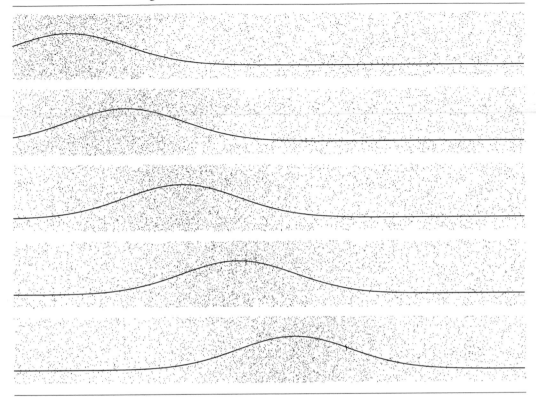

and the resulting pressure wave moves through the air until it presses against your eardrum.

Other sound sources act in similar ways. When a flute player blows across a flute, a column of air in the flute vibrates. The flute player can alter this vibration by opening and closing holes along the length of the flute. If you rub your wet finger around the top of a crystal glass, the glass will vibrate.

This vibration is sometimes complex. A human voice is the combination of vibrating vocal cords; vibrating air within the lungs, throat, mouth, and sinuses; and vibrations within the fluid of the body itself. The sound of an acoustic guitar or a violin is the result of a vibrating string that causes the air within the instrument to vibrate. A trombonist's lips cause the air within the trombone to vibrate. Most of the sound that people associate with these instruments is due to the shape and properties of the air chamber. Most sounds you hear in your everyday life are the result of a complex interaction of different vibrating parts.

Electronic Sounds

Any sound you hear is, at some point, a series of pressure waves. If you had a very sensitive pressure meter and connected it to a pen plotter, you would get a line that went up when the pressure increased and down when it decreased. Figure 1.2 shows the connection—the wavy line goes up when the pressure is high (indicated by a dark background) and down when the pressure is low.

FIGURE 1.2   Converting a Sound from Air to Electricity

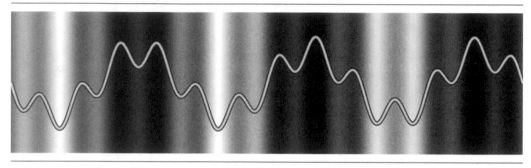

Fortunately, it's relatively easy to construct such a pressure meter. You start with a piece of paper or a thin plastic film. When the air pressure rises, the air will push against the paper and move it back. When the pressure falls, the paper will be pulled forward. You then attach a small loop of wire to the back of the paper and place a magnet nearby. As the air pressure rises and falls, it will push the paper back and forth, moving the wire with it. As the wire moves through the magnet's field, a small, varying electric current is produced. This electric signal duplicates the pressure variations in the air. Figure 1.3 shows how this works.

Conveniently, this microphone mechanism also works in reverse: A changing electric signal in the wire loop will press the paper back and forth, which will in turn generate pressure waves in the nearby air. Thus, speakers and microphones operate on the same principles.

The ability to convert sounds between pressure waves in air and varying electric signals is the basis of such everyday marvels as radio, telephone, and tape recorders. It has also provided fertile ground for people interested in experimenting with sounds. Many types of sound manipulation are easier with electronic devices than with acoustic devices, and vice versa. For example, jazz trumpeters have placed different materials—from wet rags to kazoos—into their trumpets to vary the sound. These effects are difficult to imitate electronically. Conversely, many sound manipulations that are fairly simple to

FIGURE 1.3   A Microphone in Action

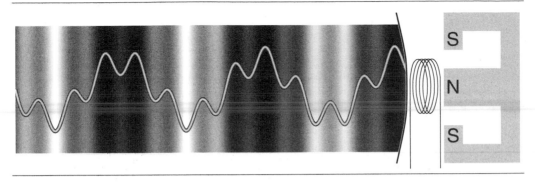

produce using electronic circuitry, including the chorus and distortion effects popular with electric guitarists, are nearly impossible to achieve with acoustic devices.

Sounds We Hear

Before I begin to discuss digital sounds in the next section, I want to introduce an important theme. Ultimately, the purpose of producing any sound is for people to hear it. As a result, you have to understand *what* people hear and *how* they hear it. For instance, although our ears are essentially pressure-sensitive organs, few people claim to hear the pressure changes associated with weather patterns. The sounds bats use to detect flying insects are equally inaudible to humans.

The fact that humans can hear only some sounds has a number of interesting repercussions. It means that you will frequently be able to simplify your sound data or processing without severely affecting the final result. This most commonly arises when you have bandwidth or storage restrictions.

For example, consider what occurs if you try to use very-high-quality sound processing techniques on mid-range computers. If your software is unable to process the data quickly enough, the sound may stop and start as data is relayed through the system. In this case, you can improve the user's experience by using less accurate techniques. Although the resulting sound data may technically be lower quality, you will be able to maintain a steady transfer, thus removing the more objectionable periodic gaps.

Although this example is simple and dramatic, it demonstrates the type of trade-off that is common in sound processing. In the next chapter, I'll begin to explore the science of *psychoacoustics*, the study of how people hear sound.

Digital Sounds

Just as it's possible to convert a sound between pressure waves in air and analog electric signals, it's possible to convert a varying electric signal into a series of digital values, and vice versa. However, because analog and digital sound are fundamentally different, you always lose information when you make this transformation. The trick is to understand what information is lost so that you can select what information to keep.

Digitally, a sound wave is represented as a series of numbers (called *samples*), which represent the air pressure or electric voltage at successive moments in time. When you sample an analog signal, you encounter two basic problems, illustrated in Figure 1.4. This figure shows two versions of a sound wave. The smooth black line is the original electronic version; the digital version is represented as a series of grey blocks. The first problem is that each successive value in the digital version represents a certain interval of time; each grey block has a certain width. The second problem is that digital numbers are discrete; there are only a certain number of possible heights for each block. As a result, the heights of the blocks don't quite match the wave either. These issues are discussed more fully in Chapter 3.

These two problems are basic sources of error in a digital sound signal. This error can be controlled by changing the detailed format of your sound representation, but it can never be eliminated. The problem is not: How do I get rid of this error? but rather: What errors can my application best tolerate? Other factors, such as data size and processing speed, may require you to accept greater error from some sources in order to reduce more objectionable types of errors.

FIGURE 1.4   Converting an Electronic Sound into Digital Samples

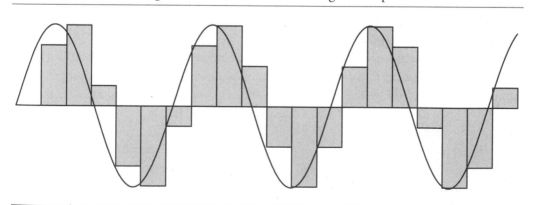

Other Resources

Audio processing is an enormous subject, and no single book can cover it in detail. After reading this book, you'll have the knowledge you need to support common sound file formats in your own software, and you'll have a collection of C++ code to help you get started. However, there are many other issues that you may need to research. Here are a few resources that I find indispensable:

- Glenn White's *The Audio Dictionary* (University of Washington Press, 1985) is a comprehensive guide to terms used in all areas of audio. The entries include both history and detailed, technical information.

- F. Richard Moore's *The Elements of Computer Music* (Prentice-Hall, 1990) is the definitive reference for computer music. Moore uses his cmusic system as a basis for describing the entire field of computer music, from low-level issues of instrument synthesis to the intriguing topic of random composition.

- Ken Pohlmann's *Principles of Digital Audio, Third Edition* (McGraw-Hill, 1995) is a detailed and thorough look at digital audio from the hardware side. In particular, Pohlmann carefully explains how hardware designs address the issues of aliasing and quantization error.

- Richard G. Lyons' *Understanding Digital Signal Processing* (Addison Wesley Longman, 1997) is a good introduction to this complex subject. I especially appreciate his coverage of digital filter design, which includes many practical programming tips.

- The *Computer Music Journal* covers all areas of computer music production, including digital audio file formats. Its web site contains sample articles and a useful archive of sounds: http://www-mitpress.mit.edu/Computer-Music-Journal/

Human Sound Perception 2

As you pick and choose among different sound formats and processing techniques, you have to juggle many criteria, including data size and processor speed. One of the most important questions is always: How good will it sound?

It would be convenient if you could simply buy a meter, point it at a speaker playing a sound, and read off the sound quality. Manufacturers of expensive stereo equipment could boast that their system "preserves 99.2 percent of the sound quality," and sound algorithms could accurately measure how much sound quality was lost. Of course, such a useful device can't be built, in part because of a fundamental, but subtle, difference between sound properties that can be *measured* and those that can be *heard*. Ultimately, the only instruments that matter are the ones attached to your head.

Psychoacoustics (a branch of *psychophysics*) is the scientific study of human hearing. Over the past century, scientists have built up a fairly detailed picture of how humans hear. The process is remarkably complex.

In the subsequent discussion, I'll distinguish between *perceptual* measures—terms that refer to perceived qualities of a sound—and terms that refer to mathematical or physical properties of a sound.

Frequency and Pitch

A trumpet and a tuba are similar instruments, but the trumpet sounds "higher" than the tuba. This perception is called *pitch*—we say that a trumpet has a "higher pitch" than a tuba. Pitch is closely related to a physical property called *frequency*.

The frequency of a sine wave is the time it takes for one complete cycle. Frequency is specified in *hertz* (abbreviated Hz), the number of complete cycles that occur in one second. (I'll also refer to *kilohertz* [kHz], which are thousands of hertz.) For reference, humans can hear sine waves roughly between 30 Hz and 20,000 Hz.

This definition of frequency relies on the fact that sine waves are *periodic*: they repeat exactly. Although much of the mathematics that is used to work with sound is based on a

FIGURE 2.1 Adding Together Two Sine Waves Creates a New Sound

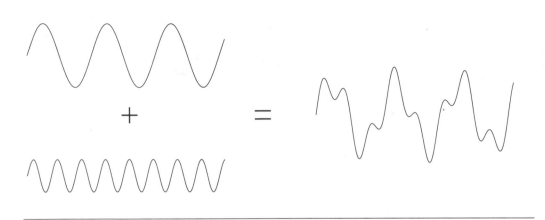

general idea of repeating signals—in particular, the Fourier transform I discuss in Chapter 24—very few real sounds are truly periodic. In practice, frequency is directly meaningful only for sine waves.

Fortunately, every sound can be broken down into a collection of sine waves. Conversely, you can build any sound by adding together a suitable collection of sine waves. The equation illustrated in Figure 2.1 works both ways: Viewed left to right, it shows how to build a new sound by adding sine waves; viewed right to left, it shows that you can break a complex sound into individual sine waves.

FIGURE 2.2 Frequency Spectrum of Figure 2.1

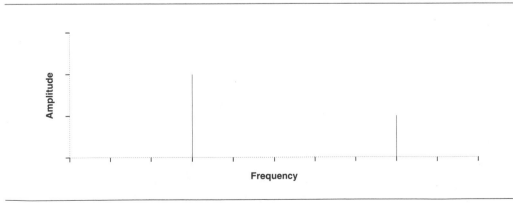

Because any sound can be broken down into sine waves, you can describe the *frequency spectrum* of a sound. The frequency spectrum of a sound is a graph of frequency versus amplitude. Figure 2.2 shows the amplitude of the composite sound in Figure 2.1. This particular spectrum is simple. It shows that there are only two frequencies, and one is twice as strong as the other. Chapter 24 describes how you can compute the frequency spectrum of a sound.

Informally, people often do refer to the frequency of a complex sound. Usually, you can measure this by computing the frequency spectrum and noting the frequency of the strongest sine wave. But this doesn't always work.

Consider Figure 2.3. Like most instrument sounds, this spectrum contains a series of evenly spaced spikes. These spikes, called *harmonics*, all appear near multiples of some *fundamental* frequency. The characteristic sound (or *timbre*—pronounced "TAM-ber") of an instrument can often be explained by the relative loudness of the different harmonics. Usually, the fundamental frequency is also the strongest frequency that appears in the sound.

The fundamental frequency seems to most closely indicate the perceived pitch of the total sound. This works well enough that some computerized instruments use a process known as *fundamental-tracking* or *pitch-tracking* to identify played notes based on the fundamental frequency of a sound. This allows computerized instruments to automatically follow a tune played on another instrument.

When discussing the frequency of a complex sound, it's probably more useful to think of it in perceptual terms: The frequency of a complex sound is the frequency of a sine wave with the same perceived pitch.

FIGURE 2.3   The Frequency Spectrum of a Real Instrument

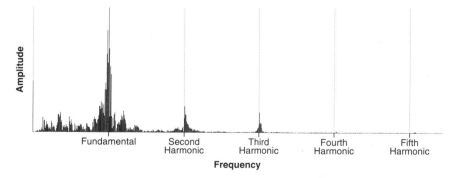

Musical Pitch

Most Western musicians work with a specific collection of pitches, called *notes*. The collection of notes currently in widespread use is called *equal tempering*, a system that has gradually evolved from the musical theories of ancient Greek mathematicians.

The Greeks are generally credited with having realized the connection between frequency and pitch. They realized that a plucked string produced different pitches, depending on its length (the length corresponds directly to the frequency), and they developed an elaborate mathematical theory to explain why certain frequencies sounded good in combination. For example, they discovered that when one sound has exactly twice the frequency of another, those sounds are especially compatible. This relation is now known as an *octave* and is so basic that today we often think of notes separated by an octave as the same note. Over time, Western musicians agreed that each octave should be divided into 12 notes. However, as I'll explain in a moment, there has been some disagreement about the exact frequency that each of those 12 notes should have.

The Greeks attempted to explain why some pairs of sounds were *consonant*—they sounded good together—while others were *dissonant*. The theory they developed is based on relative frequencies. This theory says that two sounds will be consonant if the ratio of their frequencies can be reduced to small numbers. For example, if you have two perfect sine waves, one at 660 Hz and one at 440 Hz, the ratio of their frequencies is 660:440 or 3:2. Because 3 and 2 are small numbers, you would expect these two notes to sound quite pleasant together. Following this theory, you can define note pitches relatively. You start with a single note (the *tonic*) and identify other notes according to the ratios of their frequencies to the tonic frequency.

The most important of these ratios are the *fifth* (a ratio of 3:2) and the *third* (a ratio of 5:4). If you call your starting note C, you can use these Greek ratios to define a system of 12 pitches, called *just intonation*, shown in Table 2.1. The first column gives the common names for Western notes. (The symbol ♯ is pronounced *sharp* and ♭ is pronounced *flat*.) The second and third columns give the names and ratios for the various musical *intervals*. For example, E is the "third above C."

Just intonation produces very pleasant chords. For example, the ratio of 4:5:6 is called the *major triad* and arises by combining a tonic with its third and fifth (such as C-E-G).

However, just intonation isn't very flexible. For example, if you tune an instrument so that the keys have exactly the correct ratios for just intonation, then not all notes have thirds. In the C Major tuning shown in Table 2.1, you can't play a third above E (which would have a ratio of 5:4 compared to E and 25:16 compared to C). The closest note is G♯, whose frequency is about 3 percent too high.

There are definite musical consequences of this discrepancy. For example, if you tune your favorite instrument to the just C Major scale provided in Table 2.1 and try to play a

TABLE 2.1   Frequency Ratios for Just Intonation

Note	Interval	Ratio to Tonic
C	Tonic	1:1
C♯/D♭		16:15
D	Second	9:8
D♯/E♭	Minor third	6:5
E/F♭	Third	5:4
F/E♯	Fourth	4:3
F♯/G♭		7:5
G	Fifth	3:2
G♯/A♭		8:5
A	Sixth	5:3
A♯/B♭		9:5
B/C♭	Seventh	15:8
C/B♯	Octave	2:1

major triad starting with E, the resulting chord will sound slightly "off." Depending on your point of view, this is either a serious problem or the opportunity to provide a distinctive color to your musical compositions. Historically, both points of view have been well represented.

With the rise of a standard music notation (*common practice notation*), people increasingly thought of the 12-tone scale as a series of 12 ratios, called *halftones*. Each halftone is the ratio between successive notes. Of course, with just intonation, not all halftones are the same. Table 2.2 shows just intonation again, with a column showing the ratios between successive notes (C♯ to C, for instance).

There have been many efforts to "fix" the arrangement of notes by shifting certain notes slightly. In fact, just intonation as I've presented it wasn't formulated until the 16th century. The tuning originally proposed by the Greek mathematician Pythagoras constructed the entire scale from successive fifths. His *Pythagorean tuning* scale is also shown in Table 2.2. Later attempts to reconcile Pythagorean tuning and just intonation were called *temperaments*.

The pressure to adopt a common temperament eventually led to equal tempering, which makes all halftones exactly the same. To accomplish this, you adjust the notes so that each successive pair of notes has the same ratio. Because there are 12 notes, and the octave is still a 2:1 frequency ratio, you end up with the ratio between successive keys

TABLE 2.2 Frequency Ratios for Various Tunings

Note	Just Intervals	Just Halftones	Pythagorean Intervals	Pythagorean Halftones
C	1.0		1.0	
		1.0667		1.0679
C♯/D♭	1.0667		1.0679	
		1.0547		1.0535
D	1.125		1.125	
		1.0667		1.0679
D♯/E♭	1.2		1.2013	
		1.0417		1.0535
E	1.25		1.2656	
		1.0667		1.0679
F	1.3333		1.3515	
		1.05		1.0535
F♯/G♭	1.4		1.4238	
		1.0714		1.0535
G	1.5		1.5	
		1.0667		1.0679
G♯/A♭	1.6		1.6018	
		1.0417		1.0535
A	1.6667		1.6875	
		1.08		1.0679
A♯/B♭	1.8		1.8020	
		1.0417		1.0535
B	1.875		1.8984	
		1.0667		1.0535
C	2.0		2.0	

being $\sqrt[12]{2}$, an irrational number approximately equal to 1.0595. Table 2.3 compares the frequency ratios for just intonation, Pythagorean tuning, and equal tempering.

Equal tempering is a dramatic compromise. It allows any note to serve as the basis for the scale but, in the process, erases the differences between keys. Historically, certain keys have been associated with a particular mood, in large part because of the inherent discrepancies you encounter when you try to build a 12-tone scale using perfect thirds and fifths.

Once you've decided on the frequency of your starting note, you can use the ratios described above to define a complete musical scale. The most common reference used by musicians is A440, an A note with a frequency of 440 Hz. If you use equal tempering, this gives you the frequencies shown in Table 2.4.

One reason for the adoption of equal tempering was to permit a single physical instrument to play in a variety of keys without constant retuning. However, this problem essentially evaporates with electronic instruments. Although a single physical instrument can't easily shift from C Major with just intonation to E Major with just intonation, an electronic instrument can instantly retune itself to allow such shifts even within a single song. Some modern compositions have even abandoned the 12-tone scale completely, using electronic instruments to play *micro-tonal* compositions with different numbers of divisions in the scale or *atonal* compositions that do not use fixed note pitches at all.

TABLE 2.3   Frequency Ratios for Various Tunings

Note	Just Intonation	Pythagorean Tuning	Equal Tempering
C	1.0	1.0	1.0
C♯/D♭	1.0667	1.0679	1.0595
D	1.125	1.125	1.1225
D♯/E♭	1.2	1.2013	1.1892
E	1.25	1.2656	1.2599
F	1.3333	1.3515	1.3348
F♯/G♭	1.4	1.4238	1.4142
G	1.5	1.5	1.4983
G♯/A♭	1.6	1.6018	1.5874
A	1.6667	1.6875	1.6818
A♯/B♭	1.8	1.8020	1.7818
B	1.875	1.8984	1.8877
C	2.0	2.0	2.0

Pitch and Frequency Aren't the Same

The Greek theory that pitch and frequency are essentially the same is attractively simple. However, recent experiments that attempt to measure people's sense of pitch have uncovered a number of ways in which this simple idea doesn't quite work. For example, loud sounds have a lower pitch than quiet sounds of the same frequency.

The Greek theory of sound also breaks down with very high or very low frequencies. If you carefully test a properly tuned piano, you'll discover that the high notes are tuned to a slightly higher frequency than you might expect and the low notes are tuned to a slightly lower frequency. Researchers have recently verified what piano tuners have known for a long time: People tend to hear high notes as slightly lower than they are, and similarly hear low notes as slightly higher. The Greek relation between pitch and frequency is correct only for the middle range of notes and becomes less accurate for higher and lower sounds.

For complex sounds, the picture becomes even muddier. I mentioned earlier that most instrument sounds contain strong components at multiples (harmonics) of some fundamental frequency. Typically, this fundamental frequency is also the frequency of the strongest sine wave in the sound. As a result, you can often predict the pitch of a sound by measuring the frequency spectrum and picking the loudest component. However, in some cases, the fundamental frequency is very quiet or even completely absent, and we

TABLE 2.4   Note Frequencies in Hertz Using Equal Tempering

C	32.70	65.41	130.81	261.63	523.25	1046.50	2093.00
C♯	34.65	69.30	138.59	277.18	554.36	1108.73	2217.46
D	36.71	73.42	146.83	293.66	587.33	1174.66	2349.32
D♯	38.89	77.78	155.56	311.13	622.25	1244.51	2489.02
E	41.20	82.41	164.81	329.63	659.25	1318.51	2637.02
F	43.65	87.31	174.61	349.23	698.46	1396.91	2793.83
F♯	46.25	92.50	185.00	369.99	739.99	1479.98	2959.96
G	49.00	98.00	196.00	391.99	783.99	1567.98	3135.96
G♯	51.91	103.83	207.65	415.31	830.61	1661.22	3322.44
A	55.00	110.00	220.00	**440.00**	880.00	1760.00	3520.00
A♯	58.27	116.54	233.08	466.16	932.33	1864.65	3729.31
B	61.74	123.47	246.94	493.88	987.77	1975.53	3951.07
C	65.41	130.81	261.63	523.25	1046.50	2093.00	4186.01

still hear the same pitch. Some instruments, including the piano, are known for having *stretched partials*, in which the harmonics don't appear at precise multiples of the fundamental.

Noise

If you have a frequency spectrum like the one in Figure 2.2, it makes sense to identify the loudest frequencies and use them to characterize the sound. But what if your frequency spectrum looks more like Figure 2.4? In this case, there is no one frequency, nor even a small number of frequencies, that seem to characterize the sound.

A sound that has a complete range of frequencies, like the one whose spectrum is shown in Figure 2.4, is called *noise*. This technical use of the word is different from the common use. A high-pitched squeal (for example, from an old computer monitor) may be noise in the colloquial sense, but it has a well-defined frequency spectrum and is therefore *not* noise in the technical sense. I'll use the word *noise* only in this technical sense.

Noise is surprisingly common. Most percussion instruments, including drums, wood blocks, and cymbals, produce sounds that are predominantly noise. Human voices have a large amount of noise. Moving air, whether from a person blowing or the wind rustling against a microphone head, produces noise. In a sense, the sweet tones of a flute are extracted from the noise of a person blowing air. Because the noise contains all frequencies, the flute can pick out the correct frequencies and amplify them. This idea turns out to be remarkably effective at synthesizing certain instrument sounds.

FIGURE 2.4   Frequency Spectrum of Noise

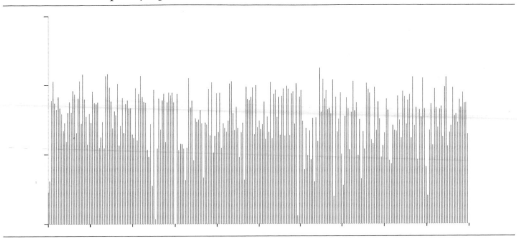

When you view noise as samples (rather than as a frequency spectrum), it consists of random data. A high-quality random-number generator is a good source of noise and forms the starting point for synthesizing many percussion sounds.

Loudness, Amplitude, and Power

In addition to pitch, the other important perceptual quality is *loudness*. The physical quantities that most closely correspond to loudness are *sound pressure* (for sounds in air) and *amplitude* (for digital or electronic sounds).

For a digital signal, the amplitude is the sample value. When confronted with millions of samples from a single sound, you're often concerned with the *peak amplitude*, the largest sample value (in absolute value) that occurs in the sound. In digital recording, you must pay attention to the peak amplitude in order to avoid *clipping distortion* (which occurs when the peak amplitude exceeds your storage format) while keeping the *signal-to-noise ratio* as high as possible. (I'll discuss both of these concepts later.) Before I define *average amplitude*, I'll digress and discuss the related concept of *power*.

The basic reason that sounds have different loudnesses is that they push on your ear with different strengths. A physicist would say that the pressure waves have different amounts of power. Waves carrying more power exert more force on the mechanisms in your ear. Electronic signals on a wire also carry power. The sound on a wire is usually carried by a varying voltage, and the instantaneous power of that sound is proportional to the square of the voltage. To determine the total power, you add up all the instantaneous power. Mathematically, this is expressed as an integral $\int v_t^2 \, dt$, where v_t is the voltage at a given time.

Because you're using sampled sounds, you don't need an integral; you can simply add up the squares of the samples. The average of the squares of the samples is proportional to the *average power*.

Because instantaneous power is related to the square of the instantaneous amplitude, it makes sense that you'd want a similar relation to hold between the average amplitude and the average power. The way to do this is to define the *average amplitude* as the *root-mean-square* (RMS) amplitude. Instead of averaging the amplitude values directly, you first square the samples, take the average (mean) of those squares, and finally take the square root of the average. This RMS technique is appropriate wherever you need to talk about the average of a rapidly changing value. In symbols, if you have N samples, and $x(i)$ is the amplitude of sample i, you have:

$$RMS \; Amplitude = \sqrt{\frac{1}{N} \sum_{i=0}^{N} (x(i))^2}$$

I've glossed over the fact that the power is only proportional to the squared sample value. That is, there's some number you need to multiply by to convert the squared sample value into the actual power. Of course, as a programmer, you probably don't ever need to know the actual electronic power, so you don't really care what this number is. What you care about is *relative power*.

Relative power is measured in *bels* or, more commonly, in *decibels* (dB) (a decibel— pronounced "DESS-a-bull"—is one-tenth of a bel). To compare two sounds, you take the ratio of their powers. The logarithm (base 10) of this ratio is the difference in bels; you multiply by 10 to get a value in decibels. For example, if one sound signal has twice as much power as another, it is $10 \log_{10}(2) \approx 3.01$ dB louder.

Notice that you can use decibels only to *compare* two different sounds. However, decibel measures are so convenient that audio engineers define a particular sound as a standard reference.[1] This sound is approximately the quietest that humans can hear. The loudest sound that humans can hear is approximately 120 dB louder (a million million times as loud as the standard reference), about the loudness of a nearby jet engine. As you can see, human hearing can deal with a very large range of loudness.

Decibel scales are also used to measure the amount of sound loss. If two different sounds with the same energy are fed through a certain electronic circuit or digital

---

[1]For the more technically inclined, this standard reference, which applies only to measuring sounds in air, is a 1,000-Hz tone producing an air pressure variation of 20 micropascals.

sound-processing algorithm, one might emerge with 6 dB less power than the other. Decibel scales are also used to measure how much noise or distortion has been (unintentionally) added to a signal.

For example, an audio compact disc uses 16-bit integers to store sound samples. This gives a total range of -32,768 to +32,767. Because the true original signal has been rounded to the nearest integer, the maximum error is 0.5, which is 2^{-16} as loud as the loudest possible sample value. Remember that power depends on the square of the amplitude, so the error has a power 2^{-32} as loud as the loudest possible signal. The ratio between the power of the loudest signal and the error (noise) is 2^{32} to 1, or $10\log_{10}(2^{32})$ ≈ 96.3 dB.

There are several ways in which decibel measurements are a good approximation of the perception of loudness. The first is that human hearing is very nearly logarithmic—the perceived difference in loudness between two sounds depends on the ratio of the powers, not the difference in power. Although not precisely correct, it's useful to think of a decibel as the minimum perceivable change in loudness.

Another way in which decibel measurements match the human perception of loudness is that perceived loudness depends very much on the relative power. In particular, there's a kind of audio illusion known as *masking*. If a sound consists of two separate components and one component is much louder than the other, then the quieter component will often be inaudible. Essentially, your hearing adjusts to the loudest sound; the quieter sound is perceived as much quieter than it actually is. This is especially pronounced when the two sounds are very close in pitch.

The masking effect is an important tool in modern audio compression. By identifying and selectively discarding quiet sounds that are masked by louder sounds, you can simplify the overall sound and make it easier to compress. A good understanding of masking allows you to identify the most audible components of a complex sound—by realizing that the most audible components are not necessarily those with the greatest amplitude.

There are other important factors that affect our perception of loudness. The first is that loudness depends in part on pitch. Human hearing is more sensitive to sounds in a certain middle range and becomes progressively less sensitive with higher and lower pitches. As a result, if you have a mid-range sound and a high-pitched sound with the same power, the mid-range sound will appear louder.

Human hearing is also less sensitive to complex sounds than it is to simple tones. In particular, high-frequency noise is relatively difficult to hear. A digital technique, called *dithering*, can convert certain types of errors into less-audible, high-frequency noise.

Overall Quality

Although there's no absolute measure for sound quality, many people use certain common audio technologies as a reference. For example, you commonly hear "CD-quality" or "voice-quality" used to describe different audio technologies. Here is a brief list of typical sound technologies, from the best sounding to the least.

Professional Professional-quality systems use high sampling rates in the digital domain and top-quality electronics in the analog parts to produce remarkably clear sound. Although few people have the luxury of dealing with these systems, it's worth keeping in mind that even CD-quality audio is not adequate for some purposes. (In particular, new systems designed for movie theaters require that the original sounds have extremely high quality.)

Compact Disc The compact disc audio system, first developed in the late 1970s, was a remarkable improvement in home audio. CDs are durable (compared with vinyl LPs), easy to use (compared with tapes), and provide clear, high-quality audio. CD technology does have some compromises, however. In particular, the 44.1-kHz sampling rate was chosen not for optimal sound quality (professional systems typically use 48 kHz), but for compatibility with early digital audio systems that used videotape.

Broadcast FM Stereo Broadcast FM became available in the 1940s. It provides good-quality sound, thanks in part to the natural noise resistance of FM receivers. FM stereo works well for typical material, where the two channels are only slightly different. It transmits a monaural signal, which is the average of the two channels, and a separate, lower-quality signal that's used to recover the stereo difference.

Broadcast AM AM radio is remarkably simple electronically and can provide reasonable audio quality if you use very good components.

Voice Speech exists primarily within a narrow band of frequencies. It's possible to design systems that can carry high-fidelity speech but aren't up to the more rigorous demands of music and other audio types.

Storing Sound Digitally 3

Digital sound storage involves two ideas that I want to discuss separately. The first idea is *sampling*. Sampling involves periodically measuring the analog signal and using these measurements (samples) instead of the original signal. The second idea is *quantization*, which is the process of taking infinite-precision analog samples and rounding them. In this chapter, I'll take a careful look at these two processes and the errors they introduce.

Sampled Sound Formats

Today, we usually think of storing samples as binary numbers, but they can be stored in other ways, as well. I'll first discuss a couple of ways to sample a sound signal and then take a careful look at exactly what the sampling process does to the sound.

Pulse Amplitude Modulation (PAM)

Sound sampling was invented by engineers to solve a variety of problems. One problem was how to put two or more sound signals on a single wire. One way to do this is to take "slices" of each sound and interleave the slices of different sounds onto the same wire. The receiver can then pick out the slices that correspond to a particular sound and reassemble them.

If you take a single sound signal from this scheme, it looks something like Figure 3.1. In this approach, the sound is transmitted as a series of pulses, with the amplitude (height) of each pulse representing the sound strength at that point, hence the name *pulse amplitude modulation* (PAM).

One of the strengths of PAM is that it is easy to convert an analog signal into PAM (a fast switch suffices) and very easy to convert a PAM signal back into its analog equivalent (just pass it through an analog low-pass filter). In fact, digital-to-analog and analog-to-digital converters frequently use PAM as an intermediate format.

FIGURE 3.1   Pulse Amplitude Modulation

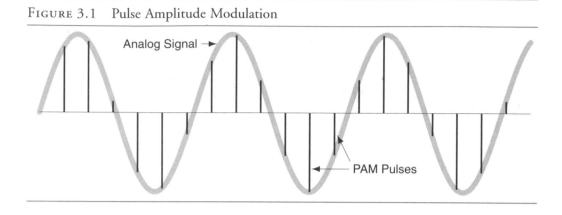

Pulse Width Modulation (PWM)

Sampling techniques are also used to reduce the degradation of sound signals as they are sent through wires or radio connections. In practice, these connections often damage the amplitude of signals that pass through them but tend to preserve the timing. A method that converts an analog sound signal into a stream of timed pulses reduces the amount of damage that such a signal can experience. *Pulse width modulation* (PWM), illustrated in Figure 3.2, does exactly this. Like PAM, PWM represents each sample as a pulse, but it uses the width or duration of the pulse, rather than the amplitude, to represent the strength.

PWM has been used in computer applications in an interesting way. By its very nature, a computer speaker has the built-in ability to roughly convert PWM into an analog signal. As a result, you can feed a PWM signal directly to computer speaker

FIGURE 3.2   Pulse Width Modulation

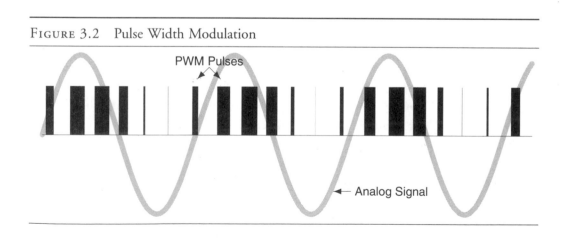

circuits. Creating a PWM signal in software merely requires careful high-speed timing and a single-bit output port. This technique allows software to produce comparatively high-quality sound even on systems such as the original IBM PC, which only supported a single-bit output to the built-in speaker.

Pulse Code Modulation (PCM)

A third alternative is to represent each sample with a series of pulses that represent its binary *code*. *Pulse code modulation* (PCM), when sent over a single wire, looks something like Figure 3.3.

FIGURE 3.3   Pulse Code Modulation for the Engineer

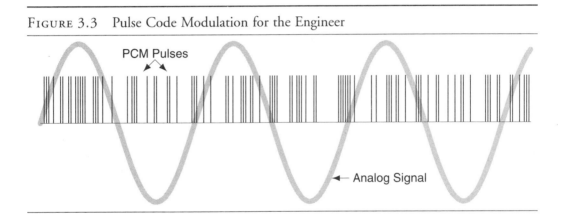

Figure 3.3 has an obvious problem: It's hard to tell where each code begins and ends. This problem can be solved by adding another wire to carry pulses indicating the beginning of each code or by designing the signal to be *self-clocking*. Self-clocking signals have special features that allow the receiver to automatically detect where each new code begins. For example, instead of using binary numbers for the codes, you might construct codes so that no code contains three consecutive ones, and then insert three consecutive ones into the signal just before each code. There are a variety of similar methods that offer various trade-offs of signal rate (how fast you can pump data through a single wire), error tolerance (how likely the data is to be unrecoverable when errors occur), and complexity. Engineers refer to these as *encoding*, or *modulation*, techniques.

For programmers, of course, the various modulation techniques are irrelevant. In a computer's memory, the successive binary values are simply stored as numbers. For most programmers, PCM can be thought of as in Figure 3.4. (Even here, issues of byte order and the format of signed numbers present compatibility problems.)

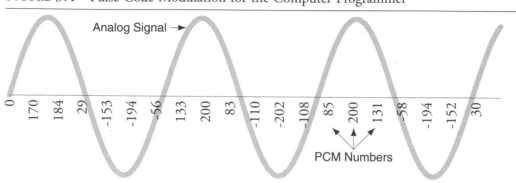

FIGURE 3.4   Pulse Code Modulation for the Computer Programmer

Side Effects of Sampling

Sampled sound systems are typically characterized by the *sampling rate*, the number of samples that are used to represent one second of sound. For example, audio compact discs store 44,100 samples for each second of sound. In contrast, most telephone systems use only 8,000 samples for one second of sound.

The effect of this sampling is easy to quantify. Harry Nyquist (1889-1976) discovered that a sampled sound signal can exactly reproduce any sound whose frequency is less than half the sampling rate. Thus, a compact disc can exactly reproduce frequencies up to 22,050 hertz[1]; a telephone connection can exactly reproduce frequencies up to 4,000 Hz. These values are not accidental, of course. Human speech is contained primarily below 3,000 Hz; few humans can hear at all above about 20,000 Hz. Half the sampling rate is often referred to as the *Nyquist limit*.

Of course, the Nyquist limit is a slight oversimplification in practice. If you have a 4,000-Hz signal and you record it at 8,000 samples per second, you'll have a digital signal that alternates between positive and negative values. If you have a 3,999-Hz signal, it will look very much like the 4,000-Hz signal unless you look at it for a long time. In theory, this means that you can distinguish the two. However, most sounds change rapidly enough that these subtle differences can be lost. As a result, digital sampling does introduce some distortion as you approach the Nyquist limit.

---

[1]It's convenient to interpret the word *hertz* as "per second." It's used to refer to both sampling rates (where it refers to samples per second) and frequency (where it refers to cycles per second).

Aliasing

The Nyquist limit I described earlier is an important restriction, with many practical repercussions. Imagine that you're working with sounds sampled at 8,000 samples per second. The Nyquist limit is then 4,000 Hz. If you try to record a 5,000-Hz signal (1,000 Hz above the Nyquist limit), you will get a 3,000-Hz sound (1,000 Hz below the Nyquist limit) when you play it back. This *aliasing* effect can cause significant problems and is one of the most important issues in dealing with digital sound.

The basic idea behind aliasing is that one set of digital samples belongs to many sine waves. The dots in Figure 3.5 represent successive digital samples. As you can see, many different sine waves go through those points. Conversely, if you sample any of these sine waves, you get the exact same samples. This ambiguity means that if you sample (or synthesize) a sound, you may be surprised. Because different signals go through those points, it's possible that the digital-to-analog output circuitry might choose a different signal than you expect.

Fortunately, the output circuitry is consistent; it will always choose frequencies less than the Nyquist limit. As a result, if you want to get the right output, you must ensure that your sound doesn't contain anything above the Nyquist frequency. This is not a practical problem if you're recording a sound, because the digital-to-analog conversion includes a low-pass filter to remove those high frequencies. However, it can be a problem if you're synthesizing sounds digitally.

FIGURE 3.5   Aliasing: Many Sine Waves Can Generate the Same Samples

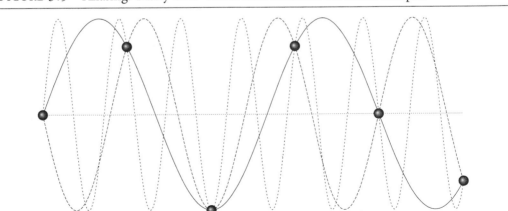

FIGURE 3.6 440-Hertz Square Wave Signal Sampled at 8,000 Hertz

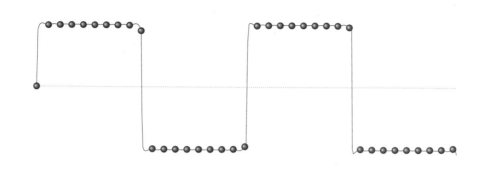

To illustrate the effect of aliasing, consider what happens when you try to digitally sample a pure 440-Hz square wave at 8,000 samples per second. Figure 3.6 shows a square wave, with dots indicating the digital samples.

The spectrum of the analog signal is shown in Figure 3.7. From left to right, the spikes appear at 440 Hz, 1,320 Hz (third harmonic), 2,200 Hz (fifth harmonic), and so on. These harmonics are fairly strong. The eleventh harmonic (4,840 Hz) is 1/11 as strong as the 440-Hz fundamental, which is only a 21 decibel difference. As you can see,

FIGURE 3.7 Frequency Spectrum of an Analog 440-Hertz Square Wave

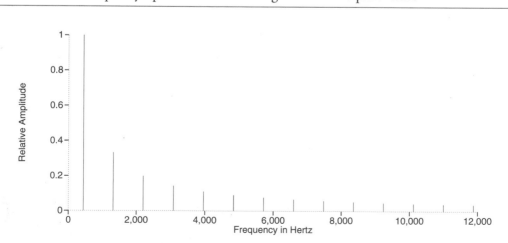

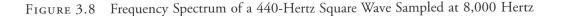

FIGURE 3.8   Frequency Spectrum of a 440-Hertz Square Wave Sampled at 8,000 Hertz

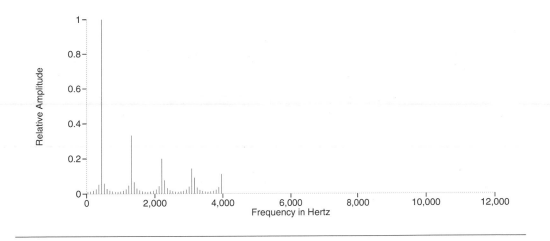

this includes frequencies well beyond the Nyquist limit. (In fact, it includes arbitrarily high frequencies.)

When you play back this signal, the output circuitry will select alias frequencies below the Nyquist limit. The resulting spectrum looks like Figure 3.8. Notice how all the components have been aliased to frequencies below the Nyquist limit of 4,000 Hz.

The important point is that neither of these spectrums is right or wrong. They're simply different ways of looking at the same samples. That's the reason the aliasing problem exists; a set of samples has no unique spectrum. However, in order to avoid ambiguity, we always choose the spectrum with frequencies below the Nyquist limit. Even though Figure 3.7 and Figure 3.8 represent the same samples, we will always use Figure 3.8 (in fact, all digital-to-analog circuitry is designed around this assumption). The catch is that although these two spectra have the same samples, they are not the same signal. In this example, the final output will look like Figure 3.9. The samples (indicated by dots) are at the exact same locations as in Figure 3.6, but the output looks (and sounds) quite different. Notice that the signal that gets played is not created by just "connecting the dots."

FIGURE 3.9   Square Wave Signal with Aliasing

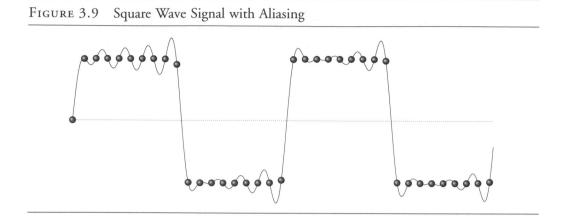

To understand one reason why this is a problem, you need an additional fact. Earlier, I used an example of a 5,000-Hz signal sampled at 8,000 Hz. Because this is 1,000 Hz above the Nyquist limit, it has an alias 1,000 Hz below the Nyquist limit. It also has infinitely many other aliases, which occur in pairs.

$$4{,}000 \pm 1{,}000 \text{ Hz}$$
$$12{,}000 \pm 1{,}000 \text{ Hz}$$
$$20{,}000 \pm 1{,}000 \text{ Hz}$$
$$28{,}000 \pm 1{,}000 \text{ Hz}$$
$$36{,}000 \pm 1{,}000 \text{ Hz}$$
$$\vdots$$

Note that the center frequencies of these pairs are spaced 8,000 Hz apart. If you gradually increase this 3,000-Hz sine wave, some aliases will increase while others decrease. Similarly, if you sample a decreasing 5,000-Hz signal, you'll end up playing back an increasing 3,000-Hz signal.

This effect is particularly objectionable with more complex wave forms. For example, if you play a square wave with an ascending pitch, some of the aliased harmonics will decrease in frequency while others will increase. The decreasing harmonics in this case will be quite distracting.

To prevent this type of problem, you need to avoid using frequencies above the Nyquist limit. In the case of the square wave in Figure 3.6, if you take only the frequencies below the Nyquist limit, you'll end up with the *band-limited square wave* shown in Figure 3.10. Although this may not look any more square than Figure 3.9, it is actually much better and sounds as much like a real square wave as you can get. To get a better signal, you need to use a higher sampling rate, with its correspondingly higher Nyquist limit so that you can use those higher frequencies.

FIGURE 3.10   440-Hertz Square Wave Signal, Band-Limited to 4,000 Hertz

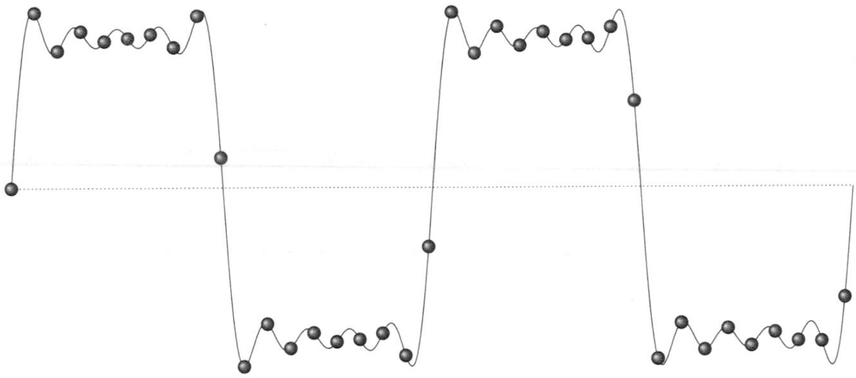

Output Aliasing

In the previous section, I described aliasing as a problem for recording or synthesizing sounds: If you're careless, you may end up playing back something different than you intended. This is also an issue for output. In theory, the first stage of the digital-to-analog conversion actually produces all aliases of the digital signal. The unwanted aliases must somehow be removed. There are two approaches.

One way to remove output aliases is to use an analog filter on the output. Unfortunately, analog filters are not very sharp. You want a filter that effectively removes signals above the 22,050-Hz Nyquist frequency but leaves lower frequencies intact. In addition, high-quality analog filters are expensive to mass produce. As a result, most modern digital systems use *oversampling*.

An oversampling system uses digital techniques to raise the sampling rate. For example, a "4x oversampling" CD player might convert sound from 44,100 samples per second to 176,400 samples per second.

The precise oversampling process involves inserting additional zero values to obtain the required number of samples. The result is a digital sound with a higher sampling rate (176,400 samples per second, in this example) and a lot of unwanted aliases. A digital filter (much less expensive than an analog filter to mass produce) is then used to remove the aliases above 22,050 Hz. This oversampled signal is then converted to analog. The analog signal still has aliases above the new 88,200-Hz Nyquist limit, but it's relatively inexpensive to build an analog filter that will remove those aliases without damaging the desired sound below 22,050 Hz. The net effect of this process, then, is to digitally remove the aliases between 22,050 Hz and 88,200 Hz in order to simplify the analog filtering.

Resampling

I've discussed aliasing primarily in the context of hardware. Of course, if you're a software engineer, you needn't worry about hardware aliasing. The analog-to-digital circuitry in your sound card contains a filter that removes frequencies above the Nyquist limit before sampling, so that aliasing won't occur. Similarly, the output circuitry contains another filter to remove aliases after the digital-to-analog conversion.

However, these issues also arise when you need to *resample*—change the sampling rate of—a sound. For example, suppose you have a voice that has been sampled at 11,025 samples per second and you want to mix it with music sampled at 44,100 samples per second. Before you can mix them, you need to convert them to the same sampling rate.

One possibility is to *down-sample* the 44,100 samples per second music to 11,025 samples per second for mixing. Start by thinking of the original analog sound, with 44,100 slices taken per second (see Figure 3.1 on page 24). It's clear that to get 11,025 slices per second, you want to pick every fourth sample.

There's a catch, of course. That 44,100 samples per second original might contain frequencies as high as 22,050 Hz, well above the Nyquist limit for your 11,025 sample per second target. To get a good result, you must first filter the music signal to remove frequencies above 5,512 Hz, then pick every fourth sample. Chapter 25, starting on page 391, discusses filtering in more detail.

The other possibility is to *up-sample* the 11,025 samples per second voice recording to 44,100 samples per second. There are two ways to think about this process. One approach is to look at your data sample by sample and consider how to create the intermediate samples you don't have. This view, known as *interpolation*, can use a variety of mathematical techniques. The problem with this approach is that it doesn't give you much insight into what happens to the frequency spectrum of your signal.

Instead, start by considering a simpler approach for converting from 11,025 samples per second to 44,100 samples per second: Just repeat each sample four times. The result is a stair-step signal that mimics the lower-resolution version and clearly contains aliases of the desired signal. In order to get a good result, you'll need to filter out these aliases after you repeat the samples.

The similarity between resampling and digital-to-analog conversion isn't a coincidence. You can think of an analog electric signal as having an infinite sampling rate. In effect, digital-to-analog or analog-to-digital conversion is just an extreme case of resampling.

Earlier, I assumed that one sampling rate was an exact multiple of the other. If neither sampling rate is an exact multiple of the other, the conversion is considerably trickier. One way to design a resampling routine is to find a sampling rate that is an exact multiple of both. You then up-sample to this common frequency, filter, and then down-sample. You'll want to try to combine these three operations into one for efficiency.

Quantization Error

Sampling and the associated aliasing problem is only one source of potential error in a digital signal. When you design a digital audio system (whether software or hardware), you have to decide how you will store the individual samples. Because we're working with computers, there are a finite number of values. For example, if you use 8-bit or 16-bit integers, you have either 256 or 65,536 discrete integer sample values.

But the original analog samples aren't integers. The process of rounding an exact sample value to a less-precise value is referred to as *quantization*, and the resulting error is called *quantization error*.

You can think of your final sampled signal as the sum of the original plus an error signal. (This is equivalent to saying the error is the difference between the original and the sampled version.) Although it may not be obvious at first, this error signal is usually quite random and is actually a form of noise.

The first question to ask about this noise is: How loud is it? Engineers refer to the amplitude of the noise as the *noise floor*. (Lower noise floor is better.) In the typical case of 8-bit integer samples, the values range from +127 to -128 and the error is at most 0.5 (assuming everything is being correctly rounded). Clearly, for 16-bit samples, the steps are much smaller, so the noise floor will be lower (the noise will be quieter).

The more important question is: How loud is the noise compared with the desired sound? This ratio is called the *signal-to-noise ratio* (SNR). (Larger SNR is better.)

The important fact about SNR is that it is quite context-dependent. People often discuss the SNR by assuming that you're using the loudest possible signal. For 8-bit digital audio, sample values range from +127 to -128, so your largest sample (in absolute value) is 128 and the error is at most 0.5. So the ratio of signal amplitude to noise amplitude is 256:1, or 2^8. The ratio of signal power to noise power is 2^{16}, or about 48 dB, on a par with a good AM radio. (The rule of thumb is that you get 6 dB SNR per bit.)

If your signal is not the loudest possible, then your SNR will be lower (worse). In the worst case, a very quiet sound will cause the sampled values to change by only one or two steps. For example, consider Figure 3.11. This shows a sine wave whose amplitude is less than one step; the sampled value switches between 0, +1, and -1.

FIGURE 3.11   Sampling a Very Quiet Signal

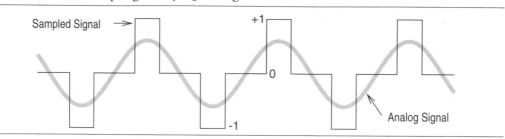

Figure 3.12 shows the error in this case. As you can see, the error is nearly as loud as the original signal. In addition, the sharp shape of this wave form suggests that it has many high-frequency components, which are likely to make the error appear even louder than the original. The worst part of this error is that it is clearly not random. In fact, it is not really noise at all. Audio engineers refer to this type of error as *distortion*.

FIGURE 3.12   Error from Sampling a Very Quiet Signal

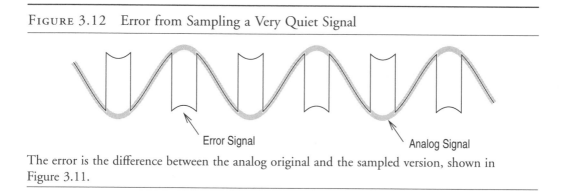

The error is the difference between the analog original and the sampled version, shown in Figure 3.11.

Distortion is usually more objectionable than noise. One reason for this is that distortion follows the signal. In the above case, if you change the frequency or amplitude of the sine wave, you'll change the nature of the distortion. This changing error draws attention to itself in a way that random noise does not. In addition, because random noise is common in our everyday world, our ears are relatively insensitive to it.

Dithering

Because our ears are less sensitive to random noise than to signal-dependent distortion, it's interesting that there's a way to convert some types of distortion into high-frequency noise. This process is called *dithering*, and it's similar to the dithering techniques used in graphics. (In fact, graphical dithering works for the same reason as audio dithering: It converts visible quantization distortion into less-visible high-frequency noise.)

The basic idea is called *error diffusion* and works anytime you need to convert a high-resolution signal into a lower-resolution signal, such as when you convert from 16-bit audio samples down to 8-bit samples. It works by keeping a running sum of the error and using that to fudge future values.

The key point about dithering is that it works best at high sampling rates. It's especially worthwhile if you are working with very-high-resolution samples (more than 16 bits) and need to convert down to 16 bits.

Clipping

Very loud signals are subject to a type of distortion known as *clipping*. In the analog world, clipping usually occurs when an amplifier circuit becomes saturated. The result is that tall peaks are squared off, as shown in Figure 3.13. As you've already seen, square waves have strong harmonics, and this type of clipping causes a similar-sounding distortion.

FIGURE 3.13   An Increasing Sine Wave Subject to Saturation Clipping

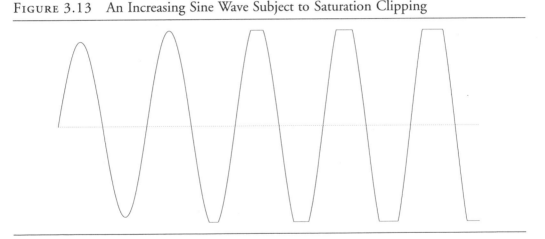

In digital work, a similar type of problem appears as overflow. Most audio work is done with integer or fixed-point arithmetic, which is subject to wrap-around: If you exceed the largest positive value, you end up with a large negative value. The result is even worse than saturation clipping; witness the sharp transitions in Figure 3.14.

Saturation clipping is arguably less bad than wrap-around, but it's best to avoid both by ensuring that your signal levels don't overflow in the first place.

FIGURE 3.14   An Increasing Sine Wave Subject to Wrap-Around

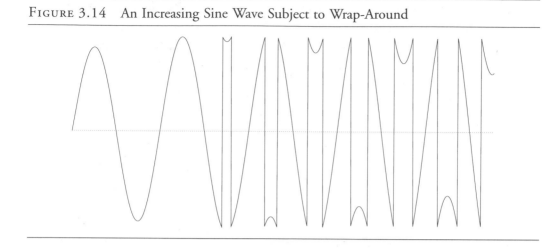

Floating-Point Samples

To reduce quantization errors, many people have considered using floating-point numbers to represent sound samples. Because floating-point numbers allow greater precision for smaller values, they address the problem of distortion with low-level signals. Unfortunately, floating-point numbers also have several disadvantages.

- Floating-point numbers are usually stored in 32-bit or larger formats, which is double the memory and storage requirements of more common 16-bit integer samples.

- Floating-point formats are not very standard, which creates problems if you want to exchange them among different platforms.

- Floating-point arithmetic is often slower than integer arithmetic. Although newer processors are addressing this issue, it's still a significant concern for many systems.

- Digital-to-analog converters always use integer inputs, which means the samples must be converted to integers before they can be played.

Taken together, these considerations mean that floating-point is rarely used in sound processing. It is primarily useful for off-line processing, for which the additional accuracy is useful and speed and storage space are not a concern. (However, the μ-Law and A-Law formats are essentially floating-point formats; see page 111.)

A C++ Sound Framework

4

One of the goals of this book is to develop a collection of sample tools for manipulating sound. These tools should be useful on a variety of computer systems, and it should be easy to combine different sound-processing tools to obtain specific effects. It should also be easy to create new tools and to modify existing tools.

I've taken the approach of developing software components that can be easily combined. This approach is a natural fit for object-oriented programming techniques. Because C++ is currently the most widely available object-oriented language, I've chosen to develop these tools as a collection of C++ classes. (If you're unfamiliar with C++, Appendix B, starting on page 407, gives a quick orientation for C programmers.)

Just as audio engineers connect microphones to sound-effects boxes to tape recorders, you should be able to connect a series of objects that produce, modify, and ultimately record or play the resulting sound.

As an example, here's a simple main function that reads an AU format audio file from cin and plays it to the speaker.

LISTING 4.1   playau.cpp

```
Copyright © 1998, Tim Kientzle (Listing E.1)
```
```cpp
#include <fstream>
#include "au.h"
#include "aplayer.h"

// Try to select appropriate player for Win32, Macintosh, or UNIX/NAS
#if defined(_WIN32)
#include "winplayr.h"
typedef WinPlayer Player;
#elif defined(macintosh)
#include "macplayr.h"
typedef MacPlayer Player;
#else
#include "nasplayr.h"
typedef NasPlayer Player;
#endif
```

```
int main() {
   AuRead auRead(cin);  // Create AuRead object
   Player player(&auRead); // Connect auRead output to player input
   player.Play(); // Now run player
   return 0;
}
```

A file isn't the only possible source of sound, nor is a speaker the only possible output. Here's another example, which plays a sine wave to an AU output file. Notice that because the `SineWave` class can generate any output format, you need to specify the format you want. If you don't specify, the `sinewave` and `player` objects will negotiate some reasonable defaults.

LISTING 4.2   sinetoau.cpp

Copyright © 1998, Tim Kientzle (Listing E.1)

```
#include "sinewave.h"
#include "aplayer.h"
#include "au.h"
int main(int, char **) {
   SineWave sinewave(440);  // 440-Hz sine wave
   sinewave.SamplingRate(11025); // 11025-Hz sampling rate
   AuWrite player(&sinewave); // Connect sinewave to player
   player.Play();
   return 0;
}
```

This approach has a number of benefits.

- It is remarkably portable. The only system-specific portion is one class that feeds PCM samples to the speaker. I've ported the code from this book to three different systems (Windows, Mac OS, and UNIX) with minimal changes. (Only 5 percent of the sample *playsnd* application is system specific.)

- It is flexible. Objects can be combined easily in different ways.

- Because the objects aren't separate programs, they can query each other up and down the chain to determine the best parameters. For example, the `SineWave` class that simply generates a sine wave can query the objects that come after it in the chain to find out the preferred sampling rate. Conversely, the class that communicates with the speaker can query the objects that come before it in the chain to find out the parameters they prefer.

Working with C++ does have some pitfalls. The ANSI standard is relatively new, and not all C++ compilers comply with it. Although the code in this book has been tested with a variety of compilers on different systems, I can't guarantee it will work unaltered on your favorite compiler. In addition, C++ is more complex than some other languages. Although I've tried to keep the code in this book as simple as possible, people unfamiliar with basic C++ concepts might want to refer to Appendix B or read the first few chapters of any good book on C++.

The AudioAbstract Class

Almost all the audio processors inherit from class `AudioAbstract`. The capabilities of `AudioAbstract` are thus shared by the audio processors I'm going to define in this book. This class is defined in `audio.h`, which is a pretty generic C++ class definition. I'll start with an overview of the class and then develop the various facilities, one at a time.

LISTING 4.3   audio.h

```
Copyright © 1998, Tim Kientzle (Listing E.1)
#ifndef AUDIO_H_INCLUDED
#define AUDIO_H_INCLUDED

#include <typeinfo>
#include <iostream>
#include <cstddef>

// The following line is necessary if your compiler
//    strictly follows the ANSI C++ Standard (almost none do).
// However, some compilers don't implement this feature at all.
// If your compiler complains about this line,
//    simply comment it out and try again.
using namespace std;

   AudioAbstract Utility Declarations (Listing 4.5)

class AudioAbstract {
      AudioAbstract Interface (Listing 4.6)

      AudioAbstract Sampling Rate Negotiation Interface (Listing 4.7)

      AudioAbstract Channel Negotiation Interface (Listing 4.9)
};

#endif
```

The header file above contains the class definition for `AudioAbstract` and has space for a few additional helpful functions. I define a few nontrivial member functions (methods) in an associated `.cpp` file.

LISTING 4.4   audio.cpp

```
Copyright © 1998, Tim Kientzle (Listing E.1)
#include "audio.h"

AudioAbstract Sampling Rate Negotiation Implementation (Listing 4.8)

AudioAbstract Channel Negotiation Implementation (Listing 4.10)

AudioAbstract Utility Definitions (Listing 4.11)
```

First, I define a couple of useful types. These are especially important in the decompression classes, which convert streams of bytes into streams of samples. By making these definitions part of the `AudioAbstract` class, I avoid conflicts with other definitions that may appear in your environment. Windows, for instance, defines `BYTE`.

LISTING 4.5   AudioAbstract Utility Declarations

```
typedef short AudioSample; // A single audio sample
typedef unsigned char AudioByte; // an 8-bit unsigned byte
```

All `AudioAbstract` objects share the ability to pass information along from one object to the next. The actual audio data is transferred by having an object request it from the previous object.

LISTING 4.6   AudioAbstract Interface

```
private:
    AudioAbstract *_previous; // object to get data from
    AudioAbstract *_next; // object pulling data from us
public:
    AudioAbstract *Previous(void) { return _previous; }
    void Previous(AudioAbstract *a) { _previous = a; }
    AudioAbstract *Next(void) { return _next; }
    void Next(AudioAbstract *a) {_next = a;}
```

By default, these are initialized to null pointers in the constructor. I'll discuss the `_samplingRate` and `_channels` variables in a moment.

LISTING 4.6 (CONTINUED)   AudioAbstract Interface

```
public:
    AudioAbstract(void) {
        _previous = 0;
        _next = 0;
        _samplingRate = 0;   _samplingRateFrozen = false;
        _channels = 0;       _channelsFrozen = false;
    };
```

The usual constructor initializes _previous and then sets the forward pointer in the previous member. The result is a doubly linked list of audio processors so that the processors can relay information back and forth along the chain.

LISTING 4.6 (CONTINUED)   AudioAbstract Interface

```
public:
    AudioAbstract(AudioAbstract *audio) {
        _previous = audio;
        _next = 0;
        audio->Next(this);
        _samplingRate = 0;   _samplingRateFrozen = false;
        _channels = 0;       _channelsFrozen = false;
    };
```

The **AudioAbstract** destructor does nothing, but it needs to be declared virtual to avoid complications with subclasses.

LISTING 4.6 (CONTINUED)   AudioAbstract Interface

```
public:
    virtual ~AudioAbstract(void) {};
```

The **GetSamples** method is the heart of the audio processors. To create a new audio processor, you'll need to override this method to do whatever processing is appropriate. You will also need to provide a constructor that performs any necessary initialization.

LISTING 4.6 (CONTINUED)   AudioAbstract Interface

```
public:
    // Returns number of samples actually read, 0 on error.
    // This should always return the full request unless there is
    // an error or end-of-data.
    virtual size_t GetSamples(AudioSample *, size_t) = 0;
```

As a practical matter, audio objects that read from a file usually implement the GetSamples method in terms of ReadBytes, which provides raw bytes. By default, ReadBytes simply passes the request along to the next audio object. (See Chapter 10, starting on page 101, for a description of how file-reading classes use this to support a variety of decompression techniques.)

LISTING 4.6 (CONTINUED)   AudioAbstract Interface

```
public:
    virtual size_t ReadBytes(AudioByte * buff, size_t length) {
        return Previous()->ReadBytes(buff,length);
    };
```

Stereo

To support multi-channel sound, including stereo, I need to specify how such sounds will be represented. I've adopted the convention that multi-channel sounds are stored in *frames*. A frame contains one sample for each channel.

In the case of stereo, that means that I *interleave* the channels: alternating one sample for the left channel and one sample for the right channel. This is common for PCM data; every sound file format I've seen assumes that PCM stereo data is interleaved. Further, there seems to be widespread agreement that the left channel precedes the right channel. In practice, this means that many of my audio classes won't need to worry about multi-channel data. If the file and system audio interface agree, I won't need to do any explicit conversion along the way.

However, this applies only to PCM data. Various audio compression algorithms store multi-channel sounds in different ways. It's common, for instance, to compress each channel separately and to alternate blocks of compressed data.

Note that all calls to GetSamples should specify a sample count that's an exact multiple of the number of channels. That allows all the audio classes to deal with whole frames at a time.

Negotiation

Each processor needs to agree on two basic facts about the audio stream that is being relayed: the sampling rate and the number of channels (one for mono, two for stereo).

In order to simplify the use of these objects, they automatically negotiate these parameters. For instance, the first time one of the objects requests the sampling rate (from the AudioAbstract base class), a message will be relayed to the last element of the chain. This final object will query all the objects in the chain and then set the basic parameters for all of those objects.

The negotiation rests on two variables for each parameter. The `_samplingRate` variable holds the current sampling rate; the corresponding `_samplingRateFrozen` variable indicates whether that value has been set through negotiation.

The negotiation is triggered whenever the sampling rate is requested. If the current sampling rate is not already frozen, you need to negotiate the correct sampling rate before you can return it. Similarly, an attempt to change the sampling rate will fail if the sampling rate has already been negotiated.

LISTING 4.7   AudioAbstract Sampling Rate Negotiation Interface

```
private:
   long _samplingRate;
   bool _samplingRateFrozen;
public:
   virtual long SamplingRate(void) {
      if (!_samplingRateFrozen)  // Not frozen?
         NegotiateSamplingRate(); // Go figure it out
      return _samplingRate; // Return it
   };

   virtual void SamplingRate(long s) { // Set the sampling rate
      if (_samplingRateFrozen) {
         cerr << "Can't change sampling rate.\n";
         exit(1);
      }
      _samplingRate = s;
   };
```

The negotiation procedure to determine a common audio format is more complex than you might think. The problem is that there are a variety of possible constraints. In some cases, the first object will determine much of the format (for example, when reading an audio file); at other times, the last object will determine the format. I also want to make it possible for you to set any one object and have the rest of the objects simply accept this restriction.

The overall approach I've chosen involves several methods. Figure 4.1 is a *ladder diagram* illustrating how these relate. It shows the messages exchanged by three objects (represented by vertical lines) over time (time increases as you go down). As you can see, this figure starts when the sampling rate is requested from the center object. Because the sampling rate has not been frozen, this object sends `NegotiateSamplingRate` to its left, prompting the last object (the sound player) to initiate the full negotiation.

In the first phase of this negotiation, `NegotiateSamplingRate` recursively propagates to the left. Eventually, it reaches the left-most object, which manages the actual negotiation.

FIGURE 4.1   Negotiating the Sampling Rate

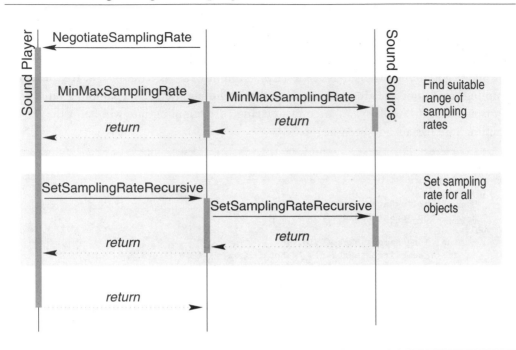

LISTING 4.7 (CONTINUED)   AudioAbstract Sampling Rate Negotiation Interface

```
public:
   virtual void NegotiateSamplingRate(void);
```

LISTING 4.8   AudioAbstract Sampling Rate Negotiation Implementation

```
void AudioAbstract::NegotiateSamplingRate(void) {
   if (Next()) // Are we the leftmost?
      Next()->NegotiateSamplingRate(); // No, keep going
   else { // Yes, we are
      long min = 8000, max = 44100, preferred = 44100;
      MinMaxSamplingRate(&min,&max,&preferred); // Get preferred values
      if (min > max) { // Check for ridiculous answers
         cerr << "Couldn't negotiate sampling rate.\n";
         exit(1);
      }
      SetSamplingRateRecursive(preferred); // Set them everywhere
   }
}
```

The negotiation consists of selecting a range that all objects can accept. An object can also specify a `preferred` value within that range. An object that must force a particular sampling rate can set the maximum and minimum to the same value.

Many classes will override `MinMaxSamplingRate` to compute their preferences, then call `AudioAbstract::MinMaxSamplingRate` to continue the negotiation. For example, an object that reads data from a file may want to delay reading the header from the file until it receives a message that requires information from the file.

Once the preferred value has been selected, `SetSamplingRateRecursive` sets it for all of the objects.

LISTING 4.7 (CONTINUED)   AudioAbstract Sampling Rate Negotiation Interface

```
public:
    virtual void MinMaxSamplingRate(long *min, long *max, long *prefer);
    virtual void SetSamplingRateRecursive(long s);
```

LISTING 4.8 (CONTINUED)   AudioAbstract Sampling Rate Negotiation
                           Implementation

```
void AudioAbstract::MinMaxSamplingRate(long *min, long *max,
                                       long *preferred) {
    if (Previous()) Previous()->MinMaxSamplingRate(min,max,preferred);
    if (_samplingRate) *preferred = _samplingRate;
    if (*preferred < *min) *preferred = *min;
    if (*preferred > *max) *preferred = *max;
}

void AudioAbstract::SetSamplingRateRecursive(long s) {
    if (Previous()) // Set towards the right first
        Previous()->SetSamplingRateRecursive(s);
    SamplingRate(s); // Set it
    _samplingRateFrozen = true; // Yes, we've negotiated
}
```

Most of the messages involved in the negotiation are `virtual`, which allows individual subclasses to override specific details of the negotiation.

The number of channels is negotiated similarly. Some applications might benefit from having a variety of `AudioSample` formats (such as 8-bit and 16-bit). You could easily add a sample width negotiation in a similar fashion.

LISTING 4.9   AudioAbstract Channel Negotiation Interface

```
private:
   long _channels;
   bool _channelsFrozen;
public:
   virtual int Channels(void) {
      if (!_channelsFrozen) NegotiateChannels();
      return _channels;
   };

   virtual void Channels(int ch) {
      if (_channelsFrozen) {
         cerr << "Can't change number of channels.\n";
         exit(1);
      }
      _channels = ch;
   };

   virtual void NegotiateChannels(void);
   virtual void MinMaxChannels(int *min, int *max, int *preferred) ;
   virtual void SetChannelsRecursive(int s);
```

LISTING 4.10   AudioAbstract Channel Negotiation Implementation

```
void AudioAbstract::NegotiateChannels(void) {
   if (Next())
      Next()->NegotiateChannels();
   else {
      int min=1, max=2, preferred=1; // Some reasonable default
      MinMaxChannels(&min,&max,&preferred);
      if (min > max) {
         cerr << "Couldn't negotiate sampling rate.\n";
         exit(1);
      }
      SetChannelsRecursive(preferred);
   }
}

void AudioAbstract::MinMaxChannels(int *min, int *max, int *preferred) {
   if (Previous())  Previous()->MinMaxChannels(min,max,preferred);
   if (_channels) *preferred = _channels;
   if (*preferred < *min) *preferred = *min;
   if (*preferred > *max) *preferred = *max;
}

void AudioAbstract::SetChannelsRecursive(int ch) {
   if (Previous()) Previous()->SetChannelsRecursive(ch);
   Channels(ch);
   _channelsFrozen = true;
}
```

Reading and Writing Integers

Reading and writing multi-byte integers requires some care. To ensure portability, you should always read one byte at a time and assemble multi-byte integers carefully.

`ReadIntMsb` reads an integer starting with the most significant byte. This format is also known as big-endian, network, or Motorola format. Conversely, `ReadIntLsb` reads an integer starting with the least significant byte. This format is also known as little-endian, VAX, or Intel format. The `BytesToIntXxx` forms accept a pointer rather than an `istream`.

LISTING 4.5 (CONTINUED)   AudioAbstract Utility Declarations

```
long ReadIntMsb(istream &in, int bytes);
long BytesToIntMsb(void *buff, int bytes);
long ReadIntLsb(istream &in, int bytes);
long BytesToIntLsb(void *buff, int bytes);
void SkipBytes(istream &in, int bytes);
```

LISTING 4.11   AudioAbstract Utility Definitions

```
long ReadIntMsb(istream &in, int size) {
   if (size <= 0) return 0;
   long l = ReadIntMsb(in,size-1) << 8;
   l |= static_cast<long>(in.get()) & 255;
   return l;
}

long BytesToIntMsb(void *vBuff, int size) {
   unsigned char *buff = reinterpret_cast<unsigned char *>(vBuff);
   if (size <= 0) return 0;
   long l = BytesToIntMsb(buff,size-1) << 8;
   l |= static_cast<long>(buff[size-1]) & 255;
   return l;
}

long ReadIntLsb(istream &in, int size) {
   if (size <= 0) return 0;
   long l = static_cast<long>(in.get()) & 255;
   l |= ReadIntLsb(in,size-1)<<8;
   return l;
}

long BytesToIntLsb(void *vBuff, int size) {
   unsigned char *buff = reinterpret_cast<unsigned char *>(vBuff);
   if (size <= 0) return 0;
   long l = static_cast<long>(*buff) & 255;
   l |= BytesToIntLsb(buff+1,size-1)<<8;
   return l;
}
```

```
void SkipBytes(istream &in, int size) {
   while (size-- > 0)
      in.get();
}
```

Writing multi-byte integers requires similar care.

LISTING 4.5 (CONTINUED)   AudioAbstract Utility Declarations

```
void WriteIntMsb(ostream &out, long l, int bytes);
void WriteIntLsb(ostream &out, long l, int bytes);
```

LISTING 4.11 (CONTINUED)   AudioAbstract Utility Definitions

```
void WriteIntMsb(ostream &out, long l, int size) {
   if (size <= 0) return;
   WriteIntMsb(out, l>>8, size-1); // Write MS Bytes
   out.put(l&255); // Write LS Byte
}

void WriteIntLsb(ostream &out, long l, int size) {
   if (size <= 0) return;
   out.put(l&255);  // Write LS Byte
   WriteIntLsb(out, l>>8, size-1); // Write rest
}
```

A SineWave Class

To illustrate how to use `AudioAbstract`, here's a simple class that generates a sine wave at any specific frequency. This is an example of how to implement real audio processors and also an example of a common audio synthesis technique.

LISTING 4.12   sinewave.h

```
Copyright © 1998, Tim Kientzle (Listing E.1)
#ifndef SINEWAVE_H_INCLUDED
#define SINEWAVE_H_INCLUDED

#include "audio.h"

class SineWave:  public AudioAbstract {
   SineWave Members (Listing 4.14)
};
#endif
```

LISTING 4.13   sinewave.cpp

```
Copyright © 1998, Tim Kientzle (Listing E.1)
#include "audio.h"
#include "sinewave.h"
#include <cmath>


SineWave Implementation (Listing 4.15)
```

In order to keep this class simple, I'll restrict it to mono output. Note that forcing a format simply requires overriding the appropriate `MinMaxXxxxx` message. Because a `SineWave` object will always be the first object in a chain, I don't even need to call the parent `AudioAbstract::MinMaxXxxxx` methods.

LISTING 4.14   SineWave Members

```
protected:
    void MinMaxChannels(int *min, int *max, int *preferred) {
        *min = *max = *preferred = 1;
    };
```

The core of `SineWave`, as with any audio processor object, is to override the `GetSamples` method to provide the audio data. For `SineWave`, this is particularly simple. When `SineWave` is initialized, it builds a table of values for a 1-Hz wave. By simply using the desired frequency to step through the table, you get the appropriate output data. Most of this `GetSamples` is just bookkeeping to make sure that successive calls pick up at the correct place.

LISTING 4.14 (CONTINUED)   SineWave Members

```
protected:
    size_t GetSamples(AudioSample *buff, size_t bytesWanted);
```

LISTING 4.15   SineWave Implementation

```
size_t SineWave::GetSamples(AudioSample *buff, size_t samplesWanted)
{
    AudioSample *p = buff;
    long samplesCopied = 0;
```

```
   while((samplesWanted > 1)) {
     *p = sine[pos];
     pos += frequency;
     if (pos > length) pos -= length;
     samplesWanted --;
     samplesCopied ++;
     p++;
   }

   return samplesCopied;
}
```

The above code depends on four variables, which need to be declared and properly initialized. The Init method handles the common initialization and is called from within the constructors.

LISTING 4.14 (CONTINUED)   SineWave Members

```
private:
   AudioSample *sine; // table of sine values
   int length; // length of above table
   int pos; // current position in table
   int frequency; // desired output frequency
public:
   void Frequency(int f) { frequency = f; }
private:
   void Init(void) {
      sine = (AudioSample *)0;
      length=0; pos=0; frequency=1;
   }
public:
   SineWave(void):AudioAbstract() { Init(); }

   SineWave(int f):AudioAbstract() {
      Init();
      Frequency(f);
   };

   ~SineWave(void) {
      if (sine) delete [] sine;
   }
```

The initialization of the table is simple. Because this is done only once and speed isn't critical, I use standard floating-point library routines.

LISTING 4.14 (CONTINUED)   SineWave Members

```
private:
   void BuildTable(long rate);
```

LISTING 4.15 (CONTINUED)   SineWave Implementation

```
void SineWave::BuildTable(long rate) {
   if (sine) {delete [] sine;}
   length = rate;
   sine = new AudioSample[length];
   double scale = 2.0*(3.14159265358)/
         static_cast<double>(length);
   for (int i=0; i<length; i++) {
      sine[i] = int(32767 * sin(static_cast<double>(i)*scale) );
   }
}
```

The tricky part is initializing the table at the proper time. In particular, it can't be initialized until the sampling rate is known. The easiest way to accomplish this is to override `SamplingRate`. This way, the table will be computed or recomputed whenever the sampling rate changes.

LISTING 4.14 (CONTINUED)   SineWave Members

```
public:
   void SamplingRate(long rate) {
      AudioAbstract::SamplingRate(rate);
      BuildTable(rate);
   }
```

Part Two
System Specifics

Player Objects 5

Before you can really appreciate any audio technique, you need to be able to feed the audio data to a speaker so that you can hear it. The next few chapters will show how to do that on several systems. In this chapter, I'll develop some common code that's useful on many systems.

As you'll see, all three of the systems I'll consider follow the same model: You first ask the system what types of sound it can handle. This often takes the form of different logical sound devices. You then select the format that works best for the sound you want to play. Finally, you must interleave writing sound data and obtaining new data so that the final playback is uninterrupted.

The *player* classes are responsible for feeding audio data to the speaker on a particular system. The common capabilities are defined in the `AbstractPlayer` class that I'll develop in this chapter.

LISTING 5.1   aplayer.h

```
Copyright © 1998, Tim Kientzle (Listing E.1)
#ifndef ABSTRACTPLAYER_H_INCLUDED
#define ABSTRACTPLAYER_H_INCLUDED
#include "audio.h"

AbstractPlayer Class (Listing 5.2)
#endif
```

Player Basics

Many system libraries contain simple functions to play a single sound from a file or a block of memory. Although this works well for simple alerts and other short fragments, it presents a problem if you're dynamically assembling complex sounds as you play them. When you ask the system to play a single sound, it first performs a significant amount of setup work, including allocating memory and configuring the sound hardware. This setup is performed at the beginning of each sound request and then undone at the end of the request. If you make several successive calls, the result is a small gap between each block of sound played.

Depending on the system, this gap can range from a hundredth of a second to as much as half a second. Even the shortest gap is audible and can cause severe problems if you need to synchronize sound playback with video or other timed actions.

The only way to avoid this problem is to ensure that the system always has more data available. The technique used by most systems is called *double buffering:* You set up two buffers and the system reads data from one at a time. When it empties a buffer, it automatically switches to the next one, and you have a chance to refill the just-emptied buffer. You need only to ensure that you can refill the buffer before the system needs it.

It's possible to do a similar trick with a single circular buffer. The system tracks the amount of data in the buffer, and when it falls below a *low-water mark*, the system asks you to write more data into the buffer. The net effect is similar to double buffering.

With either of these schemes, you need to be able to provide data to the system quickly when it needs it. The `AbstractPlayer` class supports this by providing a queue of audio data. To use it, you periodically call `FillQueue`, which requests data from the rest of the audio chain and uses it to top off the queue. You then call `FromQueue` to copy data out of the queue into whatever system data structure you're using.

Of course, that system data structure probably doesn't store `AudioSample` values. So the `AbstractPlayer` class defines two new data types: `Sample16` holds 16-bit samples; `Sample8` holds 8-bit samples. `FromQueue`, which copies data out of the queue, is overloaded to return data in either format.

LISTING 5.2   AbstractPlayer Class

```
class AbstractPlayer :  public AudioAbstract {
protected:
   typedef short Sample16;
   typedef signed char Sample8;

   volatile AudioSample *_queue, *_queueEnd; // Begin/end of queue memory
   volatile AudioSample * volatile _queueFirst;  // First sample
   volatile AudioSample * volatile _queueLast; // Last sample

   void InitializeQueue(unsigned long queueSize); // Create Queue
   void FillQueue(void); // Fill it up
   long FromQueue(Sample8 *pDest,long bytes);
   long FromQueue(Sample16 *pDest,long bytes);
private:
   void DataToQueue(long); // Used by FillQueue
   void DataFromQueue(Sample8 *,long); // Used by FromQueue(Sample8...)
   void DataFromQueue(Sample16 *,long); // Used by FromQueue(Sample16...)
private:
   size_t GetSamples(AudioSample *,size_t) { exit(1); return 0; };
```

Determining when the sound has ended can be complex. When the sound source is emptied, there will still be data in the queue. After the queue is emptied, the system may continue to play from its internal buffers. The `AbstractPlayer` class uses two flags to mark when the source data is exhausted and when the queue is empty.

LISTING 5.2 (CONTINUED)   AbstractPlayer Class

```
protected:
    bool _endOfSource; // true -> last data read from source
    bool _endOfQueue; // true -> last data read from queue
public:
    AbstractPlayer(AudioAbstract *a);
    ~AbstractPlayer();
    virtual void Play() = 0;  // Actually play the sound source
};
```

LISTING 5.3   aplayer.cpp

Copyright © 1998, Tim Kientzle (Listing E.1)

```
#include "aplayer.h"

AbstractPlayer::AbstractPlayer(AudioAbstract *a) :  AudioAbstract(a) {
    _endOfSource = _endOfQueue = false;
    _queue = _queueEnd = _queueFirst = _queueLast = 0;
}

AbstractPlayer::~AbstractPlayer(void) {
    if (_queue) delete [] const_cast<AudioSample *>(_queue);
}
```

Implementing the Queue

A queue (also known as a *circular buffer*) is a standard tool when a consumer of data and a source of data don't agree about timing issues. In this case, the data consumer is the sound hardware, which has rigid timing constraints. The rest of the program provides data by using unpredictable file I/O, compression, and other operations.

LISTING 5.3 (CONTINUED)   aplayer.cpp

```
void AbstractPlayer::InitializeQueue(unsigned long queueSize) {
    _queue = new AudioSample[queueSize];
    _queueEnd = _queue+queueSize;
    _queueFirst = _queueLast = _queue;
    FillQueue();
}
```

In Mac OS and Windows, the queue is called from different threads. Multi-threaded programming requires care. Note that the relevant pointers are marked volatile. Also note that the order in which the pointers are updated is important. When adding data to the queue, for instance, the data is first copied into the queue memory, then the pointers are adjusted. This way, if someone reads data from the queue in the middle of this process, they can read as much data as the pointers say is available.

Keep in mind the difference between _queue and _queueEnd, which mark the beginning and end of the memory used for the queue, and _queueFirst and _queueLast, which mark the first and last bytes of active data in the queue. (Actually, _queueLast marks the first byte past the end of the active data.) There are two important situations: When _queueFirst is less than _queueLast, the active data is one contiguous block in the middle of the queue. When _queueLast is greater than _queueFirst, the queue has wrapped.

It's important to never allow the queue to be completely full or you'll run into an ambiguous situation. The _queueLast and _queueFirst variables are equal when the queue is empty and when it's completely full. If you try to fill the queue exactly, it will look empty and you'll lose precisely one queue's worth of data.

Also note that because multi-channel data is provided in frames (see page 42), it's important to ensure that the request is a multiple of the number of channels.

LISTING 5.3 (CONTINUED)   aplayer.cpp

```cpp
void AbstractPlayer::FillQueue() {
    if (!_endOfSource && (_queueLast >= _queueFirst)) {
        if (_queueFirst == _queue) // Don't fill buffer
            DataToQueue(_queueEnd - _queueLast - 1);
        else
            DataToQueue(_queueEnd - _queueLast);
    }
    if (!_endOfSource && (_queueFirst > (_queueLast+1)))
        DataToQueue(_queueFirst - _queueLast - 1);
}

void AbstractPlayer::DataToQueue(long samplesNeeded) {
    long samplesRead;
    volatile AudioSample *pDest = _queueLast;

    // Make sure request is a multiple of channels
    samplesNeeded -= samplesNeeded % Channels();

    samplesRead = Previous()->GetSamples(
                    const_cast<AudioSample*>(pDest),samplesNeeded);
    pDest += samplesRead;
    if (pDest >= _queueEnd) pDest = _queue;
    _queueLast = pDest;
    if (samplesRead < samplesNeeded)
        _endOfSource = true;
}
```

Reading data from the queue is similar. There's one minor complicating issue, however. System sound managers have different requirements for the sample size they expect. For simplicity, all of my audio components use `AudioSample` to hold samples, but specific systems may require 8-bit or 16-bit samples. For that reason, there are two versions of `FromQueue`. They differ only in the type of pointer they accept.

LISTING 5.3 (CONTINUED)   aplayer.cpp

```cpp
long AbstractPlayer::FromQueue(Sample16 *pDest, long destSize) {
   long destRemaining = destSize;

   if (_queueLast < _queueFirst) {
      int copySize = _queueEnd - _queueFirst; // Number samples avail
      if (copySize > destRemaining)
         copySize = destRemaining;
      DataFromQueue(pDest,copySize);
      destRemaining -= copySize;
      pDest += copySize;
   }

   if ((destRemaining > 0) && (_queueLast > _queueFirst)) {
      int copySize = _queueLast - _queueFirst;
      if (copySize > destRemaining)
         copySize = destRemaining;
      DataFromQueue(pDest, copySize);
      destRemaining -= copySize;
      pDest += copySize;
   }

   if ((destRemaining > 0) && _endOfSource)
      _endOfQueue = true;

   return (destSize - destRemaining);
};

long AbstractPlayer::FromQueue(Sample8 *pDest, long destSize) {
   long destRemaining = destSize;

   if (_queueLast < _queueFirst) {
      int copySize = _queueEnd - _queueFirst; // Number samples avail
      if (copySize > destRemaining)
         copySize = destRemaining;
      DataFromQueue(pDest,copySize);
      destRemaining -= copySize;
      pDest += copySize;
   }

   if ((destRemaining > 0) && (_queueLast > _queueFirst)) {
      int copySize = _queueLast - _queueFirst;
      if (copySize > destRemaining)
         copySize = destRemaining;
      DataFromQueue(pDest, copySize);
      destRemaining -= copySize;
      pDest += copySize;
   }
```

```
    if ((destRemaining > 0) && _endOfSource)
      _endOfQueue = true;

    return (destSize - destRemaining);
};
```

DataFromQueue just copies a contiguous block of data from the queue. It's used twice in FromQueue.

LISTING 5.3 (CONTINUED)   aplayer.cpp

```
/* private: */
void AbstractPlayer::DataFromQueue(Sample16 *pDest, long copySize) {
    volatile AudioSample *newQueueFirst = _queueFirst;
    for(int i=0;i<copySize;i++)
      *pDest++ = *newQueueFirst++
         >> ((sizeof(*newQueueFirst) - sizeof(*pDest)) * 8 );
    if (newQueueFirst >= _queueEnd)
      newQueueFirst = _queue;
    _queueFirst = newQueueFirst;
}

/* private: */
void AbstractPlayer::DataFromQueue(Sample8 *pDest, long copySize) {
    volatile AudioSample *newQueueFirst = _queueFirst;
    for(int i=0;i<copySize;i++)
      *pDest++ = *newQueueFirst++
         >> ((sizeof(*newQueueFirst) - sizeof(*pDest)) * 8 );
    if (newQueueFirst >= _queueEnd)
      newQueueFirst = _queue;
    _queueFirst = newQueueFirst;
}
```

Opening an Unknown Sound File

Generally, users don't care about file formats. They just expect that if a file contains audio data, they can play it. This function simplifies things by creating an appropriate reader object for any supported file type. It relies on the IsXxxxFile functions defined for each file type.

LISTING 5.4   open.h

Copyright © 1998, Tim Kientzle (Listing E.1)

```
#include "audio.h"
#include <istream>
AudioAbstract *OpenFormat(istream &file);
```

Most of the file format handlers I'll discuss support streaming data: The code can read and process data on the fly, as it becomes available. This allows these classes to read data from UNIX pipes or network connections just as easily as from a local file. However, in order to determine the format of a file, you need to repeatedly seek to the beginning of the data. This doesn't rule out reading from a pipe or network connection (none of these seeks involves moving backward more than 1,024 bytes, so a suitably buffered `istream` class will allow this trick), but it is something to consider if you want to use this code with streaming data.

LISTING 5.5   open.cpp

```cpp
#include "open.h"

// Include headers for various formats
#include "mpeg.h" // MPEG Audio File
#include "au.h"   // Sun AU / NeXT SND
#include "voc.h"  // Creative Labs VOC
#include "wav.h"  // Microsoft RIFF WAVE
#include "aiff.h" // Apple AIFF, Apple AIFF-C
#include "iff.h"  // Electronic Arts IFF/8SVX
#include "midi.h" // MIDI File
#include "mod.h"  // ProTracker MOD

AudioAbstract *OpenFormat(istream &file) {
    if (IsVocFile(file)) {
        file.seekg(0);
        return new VocRead(file);
    }
    if (IsAuFile(file)) {
        file.seekg(0);
        return new AuRead(file);
    }
    if (IsWaveFile(file)) {
        file.seekg(0);
        return new WaveRead(file);
    }
    if (IsAiffFile(file)) {
        file.seekg(0);
        return new AiffRead(file);
    }
    if (IsIffFile(file)) {
        file.seekg(0);
        return new IffRead(file);
    }
    if (IsMidiFile(file)) {
        file.seekg(0);
        return new MidiRead(file);
    }
    if (IsModFile(file)) {
        file.seekg(0);
        return new ModRead(file);
    }
```

```
    if (IsMpegFile(file)) {
        file.seekg(0);
        return new MpegRead(file);
    }
    cerr << "I don't recognize this format.\n";
    return 0;
}
```

The ordering of the file tests is not completely arbitrary. Formats with well-defined signatures are tested first because the odds of a false identification are low. The formats with less-well-defined signatures are tested last. MPEG and MOD are especially troublesome. MPEG's signature is less than 2 bytes (12 bits). MOD has a 4-byte signature, but it is not at the beginning of the file. This increases the odds that some other type of file will coincidentally contain those 4 bytes.

Most of these formats have their signatures at the beginning, which reduces the chances that one file type will masquerade as another. VOC is especially good in this regard. It has a 20-byte signature at the beginning of the file; the chance that this sequence will coincidentally appear at the beginning of a non-VOC file is very low.

Playing Audio on Windows 6

As I'm writing this, Microsoft is encouraging the use of its new *DirectSound* interface. Unfortunately, DirectSound is new enough that it's not yet widely supported. For that reason, I'll discuss only the older wave interface here. The primary difference between the two is latency; the DirectSound interface offers lower overhead, which allows you to start playing sounds very quickly. Although this is necessary for games, it's not as important for other applications.

Windows uses double buffering to maintain a continuous flow of sound data. At least two buffers are created. While one is being played, the other can be filled with sound. Internally, Windows keeps a linked list of the buffers you give it. Whenever one of these buffers becomes empty, it switches to the next one and calls a callback function to refill the buffer that has emptied.

One important detail: The system creates a new thread for managing the sound playback. Your callback function is called within this new thread. Unless you're comfortable with multi-threaded programming, you should limit what you do within the callback function. In my implementation, the callback function only reads data from the queue. The queue is kept full in the main thread. And the queue routines themselves are thread-safe.

LISTING 6.1 winplayr.h

```
Copyright © 1998, Tim Kientzle (Listing E.1)
/*
 * Player class for Win32
 */
#ifndef WIN_PLAYER_H_INCLUDED
#define WIN_PLAYER_H_INCLUDED
#include "audio.h"
#include "aplayer.h"
#include <windows.h>
#include <mmsystem.h>

#define winBufferSize 10000  // Number of samples per buffer
```

```
class WinPlayer :  public AbstractPlayer {
private:
   HWAVEOUT _device;   // Windows audio device to open
   volatile bool _paused; // true -> device is paused
   int   _sampleWidth; // width of data to output

   int SelectDevice(void); // Open a suitable device

   // Allow the callback to see our members
   friend void CALLBACK WaveOutCallback(HWAVEOUT hwo, UINT uMsg,
            DWORD dwInstance, DWORD dwParam1, DWORD dwParam2);

   // The callback function defined above is just a wrapper that
   // invokes this method
   void NextBuff(WAVEHDR *);
public:
   WinPlayer(AudioAbstract *a):  AbstractPlayer(a) {
      _device = 0;
      _paused = true;
      _sampleWidth = 0;
   };
   ~WinPlayer() {};

   void Play();  // Actually play the sound source
};
#endif
```

By declaring `WaveOutCallback` a `friend`, I allow it to see the private data of
`WinPlayer`. (Note that `WaveOutCallback` is not a member of `WinPlayer`.)

LISTING 6.2   winplayr.cpp

```
#include <windows.h>
#include <mmsystem.h>
#include <iostream>
#include "aplayer.h"
#include "winplayr.h"
```

WinPlayer Implementation (Listing 6.3)

Play

The callback is called only when a buffer becomes empty. As a result, the first buffers
need to be output before the main loop starts. The callback must be certain always to
write the buffer back to the system even if there is no data in it.

Consider what happens if the program is unable to provide data quickly enough. At some point, the callback will be called to refill a buffer, but the queue will be empty. That buffer must be written back to the system or that buffer is effectively dead. The callback could write the buffer back empty, but that would prompt the system to call again immediately. If the program is having trouble keeping up, the last thing you want is to needlessly use up CPU time swapping empty buffers. The callback could just fill the buffer with zeroes and write it back, but that also needlessly consumes CPU time by playing silence.

The best approach is to pause the output in this situation. This requires some cooperation from the main loop, which has to watch the _paused variable and resume playback after the queue is refilled.

Because the _paused variable is being manipulated from two threads, the order is very important. The callback always pauses before setting _paused to true, and the main loop sets _paused to false before restarting the sound output.

LISTING 6.3   WinPlayer Implementation

```
void WinPlayer::Play(void) {
   if (SelectDevice()) return; // Open a suitable device
   waveOutPause(_device); // Don't start playing yet
   _paused = true;

   InitializeQueue(128*1024L); // Allocate 128k queue

   WAVEHDR waveHdr[2];
   for (int i=0; i<2; i++) {
      waveHdr[i].dwBufferLength  // Size in bytes
            = winBufferSize * _sampleWidth/8;
      waveHdr[i].dwFlags = 0;
      waveHdr[i].dwLoops = 0;
      waveHdr[i].lpData
          = reinterpret_cast<LPSTR>(
             new BYTE[waveHdr[i].dwBufferLength * Channels()]);
      waveOutPrepareHeader(_device,&waveHdr[i],sizeof(waveHdr[i]));
      NextBuff(&waveHdr[i]); // Fill and write buffer to output
   }

   // Wait until finished and both buffers become free
   _paused = false;
   waveOutRestart(_device); // Start playing now
   while(!_endOfQueue  // queue empty??
         || ((waveHdr[0].dwFlags & WHDR_DONE) == 0) // buffers finished?
         || ((waveHdr[1].dwFlags & WHDR_DONE) == 0)) {
      FillQueue(); // Top off the queue
      if (_paused) { // If server thread paused, restart it
         _paused = false;
         cerr << "Sound output restarted.\n";
         waveOutRestart(_device);
      }
```

```
        Sleep(50 /* ms */); // Loop about 20 times a second
    }

    MMRESULT err = waveOutClose(_device);
    while (err == WAVERR_STILLPLAYING) { // If it's still playing...
        Sleep(250); // Wait for a bit...
        waveOutClose(_device); // try again...
    };

    for(int i1=0; i1<2; i1++) {
        waveOutUnprepareHeader(_device,&waveHdr[i1],sizeof(waveHdr[i1]));
        delete [] waveHdr[i1].lpData;
    }
}
```

The Callback

The callback uses a standard trick for interfacing C-style callback mechanisms with C++ classes. As with most callback schemes, Windows accepts a single pointer that will be passed into the callback function. (Windows declares the `dwInstance` parameter as a `DWORD`, but it's almost always used to hold a pointer.) I've chosen to store `this` in that pointer. The callback recovers that pointer and uses it to send a message into the object. In this way, `WaveOutCallback` converts a C function call into a C++ method invocation.

LISTING 6.3 (CONTINUED)   WinPlayer Implementation

```
// CallBack
void CALLBACK WaveOutCallback(HWAVEOUT hwo, UINT uMsg,
    DWORD dwInstance, DWORD dwParam1, DWORD dwParam2) {
    WinPlayer *me = reinterpret_cast<WinPlayer *>(dwInstance);
    switch(uMsg) {
    case WOM_DONE: // Done with this buffer
        {
            WAVEHDR *pWaveHdr = reinterpret_cast<WAVEHDR *>(dwParam1);
            me->NextBuff(pWaveHdr);
            break;
        }
    default:
        break;
    }
}
```

The actual callback is handled in the `NextBuff` method, which fills the buffer and gives it to Windows' sound manager.

LISTING 6.3 (CONTINUED)   WinPlayer Implementation

```
void WinPlayer::NextBuff(WAVEHDR *pWaveHdr) {
   long samplesRead = 0;
   switch(_sampleWidth) {
   case 16:
      samplesRead = FromQueue(
            reinterpret_cast<Sample16 *>(pWaveHdr->lpData),
            winBufferSize);
      break;
   case 8:
      samplesRead = FromQueue(
            reinterpret_cast<Sample8 *>(pWaveHdr->lpData),
            winBufferSize);
      break;
   }
   if (samplesRead != 0) {  // I got data, so write it
      pWaveHdr->dwBufferLength = samplesRead * _sampleWidth / 8;
      waveOutWrite(_device, pWaveHdr, sizeof(*pWaveHdr));
   } else if (!_endOfQueue) { // Whoops!  Source couldn't keep up
      waveOutPause(_device); // pause the output
      _paused = true;
      cerr << "Sound output paused due to lack of data.\n";
      // Write some zeros to keep this block in Windows' queue
      memset(pWaveHdr->lpData,0,winBufferSize);
      pWaveHdr->dwBufferLength = 256;
      waveOutWrite(_device,pWaveHdr,sizeof(*pWaveHdr));
   } else { // No data, everything's done.
      pWaveHdr->dwFlags |= WHDR_DONE; // Mark buffer as finished
   }
}
```

Selecting an Audio Device

Windows supports any number of audio devices, and selecting the correct one can be tricky. There are two ways to find out the capabilities of the device. One is to request the device capabilities (waveOutGetDevCaps) and use the bitmap to select the closest format. This limits you to only three sampling rates, which can be troublesome. You can also use a special form of the waveOutOpen call to test if any device supports the format you prefer.

SelectDevice starts by calling MinMaxChannels and MinMaxSamplingRate to determine the range of parameters acceptable to other audio objects. It then queries the system to see if the preferred format is supported. If this fails, it queries Windows to see what standard formats are supported and checks if any of those standard formats fit within the range of acceptable parameters. Assuming that one of these succeeds, it knows the parameters that will be used and can call SetSamplingRateRecursive and SetChannelsRecursive to set the final parameters for the other audio objects.

LISTING 6.3 (CONTINUED)   WinPlayer Implementation

```cpp
// These are the primary formats supported by Windows
static struct {
   DWORD format; // Constant
   UINT rate;    // break down for this constant
   UINT channels;
   UINT width;
} winFormats[] = {
   {WAVE_FORMAT_1S16, 11025, 2, 16},
   {WAVE_FORMAT_1S08, 11025, 2, 8},
   {WAVE_FORMAT_1M16, 11025, 1, 16},
   {WAVE_FORMAT_1M08, 11025, 1, 8},
   {WAVE_FORMAT_2S16, 22050, 2, 16},
   {WAVE_FORMAT_2S08, 22050, 2, 8},
   {WAVE_FORMAT_2M16, 22050, 1, 16},
   {WAVE_FORMAT_2M08, 22050, 1, 8},
   {WAVE_FORMAT_4S16, 44100, 2, 16},
   {WAVE_FORMAT_4S08, 44100, 2, 8},
   {WAVE_FORMAT_4M16, 44100, 1, 16},
   {WAVE_FORMAT_4M08, 44100, 1, 8},
   {0,0,0,0}
};

//
// Negotiate the sound format and open a suitable output device
//
int WinPlayer::SelectDevice(void) {
   // Get everyone else's idea of format
   int channelsMin = 1, channelsMax = 2, channelsPreferred = 0;
   long rateMin = 8000, rateMax = 44100, ratePreferred = 22050;

   MinMaxChannels(&channelsMin,&channelsMax,&channelsPreferred);
   if (channelsMin > channelsMax) {
      cerr << "Couldn't negotiate channels.\n";
      exit(1);
   }

   MinMaxSamplingRate(&rateMin,&rateMax,&ratePreferred);
   if (rateMin > rateMax) {
      cerr << "Couldn't negotiate rate.\n";
      exit(1);
   }

   // First, try for an exact match
   static const int NO_MATCH=100000;
   UINT matchingDevice = NO_MATCH;
   WAVEFORMATEX waveFormat;
   waveFormat.wFormatTag = WAVE_FORMAT_PCM;
   waveFormat.nChannels = channelsPreferred;
   waveFormat.nSamplesPerSec = ratePreferred;
   waveFormat.wBitsPerSample = 8 * sizeof(Sample16);
   waveFormat.nBlockAlign = waveFormat.nChannels
               * waveFormat.wBitsPerSample / 8;
```

```
waveFormat.nAvgBytesPerSec = waveFormat.nBlockAlign
               * waveFormat.nSamplesPerSec;
waveFormat.cbSize = 0;
MMRESULT err = waveOutOpen(0,WAVE_MAPPER,&waveFormat,
                           0,0,WAVE_FORMAT_QUERY);
if (err == 0) {
   matchingDevice = WAVE_MAPPER;
   channelsMax = channelsMin = channelsPreferred;
   rateMax = rateMin = ratePreferred;
   _sampleWidth = 16;
} else {
   cerr << "WinPlay:  Custom format failed, ";
   cerr << "trying standard formats.\n";
}

// Get count of available devices
UINT numDevs = waveOutGetNumDevs();
if (numDevs == 0) {
   cerr << "No sound output devices found!?\n";
   exit(1);
}

// Check each available device
for (UINT i=0; (i<numDevs) && (matchingDevice == NO_MATCH); i++) {
   // What formats does this device support?
   WAVEOUTCAPS waveOutCaps;
   MMRESULT err =
            waveOutGetDevCaps(i,&waveOutCaps,sizeof(waveOutCaps));
   if (err != MMSYSERR_NOERROR) {
      cerr << "Couldn't get capabilities of device " << i << "\n";
      continue;
   }
   // Check each standard format
   for(UINT j=0; winFormats[j].format != 0; j++) {
      if ((winFormats[j].format & waveOutCaps.dwFormats) // supported?
         &&(rateMin <= winFormats[j].rate) // Rate ok?
         &&(rateMax >= winFormats[j].rate)
         &&(channelsMin <= winFormats[j].channels) // channels ok?
         &&(channelsMax >= winFormats[j].channels)) {

         // Set up my parameters
         matchingDevice = i;
         rateMin = rateMax = ratePreferred = winFormats[j].rate;
         channelsPreferred = winFormats[j].channels;
         channelsMin = channelsMax = channelsPreferred;
         _sampleWidth = winFormats[j].width;

         // Set up WAVEFORMATEX structure accordingly
         waveFormat.wFormatTag = WAVE_FORMAT_PCM;
         waveFormat.nChannels = winFormats[j].channels;
         waveFormat.nSamplesPerSec = winFormats[j].rate;
         waveFormat.wBitsPerSample = winFormats[j].width;
         waveFormat.nBlockAlign = waveFormat.wBitsPerSample / 8
                           * waveFormat.nChannels;
         waveFormat.nAvgBytesPerSec = waveFormat.nBlockAlign
                           * waveFormat.nSamplesPerSec;
```

```
                waveFormat.cbSize = 0;
            }
        }
    }

    if (matchingDevice == NO_MATCH) {
        cerr << "Can't handle this sound format.\n";
        cerr << "Rate:  " << rateMin << "-" << rateMax << "\n";
        cerr << "Channels:  " << channelsMin << "-" << channelsMax << "\n";
        return 1;
    }

    // If we found a match, set everything
    SetChannelsRecursive(channelsPreferred);
    SetSamplingRateRecursive(ratePreferred);

    // Open the matching device
    MMRESULT err2 = waveOutOpen(&_device,matchingDevice,
        &waveFormat,  reinterpret_cast<DWORD>(WaveOutCallback),
        reinterpret_cast<DWORD>(this),CALLBACK_FUNCTION);

    if (err2) {
        cerr << "Couldn't open WAVE output device.\n";
        exit(1);
    }

    return 0;
}
```

A Sample Windows Application

The sample Windows application is deliberately simple. Rather than develop a sophisticated graphical interface, I've provided you with a basic console application. This can be used from an MS-DOS box to play any number of files (*batch* mode) or run within Windows (*interactive* mode).

Interactive mode uses the standard file selection dialog to let the user pick files. Batch mode plays the files listed on the command line.

LISTING 6.4   winmain.cpp

```
#include <fstream>
#include "audio.h"
#include "open.h"
#include "aplayer.h"
#include "winplayr.h"
#include <commdlg.h>
#include <winbase.h>
```

```
#include <crtdbg.h>
#include <cassert>
```

Play One File under Windows (Listing 6.7)

Play Files Interactively under Windows (Listing 6.5)

Play Files Non-Interactively under Windows (Listing 6.6)

```
int main(int argc, char **argv) {
   // For testing, you can hard-wire a collection of files by
   // uncommenting and editing these two lines:
   // Batch("C:\\samples\\*.*");
   // exit(0);

   if (argc == 1) Interactive();
   else
      while (--argc)
         Batch(*++argv);
   return 0;
}
```

Note that distinguishing between batch and interactive mode is pretty easy: If there are no command-line arguments, then it must be interactive mode. Interactive mode is handled by repeatedly calling `GetOpenFileName` to get file names from the user.

LISTING 6.5   Play Files Interactively under Windows

```
void Interactive() {
   while (1) {
      OPENFILENAME ofn;
      char fileName[512] = "";
      memset(&ofn,0,sizeof(ofn));
      ofn.lStructSize = sizeof(OPENFILENAME);
      ofn.lpstrFile = fileName;
      ofn.lpstrTitle = "Play Sound File";
      ofn.nMaxFile =      512;
      if (GetOpenFileName(&ofn)) // Throw up dialog
         PlayFile(fileName);
      else
         return;
   }
}
```

Batch mode is trickier. In Windows, as in MS-DOS, individual applications are responsible for expanding wildcards. The system functions `FindFirstFile`, `FindNextFile`, and `FindClose` allow you to list all files that match the given pattern.

LISTING 6.6   Play Files Non-Interactively under Windows

```
void Batch(char *filePattern) {
  WIN32_FIND_DATA fileData;
  bool finished = false;
  HANDLE hSearch = FindFirstFile(filePattern,&fileData);
  if (hSearch == INVALID_HANDLE_VALUE) {
    cerr << "Can't find " << filePattern << "\n";
    finished = true;
  }
  while (!finished) {
    // Skip directories, especially . and ..
    if (!(fileData.dwFileAttributes & FILE_ATTRIBUTE_DIRECTORY)) {
      char fileName[2048];
      strcpy(fileName,filePattern);
      char *p=fileName + strlen(fileName) - 1;
      while ((p > fileName) && (*p != '\\') && (*p != '/'))
        p--;
      strcpy(p+1,fileData.cFileName);
      PlayFile(fileName);
    }
    finished = !FindNextFile(hSearch,&fileData);
  }
  FindClose(hSearch);
}
```

Both of the above functions ultimately call `PlayFile` to actually play the file. Note that the input file is opened using the `ios::binary` flag. This is necessary for correctly handling binary files such as audio files.

LISTING 6.7   Play One File under Windows

```
void PlayFile(char *fileName) {
  cerr << "File:  " << fileName << "\n";
  ifstream input(fileName,ios::in|ios::binary);
  if (!input.is_open()) {
    cerr << "Couldn't open file " << fileName << "\n";
    return;
  }
  AudioAbstract *audioFile = OpenFormat(input);
  if (audioFile) {
    WinPlayer player(audioFile);
    player.Play();
    delete audioFile;
    cerr << "Finished playing " << fileName << ".\n";
  }
  cerr << "\n";
  // Paranoia:  Check that the Heap is still okay
  assert(_CrtCheckMemory());
}
```

Playing Audio on Mac OS

Although Mac OS is not technically multi-threaded, the handling of sound is remarkably similar to Windows. Rather than having a separate thread, the callback is called from within an interrupt service routine. This places even more severe limits on what you can do in the callback; interrupt service routines must complete quickly.

LISTING 7.1   macplayr.h

```
/*
 * Player class for Mac OS
 */
#ifndef MAC_PLAYER_H_INCLUDED
#define MAC_PLAYER_H_INCLUDED
#include "audio.h"
#include "aplayer.h"
#include <Resources.h>
#include <Sound.h>
#include <Memory.h>
#include <Events.h>
#include <StandardFile.h>

#define doubleBufferSize 0x1000

class MacPlayer :  public AbstractPlayer {
private:
   friend pascal void NextBlockCallback(SndChannelPtr,
              SndDoubleBufferPtr);
   void NextBlock(SndChannelPtr, SndDoubleBufferPtr);
public:
   MacPlayer(AudioAbstract *a):AbstractPlayer(a) {};
   ~MacPlayer() {};
   void Play() { Play(0); }
   void Play(void (*serviceFunc)(void));  // Actually play the sound source
};
#endif
```

Again, note that the callback function is declared a `friend` so that it can call the private `NextBlock` method.

LISTING 7.2   macplayr.cpp

```
Copyright © 1998, Tim Kientzle (Listing E.1)

#include <Resources.h>
#include <Sound.h>
#include <Memory.h>
#include <Menus.h>
#include <istream>
#include <fstream>

#include "audio.h"
#include "aplayer.h"
#include "macplayr.h"

MacPlayer Implementation (Listing 7.3)
```

Callback

The `NextBlockCallback` is called by the Sound Manager when one of the double buffers becomes empty. Note that this occurs at interrupt time; this routine must be relatively fast and must not make any calls that might allocate or free memory on the system heap. (In particular, it must not call the C++ `new` or `delete` operators, which must occasionally request or free memory on the system heap.)

The `NextBlockCallback` simply recovers the object pointer and invokes a method; the rest of the work is done in `FromQueue`, which is careful not to call any operating-system services.

Right now, this code uses only 16-bit samples. If you want a more efficient program, you might want to use 8-bit samples instead. If you do, be aware that the Mac Sound Manager expects 8-bit samples to be in unsigned format (see page 104). The following two lines convert a byte buffer from signed 8-bit data to unsigned (or vice versa):

```
for(long i=0;i<copied;i++)
    pDest[i] ^= 0x80;
```

LISTING 7.3   MacPlayer Implementation

```
pascal void NextBlockCallback(SndChannelPtr scp,
        SndDoubleBufferPtr doubleBuffer)
{
  MacPlayer *me
    = reinterpret_cast<MacPlayer *>(doubleBuffer->dbUserInfo[0]);
```

```
      me->NextBlock(scp,doubleBuffer);
}

void MacPlayer::NextBlock(SndChannelPtr, SndDoubleBufferPtr doubleBuffer) {
   AudioSample *pDest =
      reinterpret_cast<Sample16 *>(doubleBuffer->dbSoundData);
   long copied = FromQueue(pDest,doubleBufferSize);

   doubleBuffer->dbNumFrames = copied/Channels();
   doubleBuffer->dbFlags = (doubleBuffer->dbFlags) | dbBufferReady;
   if (_endOfQueue)
      doubleBuffer->dbFlags = (doubleBuffer->dbFlags) | dbLastBuffer;
};
```

Double Buffered Sound Under Mac OS

Selecting a sound device is simple under Mac OS. Tell the system the type of sound you're producing (in this case, `sampledSynth`), and the system will select the correct device. The double buffering requires a `SndDoubleBufferHeader` structure, which contains pointers to two `SndDoubleBuffer` structures. The latter are the actual buffers, which need to be initialized.

There are two interesting differences from other systems. The first is that the sampling rate is specified as a `Fixed` value, which allows fractional sampling rates. The second is that the callback requires special handling. Because the PowerPC Mac OS is a mixture of native PowerPC code and emulated 680x0 code, callback pointers must be *universal procedure pointers*, which allow either type of system code to correctly call native functions in your program. The same calls appear on 680x0 Mac OS, although the underlying implementation is simpler.

LISTING 7.3 (CONTINUED)   MacPlayer Implementation

```
void MacPlayer::Play(void (*serviceFunc)(void)) {
   SCStatus        Stats;
   SndChannelPtr       chan;

   chan = nil;
   OSErr err = SndNewChannel (&chan, sampledSynth, 0, nil);
   if (err != noErr)
      Debugger();

   SndDoubleBufferHeader   doubleHeader;
   doubleHeader.dbhNumChannels = Channels();
   doubleHeader.dbhSampleSize = 16; // Bits per sample
   doubleHeader.dbhCompressionID = 0; // Sound is not compressed
   doubleHeader.dbhPacketSize = 0; // Not used, since no compression
   doubleHeader.dbhSampleRate =
      static_cast<Fixed>(SamplingRate()) << 16;
```

```
/* create a UPP for the SndDoubleBackProc */
doubleHeader.dbhDoubleBack = NewSndDoubleBackProc(NextBlockCallback);

// Initialize queue _after_ above negotiations
InitializeQueue(128 * 1024L); // Allocate 128k queue

for (int i = 0; i <= 1; ++i) {
   SndDoubleBufferPtr doubleBuffer =
      reinterpret_cast<SndDoubleBufferPtr>
      (NewPtrClear(sizeof(SndDoubleBuffer) + doubleBufferSize*2));
   doubleHeader.dbhBufferPtr [i] = doubleBuffer;

   if ((doubleBuffer == nil) || (MemError() != 0))
      Debugger();

   doubleBuffer->dbNumFrames = 0;
   doubleBuffer->dbFlags = 0;
   doubleBuffer->dbUserInfo [0] = static_cast<long>(this);
   NextBlockCallback(chan, doubleBuffer); // initialize the buffers
}

err = SndPlayDoubleBuffer (chan, &doubleHeader);
if (err != noErr)
   Debugger();

do {
   FillQueue(); // Keep queue full
   if (serviceFunc)
      serviceFunc(); // Call the service function
   err = SndChannelStatus (chan, sizeof (Stats), &Stats);
} while (Stats.scChannelBusy);

DisposePtr ((Ptr) doubleHeader.dbhBufferPtr[0]);
DisposePtr ((Ptr) doubleHeader.dbhBufferPtr[1]);

err = SndDisposeChannel (chan,0);
if (err != noErr)
   Debugger();
}
```

A Sample Mac OS Program

On Windows, I kept my example program simple by using text mode. There's no similar facility in Mac OS, so I'll have to do a little more work.

LISTING 7.4   macmain.cpp

```
Copyright © 1998, Tim Kientzle (Listing E.1)
#include "audio.h"
#include "open.h"
#include "aplayer.h"
#include "macplayr.h"
#include <fstream>

static void InitializeSystem();
static void CheckEvent();
static void DoClick(EventRecord *event);
static void PlayFileSpec(FSSpec *fileSpec);

Macintosh System Support (Listing 7.5)

int main() {
   InitializeSystem();
   cout << "Select File :  Play.. to play a file.\n";
   while(1)
      CheckEvent();
   return 0;
}
```

`InitializeSystem` initializes the Macintosh Toolbox and a few other utilities. `CheckEvent` waits for an event and handles it. `DoClick` handles a mouse click event. Finally, `PlayFileSpec` accepts a Macintosh-style file specification and actually opens and plays the file. Note that the `MacPlayer::Play()` method (in macplayr.cpp) also needs to check for events regularly, so it will receive a pointer to `CheckEvent`, as well.

The SIOUX (standard input/output user extension) console support provided with the Metrowerks CodeWarrior development environment handles I/O to the standard C++ `cin`, `cout`, and `cerr` paths by managing a text window. Because I'm providing my own event loop and menus, I need to disable some of the SIOUX defaults, however.

LISTING 7.5   Macintosh System Support

```
   #include <SIOUX.h>

   static void InitializeSystem() { // Initialize system components
      InitGraf(&qd.thePort);      // QuickDraw
      InitFonts();                // Font Manager
      FlushEvents(everyEvent,0);  // Flush any pending events
      InitWindows();              // Window Manager
      InitMenus();                // Menu Manager
      TEInit();                   // Text Extensions
      InitDialogs(nil);           // Dialog Manager
      InitCursor();               // Cursor
```

```
        // Alter SIOUX defaults
        SIOUXSettings.standalone = FALSE;
        SIOUXSettings.setupmenus = FALSE;
        SIOUXSettings.initializeTB = FALSE;
        SIOUXSettings.autocloseonquit = TRUE;
        SIOUXSettings.columns = 80;
        SIOUXSettings.rows = 12;
        SIOUXSettings.asktosaveonclose = 0;
        SIOUXSetTitle("\pPlay Sound");

        // Set up my menus
        Handle menuBar = GetNewMBar(128); // Pull menu bar from resources
        SetMenuBar(menuBar);
        DisposeHandle(menuBar);
        MenuHandle appleMenu = GetMenuHandle(128); // Get Apple menu
        AppendResMenu(appleMenu,'DRVR'); // Add system entries to Apple menu
        DrawMenuBar(); // Update menu bar
    }
```

`CheckEvent` first gives the SIOUX library the chance to handle a new event. If the SIOUX library doesn't want it, `CheckEvent` processes it directly. Because I'm explicitly dealing only with menus, I need to worry only about `mouseDown` events.

LISTING 7.5 (CONTINUED)   Macintosh System Support

```
    static void CheckEvent() {
        EventRecord event;
        Boolean     eventOccured;
        eventOccured = WaitNextEvent(everyEvent, &event, 10, nil);

        if(eventOccured && !SIOUXHandleOneEvent(&event)) {
            switch(event.what) {
            case mouseDown:  DoClick(&event); break;
            default:                                        break;
            }
        }
    }
```

This sample program has only one menu (`File`), and that has only two entries, `Play...` and `Quit`. `Play...` invokes a standard file selection dialog and plays the selected file. `Quit` exits the program. A click on the Apple Menu is handled by calling the `OpenDeskAcc` system call.

LISTING 7.5 (CONTINUED)   Macintosh System Support

```
static void DoClick(EventRecord *event) {
    WindowPtr whichWindow;
    switch(FindWindow(event->where,&whichWindow)) {
    case inMenuBar:
        long select = MenuSelect(event->where);
        switch(select >> 16) {
        case 128:  // Apple Menu
        {
            MenuHandle mh = GetMenuHandle(select >> 16);
            unsigned char itemName[255];
            GetMenuItemText(mh, (select & 0xFFFF), itemName);
            OpenDeskAcc(itemName);
            HiliteMenu(0);
            break;
        }
        case 129:  // File menu
            switch(select & 0xFFFF) {
            case 1:  // Selected File :  Play...
                // Throw up a standard file selection dialog
                SFTypeList typeList;
                StandardFileReply selectedFile;
                StandardGetFile (
                    // No filtering
                    reinterpret_cast<RoutineDescriptor *>(nil),
                    -1, // All types
                    typeList, // Not used
                    &selectedFile); // return selected file info
                // Disable Play... menu item
                MenuHandle mh = GetMenuHandle(129);
                DisableItem(mh,1);
                HiliteMenu(0);
                DrawMenuBar();
                // Play file
                PlayFileSpec(&selectedFile.sfFile);
                // Re-enable Play... menu item
                EnableItem(mh,1);
                DrawMenuBar();
                break;
            case 2:  // Quit entry
                exit(0);
            }
        }
        break;
    }
}
```

Playing a Mac File

Once a file has been chosen, I need to play it. There are a few Mac Toolbox oddities involved. The first is that the name provided in an FSSpec structure is a Pascal-format string that needs to be converted to C/C++ conventions. The second is that the FSSpec structure may indicate a file in any directory available to the system. Before opening the file, I need to set the current working directory and current volume to the directory containing the file.

Listing 7.5 (continued)   Macintosh System Support

```
static void PlayFileSpec(FSSpec *fileSpec) {
   char *name = reinterpret_cast<char *>(p2cstr(fileSpec->name));
   cerr << "File:  " << name << "\n";

   short volumeId;
   OpenWD(fileSpec->vRefNum,fileSpec->parID,NULL, &volumeId);
   SetVol(NULL,volumeId);

   ifstream input(name, ios_base::in | ios_base::binary);
   if (!input.is_open()) {
      cerr << "Couldn't open file " << name << "\n";
      return;
   }
   AudioAbstract *audioRead = OpenFormat(input);
   if (audioRead) {
      MacPlayer player(audioRead);
      player.Play(CheckEvent);
      delete audioRead;
      cerr << "Finished playing " << name << ".\n";
   }
   cerr << "\n";
}
```

UNIX and the Network Audio System

With most desktop personal computers, you can assume that the display and speakers are attached to the computer running your program. This isn't always true for UNIX systems. It's quite common for the display to be in another room or even another country from the computer actually doing the work. The X window system supports this type of arrangement quite nicely. Whenever an X program runs, it first opens a network connection to the machine that will serve as a display. This has proven especially useful for researchers who want to run complex calculations on distant high-speed supercomputers and have the output displayed on the graphical workstation on their desk.

Of course, if you have a program that generates sound, you want that sound to be played through the speakers attached to the display, not the speakers that may be attached to the computer running the program. Unfortunately, X does not support audio. The *Network Audio System* (NAS) originally developed at NCD Corporation was designed to complement X by providing a similar networked model for audio services.

NAS allows the program manipulating the sound and the speakers to be on different computers. The program opens a connection to the audio server and can then request a variety of operations. Many operations can be handled without the need to transfer audio data over the network; the server can store sounds locally and replay them or can play sound from other sources. In practice, the NAS server is often on the same computer as the client. NAS support for many popular systems (including Solaris, Linux, and FreeBSD) is available from ftp.x.org.

If you're unfamiliar with the X windowing model, the terms *server* and *client* may seem backward from what you expect. In this case, the server is sitting on your desktop, and the client may be elsewhere on the network. Usually, both run on the same machine. It might help to remember that the term server simply means "a program that provides a service." The NAS server provides the service of managing the physical speakers.

This player class for NAS is similar to the ones for Mac OS and Windows. One difference is that my event loop handles events from the audio server (in an X program, these would be handled by the X event handler). Another difference is that my program

needn't be multi-threaded. All the double buffering is handled by the audio server; I just
need to respond to requests for additional data.

LISTING 8.1   nasplayr.h

```
Copyright © 1998, Tim Kientzle (Listing E.1)

/* Player class for Network Audio System */
#ifndef NASPLAYER_H_INCLUDED
#define NASPLAYER_H_INCLUDED
#include "audio.h"
#include "aplayer.h"
extern "C" { /* NAS definitions */
#include <audio/audiolib.h>
}

class NasPlayer :  public AbstractPlayer {
private:
    bool _finished; // true -> all data played

    NasPlayer Private Members (Listing 8.3)

public:
    NasPlayer(AudioAbstract *a):AbstractPlayer(a) {
        _finished = false;
    } ;
    ~NasPlayer() {};
    void Play();  // Actually play the sound source
};
#endif
```

LISTING 8.2   nasplayr.cpp

```
Copyright © 1998, Tim Kientzle (Listing E.1)

#include <typeinfo>
#include <iostream>
#include <fstream>
#include "audio.h"
#include "aplayer.h"
#include "nasplayr.h"

NasPlayer Implementation (Listing 8.4)
```

Servers and Flows

Playing audio data through NAS requires a connection to a server and a *flow* on that
server. A flow is a sound processing pipeline that connects a source of data to a
destination and allows multiple sources to be combined in various ways.

LISTING 8.3   NasPlayer Private Members

```
private:
   AuServer *_server;
   AuFlowID _flow;
```

The `Play` method first opens a connection to the server, which includes creating and registering a flow. In NAS, all flows start in a paused state. Once the flow is unpaused, the server will start sending requests for audio data. Note that under NAS, the server process takes care of the double buffering; the client simply responds to requests for data. All the `AuXxxx` functions here are from the NAS library.

LISTING 8.4   NasPlayer Implementation

```
void NasPlayer::Play(){
   OpenServer();   // Establish a connection with the server
   InitializeQueue(128*1024L); // Initialize 128k queue

   AuStartFlow(_server,_flow,NULL);   // Unpause the flow

   while (!_finished) {   // Handle events until we're done
      AuEvent ev;
      AuNextEvent(_server, AuTrue, &ev);
      AuDispatchEvent(_server, &ev);
   }
   AuCloseServer(_server); // Close connection to server
}
```

Callbacks and Events

Whenever the server needs more data, it sends an event to the client. The `Play` method above uses the `AuDispatchEvent` library function to handle these events. `AuDispatchEvent` calls the callback function. If the callback receives a *notify* event, it invokes `Notify`, which interprets the notification and invokes `SendData` to send data to the server as required.

LISTING 8.3 (CONTINUED)   NasPlayer Private Members

```
private:
   void OpenServer(); // Connect to server
   friend AuBool NasEventHandler(AuServer *server,
         AuEvent *event,  AuEventHandlerRec *eventData);
   AuBool Notify(AuElementNotifyEvent *notifyEvent);
   void SendData(AuUint32 numBytes);
```

Each request from the NAS server specifies the amount of data the server expects. The server seems very particular; the client must provide exactly the requested amount in a single write. Because the required data may not be contiguous in the queue, I copy the data out of the queue into an auxiliary buffer and then write that buffer to the server.

LISTING 8.3 (CONTINUED)   NasPlayer Private Members

```
private:
#define nasBufferSize 100000
    Sample16 _buffer[nasBufferSize];
```

The library function `AuDispatchEvent` forwards events to a callback function. `OpenServer` registers `NasEventHandler` as a callback to handle events. So whenever the audio flow needs more data, the server sends an event that ends up in the `NasEventHandler` function.

This function primarily serves to convert a function call into a method invocation. It uses the user data field to store a pointer to the `NasPlayer` object and invokes the `Notify` method to handle the event.

LISTING 8.4 (CONTINUED)   NasPlayer Implementation

```
AuBool NasEventHandler(AuServer *,  // Unused
                       AuEvent *event,
                       AuEventHandlerRec *eventData)
{
   NasPlayer *me = reinterpret_cast<NasPlayer *>(eventData -> data);
   switch (event->type) {
   case AuEventTypeElementNotify:
      return me->Notify(reinterpret_cast<AuElementNotifyEvent *>(event));
   default:    // Some other event occurred.
      break;
   }
   return AuTrue;
}
```

Identifying an event requires several layers of classification. The first layer is the event *type*, which was handled in `NasEventHandler`. The `Notify` method handles notification types, classifying according to the *kind* of notification and the *reason* for that kind of notification. The two events that are important here are when the server reaches its low-water mark and when the server is forced to pause because of an empty buffer. Both of these cases result in a call to `SendData` to obtain more data and send it to the server.

Note that in normal operation, the server shouldn't report a pause. When debugging, however, you'll notice many pauses because when your program is stopped in the debugger, the server is still running. If you see a lot of pausing in normal play, you may need to increase the buffer size and raise the low-water mark.

LISTING 8.4 (CONTINUED)   NasPlayer Implementation

```
AuBool NasPlayer::Notify(AuElementNotifyEvent *notifyEvent) {
    switch (notifyEvent->kind) {
    case AuElementNotifyKindLowWater:    // Hit low water mark
        SendData(notifyEvent->num_bytes); // Send more data
        break;
    case AuElementNotifyKindState:
        // Server paused because of too little data?
        if (  (notifyEvent->cur_state == AuStatePause)
           && (notifyEvent->reason == AuReasonUnderrun))
            SendData(notifyEvent->num_bytes);
        else // Any other state change:  just end
            _finished = true;
        break;
    }
    return AuTrue;
}
```

Sending data to the server is simple. Just pull data from the queue and pass it to the server. The only trick is that the server indicates how many bytes of data it needs, not the number of samples needed. Also note that, unlike the Windows and Mac OS versions, the queue is refilled immediately, not in some other execution thread.

LISTING 8.4 (CONTINUED)   NasPlayer Implementation

```
void NasPlayer::SendData(AuUint32 numBytes){
    unsigned long bytesRead
        = FromQueue(_buffer,numBytes/sizeof(Sample16))
          * sizeof(Sample16);
    bool allDone = ((bytesRead < numBytes) && _endOfSource);
    AuWriteElement(_server, _flow, 0, bytesRead, _buffer,
                   allDone, NULL);
    FillQueue();
}
```

The NAS server doesn't use separate width and format information. Instead, it uses a single code to indicate both. The server can accept many types of PCM data, as well as a couple of compressed formats. (Remember that the server could be running on a different machine with a different byte order, so it is necessary to specify LSB or MSB.) This function converts a sample width into an appropriate server code. I also test the byte order of the local machine so that I can tell the server what format 16-bit samples will appear in.

This does assume that `short` is a 16-bit integer format; this is true for most modern compilers.

LISTING 8.4 (CONTINUED)　NasPlayer Implementation

```
unsigned char NasFormatCode(int sampleBits)
{
    if (sampleBits == 8)
        return AuFormatLinearSigned8;

    int lsb = 0; // default:  MSB format
    { // test native storage for LSB format
        union { short int sixteen; // 16-bit value
            struct { char a, b; } eight; // two 8-bit bytes
        } lsbTest ;
        lsbTest.sixteen = 1; // Set low-order byte, clear high-order
        if (lsbTest.eight.a) { lsb = 1; } // check first byte
    }

    if (lsb) return AuFormatLinearSigned16LSB;
    else return AuFormatLinearSigned16MSB;
}
```

Configuring a Flow and Attaching to the Server

Opening a connection to the server and configuring an appropriate flow is tedious but routine. This flow consists of two elements: An *import client* holds client data and requests additional data as needed. An *export device* feeds data to some output. There may be export devices for several audio cards and network services. In this case, I just want to ensure that the output device is a physical output device (a speaker) that supports the correct number of channels (mono or stereo). The final step, after registering the flow, is to register the callback function.

The `AuOpenServer` library function looks in a number of standard places to determine which server to use. It first looks in the `AUDIOSERVER` environment variable; if that doesn't exist, it uses the `DISPLAY` environment variable. Unlike the Mac OS and Windows versions, there's no need to worry about whether the server accepts 8-bit or 16-bit data. All NAS servers accept both and convert internally as necessary.

LISTING 8.4 (CONTINUED)   NasPlayer Implementation

```
void NasPlayer::OpenServer(){
   AuDeviceID deviceID = AuNone;

   // Open a connection to the server
   const char * const NullString = (const char *)NULL;
   char *server_message;
   _server = AuOpenServer(
         NullString,0,NullString,0,NullString, // Use defaults
                      &server_message); // Error message
   if (server_message != (char *)NULL) {
      cerr << "Could not connect to audio server.\n";
      cerr << "Server:  " << server_message << "\n";
      exit(1);
   }
   if (!_server) {
      cerr << "Could not connect to audio server.\n";
      exit(1);
   }

   // Select the first suitable output device
   for (int i=0; i< AuServerNumDevices(_server); i++) {
      AuDeviceAttributes *device = AuServerDevice(_server,i);
      if ((AuDeviceKind(device) == AuComponentKindPhysicalOutput) &&
          (AuDeviceNumTracks(device) == Channels())) {
         deviceID = AuDeviceIdentifier(device);
         break;
      }
   }
   if (deviceID == AuNone) {
      cerr << "No suitable audio output device found.\n";
      exit(1);
   }

   // Request a new flow on the server
   _flow = AuGetScratchFlow(_server,NULL);
   if (_flow == AuNone) {
      cerr << "Could not create audio flow on server.\n";
      exit(1);
   }

   // We need to tell the NAS server how to size its buffer
   long requestSize = (nasBufferSize)/Channels()/2;
```

```cpp
// Create elements for our flow
AuElement elements[2];

// First element is an Import element (I supply the data)
AuMakeElementImportClient(&elements[0], // First element
    SamplingRate(),              // sample rate
    NasFormatCode(16),            // get format code
    Channels(),                  // number of Channels
    AuTrue,                      // Start paused
    requestSize,                 // Samples to request
    requestSize/2,               // Low-water mark
    0,NULL);                     // No actions

// Last element is the output device
AuMakeElementExportDevice(&elements[1],
    0,                   // Get input from prev
    deviceID,            // ID of output device
    SamplingRate(),      // sample rate
    AuUnlimitedSamples,  // play forever
    0, NULL);            // No actions

// Register this flow with the server
AuStatus status;
AuSetElements(_server,_flow,AuTrue,2,elements,&status);
if (status) {
    cerr << "Couldn't configure flow.\n";
    exit(1);
}

// Register a handler for events from the import client
AuEventHandlerRec *handler =
    AuRegisterEventHandler(_server,
        AuEventHandlerIDMask, // Handle events from a particular element
        0,                     // ... element zero (import client)
        _flow,                 // ... in this flow
        NasEventHandler,       // This is the handler
        reinterpret_cast<AuPointer>(this)); // This is the aux data

if (!handler) {
    AuReleaseScratchFlow(_server,_flow,NULL);
    cerr << "Couldn't register event handler\n";
    exit(1);
}
}
```

A Sample UNIX Application

For this basic text-mode program, the main function is simple. Note that it can't accept data from cin because the OpenFormat function must be able to seek on the file.

LISTING 8.5   nasmain.cpp

```
Copyright © 1998, Tim Kientzle (Listing E.1)
#include "open.h"
#include "aplayer.h"
#include "nasplayr.h"
#include <fstream>

int main(int argc, char **argv) {
    while (--argc) {
        ++argv;
        cerr << "File:   " << *argv << "...\n";
        ifstream input(*argv);
        if (!input.is_open()) {
            cerr << "Couldn't open file " << *argv << "\n";
            continue;
        }
        AudioAbstract *audioFile = OpenFormat(input);
        if (audioFile) {
            NasPlayer player(audioFile);
            player.Play();
            delete audioFile;
            cerr << "Finished playing " << *argv << ".\n";
        }
        cerr << "\n";
    }
    return 0;
}
```

Part Three
Compression

Audio Compression 9

The basic idea behind any compression—for sound, video, or spreadsheets—is to find a way to represent data that takes up less space. Clearly, the better you understand your data, the more compactly you'll be able to store it. Today's best audio compression techniques exploit a variety of facts about the nature of real-world sounds and human hearing.

Although it's common to distinguish between "compressed" and "uncompressed" audio data, it's probably more accurate to simply think of different ways to "encode" audio data. The simplest encoding you'll encounter in working with digital audio is the PCM format I described back in Chapter 3, starting on page 25. Even this simple format is more complex than it might appear, and there are at least four PCM formats commonly used in disk files. Chapter 10, which starts on page 101, describes these in more detail.

Most programmers think of PCM data as uncompressed. If you start with PCM data, then audio compression algorithms convert PCM into a more compact format. In the rest of this chapter, I'll give an overview of the approaches that are used. The next several chapters will take detailed looks at specific, real-world compression algorithms.

Lossless Compression

Because there are so many types of data that people want to compress, there has been a lot of work over the years on *lossless* compression techniques. These are general-purpose algorithms that look for patterns in binary data. If they can locate patterns, they can compress the data by replacing blocks of data with codes indicating the pattern. The decompressor (which knows about the same types of patterns) can then undo this process.

These algorithms are lossless because the decompressed data will be bit-for-bit identical to the original. This is an important feature for general-purpose algorithms that might be used for any type of data. However, as you'll see, it's not necessary for audio compression to be lossless.

One approach—used by such algorithms as Lempel-Ziv-Welch (LZW), deflation, and Burroughs-Wheeler—is to look for long sequences of bytes that appear in several places. This works well for text because it's common for words or even entire phrases to be repeated. Many types of structured binary data, from spreadsheets to program executables, also contain this type of repetition.

However, sound files usually do not have a lot of long, repeated sequences, primarily because of noise. Any analog process contains a small amount of random error. When you record an analog sound, this random error shows up in the least significant bits of your sound file. Because it's random, it tends to prevent exact patterns from being identified.

Other general-purpose compression algorithms—including Huffman and arithmetic coding—look for certain byte values (or pairs of byte values) that occur more often than others. When they find this kind of pattern, they build codes that are shorter for more common values. Again, this works well for text because some letters, such as lowercase *e*, occur more often than others. Many other types of binary data contain large sections that consist of only zero bytes or contain a small number of values.

Sound files do have an uneven distribution of byte values, and so these types of algorithms work reasonably well for sound. However, the compression is modest, and because sound files can be very large, something better is usually necessary.

In addition to the fact that lossless algorithms don't usually work well with audio data, they have another drawback: The compression they provide is not uniform. Many applications—including streaming Internet sound—involve transferring sound data and playing it as it is received. Frequently, there are harsh restrictions on how quickly the data can be transferred. For example, a medium-speed modem can transfer about 3,000 bytes per second. To play sound over such a connection, you need to ensure that each second of sound can fit in 3,000 bytes. However, lossless compression algorithms can't guarantee this. Even if the overall compression is adequate, some parts of the sound will typically be compressed more than others.

In contrast, most of the sound compression algorithms I'll explore in the following chapters are fixed rate. The IMA ADPCM algorithm, for example, always compresses 16-bit sound by exactly 4:1.

Nonlinear PCM

As I mentioned earlier, choosing a good sample size is a trade-off. A smaller sample size reduces the amount of data, but because there are fewer values, you don't get as much accuracy. This loss of accuracy is more of a problem for quiet sounds than for loud ones. If your range of values is -64 to +63, then any sound less than 1/128 of the loudest possible sound will disappear.

One way to address the loss of quieter sounds is to redefine your numbers. Basic PCM is *linear*, which means, for example, that a value of 32 represents exactly twice as much sound intensity as a value of 16; a value of 63 represents exactly 63 times as much sound intensity as a value of 1. To get a wider dynamic range, you can use *nonlinear* encodings, in which a value of 1 might represent much less than 1/63 of the intensity represented by 63.

This simple approach works well. It consists of using the available bits more efficiently; you use more bits for quiet sounds in which the data loss is more audible. You can also think of this as a compression technique. The popular μ-Law (pronounced "mu-law") format is often described as compressing 12-bit samples into 8-bit samples.

The biggest reason nonlinear encodings aren't used more often is that it is easier to perform basic manipulations on linear sounds. Chapter 11, starting on page 107, describes nonlinear formats in more detail.

Differential PCM

If your sampling rate is sufficiently high, the differences between successive samples are likely to be small. As a result, you may be able to store the same sound signal using fewer bits per sample by storing the differences between successive samples rather than the samples themselves.

This technique is known as *differential PCM* (DPCM), sometimes called *delta modulation*. It is rarely used in software. To keep the differences small, you need to use a higher sampling rate, but that negates the benefits of smaller samples.

However, if you're willing to accept some error, DPCM can provide marginal compression. If one difference is too large to store in your format, you can compensate with later differences. For example, if three successive samples are 17, 22, and 23, the two differences are 5 and 1. If the largest difference you can store is 3, then you should store 3 and 3. The reconstructed samples will be 17, 20, 23.

Real-world DPCM techniques go a step further. Just as normal PCM sound samples tend to have mostly small values, DPCM differences also tend to be small. This makes a nonlinear format a reasonable match for DPCM, providing good speed and marginal compression. Chapter 12 (starting on page 117) discusses two simple DPCM encodings.

Adaptive Differential PCM

Adaptive Differential PCM (ADPCM) takes this idea a step further. Rather than using a fixed set of differences, you choose a set of possible differences based on prior data. This often takes the form of a variable scaling factor. If the scaling factor is small, you can represent small differences but not large ones; if the scaling factor is large, you can represent large differences but not small ones. By adjusting the scaling factor for different sections of the sound, you can provide better quality than plain DPCM.

ADPCM techniques are a popular means of sound compression. They are easy to program, fast, and can provide around 4:1 compression with reasonable sound quality. IMA ADPCM, discussed in Chapter 13, is an example of this type of encoding.

Predictor-Based Compression

The idea behind many compression techniques is to find a way to predict the next data element by looking at data that has already appeared. Intuitively, if you can correctly guess the next element, you don't need to store that element, because the decompressor can use the same technique to guess it correctly. This idea is also referred to as *data modeling*.

You can build a simple compression engine from any predictor function. For example, have the compressor compare the predicted value with the actual value. If the prediction is right, the compressor outputs a one bit. Otherwise, it outputs a zero bit followed by the actual value. If the predictor is exactly correct much of the time, the output of this process will be smaller than the input.

Because of random errors and other factors, it's difficult to guess exactly right. Instead, most predictor-based techniques output the difference between the prediction and the actual value. If the predictor is nearly correct most of the time, these differences will be small. You can store the differences using just a few bits for each one or use another technique to compress the differences.

For example, DPCM encoding uses the simplest predictor: It guesses that a sample will be identical to the previous sample. People have experimented with a variety of predictors in attempts to build better audio compression, but the additional computational overhead has limited their widespread use.

Subband Coding

One factor that limits the effectiveness of differential encoding techniques is frequency. As you might guess, low-frequency sounds tend to produce lots of small differences while higher-frequency sounds tend to produce larger differences. One way to improve differential techniques is to divide the sound into two or more frequency ranges, or *subbands*, and compress each one separately.

By using many subbands, you can exploit facts about human hearing to achieve even better compression. Because human hearing is more sensitive to some frequency ranges than to others, you can selectively compress subbands. Subbands near the center of the human hearing range can then be preserved while those to which human hearing is less sensitive can be treated less carefully, even dropped entirely. Subband coding can be complex, relying on both sophisticated mathematics to separate and analyze the subbands and careful study of human hearing to develop the rules for handling different subbands. Subband coding can typically compress PCM audio data by a factor of 10 to 20.

The most sophisticated compression techniques currently available, including MPEG audio, Dolby AC-2 and AC-3, the Sony MiniDisc system, and RealAudio, are all based on subband coding.

Human Speech Compression

The techniques discussed so far were developed to handle all types of sound, including music and speech. If you're interested only in speech, you can use techniques developed specifically for that purpose.

The simplest speech-specific compression technique is *silence encoding*. When people speak, there are many pauses. Some are short pauses between words and phrases; others are longer pauses between sentences or when changing speakers. You can often compress speech data by as much as 50 percent by identifying these silences and replacing them with compact duration codes.

More sophisticated speech-specific compression techniques consist of two parts. The first is a mathematical model of the human vocal tract. This model is a series of equations that uses information about the larynx, throat, tongue, and lips to produce the same kinds of sounds that humans produce. The second part is an analysis engine that can take a sound and create the parameters for the model. To compress human speech, you use the analysis engine to produce a series of parameters. To decompress, you feed the parameters into the vocal tract model to recreate the sounds. These techniques can sometimes compress human speech by a factor of 100 or more while maintaining good quality.

One interesting aspect of these techniques is that by modifying the playback model slightly, you can modify certain voice characteristics. As a result, speech compression techniques often form the basis of voice modification algorithms.

Checkpointing

Sophisticated compressors accumulate information about the sound as they work. This information is used to adjust the compressor for better operation on each successive sample. The decompressor tracks this information as it decompresses. Often, the compressor will update its internal information after each compressed sample. As long as the decompressor performs an identical update after decompressing each sample, the two will maintain identical statistics.

This internal information can sometimes be complex, creating a subtle problem. For a variety of reasons, it is often necessary to start decoding a sound in the middle. For example, if you are receiving streaming audio over a network or broadcast radio, you may not have the earlier data. Alternatively, a block of data might be lost, forcing you to restart your decompressor with the next correct data.

Because the decompressor won't have the accumulated information from the previous data, it might be impossible to restart the decompressor. At the beginning of the data, this isn't a problem; the compressor and decompressor simply need to agree on reasonable starting assumptions. But when you start in the middle, you're dealing with data that was compressed with full knowledge of the preceding data.

One way around this is for the compressor to occasionally insert additional *checkpoint* information that the decompressor can use to restart at that point. Sometimes, this requires inserting blocks of uncompressed data. For example, the codecs developed by Apple for use with its Sound Manager software use blocks of uncompressed data as checkpoints. At other times, this will involve dumping the compressor's internal state information. One of the strengths of the IMA ADPCM compressor is that it can store most of its compression state in only 16 bits.

Another way to handle checkpointing is to store independent "packets" of sound data. Typically, a packet will contain initialization information for the decompressor, followed by compressed sound data. By compressing blocks of sound data independently, you can always decompress the next block even if you lack the previous block. Choosing the optimal packet size is tricky. Because each packet contains a certain amount of overhead, you want your packet size to be large. However, if a packet is lost, the sound must stop until the next packet is received. Similarly, if you want to start at a point just before the end of a packet, you may need to decompress that entire packet before you can start playing.

Progressive Compression

In many computer applications, your bandwidth limitations are thoroughly understood. A single-speed CD-ROM player can provide precisely 176,400 bytes per second of data, so if you need to retrieve several types of data, you can accurately predict how fast that data will become available and choose an appropriate compression method. But you don't always know these limits so precisely. For example, the bandwidth of a network connection can vary widely. It would be nice if you could easily vary the amount of compression. When data is flowing quickly, you could provide more data for higher quality sound. When the connection slows, you could provide less data.

One way to support this is to use *progressive compression*. A typical progressive compression scheme works like this:

- Start with a block of uncompressed data.

- Compress it using a very lossy scheme. The result will be a small packet of low-quality compressed data. Call this the *compressed original*.

- Now uncompress that packet and subtract it from your original. Call this the *first-order error*.

- Compress the first-order error.

- Uncompress the compressed first-order error and subtract it from the original first-order error. Call this the *second-order error*.

- Repeat to get the third- and higher-order errors.

The result of this process is that a single block of PCM data has been converted into several packets of compressed data. By choosing the correct degree of compression at each step, the error packets will be about the same size as the compressed original. You can uncompress just the first packet and get a poor version of the sound. If you uncompress the first two and add them together, you'll get a better version. If you uncompress and add together the first three, you'll get an even better version.

This scheme gives the sender the ability to adapt easily to different requirements. When data is moving slowly, you send only the compressed original. When data is moving more quickly, you also send one or more error packets. This scheme lets you take advantage of the available bandwidth even when that bandwidth varies. Unlike some alternative approaches, it does not require storing multiple versions of the data or decompressing and recompressing data on the fly.

This technique can also be used when you have to store one copy of your sound data and have the result playable on a range of different computer systems. Slower systems might have only enough horsepower to decompress and play the first packet; more powerful systems can decompress several packets to provide higher-quality sound.

Decompression Classes

10

In this chapter, I'll present the basic framework for a family of decompression objects and build four very simple decompressors.

The basic idea behind all audio decompressors is that they convert bytes into audio samples. In order to do this conversion, my classes accept requests for new samples via `GetSamples` and ask another object for bytes via `ReadBytes`.

The classes to read from audio files will create these decompression objects as they are needed. After a decompressor has been created, the file object can route `GetSamples` requests through the decompressor, as shown in Figure 10.1. This arrangement makes it easy for file format classes to support a variety of compression methods. My decompression objects are similar to the *codec* (compression/decompression) modules used by many audio frameworks.

The classes that handle the actual decompression will inherit from the simple `AbstractDecompressor` class below. Specific decompressors will implement the `GetSamples` method to pull raw bytes from `_dataSource.ReadBytes()` and decompress them.

FIGURE 10.1   A Decompression Object Requests Bytes and Returns Samples

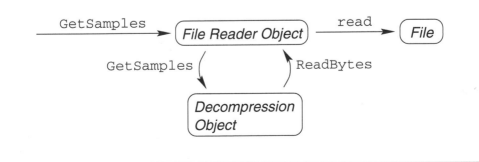

LISTING 10.1   compress.h

Copyright © 1998, Tim Kientzle (Listing E.1)

```cpp
#ifndef COMPR_H_INCLUDED
#define COMPR_H_INCLUDED

#include "audio.h"
#include <iostream>
#include <cstddef>

class AbstractDecompressor {
protected:
    AudioAbstract &_dataSource;  // The object to get raw bytes from
    size_t ReadBytes(AudioByte *buff, size_t length) {
        return _dataSource.ReadBytes(buff,length);
    };
public:
    AbstractDecompressor(AudioAbstract &a):  _dataSource(a) {};
    virtual ~AbstractDecompressor() {};
    virtual size_t GetSamples(AudioSample *, size_t) = 0;
    virtual void MinMaxSamplingRate(long *, long *, long *) {
        cerr << "MinMaxSamplingRate undefined\n";
        exit(1);
    }
    virtual void MinMaxChannels(int *, int *, int *) {
        cerr << "MinMaxChannels undefined\n";
        exit(1);
    }
};
```

8-Bit PCM Classes (Listing 10.3)

16-Bit PCM Classes (Listing 10.5)

```cpp
#endif
```

LISTING 10.2   compress.cpp

Copyright © 1998, Tim Kientzle (Listing E.1)

```cpp
#include "compress.h"
```

8-Bit PCM Implementation (Listing 10.4)

16-Bit PCM Implementation (Listing 10.6)

8-Bit PCM

As I mentioned before, although most programmers think of PCM data as "not compressed," it's more accurate to think not of compression, but of *encoding*. PCM is an encoding like any other. Unfortunately, there are many PCM encodings in common use.

Usually, PCM sound data is stored with 8 or 16 bits (1 or 2 bytes) per sample. Even with only 1 byte per sample, however, there's room for some disagreement.

Signed 8-Bit PCM

In order to store audio data, you must store both positive and negative numbers, and not everyone agrees on how to do that.

Signed format (also known as *two's complement*) uses a single byte to represent sample values from -128 to +127. Sample values from 0 to +127 are kept the same; negative sample values from -128 to -1 are converted into binary bytes by adding 256. This is the same as the internal format used by most computer systems and is generally preferred by programmers.

LISTING 10.3   8-Bit PCM Classes

```
class DecompressPcm8Signed: public AbstractDecompressor {
public:
   DecompressPcm8Signed(AudioAbstract &a): AbstractDecompressor(a) {
      cerr << "Encoding:  8-bit signed (two's complement) PCM\n";
   };
   size_t GetSamples(AudioSample * buffer, size_t length);
};
```

Although short, this implementation of `GetSamples` does use a few tricks. The first is that because 8-bit samples are smaller than the `AudioSample` type, it can reuse the same buffer. It's also careful not to overwrite unconverted data when it converts the 8-bit samples into the larger `AudioSample` type. Note the types: Any audio decompressor reads *bytes* but returns *samples*. Also notice that the short 8-bit samples are left-shifted into the most significant bits of the larger `AudioSample` values.

LISTING 10.4   8-Bit PCM Implementation

```
size_t DecompressPcm8Signed::GetSamples(AudioSample * buffer, size_t length) {
   AudioByte *byteBuff = reinterpret_cast<AudioByte *>(buffer);
   size_t samplesRead = ReadBytes(byteBuff,length);
   for(long i=samplesRead-1; i>=0; i--)
      buffer[i] = static_cast<AudioSample>(byteBuff[i])
               << ((sizeof(AudioSample)-1)*8);
   return samplesRead;
}
```

Unsigned 8-Bit PCM

Unsigned format (also known as *excess-128*) uses the same range of sample values from -128 to +127, and adds 128 to get a byte value from 0 to 255. In particular, a sample value of 0 becomes a byte value of 128. Unsigned format is specified by some telecommunications standards and is widely used in hardware designs.

LISTING 10.3 (CONTINUED)   8-Bit PCM Classes

```
class DecompressPcm8Unsigned: public AbstractDecompressor {
public:
   DecompressPcm8Unsigned(AudioAbstract &a): AbstractDecompressor(a) {
      cerr << "Encoding:  8-bit unsigned (excess-128) PCM\n";
   };
   size_t GetSamples(AudioSample * buffer, size_t length);
};
```

The only real difference between signed and unsigned numbers is the top bit. For signed format, the top bit is set for negative numbers; unsigned format sets the top bit for positive numbers. Thus, converting unsigned values requires reading a block of bytes, then toggling the top bit of each byte. This is identical to the earlier version of `GetSamples` except for the exclusive-or, which toggles the top bit.

LISTING 10.4 (CONTINUED)   8-Bit PCM Implementation

```
size_t DecompressPcm8Unsigned::GetSamples(AudioSample * buffer,
                                size_t length) {
   AudioByte *byteBuff =
      reinterpret_cast<AudioByte *>(buffer);
   size_t samplesRead = ReadBytes(byteBuff,length);
   for(long i=samplesRead-1; i>=0; i--)
      buffer[i] = static_cast<AudioSample>(byteBuff[i] ^ 0x80)
               << ((sizeof(AudioSample)-1)*8);
   return samplesRead;
}
```

16-Bit PCM

There are also signed and unsigned 16-bit formats, but the unsigned 16-bit format is rarely used. The more significant difference is the order in which the 2 bytes of a 16-bit sample are stored in a file. (This same issue arises with less common 24-bit and 32-bit samples.)

MSB 16-Bit PCM

MSB format stores the most significant byte first, followed by the least significant byte. This format is common among audio files for the Macintosh or Amiga, which use Motorola 680x0-family processors. This byte order also agrees with the network format used by many Internet standards.

LISTING 10.5   16-Bit PCM Classes

```
class DecompressPcm16MsbSigned: public AbstractDecompressor {
public:
   DecompressPcm16MsbSigned(AudioAbstract &a): AbstractDecompressor(a) {
      cerr << "Encoding:  16-bit MSB PCM\n";
   };
   size_t GetSamples(AudioSample *buffer, size_t length);
};
```

For efficiency, the 16-bit version of `GetSamples` just reads bytes into the buffer and then converts each pair of bytes into a single sample. Note that the code here is completely portable; it makes no assumptions about the byte order of the machine running this code. This code also works for any size of `AudioSample` that's at least 16 bits.

LISTING 10.6   16-Bit PCM Implementation

```
size_t DecompressPcm16MsbSigned::GetSamples(AudioSample *buffer,
                                 size_t length) {
   AudioByte *byteBuff =
      reinterpret_cast<AudioByte *>(buffer);
   size_t read = ReadBytes(byteBuff,length*2)/2;
   for(long i=read-1; i>=0; i--) {
      short s = static_cast<AudioSample>(byteBuff[2*i]) << 8;
      s |= static_cast<AudioSample>(byteBuff[2*i+1]) & 255;
      buffer[i] = static_cast<AudioSample>(s)
                  << ((sizeof(AudioSample)-2)*8);
   }
   return read;
}
```

LSB 16-Bit PCM

LSB format stores the least significant byte first, followed by the most significant byte. This is common in formats for MS-DOS, OS/2, and Microsoft Windows, which use Intel 80x86-family processors.

LISTING 10.5 (CONTINUED)   16-Bit PCM Classes

```cpp
class DecompressPcm16LsbSigned: public AbstractDecompressor {
public:
   DecompressPcm16LsbSigned(AudioAbstract &a): AbstractDecompressor(a) {
      cerr << "Encoding:  16-bit LSB PCM\n";
   };
   size_t GetSamples(AudioSample *buffer, size_t length);
};
```

LISTING 10.6 (CONTINUED)   16-Bit PCM Implementation

```cpp
size_t DecompressPcm16LsbSigned::GetSamples(AudioSample *buffer,
                                            size_t length) {
   AudioByte *byteBuff =
      reinterpret_cast<AudioByte *>(buffer);
   size_t read = ReadBytes(byteBuff,length*2)/2;
   for(long i=read-1; i>=0; i--) {
      short s = static_cast<AudioSample>(byteBuff[2*i+1]) << 8;
      s |= static_cast<AudioSample>(byteBuff[2*i]) & 255;
      buffer[i] = static_cast<AudioSample>(s)
                  << ((sizeof(AudioSample)-2)*8);
   }
   return read;
}
```

Nonlinear Sound Formats 11

Linear PCM sound storage is somewhat naive. Human hearing is relatively insensitive to small errors in loud sounds but more sensitive to similar errors in quiet sounds. PCM, however, allows the same degree of error regardless of the amplitude.

Remember that the byte value you use to store a sample is just a code. It makes sense to take a careful look at those codes and see if redefining them will improve the sound we can fit into a given sample size. This is the idea behind a couple of alternatives to plain PCM.

Linear PCM will always be preferred for manipulating sound. Whenever you mix two sounds by adding or adjust volume by multiplication, you're assuming your sound format is linear. But nonlinear formats make sense for transferring and storing sound.

Logarithmic Compression

The two most common nonlinear formats are more similar than different. Both *μ-Law* and *A-Law* compression use logarithmic formulas to convert linear PCM samples into 8-bit codes.

This approach works well for several reasons. First, most sound consists predominantly of small samples. These encodings provide more accuracy for these common values at the cost of less accuracy for relatively infrequent large samples. Second, human hearing is logarithmic; a change in the intensity of a quiet sound is more noticeable than a similar change in the intensity of a loud sound. Essentially, logarithmic encoding provides more accuracy where that accuracy is most audible.

In the rest of this chapter, I'll develop code for two common logarithmic compression schemes. These schemes were originally developed for use by telephone systems and were later incorporated into the ITU G.711 standard.

LISTING 11.1   g711.h

```
Copyright © 1998, Tim Kientzle (Listing E.1)
#ifndef G711_H_INCLUDED
#define G711_H_INCLUDED
#include "audio.h"
#include "compress.h"

Mu-Law Interface (Listing 11.3)

A-Law Interface (Listing 11.5)
#endif
```

You can think of a logarithm as computing the number of digits. It's no surprise that the starting point for logarithmic formats is a table that specifies, for every 8-bit binary value, the number of bits required for that value.

LISTING 11.2   g711.cpp

```
Copyright © 1998, Tim Kientzle (Listing E.1)
#include "audio.h"
#include "g711.h"

/* The number of bits required by each value */
static unsigned char numBits[] = {
    0,1,2,2,3,3,3,3,4,4,4,4,4,4,4,4,5,5,5,5,5,5,5,5,5,5,5,5,5,5,5,5,
    6,6,6,6,6,6,6,6,6,6,6,6,6,6,6,6,6,6,6,6,6,6,6,6,6,6,6,6,6,6,6,6,
    7,7,7,7,7,7,7,7,7,7,7,7,7,7,7,7,7,7,7,7,7,7,7,7,7,7,7,7,7,7,7,7,
    7,7,7,7,7,7,7,7,7,7,7,7,7,7,7,7,7,7,7,7,7,7,7,7,7,7,7,7,7,7,7,7,
    8,8,8,8,8,8,8,8,8,8,8,8,8,8,8,8,8,8,8,8,8,8,8,8,8,8,8,8,8,8,8,8,
    8,8,8,8,8,8,8,8,8,8,8,8,8,8,8,8,8,8,8,8,8,8,8,8,8,8,8,8,8,8,8,8,
    8,8,8,8,8,8,8,8,8,8,8,8,8,8,8,8,8,8,8,8,8,8,8,8,8,8,8,8,8,8,8,8,
    8,8,8,8,8,8,8,8,8,8,8,8,8,8,8,8,8,8,8,8,8,8,8,8,8,8,8,8,8,8,8,8,
};

Mu-Law Implementation (Listing 11.4)

A-Law Implementation (Listing 11.6)
```

μ-Law Compression

The most common nonlinear format in the United States is μ-law encoding, sometimes written "u-Law" or "mu-Law" (μ is the Greek letter *mu*). For simplicity in writing the formulas, I'll assume all samples are fractional values between -1 and 1. If you're using 16-bit samples, you'll need to divide by 32,768 before using these formulas.

If you have a sample s, the corresponding μ-Law sample s_μ is $\text{sign}(s) \log(1 + 255|s|) / \log(1 + 255)$. This is easier to remember if you consider it only for positive values, in which case it simplifies to $\log(1 + 255s) / \log(1 + 255)$. The value 255 here is sometimes replaced by other values.

To convert from μ-Law back into linear values, you just reverse this formula: $s = (256^{s_\mu} - 1) / 255$. Remember that this is only for positive values; you'll need to take the absolute value of the input and negate the output for negative values.

The formulas above are not used directly because logarithms and powers are time consuming to compute. In software, you can compensate by using precomputed lookup tables. But μ-Law was originally designed for hardware implementations, where lookup tables are less practical. For this reason, the ITU G.711 standard specifies a particular approximation that can be easily computed in hardware. This approximation matches the above formulas closely, as you can see in Figure 11.1, although there's enough difference that you don't want to mix them.

FIGURE 11.1   Two μ-Law-to-Linear Conversions

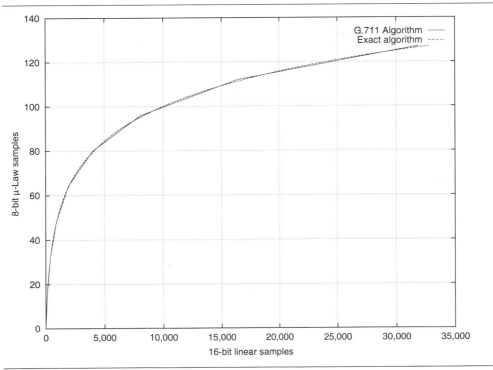

The `DecompressG711MuLaw` class below provides G.711-compatible decompression routines using the framework developed in Chapter 9.

LISTING 11.3   Mu-Law Interface

```
class DecompressG711MuLaw:  public AbstractDecompressor {
public:
   DecompressG711MuLaw(AudioAbstract &a);
   size_t GetSamples(AudioSample *buffer, size_t length);
};

AudioSample MuLawDecode(AudioByte);
AudioByte MuLawEncode(AudioSample);
```

If you'd like to experiment, I've made the `MuLawDecode` and `MuLawEncode` functions public.

For speed, the `DecompressG711MuLaw` class uses `MuLawDecode` to initialize an internal table and then uses that table for fast decoding. This table needs to be initialized only the first time a `DecompressG711MuLaw` object is created.

LISTING 11.4   Mu-Law Implementation

```
/* Mu-Law conversions */
static bool muLawDecodeTableInitialized = false;
static AudioSample muLawDecodeTable[256];

// Constructor initializes the decoding table
DecompressG711MuLaw::DecompressG711MuLaw(AudioAbstract &a)
       : AbstractDecompressor(a) {
   cerr << "Encoding:  ITU G.711 mu-Law\n";
   if (!muLawDecodeTableInitialized) {
      muLawDecodeTableInitialized = true;
      for(int i=0;i<256;i++)
         muLawDecodeTable[i] = MuLawDecode(i);
   }
}
```

The `GetSamples` method is simple. I just read the bytes and use the lookup table to decode each one. By doing the conversion from back-to-front in the buffer, I avoid accidentally overwriting data that hasn't yet been decoded.

LISTING 11.4 (CONTINUED)   Mu-Law Implementation

```
size_t DecompressG711MuLaw::GetSamples(AudioSample *buffer,
                                       size_t length) {
   AudioByte *byteBuff =
      reinterpret_cast<AudioByte *>(buffer);
   size_t read = ReadBytes(byteBuff,length);
```

```
   for(long i=read-1; i>=0; i--)
     buffer[i] = muLawDecodeTable[ byteBuff[i] ];
   return read;
};
```

The G.711 approximation uses simple bit manipulations to approximate the logarithm. After an initial adjustment, it computes the number of bits required for the upper byte and combines that with the four most significant bits.

LISTING 11.4 (CONTINUED)   Mu-Law Implementation

```
AudioByte MuLawEncode(AudioSample s) {
   unsigned char sign = (s<0)?0:0x80; // Save the sign
   if (s<0) s=-s; // make sample positive
   signed long adjusted = static_cast<long>(s) << (16-sizeof(AudioSample)*8);
   adjusted += 128L+4L;
   if (adjusted > 32767) adjusted = 32767;
   unsigned char exponent = numBits[(adjusted>>7)&0xFF] - 1;
   unsigned char mantissa = (adjusted >> (exponent + 3)) & 0xF;
   return ~(sign | (exponent << 4) | mantissa);
};
```

The decoder works similarly. It uses the top bit as a sign, and uses the next three bits to determine how to shift the bottom four bits.

LISTING 11.4 (CONTINUED)   Mu-Law Implementation

```
AudioSample MuLawDecode(AudioByte ulaw) {
   ulaw = ~ulaw;
   unsigned char exponent = (ulaw >> 4) & 0x7;
   unsigned char mantissa = (ulaw & 0xF) + 16;
   unsigned long adjusted = (mantissa << (exponent + 3)) - 128 - 4;
   return (ulaw & 0x80)? adjusted :  -adjusted;
};
```

If you're familiar with floating-point formats, you'll notice that this looks remarkably like an 8-bit floating-point representation with 1 bit for sign, 3 bits for an exponent, and 4 bits for a mantissa. Note that, as with most floating-point formats, the most significant bit of the mantissa is dropped and needs to be re-added in MuLawDecode by adding 16 to the mantissa.

If you study this algorithm carefully, you'll notice one point that requires some careful consideration. Note that in MuLawEncode, the 16-bit PCM value is offset by 128 and 4 before the rest of the conversion. Similarly, in MuLawDecode, this amount is subtracted after the conversion. If you look at this as a logarithm approximation, the 128 is used to circumvent a basic discontinuity. If you look carefully at the algorithm, you'll also notice that only the top 13 bits are ever used. Adding 4 rounds the value to the nearest multiple of 8, improving the accuracy.

A-Law

The A-Law encoding is similar in concept. Like μ-Law, it was originally designed for use in telephone systems. Where μ-Law is used by telephone systems in North America and Japan, A-Law is used predominantly in Europe. Also like μ-Law, it's defined by both a continuous function and a fast digital approximation.

A-Law actually defines a collection of encodings, depending on the precise value of a numerical coefficient A. The most common value for A is 87.6. If you have a sample s betweeen 0 and 1, the following formula gives you the A-Law sample s_A:

$$
s_A = \begin{cases} \frac{A}{1+\ln A}(s) & s \leq \frac{1}{A} \\[2mm] \frac{1+\ln(As)}{1+\ln A} & \frac{1}{A} \leq |s| \leq 1 \end{cases}
$$

The digital approximation is remarkably similar to the μ-Law approximation. The primary difference is that the A-Law encoding inverts every other bit in the output code.

LISTING 11.5   A-Law Interface

```cpp
class DecompressG711ALaw:  public AbstractDecompressor {
private:
    static AudioSample *_decodeTable;
public:
    DecompressG711ALaw(AudioAbstract &a);
    size_t GetSamples(AudioSample *buffer, size_t length);
};


AudioSample ALawDecode(AudioByte);
AudioByte ALawEncode(AudioSample);
```

LISTING 11.6   A-Law Implementation

```cpp
static bool aLawDecodeTableInitialized = false;
static AudioSample aLawDecodeTable[256];

DecompressG711ALaw::DecompressG711ALaw(AudioAbstract &a)
        :  AbstractDecompressor(a) {
    cerr << "Encoding:  ITU G.711 A-Law\n";
    if (!aLawDecodeTableInitialized) {
        aLawDecodeTableInitialized = true;
        for(int i=0;i<256;i++)
```

```
                    aLawDecodeTable[i] = ALawDecode(i);
        }
    }

    size_t DecompressG711ALaw::GetSamples(AudioSample *buffer, size_t length) {
        AudioByte *byteBuff =
            reinterpret_cast<AudioByte *>(buffer);
        size_t read = ReadBytes(byteBuff,length);
        for(long i=read-1; i>=0; i--)
            buffer[i] = aLawDecodeTable[ byteBuff[i] ];
        return read;
    }

    AudioByte ALawEncode(AudioSample s) {
        unsigned char sign = (s<0)?0:0x80; // Save the sign
        if (s<0) s=-s; // make sample positive
        signed long adjusted = static_cast<long>(s)+8L; // Round it
        if (adjusted > 32767) adjusted = 32767; // Clip it
        unsigned char exponent = numBits[(adjusted>>8)&0x7F];
        unsigned char mantissa = (adjusted >> (exponent + 4)) & 0xF;
        return sign | (((exponent << 4) | mantissa) ^ 0x55);
    };

    AudioSample ALawDecode(AudioByte alaw) {
        alaw ^= 0x55;
        unsigned char exponent = (alaw >> 4) & 0x7;
        unsigned char mantissa = (alaw & 0xF) + (exponent?16:0);
        unsigned long adjusted = (mantissa << (exponent + 4));
        return (alaw & 0x80)? -adjusted :  adjusted;
    };
```

Properties of Logarithmic Encodings

To really understand what logarithmic encodings accomplish, you have to think carefully about *signal-to-noise ratio* (SNR), which is the ratio of the signal level to the error signal, as I discussed on page 33.

For linear PCM, you're taking some analog signal and rounding each ideal sample value to the nearest integer. As a result, the difference between the ideal sample value and the PCM sample value is always less than one-half. For logarithmic encoding, things are more complex. For large samples, logarithmic encodings have more error. For small samples, logarithmic encodings have less error.

Think about how this varying error level affects the total power of the error. If your original signal becomes louder, you'll have larger samples and hence larger errors. These will cause the power of the error to go up as the signal power goes up. In fact, for a true logarithmic encoding, the signal-to-noise ratio is relatively constant.

To see this, you can use a program similar to logtest.cpp, shown in Listing 11.7. This takes 1,000 samples of a sine wave and computes the total error power for PCM and μ-Law encodings. It does this for peak sample levels ranging from 100 to 32,000.

LISTING 11.7   logtest.cpp

```cpp
#include "audio.h"
#include "g711.h"
#include <math.h>

void SNR(AudioSample magnitude) {
   // Build a one-cycle sine wave
   float original[1000];
   for(int i=0;i<1000;i++)
      original[i] = sin(i*2.0*3.14159265/1000.0)*magnitude;

   // Compress it
   AudioByte compressed[1000];
   for(int i=0;i<1000;i++)
      compressed[i] = MuLawEncode(static_cast<AudioSample>(original[i]));

   // Uncompress it
   AudioSample uncompressed[1000];
   for(int i=0;i<1000;i++)
      uncompressed[i] = MuLawDecode(compressed[i]);

   // Figure the error
   float error[1000];
   for(int i=0;i<1000;i++)
      error[i] = original[i] - uncompressed[i];

   // Compute total power
   float originalPower = 0.0,  errorPower = 0.0, pcmErrorPower = 0.0;
   for(int i=0;i<1000;i++) {
      originalPower += original[i] * original[i];
      errorPower += error[i] * error[i];
      float pcmError = original[i] - static_cast<AudioSample>(original[i]);
      pcmErrorPower += pcmError * pcmError;
   }
   // output magnitude and SNR
   cout << magnitude;
   cout << " " << 10*log10(originalPower/errorPower);
   cout << " " << 10*log10(originalPower/pcmErrorPower);
   cout << "\n";
}

int main() {
   int magnitude = 100;
   for (; magnitude < 32000; magnitude += 100)
      SNR(magnitude);
   return 0;
}
```

Figure 11.2 plots the output of this program. The horizontal axis is the maximum amplitude of the test sine wave; the vertical axis represents the SNR in decibels. Because PCM has a fixed noise floor, you expect the SNR to increase logarithmically (because decibels are measured logarithmically). Note that the SNR for the logarithmic encoding is nearly constant around 30 dB, regardless of the signal level. The wobble occurs primarily because G.711 μ-Law is only an approximation to a logarithmic encoding.

FIGURE 11.2   Signal-to-Noise Ratio for PCM and Logarithmic Encodings

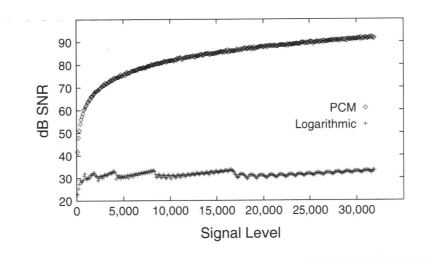

Differential PCM

12

Differential PCM (DPCM, sometimes called *delta encoding*) is a simple way to achieve modest compression. Instead of storing the samples directly, DPCM stores the differences between successive samples. If your sampling rate is fairly high, these differences will tend to be small. As a result, you can use fewer bits per sample to store just the differences.

For example, suppose you want to reduce 8-bit PCM data to a series of 4-bit differences. This is simple as long as you're careful to handle overflows correctly. In particular, consider the three samples 17, 28, 30. The two differences are 11 and 2. Because you're using 4 bits for each difference, you can only store values from -8 to +7. If you naively clip the 11 down to 7 and store the differences as 7 and 2, the decoder will decode 17, 24, 26. However, if you store the differences as 7 and 6, the decoder will decode 17, 24, 30. In this case, only one sample is in error.

The trick here is that the compressor always uses the difference between the next actual sample and the previous decoded sample. As you'll see, this is common; many compressors must decompress their own output as they go along.

Another potential pitfall in handling DPCM is that the range of possible differences may be larger than you expect. If you have 8-bit samples that range from -128 to +127, your largest difference is 255 and your smallest difference is -255. Just because your sound samples fit into a single byte does not mean the differences will fit into a single byte.

Two DPCM Encodings

The challenge in designing a good DPCM technique is balancing two requirements. For high fidelity, you want to be able to accurately represent each difference, especially small differences. But the large range of possible differences means you also need to be able to store occasional large differences. Usually, this means that the difference is itself encoded. For example, Table 12.1 shows the encodings used by two compression methods for the Amiga. Each of these schemes compresses 8-bit samples to 4-bit encoded differences.

TABLE 12.1   Coded Differences for IFF/8SVX Type 1 and 2 Compression

Code Value	-8	-7	-6	-5	-4	-3	-2	-1	0	1	2	3	4	5	6	7
Fibonacci	-34	-21	-13	-8	-5	-3	-2	-1	0	1	2	3	5	8	13	21
Exponential	-128	-64	-32	-16	-8	-4	-2	-1	0	1	2	4	8	16	32	64

Note that both of these encodings provide many small values (small differences are generally more common) and a few larger values.

In particular, note that the exponential encoding used here (which uses powers of 2) is similar in concept to the step-size table used by the more sophisticated IMA ADPCM encoding (which uses powers of 1.1; see Chapter 13 on page 122).

LISTING 12.1   dpcm.h

```
Copyright © 1998, Tim Kientzle (Listing E.1)
#ifndef DPCM_H_INCLUDED
#define DPCM_H_INCLUDED

#include "audio.h"
#include "compress.h"

class DecompressDpcmFibonacci: public AbstractDecompressor {
private:
   AudioSample _previousValue;
public:
   DecompressDpcmFibonacci(AudioAbstract &a):  AbstractDecompressor(a) {
      cerr << "Encoding:  Fibonacci Dpcm\n";
      _previousValue = 0;
   };
   size_t GetSamples(AudioSample * buffer, size_t length);
};

class DecompressDpcmExponential: public AbstractDecompressor {
private:
   AudioSample _previousValue;
public:
   DecompressDpcmExponential(AudioAbstract &a):  AbstractDecompressor(a) {
      cerr << "Encoding:  Exponential Dpcm\n";
      _previousValue = 0;
   };
   size_t GetSamples(AudioSample * buffer, size_t length);
};
#endif
```

LISTING 12.2   dpcm.cpp

```
Copyright © 1998, Tim Kientzle (Listing E.1)
#include "audio.h"
#include "compress.h"
#include "dpcm.h"

static const signed char fibonacci[] = {
   -34, -21, -13, -8, -5, -3, -2, -1, 0, 1, 2, 3, 5, 8, 13, 21
};

static const signed char exponential[] = {
   -128, -64, -32, -16, -8, -4, -2, -1, 0, 1, 2, 4, 8, 16, 32, 64
};

Fibonacci DPCM GetSamples (Listing 12.3)

Exponential DPCM GetSamples (Listing 12.4)
```

The actual decompression process is simple. For each nybble, you look up the decoded increment in a table and add it to _previousValue to get the next sample. This routine economizes by reading the compressed bytes into the end of the provided buffer and then converting the data in place. You need to read the compressed data into the end of the buffer so that you don't overwrite it as you convert. Also, note that because the Amiga hardware supports only 8-bit samples, all Amiga compression routines assume 8-bit samples; I need to shift the difference into the upper byte before adding.

LISTING 12.3   Fibonacci DPCM GetSamples

```
size_t DecompressDpcmFibonacci::GetSamples(AudioSample * buffer,
                                 size_t length) {
   AudioByte *byteBuffer =
       reinterpret_cast<AudioByte *>(buffer)
       + length * sizeof(AudioSample) // buffer length
       - length / 2 ; // Space needed for compressed data
   AudioSample *sampleBuffer = buffer;

   // Read encoded data into the buffer
   size_t bytesRead = ReadBytes(byteBuffer,length/2);
   for(size_t i=0; i<bytesRead; i++) {
      // Decode low-order nybble
      int nybble = (static_cast<int>(*byteBuffer>>4)+8)&0xF;
      _previousValue +=
            static_cast<AudioSample>(fibonacci[nybble])
            << ((sizeof(AudioSample)-1)*8);
      *sampleBuffer++ = _previousValue;
      // Decode high-order nybble
      nybble = (static_cast<int>(*byteBuffer)+8)&0xF;
```

```
    _previousValue +=
            static_cast<AudioSample>(fibonacci[nybble])
            << ((sizeof(AudioSample)-1)*8);
    *sampleBuffer++ = _previousValue;
  }
  return bytesRead * 2;
}
```

The decoder for exponential DPCM is identical except that it uses a different table.

LISTING 12.4   Exponential DPCM GetSamples

```
size_t DecompressDpcmExponential::GetSamples(AudioSample * buffer,
                            size_t length) {
  AudioByte *byteBuffer =
        reinterpret_cast<AudioByte *>(buffer)
        + length * sizeof(AudioSample) // buffer length
        - length / 2 ; // Space needed for compressed data
  AudioSample *sampleBuffer = buffer;

  // Read encoded data into the buffer
  size_t bytesRead = ReadBytes(byteBuffer,length/2);
  for(size_t i=0; i<bytesRead; i++) {
    // Decode low-order nybble
    int nybble = (static_cast<int>(*byteBuffer>>4)+8)&0xF;
    _previousValue +=
            static_cast<AudioSample>(exponential[nybble])
            << ((sizeof(AudioSample)-1)*8);
    *sampleBuffer++ = _previousValue;
    // Decode high-order nybble
    nybble = (static_cast<int>(*byteBuffer)+8)&0xF;
    _previousValue +=
            static_cast<AudioSample>(exponential[nybble])
            << ((sizeof(AudioSample)-1)*8);
    *sampleBuffer++ = _previousValue;
  }
  return bytesRead * 2;
}
```

IMA ADPCM Compression

The *Interactive Multimedia Association* (IMA) is an industry organization established to set standards for multimedia storage. Unlike many international standards, which are designed for hardware implementation, the IMA standards are specifically designed to be easy to support on desktop PCs. To date, IMA has produced a single standard covering both audio and video compression. This standard is based on Intel's earlier DVI compression engine. The audio compression method is widely known as IMA ADPCM.

Although many details are left open in the standard, current IMA ADPCM implementations all work roughly the same way. They encode a stream of audio data into a series of *packets*. Each packet contains a header (2 to 8 bytes) with state information and a series of 4-bit compressed samples. Each 4-bit value encodes the difference between two successive 16-bit samples of uncompressed data.

IMA ADPCM is very fast. It was originally designed as part of a video compression engine, so it was important that the audio compression and decompression require an absolute minimum of CPU time.

Another nice feature of IMA ADPCM is that it has very little state information. As a practical matter, people want to be able to access data from different parts of a sound file. This requires that you be able to start decompressing from almost anywhere in the file. Sophisticated compressors and decompressors keep a variety of information about the compressed data, so you can't just start decompressing in the middle of the file. You need to start from the beginning to build up the necessary information or the compressor needs to occasionally insert additional information.

IMA ADPCM requires only 23 bits of state information. Compressors store their state at the beginning of each packet, which allows the player to decompress any complete packet independently. As long as packet sizes are reasonably small, the player can easily start playing at almost any sample.

Unfortunately, the standard doesn't specify how to store the state information in the file, nor does it specify how to handle stereo streams. Two popular implementations of IMA ADPCM, one by Microsoft and another by Apple, store slightly different information and treat it slightly differently on playback.

General Operation

IMA ADPCM stores 4 bits for each sample. The compressor takes the difference between two samples, divides it by the current *step size*, and uses that as the next 4-bit compressed output. Conversely, the decompressor takes this 4-bit value, multiplies it by the current step size, and adds the result to the previous sample to create the next sample. By varying the step size, the 4-bit code can represent a wide range of values.

To keep the amount of state information low, the step size is not stored directly. Rather, there is a table of 88 possible step sizes, and the decompressor maintains an index into this table. These step sizes follow a roughly exponential curve; it's interesting to compare these values to the curve 1.1^n.

LISTING 13.1   IMA ADPCM Step-Size Table

```
static const int _stepSizeTable[89] = {
    7, 8, 9, 10, 11, 12, 13, 14, 16, 17, 19, 21, 23, 25, 28, 31, 34,
    37, 41, 45, 50, 55, 60, 66, 73, 80, 88, 97, 107, 118, 130, 143,
    157, 173, 190, 209, 230, 253, 279, 307, 337, 371, 408, 449, 494,
    544, 598, 658, 724, 796, 876, 963, 1060, 1166, 1282, 1411, 1552,
    1707, 1878, 2066, 2272, 2499, 2749, 3024, 3327, 3660, 4026,
    4428, 4871, 5358, 5894, 6484, 7132, 7845, 8630, 9493, 10442,
    11487, 12635, 13899, 15289, 16818, 18500, 20350, 22385, 24623,
    27086, 29794, 32767
};
```

Thanks to this table, the state information requires only 7 bits for the index into the step-size table and 16 bits for the current decompressed value. Actual compressors drop the least significant bits of the current decompressed sample to save space; this allows them to fit the state information into as little as 16 bits.

LISTING 13.2   IMA ADPCM State Information

```
struct ImaState {
    int index;    // Index into step size table
    int previousValue; // Most recent sample value
};
```

The important part of IMA ADPCM is how it manages the step size. The 4-bit sample represents a signed magnitude number from -7 to +7. Because the decompressor doesn't know the next sample, it has to choose a step size based on previous values. If the 4-bit scaled difference is large, the next might be larger, overflowing the 4-bit value. If the 4-bit scaled difference is small, then you're not taking advantage of the 4 bits of information you have. As a result, the step size is decreased when the scaled difference gets closer to zero, and it is increased when the scaled difference gets large.

Each 4-bit nybble is a *signed-magnitude* value; the high-order bit is the sign, the remaining bits are the value from zero to 7. (Unlike the more familiar two's-complement format, signed magnitude format distinguishes between +0 and -0.)

LISTING 13.3   IMA ADPCM Index Adjustment Table

```
static const int indexAdjustTable[16] = {
    -1, -1, -1, -1,   // +0 - +3, decrease the step size
     2, 4, 6, 8,      // +4 - +7, increase the step size
    -1, -1, -1, -1,   // -0 - -3, decrease the step size
     2, 4, 6, 8,      // -4 - -7, increase the step size
};
```

Decompression

The trickiest part of the `ImaAdpcmDecode` function is that it does not directly multiply the 4-bit encoded value by the current step size. Rather, it uses a series of bit manipulations that has roughly the same effect. However, these bit manipulations are not an actual multiplication; you can't use an actual multiplication if you want to get the correct output.

LISTING 13.4   IMA ADPCM Decode Function

```
AudioSample ImaAdpcmDecode(AudioByte deltaCode, ImaState &state) {
    // Get the current step size
    int step = _stepSizeTable[state.index];

    // Construct the difference by scaling the current step size
    // This is approximately:  difference = (deltaCode+.5)*step/4
    int difference = step>>3;
    if ( deltaCode & 1 ) difference += step>>2;
    if ( deltaCode & 2 ) difference += step>>1;
    if ( deltaCode & 4 ) difference += step;
    if ( deltaCode & 8 ) difference = -difference;

    // Build the new sample
    state.previousValue += difference;
    if (state.previousValue > 32767) state.previousValue = 32767;
    else if (state.previousValue < -32768) state.previousValue = -32768;

    // Update the step for the next sample
    state.index += indexAdjustTable[deltaCode];
    if (state.index < 0) state.index = 0;
    else if (state.index > 88) state.index = 88;

    return state.previousValue;
}
```

Compression

The compressor works much as you'd expect. It first computes the difference and then uses a series of bit manipulations to approximately divide the difference by the current step size. (These bit manipulations are much faster than a real division on many microprocessors.) Note that I call the `ImaAdpcmDecode` function directly to make sure the state information is updated correctly.

LISTING 13.5   IMA ADPCM Encode Function

```
AudioByte ImaAdpcmEncode(AudioSample sample, ImaState &state) {
    int diff = sample - state.previousValue;
    int step = _stepSizeTable[state.index];
    int deltaCode = 0;

    // Set sign bit
    if (diff < 0) { deltaCode = 8; diff = -diff; }

    // This is essentially deltaCode = (diff<<2)/step,
    // except the roundoff is handled differently.
    if ( diff >= step ) {  deltaCode |= 4;  diff -= step;  }
    step >>= 1;
    if ( diff >= step ) {  deltaCode |= 2;  diff -= step;  }
    step >>= 1;
    if ( diff >= step ) {  deltaCode |= 1;  diff -= step;  }

    ImaAdpcmDecode(deltaCode,state);  // update state
    return deltaCode;
}
```

Practical IMA ADPCM Decompression

Now that you've seen the basic sample-by-sample decompression, I'll explain the detailed format of two subtly different implementations of this algorithm. The first is the one developed by Microsoft for compressing WAVE files. The other was developed by Apple for use with AIFF-C and QuickTime files.

LISTING 13.6   imaadpcm.h

```
Copyright © 1998, Tim Kientzle (Listing E.1)
#ifndef IMAADPCM_H_INCLUDED
#define IMAADPCM_H_INCLUDED
#include "audio.h"
#include "compress.h"

IMA ADPCM State Information (Listing 13.2)
```

```
// Decode/Encode a single sample and update state
AudioSample ImaAdpcmDecode(AudioByte deltaCode, ImaState &);
AudioByte ImaAdpcmEncode(AudioSample, ImaState &);
```

Microsoft IMA ADPCM Definition (Listing 13.8)

Apple IMA ADPCM Definition (Listing 13.10)
```
#endif
```

I've already explained the generic parts of the IMA ADPCM decompression code. The next two sections will explain the detailed packet formats and other information used by the Microsoft and Apple implementations of IMA ADPCM.

LISTING 13.7   imaadpcm.cpp

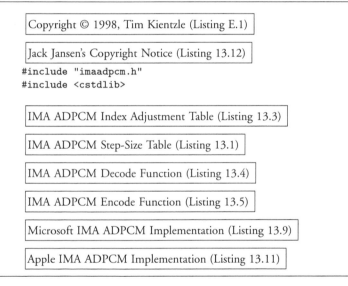

Copyright © 1998, Tim Kientzle (Listing E.1)

Jack Jansen's Copyright Notice (Listing 13.12)
```
#include "imaadpcm.h"
#include <cstdlib>
```

IMA ADPCM Index Adjustment Table (Listing 13.3)

IMA ADPCM Step-Size Table (Listing 13.1)

IMA ADPCM Decode Function (Listing 13.4)

IMA ADPCM Encode Function (Listing 13.5)

Microsoft IMA ADPCM Implementation (Listing 13.9)

Apple IMA ADPCM Implementation (Listing 13.11)

Microsoft's IMA ADPCM Variant

As I mentioned, the IMA standard does not specify the size or format of packets. Microsoft's implementation uses two distinct packet formats: one for mono sound files and the other for stereo sound files.

Microsoft uses two fields in the WAVE file header to specify the size of each packet. The Block Alignment field (see Table 17.2 on page 212) is the number of bytes in each packet. The Number of Channels field specifies the number of channels and hence the precise packet format. In addition, WAVE IMA ADPCM files add 2 bytes of

TABLE 13.1   Microsoft IMA ADPCM Mono Packet Format

Bytes	Description
1	LSB of current sample (always zero for MS compressor)
1	MSB of current sample
1	Current step size
1	Always zero
n	Compressed samples

compressor-specific information, which are used to specify the number of samples stored in the packet. Note that the Bits per Sample field is always set to 4.

The mono packet has the format shown in Table 13.1. It begins with a 4-byte header, followed by the compressed data. When you decompress a packet, you emit one sample for the header itself, and then one sample for each nybble. For example, if the Block Alignment is 256, the packet will contain 505 samples (504 samples in 252 bytes plus one sample for the 4-byte header).

Microsoft resets the decompressor at the beginning of each packet. Although the header has space for the complete 16-bit current sample value, the mono files I've inspected (compressed with the IMA ADPCM compressor included with Windows 95) always set the least significant byte to zero.

TABLE 13.2   Microsoft IMA ADPCM Stereo Packet Format

Bytes	Description
4	Decompressor state for left channel
4	Decompressor state for right channel
4	Compressed left samples
4	Compressed right samples
4	Compressed left samples
4	Compressed right samples
4	Compressed left samples
4	Compressed right samples
⋮	⋮

A stereo packet looks very much like two mono packets that have been combined by alternating 32-bit words, as shown in Table 13.2. In particular, the extended field in the WAVE header contains the number of samples contained in a packet for each channel. For example, a packet size of 2,048 bytes corresponds to 2,041 samples in the WAVE header (one for the 4-byte decompressor state plus 2,040 samples from 1,020 compressed bytes).

To actually implement the decompressor, I'll need a temporary buffer to hold packets that are read from disk, as well as two buffers to hold left and right samples as they are decoded. The `GetSamples` method will call `NextPacket` to read and decode the next packet whenever the two buffers are empty.

LISTING 13.8   Microsoft IMA ADPCM Definition

```
class DecompressImaAdpcmMs: public AbstractDecompressor {
private:
   int  _channels;
   AudioSample *_samples[2];  // Left and right sample buffers
   AudioSample *_samplePtr[2]; // Pointers to current samples
   size_t  _samplesRemaining; // Samples remaining in each channel
   size_t  _samplesPerPacket; // Total samples per packet
public:
   DecompressImaAdpcmMs(AudioAbstract &a, int packetLength, int channels);
   ~DecompressImaAdpcmMs();
   size_t GetSamples(AudioSample *outBuff, size_t len);
private:
   AudioByte *_packet;   // Temporary buffer for packets
   size_t  _bytesPerPacket; // Size of a packet
   size_t  NextPacket();
};
```

To create a `DecompressImaAdpcmMs` decompressor, you need to specify the packet length (I use the number of samples in a packet, as given in the additional WAVE header information) and the number of channels. Although the number of bytes per packet is also available in the WAVE header, I prefer to calculate it directly. I also allocate the various buffers here. The destructor needs to delete the buffers.

LISTING 13.9   Microsoft IMA ADPCM Implementation

```
DecompressImaAdpcmMs::DecompressImaAdpcmMs
         (AudioAbstract &a, int packetLength, int channels)
         :  AbstractDecompressor(a) {
   cerr << "Encoding:  IMA ADPCM (Microsoft variant)";
   if (channels == 2) { cerr << " (stereo)"; }
   cerr << "\n";
   _channels = channels;
   _samplesPerPacket = packetLength;
   _bytesPerPacket = (_samplesPerPacket + 7 )/2 * channels;
   _packet = new AudioByte[_bytesPerPacket];
   _samples[1] = _samples[0] = 0;
   while (channels-- > 0)
      _samples[channels] = new AudioSample[_samplesPerPacket];
   _samplesRemaining = 0;
};
```

```
DecompressImaAdpcmMs::~DecompressImaAdpcmMs() {
    if (_samples[0]) delete [] _samples[0];
    if (_samples[1]) delete [] _samples[1];
    if (_packet) delete [] _packet;
};
```

Having two packet formats makes reading the next packet a bit tricky. Because Microsoft chose to reset the decompressor for every packet, I need to create and initialize one decompressor state for each channel. During the decompression, I need to be careful to use the correct state for each channel.

LISTING 13.9 (CONTINUED)   Microsoft IMA ADPCM Implementation

```
size_t  DecompressImaAdpcmMs::NextPacket() {
    // Pull in the packet and check the header
    size_t bytesRead = ReadBytes(_packet,_bytesPerPacket);
    if (bytesRead < _bytesPerPacket) { return 0; }
    AudioByte *bytePtr = _packet;

    // Reset the decompressor
    ImaState state[2];  // One decompressor state for each channel
    // Read the four-byte header for each channel
    for(int ch=0;ch < _channels; ch++) {
        state[ch].previousValue =
                static_cast<signed char>(bytePtr[1])*0x100
                  + static_cast<signed char>(bytePtr[0]);

        if (bytePtr[2] > 88)
            cerr << "IMA ADPCM Format Error (bad index value)\n";
        else
            state[ch].index = bytePtr[2];
        if (bytePtr[3])
            cerr << "IMA ADPCM Format Error (synchronization error)\n";
        bytePtr+=4; // Skip this header

        _samplePtr[ch] = _samples[ch];
        // Decode one sample for the header
        *_samplePtr[ch]++ = state[ch].previousValue;
    }

    // Decompress nybbles
    size_t remaining = _samplesPerPacket-1;

    while (remaining>0) {
        remaining-=8;

        int i;
        // Decode 8 left samples
        for (i=0;i<4;i++) {
            AudioByte b = *bytePtr++;
            *_samplePtr[0]++ = ImaAdpcmDecode(b & 0xF,state[0]);
            *_samplePtr[0]++ = ImaAdpcmDecode((b>>4) & 0xF,state[0]);
```

```
        }
        if (_channels < 2)
            continue; // If mono, skip rest of loop
        // Decode 8 right samples
        for (i=0;i<4;i++) {
            AudioByte b = *bytePtr++;
            *_samplePtr[1]++ = ImaAdpcmDecode(b & 0xF,state[1]);
            *_samplePtr[1]++ = ImaAdpcmDecode((b>>4) & 0xF,state[1]);
        }
    };
    return _samplesPerPacket;
};
```

Because of the alternate packet formats for mono and stereo, `GetSamples` needs to request only one packet at a time and then copy the decoded data into the request buffer.

LISTING 13.9 (CONTINUED) Microsoft IMA ADPCM Implementation

```
size_t DecompressImaAdpcmMs::GetSamples(AudioSample *outBuff, size_t len) {
    size_t wanted = len;
    while (wanted > 0) { // Still want data?
        if (_samplesRemaining == 0) { // Need to read more from disk?
            _samplesRemaining = NextPacket();
            if (_samplesRemaining == 0) { return len - wanted; }
            _samplePtr[0] = _samples[0];
            _samplePtr[1] = _samples[1];
        }
        switch(_channels) { // Copy data into outBuff
        case 1:  // Mono:  Just copy left channel data
            while((_samplesRemaining > 0) && (wanted > 0)) {
                *outBuff++ = *_samplePtr[0]++;
                _samplesRemaining--;
                wanted--;
            }
            break;
        case 2:  // Stereo:  Interleave samples
            while((_samplesRemaining > 0) && (wanted > 0)) {
                *outBuff++ = *_samplePtr[0]++; // left
                *outBuff++ = *_samplePtr[1]++; // right
                _samplesRemaining--;
                wanted -= 2;
            }
            break;
        default:  exit(1);
        }
    }
    return len - wanted;
}
```

Apple's IMA ADPCM Variant

Apple and Microsoft use the same low-level compression, but the packet formats are quite different.

- Apple uses the same packet format for mono and stereo. Stereo files alternate one packet of left data with one packet of right data.

- Microsoft emits one sample for the header, Apple does not. (A Microsoft packet always contains an odd number of samples. An Apple packet always contains an even number of samples.)

- The Microsoft packet header uses 8 bits for the step-size index and stores 8 or 16 bits of the current sample. Apple uses only 7 bits for the step-size index and stores the upper 9 bits of the current sample.

- Microsoft's decompressor completely resets at the start of each packet. Apple's does not.

- The Microsoft packet header contains a zero byte for detecting synchronization errors. Apple does not provide a means for detecting these errors (apart from checking that the 7-bit index value falls in the range 0 to 88).

- An Apple packet is always 34 bytes (64 samples). Microsoft chose to allow the compressor to choose a packet size; it stores the number of samples per packet in the file header.

With this laundry list in hand, it's not hard to adapt the earlier Microsoft IMA ADPCM compressor to handle Apple IMA ADPCM files.

LISTING 13.10   Apple IMA ADPCM Definition

```
class DecompressImaAdpcmApple:  public AbstractDecompressor {
private:
   int _channels;

   ImaState _state[2];
   AudioSample _samples[2][64];
   AudioSample *_samplePtr[2];

   size_t   _samplesRemaining;
   size_t   NextPacket(AudioSample *sampleBuffer, ImaState &state);

public:
   DecompressImaAdpcmApple(AudioAbstract &a, int channels);
   size_t GetSamples(AudioSample *outBuff, size_t len);
};
```

Because Apple always uses the same packet size, I can use arrays; I don't need to worry about allocating and freeing memory.

LISTING 13.11   Apple IMA ADPCM Implementation

```
DecompressImaAdpcmApple::DecompressImaAdpcmApple
    (AudioAbstract &a, int channels) : AbstractDecompressor(a) {
  cerr << "Encoding:  IMA ADPCM (Apple variant)";
  if (channels == 2) { cerr << " (stereo)"; }
  cerr << "\n";
  _samplesRemaining = 0;
  _state[0].previousValue = 0;
  _state[0].index = 0;
  _state[1] = _state[0];
  _channels = channels;
};
```

Reading a packet is fairly direct. Note that unlike Microsoft, Apple does not reset the decompressor with each packet. This means that I need to keep the decompressor state in the object (rather than keep it local to `NextPacket`). It also means that when I pull the upper 9 bits of the last sample from the packet, I need to decide whether to continue with the previous state or use the value provided in the packet. For example, when I get the first packet from a file, I probably need to use the value from the file. In this code, I compare the upper 9 bits and see if they agree. If they do, I keep my value because it's more accurate.

LISTING 13.11 (CONTINUED) Apple IMA ADPCM Implementation

```
size_t DecompressImaAdpcmApple::NextPacket(AudioSample *sampleBuffer,
                                           ImaState &state) {
  AudioByte _packet[34];
  // Pull in the packet and check the header
  size_t bytesRead = ReadBytes(_packet,34);
  if (bytesRead < 34) return 0;

  // Check the decompressor state
  state.index = _packet[1] & 0x7F;
  if (state.index > 88) {
    cerr << "Synchronization error.\n";
    exit(1);
  }

  // Recover upper nine bits of last sample
  AudioSample lastSample =
    (static_cast<signed char>(_packet[0])*0x100 +
     static_cast<signed char>(_packet[1])) & 0xFF80;

  // If ours doesn't match, reset to the value in the file
  if ((state.previousValue & 0xFF80) != lastSample)
    state.previousValue = lastSample;
```

```
   // Decompress nybbles
   for(int i=0; i<32; i++) {
      *sampleBuffer++ = ImaAdpcmDecode(_packet[i+2] & 0xF, state);
      *sampleBuffer++ = ImaAdpcmDecode((_packet[i+2]>>4) & 0xF, state);
   }
   return 64;
};
```

This `GetSamples` is similar to the one I used for the Microsoft version. The only difference is that I need to call `NextPacket` once for each channel. I also need to tell `NextPacket` which state to use (so that the decompressor state is maintained separately for each channel) and where to put the decoded results.

LISTING 13.11 (CONTINUED)   Apple IMA ADPCM Implementation

```
   size_t DecompressImaAdpcmApple::GetSamples(AudioSample *outBuff,
                                              size_t wanted) {
      size_t remaining = wanted;
      while (remaining > 0) {
         if (_samplesRemaining == 0) {
            for(int i=0; i<_channels; i++) {
               _samplesRemaining = NextPacket(_samples[i],_state[i]);
               if (_samplesRemaining == 0) { return wanted-remaining; }
               _samplePtr[i] = _samples[i];
            }
         }
         switch(_channels) {
         case 1:
            while((_samplesRemaining > 0) && (remaining > 0)) {
               *outBuff++ = *_samplePtr[0]++;
               _samplesRemaining--;
               remaining--;
            }
            break;
         case 2:
            while((_samplesRemaining > 0) && (remaining > 0)) {
               *outBuff++ = *_samplePtr[0]++; // Left
               *outBuff++ = *_samplePtr[1]++; // Right
               _samplesRemaining--;
               remaining -= 2;
            }
            break;
         }
      }
      return wanted - remaining;
   };
```

Comparing Microsoft's and Apple's IMA ADPCM Codecs

From a coding point of view, Apple's implementation of IMA ADPCM is quite a bit simpler, mostly because you don't need to worry about two packet formats. It also provides better quality; Microsoft throws away 8 bits of decompressor state at the beginning of each mono packet, which results in a small jump in sample value at the start of each packet.

Microsoft's approach is more compact. Assuming 2,048-byte stereo packets, Microsoft's approach incurs only 8 bytes of overhead for each 2,041 bytes of compressed data (less than 0.4 percent overhead); Apple incurs 2 bytes for each 32 bytes of compressed data (more than 6 percent overhead). It also provides lower latency; if stereo data is being compressed and decompressed simultaneously, Microsoft incurs only an 8-sample delay, while Apple must wait for a complete 64-sample packet before it can have stereo data available. However, this is not a serious issue even at low sampling rates; at 11,025 samples per second, 64 samples is less than 6 milliseconds.

Notes on IMA ADPCM

Although originally defined to be a platform-independent standard for audio file compression, the IMA ADPCM format doesn't quite meet that requirement. The low-level compression is not a concern; it's independent of byte order and is defined using only low-level bit manipulations, which gives it good performance even on processors that don't have fast integer division.

However, the differences between the Microsoft and Apple versions make it impossible to mix their codecs. You can't extract IMA ADPCM compressed data from an AIFF-C file and feed it to the Microsoft codec, nor can you feed IMA ADPCM WAVE data to the Apple codec. Fortunately, IMA ADPCM codecs are compact; the code in this chapter should allow you to easily support both common variants, and you should also be able to adapt this code to suport any other IMA ADPCM variants you may encounter.

Unraveling ADPCM Formats

The IMA does provide complete specifications for IMA ADPCM, including sample source implementations. However, I was unable to find detailed information for the Microsoft and Apple implementations. Also, to avoid any possible infringement of the IMA's copyright, I deliberately avoided its sample source. I did find some useful material on the Internet, including Jack Jansen's implementation of the basic algorithm and Apple

Developer Support TechNote 1081, which outlines some of the fundamental differences between Apple and Microsoft implementations.

However, none of this was sufficient to actually implement the decompressors I've given in this chapter. As a result, I had to experiment with actual files to uncover the necessary details. The techniques I used may be helpful if you need to analyze other similar formats.

I started by using common utilities (included with Mac OS 7.6 and Windows 95) to convert a short sample file to IMA ADPCM compressed format. I then decompressed the file into a 16-bit PCM format. Because IMA ADPCM is a lossy algorithm, it's more useful to compare the compressed data to the data after decompression rather than the data before compression.

The key to unraveling IMA ADPCM is that each nybble represents a signed difference. It's easy to write a short program that dumps out the nybbles from the compressed data and the differences from the decompressed data side-by-side. By comparing the pattern of positive and negative values, it took only a short time for me to verify the order of the nybbles within each byte (IMA ADPCM stores the low-order nybble first) and to find where blocks of nybbles aligned with blocks of differences. Mismatches within the sequence of positive and negative values pointed out the location of packet headers and, hence, the size of packets themselves.

If you need to analyze an ADPCM algorithm that uses 4 bits per sample, this method may be a good start. Determining how a 4-bit compressed value corresponds to a difference is a more complex task, although you can find clues in a variety of places. The first step is to be familiar with a variety of related algorithms. In addition to the IMA ADPCM algorithm, there is also a family of ITU algorithms (especially G.721 and G.723) that you can study. You can often find fragmentary source code (as I did with IMA ADPCM) that will give you important clues.

Thanks to these techniques, I was able to implement the code in this chapter that exactly matches the output of the official decompressors for all files I've tested. (Since my initial work, I have been able to verify many of my early guesses with official documentation.) Such sleuthing is not always easy—one friend of mine likens it to cryptanalysis—but it is often the only way to find the detailed information you need.

Credits

The code in this chapter is partially based on an implementation of Intel's DVI ADPCM algorithm developed by Jack Jansen. The original source code contains the following copyright notice:

LISTING 13.12   Jack Jansen's Copyright Notice

MPEG Audio

14

The Moving Pictures Expert Group (MPEG) first met in May of 1988. It had been formed by the ISO (International Organization for Standardization) to develop a standard way to compress video sequences. By the end of 1992, the first of a series of standards—also known as MPEG—was officially approved by the ISO. Although the MPEG standards are best known for their video compression, they also support high-quality audio compression.

An impressive array of companies, research organizations, and standards groups have participated in the creation of the MPEG standards. This has occurred, in part, because of the converging needs of a variety of industries. Commercial broadcasters are interested in high-quality digital video for satellite, cable, and standard broadcast; consumer electronics manufacturers want to distribute movies on compact digital media; and computer developers want to use audio/video content in a variety of software products. A standard for high-quality digital compression is essential to all of these industries.

A Survey of the MPEG Standards

MPEG standardization is an ongoing process. As interest builds in new technologies and new consumer devices, the MPEG committees have responded by examining the existing standards and, where appropriate, developing extensions and improvements. In addition, as more people gain experience with the standards, new refinements have appeared that are incorporated into the succeeding work. There are currently three MPEG standards in various stages of completion. Each consists of numerous parts addressing aspects of video compression, storage, and delivery.

MPEG-1

ISO-11172, entitled *Coding of Moving Pictures and Associated Audio for Digital Storage Media at up to About 1.5 Mbit/s*, is the first of the MPEG standards. Commonly called MPEG-1, it contains the five parts outlined in Table 14.1.

TABLE 14.1   Parts of the MPEG-1 Standard

Part 1: Systems	How to combine multiple video and audio streams
Part 2: Video	How to compress a sequence of images
Part 3: Audio	How to compress one- or two-channel audio
Part 4: Conformance	How to test an implementation for conformance
Part 5: Software	A full reference implementation of the standard, released in part to correct misunderstandings caused by the poor quality of some early implementations

As the title of the standard suggests, MPEG-1 is targeted at systems that can transfer data at about 1.5 megabits per second (187.5 kilobytes per second). This includes CD-ROM, ISDN, and some broadcasting systems. Overall, MPEG-1 is usually considered to have the same quality as VHS videotape. Because a raw television-quality audio/video signal requires nearly 200 megabits per second, this represents an overall compression ratio of about 150 to 1.

The audio portion of MPEG-1 is itself divided into three *layers*. Each layer provides successively better quality at the cost of a more complex implementation. Layer 1 is the simplest. It's best suited to situations in which data can be transferred quickly (such as from a hard disk) but computation speed is limited. Layer 3 offers the best quality when data size is critical, but it requires more computational power to compress and decompress.

The different numbered parts of the MPEG standards has caused some confusion with filenames. In particular, people commonly use filename extensions that incorporate digits. For example, .MP3 is commonly used for Layer 3 audio files. But it may not be clear (except from context) whether an .MP2 file is MPEG-2 video or MPEG-1 Layer 2 audio.

The distinction between MPEG audio and video files is important. The MPEG standards define three storage formats. A file might contain a *video stream*, an *audio stream*, or a *system stream* which interleaves some combination of audio and video streams. All three file types are widely distributed.

MPEG-2

The relative success of MPEG-1 led to interest in extending the standard to support other applications. The result is ISO 13818, commonly known as MPEG-2. MPEG-2 extends and clarifies MPEG-1 to support a wider variety of applications. In particular, the standard specifies that any MPEG-2 decoder must also support MPEG-1.

For example, Part 3 of MPEG-2 extends the MPEG-1 audio encoding in two directions. For high-quality surround-sound applications, it adds support for up to five-channel audio. For low-bandwidth applications, such as Internet audio, it adds support for lower bit rates (down to 8 kilobits per second) and lower sampling frequencies (down to 16,000 samples per second).

MPEG-2 is organized into nine parts. The first five have the same titles as the corresponding parts of MPEG-1; Parts 6 through 9 provide additional features and clarification. Part 7: NBC Audio is particularly interesting here. The NBC (non-backward-compatible) audio format is intended to address some problems with the multi-channel support in MPEG-2 Part 3. (In contrast, the MPEG-2 Part 3 audio format is sometimes called BC audio.)

In order to maintain backward compatibility, the multi-channel extensions in MPEG-2 Part 3 first mix the various channels into a single stereo stream and encode that using the techniques of MPEG-1 Part 3. They then encode additional information and hide it in the bitstream so that an MPEG-1 decoder will not see this information. The result is that an MPEG-1 decoder will see and extract the stereo version, and a decoder that understands the multi-channel extensions will be able to extract the full signal (with up to 5 channels).

In practice, this multi-channel scheme doesn't work as well as expected, and competing schemes such as Dolby AC-3 compression are preferred by many people. The NBC audio drops the requirement for MPEG-1 compatibility and should provide better quality for surround-sound applications. The final version of the NBC audio standard should be available in 1997.

MPEG-3

MPEG-3 was originally intended to support high definition television (HDTV) but was dropped when it became clear that MPEG-2 would suffice.

MPEG-4

MPEG-4 is an ongoing effort to produce a standard for very low bit rate systems. This would allow for low-quality video over modem-speed connections.

MPEG Audio

In the rest of this chapter, I'll focus on the MPEG-1 Part 3 audio specification. I'll develop code for a complete Layer 1 and Layer 2 audio decompression engine to illustrate the principles involved.

The MPEG standard takes a different approach from some other standards. MPEG Part 3 details the format of a legal MPEG bitstream and explains how to correctly decode that bitstream, but it does *not* specify a compression technique. This may seem odd at first, but it's actually an important feature of the standard.

Essentially, an MPEG audio bitstream specifies the frequency content of a sound and how that content varies over time. In order to conserve space, the compressor selectively discards information. The standard specifies how the remaining information is encoded and how the decoder can construct PCM audio samples from the MPEG bitstream. By leaving the encoding process unspecified, implementors are free to use a variety of techniques to decide which information is important. This variety might include simplified encoders for lower-quality applications and encoders that are tailored for specific types of sound (top-quality compression of orchestral music might be different from top-quality compression of speech, for instance).

General Structure

Like many hardware-oriented compression techniques, MPEG compressed data is defined as a stream of bits. Fortunately for software developers, key points in the bitstream must occur on byte boundaries.

An MPEG bitstream consists of *frames* of compressed data. Each frame contains a *frame header* that defines the format of that data. To decode the data, you need to track the incoming bytes, identify and parse the frame headers, and use the information in the headers to decompress individual frames.

LISTING 14.1   mpeg.h

Copyright © 1998, Tim Kientzle (Listing E.1)

```
#ifndef MPEG_H_INCLUDED
#define MPEG_H_INCLUDED
#include "audio.h"
#include "compress.h"

class DecompressMpeg:  public AbstractDecompressor {
private:
```

MPEG Incoming Byte Storage Variables (Listing 14.4)

```
   ┌─────────────────────────────────────────────┐
   │ MPEG Frame Header Variables (Listing 14.7)   │
   └─────────────────────────────────────────────┘
   ┌──────────────────────────────────────────────────────┐
   │ Layer 1/Layer 2 Decompression Variables (Listing 14.12) │
   └──────────────────────────────────────────────────────┘
   ┌──────────────────────────────────────────────┐
   │ Layer 3 Decompression Variables (Listing 14.31) │
   └──────────────────────────────────────────────┘
   AudioSample _sampleStorage[2][1152];
   AudioSample *_pcmSamples[2]; // Samples for left/right channels
   int _samplesRemaining; // Samples remaining from last frame

   void NextFrame(); // Read and decompress next frame
public:
   DecompressMpeg(AudioAbstract &a);
   ~DecompressMpeg();
   size_t GetSamples(AudioSample *outBuff, size_t len);
   void MinMaxSamplingRate(long *min, long *max, long *preferred) {
      *min=*max=*preferred=_samplingRate;
   };
   void MinMaxChannels(int *min, int *max, int *preferred) {
      *min=*max=*preferred=_channels;
   };
};

   ┌──────────────────────────────────────┐
   │ MPEG File Reader (Listing 14.33)      │
   └──────────────────────────────────────┘
   #endif
```

The public parts of the `DecompressMpeg` class are generic. The `GetSamples` method, for instance, copies samples from the sample buffers, calling `NextFrame` to refill them.

LISTING 14.2   MPEG GetSamples

```
size_t DecompressMpeg::GetSamples(AudioSample *outBuff, size_t wanted) {
   long remaining = wanted;
   while(remaining > 0) {
      if(_samplesRemaining == 0) { // buffer empty?
         NextFrame();  // Get more data from MPEG stream
         if(_samplesRemaining == 0) // End of data?
            return wanted-remaining;
      }
      switch(_channels) {
      case 1:  // Mono, just copy left channel
         while((_samplesRemaining > 0) && (remaining > 0)) {
            *outBuff++ = *_pcmSamples[0]++;
            _samplesRemaining--;
            remaining--;
         }
         break;
      case 2:  // Stereo, copy both channels
         while((_samplesRemaining > 0) && (remaining > 0)) {
            *outBuff++ = *_pcmSamples[0]++; // Left
            *outBuff++ = *_pcmSamples[1]++; // Right
            _samplesRemaining--;
```

```
            remaining -= 2;
        }
        break;
    }
}
return wanted-remaining;
}
```

There's a lot of machinery behind this. In the remainder of this chapter, I'll develop the various pieces in more detail.

LISTING 14.3   mpeg.cpp

```
Copyright © 1998, Tim Kientzle (Listing E.1)

#include <iostream> // #include <iostream.h> for old compilers
#include <cstring> // #include <string.h>  for old compilers
#include <cmath>    // #include <math.h> for old compilers
#include <cstdio>   // #include <stdio.h> for old compilers
#include "audio.h"
#include "compress.h"
#include "mpeg.h"

MPEG GetSamples (Listing 14.2)

Read and Decompress Next MPEG Frame (Listing 14.11)

MPEG Buffer Management (Listing 14.6)

MPEG Frame Header Decoding (Listing 14.8)

Layer 1/Layer 2 Synthesis Window Coefficients (Listing 14.18)

Layer 1/Layer 2 Subband Synthesis (Listing 14.15)

Layer 1 Requantization Function (Listing 14.24)

Layer 1 Frame Decoding (Listing 14.19)

Layer 2 Quantization Class Tables (Listing 14.30)

Layer 2 Bit Allocation Tables (Listing 14.26)

Layer 2 Frame Decoding (Listing 14.25)

Layer 3 Frame Decoding (Listing 14.32)
```

```
// Constructor
DecompressMpeg::DecompressMpeg(AudioAbstract &a) :AbstractDecompressor(a) {

    _samplesRemaining = 0;
```
Initialize MPEG Buffer Variables (Listing 14.5)

Initialize Layer 1/Layer 2 Shared Variables (Listing 14.13)
```
    NextFrame(); // Read first frame
    cerr << "Encoding:  MPEG-" << ((_id==0)?"2":"1");
    cerr << " Layer " << static_cast<int>(_layer) << "\n";

    cerr << "Sampling Rate:  " << _samplingRate << "\n";
    switch(_mode) {
    case 0:  cerr << "Mode:  Stereo\n"; break;
    case 1:  cerr << "Mode:  Joint Stereo\n"; break;
    case 2:  cerr << "Mode:  Dual Channel\n"; break;
    case 3:  cerr << "Mode:  Single Channel\n"; break;
    }
    cerr << "Bit rate:  " << _bitRate << "\n";
    switch(_emphasis) {
    case 0:    cerr << "Emphasis:  none\n"; break;
    case 1:    cerr << "Emphasis:  50/15\n"; break;
    case 2:    cerr << "Emphasis:  reserved\n"; break;
    case 3:    cerr << "Emphasis:  ITU J.17\n"; break;
    }
    fprintf(stderr,"Approximate Compression Ratio:  %5.1f:1\n",
        _samplingRate*16.0*_channels/_bitRate);
}

// Destructor
DecompressMpeg::~DecompressMpeg() {
```
MPEG Cleanup (Listing 14.14)
```
}
```

Managing the Byte Stream

To simplify parsing bits out of the data, I use a single buffer of bytes and slide it forward so that I'm always working with a contiguous block of memory. The _bufferStorage variable is a block of memory for this storage; other methods will move the _buffer variable forward past data that's been used. The _header variable indicates the location of the next frame header.

For simplicity, both Layer 1 and Layer 2 require that the compressed data follow the frame header. In essence, you can work with packets of compressed data. Layer 3 goes a step further, however. Because some parts of the audio data may be easier to compress than others, Layer 3 compression allows the compressed data to slop over; a single frame may have data both before and after the frame header. All three layers require that the frame headers be evenly spaced.

LISTING 14.4 MPEG Incoming Byte Storage Variables

```
private:
    void FillBuffer(); // Keep byte buffer full
    void ResetBits(); // Reset bit extraction
    long GetBits(int numBits); // Extract bits

    AudioByte _bufferStorage[2048];
    AudioByte *_buffer; // Beginning of live data in buffer
    int       _bitsRemaining; // bits left in top byte
    AudioByte *_bufferEnd; // End of live data in buffer
    AudioByte *_header; // Location of header in buffer
```

LISTING 14.5 Initialize MPEG Buffer Variables

```
_buffer = _bufferStorage + sizeof(_bufferStorage);
_header = _bufferEnd = _buffer;
_headerSpacing = 0; // Unknown
```

LISTING 14.6 MPEG Buffer Management

```
// Move data to start of buffer and fill up rest
void DecompressMpeg::FillBuffer() {
    // We ran off the end of the buffer?!
    if (_header > _bufferStorage+sizeof(_bufferStorage)) {
        cerr << "Internal error; buffer exhausted!\n";
        _buffer = _header;
    }
    if (_buffer > _header) { // We skipped past the next header?!?!
        cerr << "Synchronization error; frame too big!\n";
        _buffer = _header;
    }
    // Avoid frequent small calls to ReadBytes()
    if (_buffer < (_bufferStorage+512)) return;

    int totalBufferSize = sizeof(_bufferStorage);
    int bufferSize = _bufferEnd - _buffer;
    memmove(_bufferStorage,_buffer, bufferSize);
    _header -= _buffer - _bufferStorage;
    _bufferEnd -= _buffer - _bufferStorage;
    _buffer = _bufferStorage;
    _bufferEnd += ReadBytes(_bufferEnd, totalBufferSize - bufferSize);
}
```

The `FillBuffer` method above ensures that I always have a contiguous block of data to play with. The next step is to assemble the machinery to pull variable numbers of bits from the bitstream. The key part of this is the `_bitsRemaining` variable, which tracks the number of unused bits in the first byte in the buffer.

LISTING 14.6 (CONTINUED) MPEG Buffer Management

```
void DecompressMpeg::ResetBits() {
   _bitsRemaining = 8;
}

int masks[] = {0,1,3,7,0xF,0x1F,0x3F,0x7F,0xFF};

long DecompressMpeg::GetBits(int numBits) {
   if(_bitsRemaining == 0) { // If no bits in this byte ...
      _buffer++;             // ... move to the next
      _bitsRemaining = 8;
   }
   if(_bitsRemaining >= numBits) { // Can I fill it from this byte?
      _bitsRemaining -= numBits;
      return (*_buffer>>_bitsRemaining)&masks[numBits];
   }
   // Use up rest of this byte, then recurse to get more bits
   long result = (*_buffer & masks[_bitsRemaining])
               << (numBits - _bitsRemaining);
   numBits -= _bitsRemaining; // I don't need as many bits now
   _bitsRemaining = 8;  // Move to next bit
   _buffer++;
   return result | GetBits(numBits);
}
```

MPEG's Frame Header

The frame header is always 32 bits and aligned on a byte boundary. The first 12 bits are all ones, for synchronization; the remaining bits are outlined in Table 14.2. The 12 bits of ones are the *syncword*. If the decoder loses track of where it is, it can search forward for the next syncword and restart from there.

Fake syncwords can potentially make it difficult for the decoder to reliably resynchronize. Although the standard does ensure that fake syncwords won't appear in a valid audio stream, they can occur if the encoded data is damaged by errors. If the decoder knows additional information about the incoming bitstream (for example, it might already know to expect an MPEG-1 Layer 1 bitstream), it can use those additional header bits as an extended syncword. The standard also provides for a CRC to be stored following the header. This CRC provides an error check for the header and the most sensitive encoded sound data. If the CRC check fails, the decoder can simply ignore this

TABLE 14.2   MPEG Frame Header

Byte	Bits	Description
0	8	All ones, for synchronization
1	4	All ones, for synchronization
	1	ID: zero indicates MPEG-2 extensions are being used
	2	Layer: 11=Layer 1, 10=Layer 2, 01=Layer 3, 00=reserved
	1	Protection bit: zero if CRC included
2	4	Bit rate index, see Table 14.4
	2	Sampling-rate index, see Table 14.3
	1	Padding: one if there's an extra slot
	1	Private
3	2	Mode: 00=stereo, 01=joint stereo, 10=dual channel, 11=mono
	2	Mode extension: lowest subband for intensity stereo
	1	Copyright: one if copyrighted
	1	Original: one if this is original
	2	Emphasis

TABLE 14.3   MPEG Sampling-Rate Codes

Code	MPEG-1 Sampling Rate	MPEG-2 Sampling Rate
00	44,100	22,050
01	48,000	24,000
10	32,000	16,000
11	reserved	reserved

frame (silencing the output or duplicating the previous frame to obscure the lost data), resynchronize, and continue with the next valid frame.

The frame header indicates the sampling rate of the uncompressed data (in samples per second) and the data rate of the compressed data (in bits per second). These values are stored as indexes into Tables 14.3 and 14.4. These values are stored in the header of each frame. Although it's unusual for encoders to vary the sample rate between frames, it's quite reasonable to vary the bit rate between frames. By varying the bit rate between frames, MPEG can use actual bit rates that are between rates in these tables. In unusual circumstances, the *free* bit rate can be used, although there are some restrictions (see page 150).

The all-ones value is forbidden, to avoid false syncwords.

TABLE 14.4   MPEG Bit Rate Codes

Code	MPEG-1 Bit Rate			MPEG-2 Bit Rate		
	Layer 1	**Layer 2**	**Layer 3**	**Layer 1**	**Layer 2**	**Layer 3**
0000	free	free	free	free	free	free
0001	32	32	32	32	8	8
0010	64	48	40	48	16	16
0011	96	56	48	56	24	24
0100	128	64	56	64	32	32
0101	160	80	64	80	40	40
0110	192	96	80	96	48	48
0111	224	112	96	112	56	56
1000	256	128	112	128	64	64
1001	288	160	128	144	80	80
1010	320	192	160	160	96	96
1011	352	224	192	176	112	112
1100	384	256	224	192	128	128
1101	416	320	256	224	144	144
1110	448	384	320	256	160	160
1111	*	*	*	*	*	*

MPEG-2 Part 3 provides two extensions to MPEG-1 Part 3 audio. The simplest is that it adds additional low bit rates and new sampling rates. It also adds support for surround-sound multi-channel audio. The multi-channel extension is stored as an ordinary stereo stream with the additional data placed between frames. A normal MPEG-1 decoder will completely ignore this additional data.

LISTING 14.7   MPEG Frame Header Variables

```
private:
    bool ParseHeader(); // Parse header for next frame

    char _id; // 1 for MPEG-1, 0 for MPEG-2 extensions
    char _layer;
    char _protection; // 1 if CRC check omitted
    long _bitRate; // total bits/second
    long _samplingRate; // samples/second
    bool _padding; // this packet has an extra slot
    char _private; // private bit
```

```
char _mode;    // single-channel, dual-channel, stereo, etc.
char _modeExtension; // Type of stereo encoding
char _bound; // subband where stereo encoding changes
bool _copyright; // true if copyrighted
bool _original; // true if original
char _emphasis; // How to post-process audio
int _channels; // Number channels
int _headerSpacing; // in bytes
```

Most of these variables are fairly obvious, except that the sense is sometimes inverted from what you might expect (for example, the protection bit is set to one if the frame is *un*protected). The mode values require some additional explanation.

MPEG-1 supports four channel settings. The ordinary stereo and dual channel modes each store two independently compressed data streams. The joint stereo setting uses less data by sharing some information between the two channels. This works well for typical stereo programs where the difference between the left and right channels is fairly small. I'll explain this in more detail later.

LISTING 14.8   MPEG Frame Header Decoding

```
static short bitRateTable[2][4][16] = { // ID, Layer, Code
{ // ID bit == 0 for MPEG 2 lower bit rates
  {0 }, // Reserved
  // Layer 1
  {0,32,48,56,64,80,96,112,128,144,160,176,192,224,256,0 },
  // Layer 2 and 3 are the same
  {0,8,16,24,32,40,48,56,64,80,96,112,128,144,160,0 },
  {0,8,16,24,32,40,48,56,64,80,96,112,128,144,160,0 },
}, { // ID bit == 1 for MPEG 1 bit rates
  {0 }, // Reserved
  // Layer 1
  {0,32,64,96,128,160,192,224,256,288,320,352,384,416,448,0 },
  // Layer 2
  {0,32,48,56,64,80,96,112,128,160,192,224,256,320,384,0 },
  // Layer 3
  {0,32,40,48,56,64,80,96,112,128,160,192,224,256,320,0 },
}};

static long samplingRateTable[2][4] = { // ID, Code
  {22050,24000,16000,0},  // MPEG 2 sampling rates
  {44100,48000,32000,0}   // MPEG 1 sampling rates
};

// Parse header, return true if no more headers
bool DecompressMpeg::ParseHeader() {
  FillBuffer(); // Advance buffer
  if (_bufferEnd - _header < 4)
    return true; // No more frames

  if((_header[0] != 0xFF)||((_header[1] & 0xF0) != 0xF0)) {
    cerr << "Syncword not found.";
```

```
      return true; // no more frames
   }
   _id = (_header[1] & 8)>>3; // 1 if MPEG-1, 0 if MPEG-2
   _layer = -(_header[1] >> 1) & 3; // Decode
   _protection = (~_header[1] & 1); // 0->CRC, 1->no CRC

   int bitRateIndex = (_header[2] & 0xF0)>>4;
   _bitRate = bitRateTable[_id][_layer][bitRateIndex] * 1000;

   int samplingRateIndex = (_header[2] & 0x0C)>>2;
   _samplingRate = samplingRateTable[_id][samplingRateIndex];

   _padding = (_header[2] & 0x02)>>1;
   _private = (_header[2] & 0x01);

   _mode = (_header[3] & 0xC0) >> 6;
   _modeExtension = (_header[3] & 0x30)>>4;

   switch(_mode) {
   case 0:  // Stereo:  all subbands
           _channels = 2;
           _bound = 32;
           break;
   case 1:  // Joint stereo:  some subbands use intensity coding
           _channels = 2;
           _bound = (_modeExtension + 1)<<2;
           break;
   case 2:  // Dual channel:  two independent channels
           _channels = 2;
           _bound = 32;
           break;
   case 3:  // single channel
           _channels = 1;
           _bound = 0;
           break;
   }

   _copyright = (_header[3] & 0x08);
   _original = (_header[3] & 0x04);
   _emphasis = (_header[3] & 0x03);

   _buffer = _header+4;
   if (_protection) _buffer += 2; // Skip 2-byte CRC
```

Locate Next Header (Listing 14.9)

```
   return false; // Read header successfully
}
```

For simplicity, I'm not going to verify the CRC, but simply ignore it when it appears.

Slots and Frames

MPEG frames are measured in *slots*. For Layer 1, a slot is 4 bytes; for Layers 2 and 3, a slot is 1 byte. Locating the next header is straightforward. You know the bit rate of the incoming data, and you know the sampling rate of the outgoing audio. You also know the number of samples that occur in one packet: 384 for Layer 1, 1,152 for Layers 2 and 3. From this, you can calculate the average frame length. MPEG guarantees that the frame headers will be evenly spaced.

It's not always possible to space them perfectly, so a special bit in the header indicates if an extra slot has been added to this frame.

LISTING 14.9   Locate Next Header

```
if (_bitRate == 0) { // Other bit rate
    Locate Next Header with Free Bit Rate (Listing 14.10)
} else if (_layer==1) { // Layer 1 has 4-byte slots
    _headerSpacing =    // slots/packet =
            384         // samples/packet
        /  32          // bits/slot
        * _bitRate // bits/second
        / _samplingRate;   // samples/second
    _header += _headerSpacing*4;  // 4 bytes/slot
    if(_padding) _header += 4; // extra slot
} else { // Layer 2 and 3 have 1-byte slots
    _headerSpacing =
            1152        // samples/packet
        /  8           // bits/slot
        * _bitRate // bits/second
        / _samplingRate;   // samples/second
    _header += _headerSpacing;  // 1 byte/slot
    if(_padding) _header += 1; // Extra slot
}
```

Remember that all of the header information is repeated with each frame. Most of that information is allowed to change with each frame (although the layer, id, and sampling rate should not change). In particular, it's possible for the bit rate to vary from header to header so that, over the long term, you get a bit rate different from any of the standard bit rates.

Another way to use a nonstandard bit rate is to use the special *free bit rate* code. Of course, this makes it impossible to directly compute the frame length, so the standard also specifies that if the bit rate is free, the frame length must not change (except for the indicated slot of padding). This allows you to measure the length of the first frame by searching ahead for the next header and then reusing that value for the remaining frames. I use the `_headerSpacing` variable to indicate the number of slots in a frame.

LISTING 14.10   Locate Next Header with Free Bit Rate

```
if (_headerSpacing) { // Already know header spacing
   if (_layer == 1) { // Layer 1 has 4-byte slots
      _header += _headerSpacing * 4;
      if(_padding) _header += 4;
   } else {   // Layers 2 and 3 have 1-byte slots
      _header += _headerSpacing;
      if(_padding) _header += 1;
   }
} else {  // Need to search for next header
   int slotLength = (_layer == 1)?4:1;
   _headerSpacing = 1;
   _header+=slotLength;
   while( (_header[0] != 0xFF) || ((_header[1]&0xF0) != 0xF0) ) {
      _header+=slotLength;
      _headerSpacing++;
   }
   if (_padding) _headerSpacing--;
}
```

If you look carefully throughout the standard, you'll notice that the bit pattern of all ones is routinely omitted, so a false syncword can't appear unless there are errors.

LISTING 14.11   Read and Decompress Next MPEG Frame

```
// Read and decompress next frame
void DecompressMpeg::NextFrame() {
   if (ParseHeader()) { // If no more headers
      _samplesRemaining = 0;
      return;
   }

   // Initialize for decoding
   _pcmSamples[0] = _sampleStorage[0];
   _pcmSamples[1] = _sampleStorage[1];

   switch(_layer) {
   case 1:  Layer1Decode(); break;
   case 2:  Layer2Decode(); break;
   case 3:  Layer3Decode(); break;
   }

   // Initialize for reading samples
   _pcmSamples[0] = _sampleStorage[0];
   _pcmSamples[1] = _sampleStorage[1];
}
```

Layer 1/Layer 2 Subband Synthesis

Although they store the data differently, Layers 1 and 2 work on the same basic principles. I'll start by explaining how you reconstruct PCM audio after you've decoded the bits. In the next sections, I'll show how Layers 1 and 2 store the bits in the file.

The initial decoding gives you groups of 32 subband samples. Each sample is the amplitude of a particular frequency subband. To reconstruct the output, you first convert 32 subband samples to 64 PCM samples by summing a collection of cosine waves. You then blend successive sets of these PCM samples to obtain 32 output samples.

LISTING 14.12   Layer 1/Layer 2 Decompression Variables

```
private:
   long *_V[2][16];  // Synthesis window for left/right channel
   void Layer12Synthesis(long *V[16], long *in, int inSamples,
                         AudioSample *out);
   void Layer1Decode(); // Decompress layer 1 data
   void Layer2Decode(); // Decompress layer 2 data
```

The V arrays store 16 groups of 64 PCM samples. Each set of 32 subband (frequency-domain) samples is reconstructed to form 64 PCM samples. The V arrays keep the most recent 16 sets of these samples.

LISTING 14.13   Initialize Layer 1/Layer 2 Shared Variables

```
for(int ch=0;ch<2;ch++) {     // V is stored in object
   for(int i=0;i<16;i++) {
      _V[ch][i] = new long[64];
      for(int j=0;j<64;j++)
         _V[ch][i][j] = 0;
   }
}
```

Because the V array is stored in the object, it needs to be deleted when the object is deleted.

LISTING 14.14   MPEG Cleanup

```
for(int ch=0;ch<2;ch++)
   for(int i=0;i<16;i++)
      delete [] _V[ch][i];
```

For speed, I've implemented the subband synthesis using 32-bit fixed-point arithmetic. I've indicated in comments my assumptions about various values. For example, I assume the subband samples are 2.16—there are 2 bits before the decimal place and 16 after. This notation is convenient for tracking the precision of values. For example, if you multiply a 2.15 value by a 2.13 value, the result will have 28 bits after the decimal place (15 + 13) and 3 before (each 2 represents 1 bit plus a sign, the new number has 2 bits plus sign), which I write as 3.28. Because 3 + 28 is only 31 bits, it won't overflow a 32-bit value. Similar considerations appear throughout this code.

LISTING 14.15   Layer 1/Layer 2 Subband Synthesis

Layer 1/Layer 2 Matrix Samples–Fast Version (Listing 14.17)

```
void DecompressMpeg::Layer12Synthesis(
                    long *V[16],
                    long *subbandSamples,
                    int numSubbandSamples,
                    AudioSample *pcmSamples) {
   long *t = V[15];
   for(int i=15;i>0;i--) // Shift V buffers over
      V[i] = V[i-1];
   V[0] = t;

   // Convert subband samples into PCM samples in V[0]
   Matrix(V[0],subbandSamples,numSubbandSamples);

   // Rearrange synthesis window coefficients into a more
   // useful order, and scale them to 3.12
   static long D[512];
   static bool initializedD = false;
   if (!initializedD) {
      long *nextD = D;
      for(int j=0;j<32;j++)
         for(int i=0;i<16;i+=2) {
            *nextD++ = SynthesisWindowCoefficients[j+32*i]>>4;
            *nextD++ = SynthesisWindowCoefficients[j+32*i+32]>>4;
         }
      initializedD = true;
   }

   // D is 3.12, V is 6.9, want 16 bit output
   long *nextD = D;
   for(int j=0;j<32;j++) {
      long sample = 0; // 8.16
      for(int i=0;i<16;i+=2) {
         sample += (*nextD++ * V[i][j]) >> 8;
         sample += (*nextD++ * V[i+1][j+32]) >> 8;
      }
      *pcmSamples++ = sample >> 1; // Output samples are 16 bit
   }
}
```

Matrixing

The 32 subband samples represent the amplitude of 32 different frequencies. The *matrixing* step converts them into 64 PCM samples. This is the core of the entire decoder process.

The term *matrixing* comes from the way this reconstruction is defined within the ISO standard. The standard defines a particular 64×32 matrix, and presents the reconstruction as a matrix multiplication; a vector of 32 subband samples is multiplied by this matrix to form 64 PCM samples. Those 64 samples go through some further processing to emerge as the final, reconstructed 32 PCM samples.

The specific definition of matrixing is that it generates 64 outputs $V_0, V_1, \ldots, V_{63}$ from 32 subband samples $S_0, \ldots, S_{31}$ according to the following formula:

$$V_n = \sum_{k=0}^{31} S_k \cos[(16 + n)(2k + 1)\pi/64]$$

Note that each row of the matrix represents a different cosine wave. This formula simply scales each cosine wave by the corresponding S_k and then adds them together to get the 64 output values.

Slow Matrixing

Since the 64×32 cosine values are fixed, you can precompute them in a table and implement the above formula directly, as in the following code:

LISTING 14.16   Layer 1/Layer 2 Matrix Samples–Slow Version

```
static void Matrix(long *V, long *subbandSamples, int numSubbandSamples) {
    // N is constant, so it's stored in a static variable
    static long N[64][32];
    static bool initializedN = false;

    if (!initializedN) {
        for(int n=0;n<64;n++) {
            for(int k=0;k<32;k++)
                N[n][k] = static_cast<long>
                    (8192.0*cos((16+n)*(2*k+1)*(3.14159265358979/64.0)));
        }
        initializedN = true;
    }

    for(int n=0; n<64;n++) { // Matrixing
        long t=0; // sum of 32 numbers, each 2.21
        long *samples = subbandSamples; // 1.16
        long *matrix = N[n]; // 2.13
        for(int k=0;k<numSubbandSamples;k++)
```

```
        t += (*samples++ * *matrix++) >> 8;
      V[n] = t>>10; // V is 5.12
    }
  }
```

The code above has two serious problems. The first is accuracy. Every time you add or multiply two fixed-point numbers, you potentially lose one bit of accuracy to roundoff errors. Since each output requires 32 multiplications and 32 additions, accuracy is a serious concern.

The bigger problem is speed. Each matrix multiplication requires over 2,000 multiplications. On a 486/66, the matrixing code above requires about 2 milliseconds. Unfortunately, even at the lowest MPEG-1 sampling rate of 32,000 samples per second, you have only 1 millisecond to decompress each group of 32 samples (and remember that matrixing is only one step of the entire decompression).

With higher sampling rates or stereo, the timing is even tighter. While a sufficiently fast processor could decode a CD-quality stereo MPEG file using this approach, it would be hard to do anything else while decoding.

Fast Matrixing

To develop a faster version of the matrixing operation, I'll use a number of tricks from Chapter 24. If you're not at least passingly familiar with Fourier transforms in general, and the Fast Fourier Transform (FFT) algorithm in specific, you may want to read Chapter 24 before reading this section. (If you are uncomfortable with complex numbers, you may want to skip this section entirely.)

By rewriting the matrixing formula, you can convert it into something similar to the Discrete Fourier Transform (DFT). I can then use the techniques from Chapter 24 to develop an algorithm similar to the FFT algorithm.

To see that the matrixing formula is similar in form to the DFT, remember that $\cos(x)$ is the real part of the complex exponential e^{ix}. (Where i is the square root of -1.) So, I can rewrite the matrixing calculation in the following form:

$$V_n = \text{Real}\left(\sum_{k=0}^{31} S_k e^{i(16+n)(2k+1)\pi/64}\right)$$

At first glance, it might seem counterproductive to rewrite the formula as one involving slow complex arithmetic. But exponentials are generally easier to work with than trigonometric functions. This will allow me to simplify the formula in an important way. In particular, I can easily factor out the part that doesn't depend on k:

$$V_n = \text{Real} \left(e^{i(16+n)\pi/64} \sum_{k=0}^{31} S_k e^{i(16+n)2k\pi/64} \right)$$

Now, I'm going to cheat a little, and renumber the V_n as $V_{16}, V_{17}, \ldots, V_{79}$. That allows me to drop the 16+ part:

$$V_n = \text{Real} \left(e^{in\pi/64} \sum_{k=0}^{31} S_k e^{i\pi nk/32} \right)$$

If I can find a fast way to compute the inner summation, then I can simply multiply by the fixed constants $e^{in\pi/64}$, take the real part, and renumber everything correctly to get the final answer. So, I need to find a fast way to compute the inner summation.

The inner summation looks very much like the DFT equation shown on page 374. In particular, it's one case of a more general transform:

$$\sum_{k=0}^{N-1} S_k e^{i\pi nk/N}$$

This transform is *not* a Fourier transform. However, it's similar enough that many of the same tricks can be used. In particular, you can separate this summation into odd and even terms:

$$\left(\sum_{k=0}^{(N/2)-1} S_{2k} e^{i\pi n(2k)/N} \right) + \left(\sum_{k=0}^{(N/2)-1} S_{2k+1} e^{i\pi n(2k+1)/N} \right)$$

Following the derivation of the FFT algorithm, you can rewrite this as two $N/2$-point transformations:

$$\left(\sum_{k=0}^{(N/2)-1} S_{2k} e^{i\pi nk/(N/2)} \right) + e^{i\pi n/N} \left(\sum_{k=0}^{(N/2)-1} S_{2k+1} e^{i\pi nk/(N/2)} \right)$$

If you study this equation carefully, it says that you can calculate the 32-point transformation (the one you want) by first calculating two 16-point transformations. The two 16-point transformations can be computed from four 8-point transformations, and so on. Ultimately, this formula tells you how to combine sixteen 2-point transformations into the 32-point transformation you want.

Now, remember that the 32-point transformation gives you 64 values. Similarly, the 2-point transformation gives you four values. With inputs *a* and *b*, the 2-point transformation gives you: $a + b$, $a + ib$, $a - b$, and $a - ib$.

From the above work, and the tools from Chapter 24, you can derive the algorithm I'm using here. This function uses a number of optimizations that could also be applied to the FFT code in Chapter 24.

LISTING 14.17   Layer 1/Layer 2 Matrix Samples–Fast Version

```
// subbandSamples input are 2.16
static void Matrix(long *V, long *subbandSamples, int numSamples) {
   for(int i=numSamples;i<32;i++)
      subbandSamples[i]=0;

   static const double PI=3.14159265358979323846;
   long *workR=V; // Re-use V as work storage
   long workI[64]; // Imaginary part

   static const char order[] = {0,16,8,24,4,20,12,28,2,18,10,26,6,22,14,30,
                                 1,17,9,25,5,21,13,29,3,19,11,27,7,23,15,31};

   // The initialization step here precalculates the
   // 2-point transforms (each two inputs generate four outputs)
   // I'm taking advantage of the fact that my inputs are all real
   long *pWorkR = workR; // 2.16
   long *pWorkI = workI; // 2.16
   const char *next = order;
   for(int n=0;n<16;n++) {
      long a = subbandSamples[*next++];
      long b = subbandSamples[*next++];
      *pWorkR++ = a+b;   *pWorkI++ = 0;
      *pWorkR++ = a;     *pWorkI++ = b;
      *pWorkR++ = a-b;   *pWorkI++ = 0;
      *pWorkR++ = a;     *pWorkI++ = -b;
   }

   // This is a fast version of the transform in the ISO standard.
   // It's derived using the same principles as the FFT,
   // but it's NOT a Fourier Transform. (See Chapter 24)

   // For speed, precompute all of the phase shift values
   static long phaseShiftsR[32], phaseShiftsI[32]; // 1.14
   static bool initializedPhaseShifts = false;

   if (!initializedPhaseShifts) { // Initialize it only once
      for(int i=0;i<32;i++) { // 1.14
         phaseShiftsR[i] = static_cast<long>(16384.0*cos(i*(PI/32.0)));
         phaseShiftsI[i] = static_cast<long>(16384.0*sin(i*(PI/32.0)));
      }
      initializedPhaseShifts = true;
   }
```

```
// In each iteration, I throw out one bit of accuracy
// This gives me an extra bit of headroom to avoid overflow
int phaseShiftIndex, phaseShiftStep = 8;
for(int size=4; size<64; size <<= 1) {
   // Since the first phase shfit value is always 1,
   // I can save a few multiplies by duplicating the loop
   // Note that such unrolling is actually counter-productive
   // on fast processors that have small caches.
   for(int n=0; n < 64; n += 2*size) {
      long tR = workR[n+size];
      workR[n+size] = (workR[n] - tR)>>1;
      workR[n] = (workR[n] + tR)>>1;
      long tI = workI[n+size];
      workI[n+size] = (workI[n] - tI)>>1;
      workI[n] = (workI[n] + tI)>>1;
   }
   phaseShiftIndex = phaseShiftStep;
   for(int fftStep = 1; fftStep < size; fftStep++) {
      long phaseShiftR = phaseShiftsR[phaseShiftIndex];
      long phaseShiftI = phaseShiftsI[phaseShiftIndex];
      phaseShiftIndex += phaseShiftStep;
      for(int n=fftStep; n < 64; n += 2*size) {
         long tR = (phaseShiftR*workR[n+size]
                  - phaseShiftI*workI[n+size])>>14;
         long tI = (phaseShiftR*workI[n+size]
                  + phaseShiftI*workR[n+size])>>14;
         workR[n+size] = (workR[n] - tR)>>1;
         workI[n+size] = (workI[n] - tI)>>1;
         workR[n] = (workR[n] + tR)>>1;
         workI[n] = (workI[n] + tI)>>1;
      }
   }
   phaseShiftStep /= 2;
}


// Build final V values by massaging transform output
{
   static long vShiftR[64], vShiftI[64]; // 1.13
   static bool initializedVshift = false;
   int n;

   if (!initializedVshift) { // Initialize it only once
      for(n=0;n<32;n++) { // 1.14
         vShiftR[n] = static_cast<long>(16384.0*cos((32+n)*(PI/64.0)));
         vShiftI[n] = static_cast<long>(16384.0*sin((32+n)*(PI/64.0)));
      }
      initializedVshift = true;
   }

   // Now build V values from the complex transform output
   long *pcmR = workR+33; // 6.12
   long *pcmI = workI+33; // 6.12
   V[16] = 0;    // V[16] is always 0
   for(n=1;n<32;n++) {    // V is the real part, V is 6.9
      V[n+16] = (vShiftR[n] * *pcmR++ - vShiftI[n] * *pcmI++)>>15;
   }
```

```
        V[48] = (-workR[0])>>1;   // vShift[32] is always -1
        // Exploit symmetries in the result
        for(n=0;n<16;n++) V[n] = -V[32-n];
        for(n=1;n<16;n++) V[48+n] = V[48-n];
    }
}
```

It's also possible to use this approach to develop an alternative floating-point version of the matrixing operation. The advantage of a floating-point version is accuracy; the code I've developed here gives only about 13 bits of accuracy (out of 16 bits that I want for my final output). Although new processors are fast enough to make a floating-point MPEG decoder feasible, this integer version is still noticably faster, which can be important if you need to do additional processing while the sound is being decompressed.

TABLE 14.5   Timing for Different Matrix Implementations

Processor	Compiler	OS	Integer		Floating Point	
			Fast	Slow	Fast	Slow
Intel 486DX2/66	GCC 2.7.2	FreeBSD 2.1	400	1200	720	1100
Intel 486DX2/66	VC++ 5.0	Windows 95	450	1120	1390	960
PowerPC 603e/200	CW11	Mac OS 7.6	55	90	103	113
Intel Pentium/90	VC++ 5.0	Windows 95	100	340	230	210

All times are in microseconds.

For concreteness, Table 14.5 shows the time required to matrix 32 samples using several different implementations. The "slow" version is the straightforward implementation that I presented in the previous section; the "fast" version uses the algorithm I developed in this section. Keep in mind that these timings represent just the matrixing operation. For reference, a CD-quality stereo signal requires you to process each group of 32 samples in 360 microseconds. (These values were calculated using the `testmatrix.cpp` program included on the CD-ROM.)

As you can see, this type of optimization is a black art at best. The integer version is two- to three-times faster using the algorithm in this section (providing as much as a 30 percent increase in speed for the entire decoder). However, the floating point versions behave quite differently; on system B, the "fast" floating point implementation is almost 50 percent slower than the "slow" version.

Synthesis Window Coefficients

The ISO standard gives a table of 512 9-digit floating-point numbers for the synthesis window. It fails to point out that every one of these numbers is an exact multiple of 1/65,536. It also fails to mention that the table is symmetric; entries 257–511 are the negatives of entries 1–255 in reverse order. If you divide each of the values in the following table by 65,536, you'll recover the floating point values as given in the standard.

LISTING 14.18 Layer 1/Layer 2 Synthesis Window Coefficients

```
static long SynthesisWindowCoefficients[] = // 2.16 fixed-point values
{0, -1, -1, -1, -1, -1, -1, -2, -2, -2, -2, -3, -3, -4, -4, -5, -5, -6,
-7, -7, -8, -9, -10, -11, -13, -14, -16, -17, -19, -21, -24, -26,

-29, -31, -35, -38, -41, -45, -49, -53, -58, -63, -68, -73, -79,
-85, -91, -97, -104, -111, -117, -125, -132, -139, -147, -154, -161,
-169, -176, -183, -190, -196, -202, -208,

213, 218, 222, 225, 227, 228, 228, 227, 224, 221, 215, 208, 200, 189,
177, 163, 146, 127, 106, 83, 57, 29, -2, -36, -72, -111, -153, -197,
-244, -294, -347, -401,

-459, -519, -581, -645, -711, -779, -848, -919, -991, -1064, -1137,
-1210, -1283, -1356, -1428, -1498, -1567, -1634, -1698, -1759, -1817,
-1870, -1919, -1962, -2001, -2032, -2057, -2075, -2085, -2087, -2080,
-2063,

2037, 2000, 1952, 1893, 1822, 1739, 1644, 1535, 1414, 1280, 1131, 970,
794, 605, 402, 185, -45, -288, -545, -814, -1095, -1388, -1692, -2006,
-2330, -2663, -3004, -3351, -3705, -4063, -4425, -4788,

-5153, -5517, -5879, -6237, -6589, -6935, -7271, -7597, -7910, -8209,
-8491, -8755, -8998, -9219, -9416, -9585, -9727, -9838, -9916, -9959,
-9966, -9935, -9863, -9750, -9592, -9389, -9139, -8840, -8492, -8092,
-7640, -7134,

  .
  .
  .

459, 401, 347, 294, 244, 197, 153, 111, 72, 36, 2, -29, -57, -83,
-106, -127, -146, -163, -177, -189, -200, -208, -215, -221, -224,
-227, -228, -228, -227, -225, -222, -218,

213, 208, 202, 196, 190, 183, 176, 169, 161, 154, 147, 139, 132, 125,
117, 111, 104, 97, 91, 85, 79, 73, 68, 63, 58, 53, 49, 45, 41, 38, 35,
31,

29, 26, 24, 21, 19, 17, 16, 14, 13, 11, 10, 9, 8, 7, 7, 6, 5, 5, 4, 4,
3, 3, 2, 2, 2, 2, 1, 1, 1, 1, 1, 1};
```

MPEG Stereo Encoding

Human hearing uses a variety of cues to determine the location of a sound source. The most obvious cue is volume; if a sound is louder in your left ear, it's probably located to your left. But there are other, more subtle clues. For example, a sound on your left will arrive at your left ear slightly before it arrives at your right ear. In addition, the shape of your outer ear slightly alters sounds, depending on their location. Your inner ear and brain can detect these slight changes to obtain remarkably detailed positional information.

The only way to preserve all of these cues is to record and compress the left and right channels independently. However, your ears aren't uniformly sensitive to all of the possible cues. In particular, at higher frequencies, the relative volume is more important than the other information. MPEG exploits this variation to provide better compression of stereo signals.

In ordinary stereo mode, MPEG stores two independent sets of samples, one for each channel. This obviously preserves all of the stereo cues. The alternative is *intensity stereo*, which stores only one set of samples, as well as different *scale factors* (volumes) for each channel. Intensity stereo preserves only the volume difference between left and right.

Most stereo MPEG files are stored in *joint stereo*, in which the lower-frequency subbands use ordinary stereo (there are separate samples for each channel) while higher-frequency subbands use intensity stereo (only the scale factors are different).

MPEG Layer 3 adds an additional *MS-stereo* mode that provides an intermediate choice between full stereo and intensity stereo. Essentially, MS stereo converts the separate left and right channels into a middle channel (sum of the two) and side channel (difference). To decode it, you start with the middle channel and add the side channel to get the left value and subtract the side channel to get the right value. The advantage of this scheme is that the side channel can be stored less accurately.

Layer 1

MPEG Layer 1 stores 12 groups of 32 subband samples in each frame. Each sample requires from 2 to 15 bits. In order to extract the samples, you need to first know how many bits to read for each sample (the *allocation*), and you need to know how to scale the resulting samples (the scale factors).

Layer 1 stores the allocation and scale factors in a direct fashion. The allocation values are stored as a series of 4-bit values, and the scale factors are stored as a series of 6-bit values.

LISTING 14.19   Layer 1 Frame Decoding

```
void DecompressMpeg::Layer1Decode() {
   int allocation[2][32]; // One for each channel and subband
   ResetBits();
```

┌───┐
│ Read Layer 1 Allocation Values (Listing 14.20) │
└───┘

```
   int scaleFactor[2][32]; // One for each channel and subband
```

┌───┐
│ Read Layer 1 Scale Factors (Listing 14.21) │
└───┘

```
   long sbSamples[2][32]; // samples

   for(int gr=0;gr<12;gr++) { // Read 12 groups of samples
      if(_channels == 1) {
```

┌──┐
│ Read and Decode Layer 1 Mono Subband Samples (Listing 14.22) │
└──┘

```
      } else { // Stereo
```

┌───┐
│ Read and Decode Layer 1 Stereo Subband Samples (Listing 14.23) │
└───┘

```
      }
   }
}
```

Layer 1 Allocation Storage

The 4-bit allocation value indicates how many bits will be used for each sample in that subband. If any allocation is zero, then no samples or scale factors are stored for that subband. This allows the encoder to omit certain subbands from this frame. Also, because a subband stored in intensity stereo shares a single sample among the channels, it needs only to store a single allocation value (rather than one for each channel).

In order to help avoid false sync values in the bitstream, the allocation value cannot be all ones.

LISTING 14.20   Read Layer 1 Allocation Values

```
   if(_channels == 1) {
      // Mono stores one allocation for each subband
      for(int sb=0;sb<32;sb++)
         allocation[0][sb] = GetBits(4);
   } else { // Stereo is slightly more complex
      // Retrieve separate allocations for full stereo bands
      int sb;
      for(sb=0;sb<_bound;sb++) {
         allocation[0][sb] = GetBits(4);
         allocation[1][sb] = GetBits(4);
      }
```

```
    // Retrieve shared allocation for intensity stereo bands
    for(;sb<32;sb++) {
        allocation[0][sb] = GetBits(4);
        allocation[1][sb] = allocation[0][sb];
    }
}
```

Layer 1 Scale Factors

A single frame contains 12 sets of 32 subband samples. In order to save space, the compressor can balance two parameters. The allocation value controls how many values can be stored for a given subband. If a subband does not change much across the 12 sets of samples, it makes sense to use fewer bits. To control the overall amplitude of a subband, a scale factor is used. The scale factor is an index into a table of values.

LISTING 14.21   Read Layer 1 Scale Factors

```
{
   for(int sb=0; sb<32; sb++)
      for(int ch=0; ch<_channels; ch++)
         if(allocation[ch][sb] != 0) {
            scaleFactor[ch][sb] = GetBits(6);
         }
}
```

Layer 1 Sample Storage

With the allocation values and scale factors in hand, reading the subband samples is easy. The allocation value indicates the number of bits in a sample. An allocation value of zero indicates that no bits are stored for this sample. Allocation values from 1 to 14 indicate the sample is stored with 2 to 15 bits. An allocation value of 15 is forbidden, to avoid false syncwords.

Each sample needs to be reconstituted into a full 16-bit value, and the appropriate scale factor must be applied. (The ISO standard actually specifies all calculations in floating-point arithmetic.)

Once you've retrieved a group of 32 subband samples, you use subband synthesis to re-create 32 PCM samples.

LISTING 14.22   Read and Decode Layer 1 Mono Subband Samples

```
for(int sb=0;sb<32;sb++) // Read a group of 32 samples
   if(!allocation[0][sb]) // No bits?
      sbSamples[0][sb] = 0;
   else {
```

```
        int width = allocation[0][sb]+1;
        long s = GetBits(width);
        // Requantize and Scale this sample
        sbSamples[0][sb] = Layer1Requant(s, width,
                            scaleFactor[0][sb]);
    }
  Layer12Synthesis(_V[0],sbSamples[0],32,_pcmSamples[0]);
  _pcmSamples[0] += 32;
  _samplesRemaining += 32;
```

Stereo uses the same idea, except that it's obviously complicated by the need to juggle full stereo and intensity stereo subbands. In the intensity stereo subbands, even though a single sample value is shared across the channels, the two channels must be scaled separately.

LISTING 14.23   Read and Decode Layer 1 Stereo Subband Samples

```
  { // Retrieve samples for full stereo subbands
    for(int sb=0;sb<_bound;sb++)
      for(int ch=0;ch<2;ch++)
        if(!allocation[ch][sb])
          sbSamples[ch][sb] = 0;
        else {
          int width = allocation[ch][sb]+1;
          long s = GetBits(width);
          // Requantize and Scale this sample
          sbSamples[ch][sb] = Layer1Requant(s, width,
                            scaleFactor[ch][sb]);
        }
  }

  { // Retrieve shared samples for intensity stereo subbands
    for(int sb=0;sb<_bound;sb++) {
      if(!allocation[0][sb])
        sbSamples[0][sb] = 0;
      else {
        int width = allocation[0][sb]+1;
        long s = GetBits(width);
        // Requantize and Scale this sample for each channel
        sbSamples[0][sb] = Layer1Requant(s, width,
                            scaleFactor[0][sb]);
        sbSamples[1][sb] = Layer1Requant(s, width,
                            scaleFactor[1][sb]);
      }
    }
  }

  // Now, reconstruct each channel
  for(int ch=0;ch<_channels;ch++) {
    Layer12Synthesis(_V[ch],sbSamples[ch],32,_pcmSamples[ch]);
    _pcmSamples[ch] += 32;
  }
  _samplesRemaining += 32;
```

Layer 1 Requantization and Scaling

Requantization refers to the process of converting short (2 to 15 bit) samples into a uniform range. My code converts the samples into signed 16-bit values.

The requantization process maps the possible n-bit sample codes to a collection of equally-spaced values between -1 and +1. For example, there are seven possible codes with 3 bits (the all-ones value is not allowed to prevent false syncwords). The values from 0 to 6 are mapped to -6/7, -4/7, -2/7, 0, 2/7, 4/7, and 6/7, respectively.

LISTING 14.24   Layer 1 Requantization Function

```
static long *layer1ScaleFactors = 0;    // 1.15 unsigned fixed-point

// return 2.16 requantized and scaled value
inline long Layer1Requant(long sample, int width, int scaleIndex) {
   long levels = (1<<width)-1;
   return (layer1ScaleFactors[scaleIndex]   *
     (((sample+sample+1 - levels)<<15)/levels)
          )>>14;
}
```

The scale factors follow an exponential curve.

LISTING 14.13 (CONTINUED)   Initialize Layer 1/Layer 2 Shared Variables

```
if(!layer1ScaleFactors) {
   layer1ScaleFactors = new long[63];
   for(int i=0;i<63;i++) {
      layer1ScaleFactors[i] = static_cast<long>
              (32767.0 * pow(2.0, 1.0 - i/3.0));
   }
}
```

LISTING 14.14 (CONTINUED)   MPEG Cleanup

```
delete layer1ScaleFactors;
layer1ScaleFactors = 0;
```

Layer 2

Layer 2 is similar to Layer 1 in concept. However, Layer 2 provides more opportunities for shaving bits from the result.

- Layer 2 uses fewer subbands at lower bit rates. This reduces the amount of allocation information required.

- A single Layer 2 frame stores three groups of 12 samples and allows scale factors to be shared across the three groups of samples. (A Layer 1 frame contains only one group of 12 samples.)

- Rather than store separate binary codes for each subband sample, certain samples can be grouped into a single binary code.

In outline, the Layer 2 decoder looks a lot like the Layer 1 decoder. The primary difference is that there are 36 sets of subband samples, which are divided into three groups of twelve (each of which can have different scale factors), and each group of twelve is divided into four groups of three. Figure 14.1 illustrates how sets of subband samples are collected into groups of three (to combine similar samples) and groups of twelve (to share a single set of scale factors).

LISTING 14.25   Layer 2 Frame Decoding

```
void DecompressMpeg::Layer2Decode() {
    int allocation[2][32]; // One for each channel and subband
    ResetBits();
```

> Read Layer 2 Allocation Values (Listing 14.27)

FIGURE 14.1   Diagram of Level 2 Subband Sample Storage

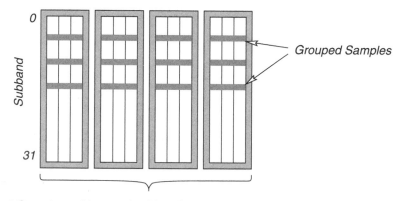

4 Granules = 12 sets of subband samples = 1/3 frame

```
int scaleFactor[3][2][32]; // One for each channel and subband
long sbSamples[3][2][32]; // Three sets of subband samples
```

> Read Layer 2 Scale Factors (Listing 14.28)

```
for(int sf=0;sf<3;sf++) { // Diff't scale factors for each 1/3
    for(int gr=0;gr<4;gr++) { // 4 groups of samples in each 1/3
```

> Read and Decode Layer 2 Subband Samples (Listing 14.29)

```
    }
  }
}
```

Layer 2 Allocation Storage

The lower-frequency subbands need more resolution than the higher-frequency subbands. Layer 2 exploits this by providing fewer allocation options for higher subbands. Depending on the bit rate and the sampling rate, Layer 2 chooses a particular strategy for storing allocation information.

For example, at a bit rate of 32,000 bits per second and a sampling rate of 32,000 samples per second, Layer 2 uses `Layer2AllocationB2d` on page 168, which is taken from Table B.2d in the ISO specification. With this strategy, 4 bits are used to specify the allocation for each of the bottom two subbands, 3 bits are used for each of the next ten, and the top twenty subbands aren't stored at all. Thus, a mono file would require only 38 bits for the allocation information, compared to 128 bits in a Layer 1 file.

In addition, the value stored for the allocation is not a direct count of the number of bits stored for each sample, but it is itself an index into a table. The entries of this latter table are pointers to *quantization classes*, which I'll explain later. The important point is that, by selecting an allocation strategy based on the bit rate, and by using indexes into tables rather than direct values, the Layer 2 compressor has many more options for adjusting the precise storage needs.

LISTING 14.26 Layer 2 Bit Allocation Tables

```
Layer2QuantClass *l2allocationA[] = {0,&l2qc3,&l2qc7,&l2qc15,
    &l2qc31,&l2qc63,&l2qc127,&l2qc255,&l2qc511,&l2qc1023,&l2qc2047,
    &l2qc4095,&l2qc8191,&l2qc16383,&l2qc32767,&l2qc65535};
Layer2QuantClass *l2allocationB[] = {0,&l2qc3,&l2qc5,&l2qc7,&l2qc9,
    &l2qc15,&l2qc31,&l2qc63,&l2qc127,&l2qc255,&l2qc511,&l2qc1023,&l2qc2047,
    &l2qc4095,&l2qc8191,&l2qc65535};
Layer2QuantClass *l2allocationC[] = {0,&l2qc3,&l2qc5,&l2qc7,
    &l2qc9,&l2qc15,&l2qc31,&l2qc65535};
Layer2QuantClass *l2allocationD[] = {0,&l2qc3,&l2qc5,&l2qc65535};
Layer2QuantClass *l2allocationE[] = {0,&l2qc3,&l2qc5,&l2qc9,
    &l2qc15,&l2qc31,&l2qc63,&l2qc127,&l2qc255,&l2qc511,&l2qc1023,&l2qc2047,
    &l2qc4095,&l2qc8191,&l2qc16383,&l2qc32767};
```

```
Layer2QuantClass *l2allocationF[] = {0,&l2qc3,&l2qc5,&l2qc7,&l2qc9,
   &l2qc15,&l2qc31,&l2qc63,&l2qc127,&l2qc255,&l2qc511,&l2qc1023,&l2qc2047,
   &l2qc4095,&l2qc8191,&l2qc16383};

struct Layer2BitAllocationTableEntry {
   char _numberBits;
   Layer2QuantClass **_quantClasses;
};

// 27 active subbands
// Mono requires 88 bits for allocation table
Layer2BitAllocationTableEntry Layer2AllocationB2a[32] = {
   { 4, l2allocationA },    { 4, l2allocationA },    { 4, l2allocationA },
   { 4, l2allocationB },    { 4, l2allocationB },    { 4, l2allocationB },
   { 4, l2allocationB },    { 4, l2allocationB },    { 4, l2allocationB },
   { 4, l2allocationB },    { 4, l2allocationB },    { 3, l2allocationC },
   { 3, l2allocationC },    { 3, l2allocationC },    { 3, l2allocationC },
   { 3, l2allocationC },    { 3, l2allocationC },    { 3, l2allocationC },
   { 3, l2allocationC },    { 3, l2allocationC },    { 3, l2allocationC },
   { 3, l2allocationC },    { 3, l2allocationC },    { 2, l2allocationD },
   { 2, l2allocationD },    { 2, l2allocationD },    { 2, l2allocationD },
   { 0,0},    { 0,0},    { 0,0},    { 0,0},    { 0,0}
};

// 30 active subbands
// Mono requires 94 bits for allocation table
// Used at highest bit rates
Layer2BitAllocationTableEntry Layer2AllocationB2b[32] = {
   { 4, l2allocationA },    { 4, l2allocationA },    { 4, l2allocationA },
   { 4, l2allocationB },    { 4, l2allocationB },    { 4, l2allocationB },
   { 4, l2allocationB },    { 4, l2allocationB },    { 4, l2allocationB },
   { 4, l2allocationB },    { 4, l2allocationB },    { 3, l2allocationC },
   { 3, l2allocationC },    { 3, l2allocationC },    { 3, l2allocationC },
   { 3, l2allocationC },    { 3, l2allocationC },    { 3, l2allocationC },
   { 3, l2allocationC },    { 3, l2allocationC },    { 3, l2allocationC },
   { 3, l2allocationC },    { 3, l2allocationC },    { 2, l2allocationD },
   { 2, l2allocationD },    { 2, l2allocationD },    { 2, l2allocationD },
   { 2, l2allocationD },    { 2, l2allocationD },    { 2, l2allocationD },
   { 0,0},    { 0,0}
};

// 7 active subbands
// Mono requires 26 bits for allocation table
// Used at lowest bit rates
Layer2BitAllocationTableEntry Layer2AllocationB2c[32] = {
   { 4, l2allocationE },    { 4, l2allocationE },    { 3, l2allocationE },
   { 3, l2allocationE },    { 3, l2allocationE },    { 3, l2allocationE },
   { 3, l2allocationE },    { 3, l2allocationE },
   {0,0},{0,0},{0,0},{0,0},{0,0},{0,0},{0,0},{0,0},
   {0,0},{0,0},{0,0},{0,0},{0,0},{0,0},{0,0},{0,0},
   {0,0},{0,0},{0,0},{0,0},{0,0},{0,0},{0,0},{0,0},
};

// 11 active subbands
// Mono requires 38 bits for allocation table
// Used at lowest bit rates
```

```
Layer2BitAllocationTableEntry Layer2AllocationB2d[32] = {
    { 4, l2allocationE },   { 4, l2allocationE },   { 3, l2allocationE },
    { 3, l2allocationE },   { 3, l2allocationE },   { 3, l2allocationE },
    { 3, l2allocationE },   { 3, l2allocationE },   { 3, l2allocationE },
    { 3, l2allocationE },   { 3, l2allocationE },   { 3, l2allocationE },
    {0,0},{0,0},{0,0},{0,0},{0,0},{0,0},{0,0},{0,0},{0,0},{0,0},
    {0,0},{0,0},{0,0},{0,0},{0,0},{0,0},{0,0},{0,0},{0,0},{0,0},
};


// 30 active subbands
// Mono requires 75 bits for allocation table
// Used at low MPEG-2 sampling rates
Layer2BitAllocationTableEntry Layer2AllocationB1[32] = {
    { 4, l2allocationF },   { 4, l2allocationF },   { 4, l2allocationF },
    { 4, l2allocationF },   { 3, l2allocationE },   { 3, l2allocationE },
    { 3, l2allocationE },   { 3, l2allocationE },   { 3, l2allocationE },
    { 3, l2allocationE },   { 3, l2allocationE },   { 2, l2allocationE },
    { 2, l2allocationE },   { 2, l2allocationE },   { 2, l2allocationE },
    { 2, l2allocationE },   { 2, l2allocationE },   { 2, l2allocationE },
    { 2, l2allocationE },   { 2, l2allocationE },   { 2, l2allocationE },
    { 2, l2allocationE },   { 2, l2allocationE },   { 2, l2allocationE },
    { 2, l2allocationE },   { 2, l2allocationE },   { 2, l2allocationE },
    { 2, l2allocationE },   { 2, l2allocationE },   { 2, l2allocationE },
    {0,0},{0,0}
};
```

To read the allocation values, you use the ID, bit rate, and sampling rate values to select the correct allocation map. With that in hand, you use the _numberBits field from each entry of the allocation map to determine how many bits to read.

LISTING 14.27   Read Layer 2 Allocation Values

```
// Select which allocation map to use
Layer2BitAllocationTableEntry *allocationMap;
long bitRatePerChannel = _bitRate/_channels;
if(_id==0) // Use MPEG-2 allocation map
      allocationMap = Layer2AllocationB1;
else if(bitRatePerChannel <= 48000) {
    if(_samplingRate == 32000) allocationMap = Layer2AllocationB2d;
    else allocationMap = Layer2AllocationB2c;
} else if (bitRatePerChannel < 96000)
    allocationMap = Layer2AllocationB2a;
else if (_samplingRate == 48000)
    allocationMap = Layer2AllocationB2a;
else
    allocationMap = Layer2AllocationB2b;

// Note:  frame header sets _bound to 0 for single-channel,
// so the following works correctly for both stereo and mono
int sblimit=0; // One past highest subband with non-empty allocation

{ // Retrieve separate allocations for full stereo bands
    for(int sb=0;sb<_bound;sb++) {
```

```
        if(allocationMap[sb]._numberBits) {
            allocation[0][sb] = GetBits(allocationMap[sb]._numberBits);
            allocation[1][sb] = GetBits(allocationMap[sb]._numberBits);
            if(  (allocation[0][sb] || allocation[1][sb])
                &&(sb >= sblimit) )
                sblimit=sb+1;
        } else {
            allocation[0][sb] = 0;
            allocation[1][sb] = 0;
        }
    }
}

{  // Retrieve shared allocation for intensity stereo bands
    for(int sb=_bound;sb<32;sb++) {
        if(allocationMap[sb]._numberBits) {
            allocation[0][sb] = GetBits(allocationMap[sb]._numberBits);
            if(allocation[0][sb] && (sb >= sblimit))
                sblimit=sb+1;
        } else
            allocation[0][sb] = 0;
        allocation[1][sb] = allocation[0][sb];
    }
}
```

Along the way, I've computed a useful statistic. Typically, a number of high-frequency bands are not stored at all. By identifying the highest band that is used in this frame, I can economize on future calculations.

Layer 2 Scale Factors

Layer 1 stores one set of scale factors for each 384-sample frame. With three times as many samples, Layer 2 uses a few tricks to economize on scale factor storage.

One Layer 2 frame holds 36 sets of subband samples. Another way to say this is: For each subband, one frame holds 36 samples. In a Layer 1 frame, a single scale factor applies to all the samples for a single subband. Because there are three times as many samples, Layer 2 provides the option of storing three scale factors (one for each group of 12), which gives the same time resolution as in Layer 1, or storing fewer scale factors (shared by the groups of 12), which conserves storage space.

To read the scale factors, you first grab the scale factor selection information. These 2-bit values indicate how the scale factors are stored. Then, for each subband, you read either one scale factor (which applies to all 36 samples), two scale factors (one applies to 12 samples, the other to 24), or three scale factors (one for each group of 12).

LISTING 14.28   Read Layer 2 Scale Factors

```
int scaleFactorSelection[2][32];

{ // Retrieve scale factor selection information
   for(int sb=0; sb<sblimit; sb++)
      for(int ch=0; ch<_channels; ch++)
         if(allocation[ch][sb] != 0)
            scaleFactorSelection[ch][sb] = GetBits(2);
}

{ // Read scale factors, using scaleFactorSelection to
  // determine which scale factors apply to more than one group
   for(int sb=0; sb<sblimit; sb++)
      for(int ch=0; ch<_channels; ch++)
         if(allocation[ch][sb] != 0) {
            switch(scaleFactorSelection[ch][sb]) {
            case 0:  // Three scale factors
               scaleFactor[0][ch][sb] = GetBits(6);
               scaleFactor[1][ch][sb] = GetBits(6);
               scaleFactor[2][ch][sb] = GetBits(6);
               break;
            case 1:  // One for first two-thirds, one for last third
               scaleFactor[0][ch][sb] = GetBits(6);
               scaleFactor[1][ch][sb] = scaleFactor[0][ch][sb];
               scaleFactor[2][ch][sb] = GetBits(6);
               break;
            case 2:  // One for all three
               scaleFactor[0][ch][sb] = GetBits(6);
               scaleFactor[1][ch][sb] = scaleFactor[0][ch][sb];
               scaleFactor[2][ch][sb] = scaleFactor[0][ch][sb];
               break;
            case 3:  // One for first third, one for last two-thirds
               scaleFactor[0][ch][sb] = GetBits(6);
               scaleFactor[1][ch][sb] = GetBits(6);
               scaleFactor[2][ch][sb] = scaleFactor[1][ch][sb];
               break;
            }
         }
}
```

Reading Layer 2 Samples

In addition to splitting the 36 sets of samples into thirds for the purpose of allocating scale factors, Layer 2 also bunches the samples into sets of three. Rather than reading one set of 32 subband samples at a time as Layer 1 does, Layer 2 stores three samples for each subband. The primary savings here is by *grouping*.

Grouping stores three individual samples into a single bit field. For instance, if you want to store three values in the range 0 to 4, you can use base-5 arithmetic to combine them into a single 7-bit field, rather than using 3 bits each for a total of 9 bits. If the three values are a, b, and c, you store $25a + 5b + c$. Separating these grouped values requires computing successive remainders.

LISTING 14.29   Read and Decode Layer 2 Subband Samples

```
for(int sb=0;sb<sblimit;sb++) { // Read 3 sets of 32 subband samples
    for(int ch=0;ch<_channels;ch++) {
        // If this is an intensity stereo band, just copy samples over
        if((sb>=_bound) && (ch == 1)) {
            sbSamples[0][1][sb] = sbSamples[0][0][sb];
            sbSamples[1][1][sb] = sbSamples[1][0][sb];
            sbSamples[2][1][sb] = sbSamples[2][0][sb];
            continue;
        }
        Layer2QuantClass *quantClass
            = allocationMap[sb]._quantClasses ?
                allocationMap[sb]._quantClasses[ allocation[ch][sb] ]
                : 0 ;
        if(!allocation[ch][sb]) { // No bits, store zero for each set
            sbSamples[0][ch][sb] = 0;
            sbSamples[1][ch][sb] = 0;
            sbSamples[2][ch][sb] = 0;
        } else if (quantClass->_grouping) { // Grouped samples
            long s = GetBits(quantClass->_bits); // Get group
            // Separate out by computing successive remainders
            sbSamples[0][ch][sb]
                = Layer2Requant(s % quantClass->_levels,quantClass,
                                scaleFactor[sf][ch][sb]);
            s /= quantClass->_levels;
            sbSamples[1][ch][sb]
                = Layer2Requant(s % quantClass->_levels,quantClass,
                                scaleFactor[sf][ch][sb]);
            s /= quantClass->_levels;
            sbSamples[2][ch][sb]
                = Layer2Requant(s % quantClass->_levels,quantClass,
                                scaleFactor[sf][ch][sb]);
        } else { // Ungrouped samples
            int width = quantClass->_bits;
            long s = GetBits(width); // Get 1st sample
            sbSamples[0][ch][sb]
                = Layer2Requant(s,quantClass,scaleFactor[sf][ch][sb]);
            s = GetBits(width); // Get 2nd sample
            sbSamples[1][ch][sb]
                = Layer2Requant(s,quantClass,scaleFactor[sf][ch][sb]);
            s = GetBits(width); // Get 3rd sample
            sbSamples[2][ch][sb]
                = Layer2Requant(s,quantClass,scaleFactor[sf][ch][sb]);
        }
    }
}

// Now, feed three sets of subband samples into synthesis engine
for(int ch=0;ch < _channels;ch++) {
```

```
        Layer12Synthesis(_V[ch],sbSamples[0][ch],sblimit,_pcmSamples[ch]);
        _pcmSamples[ch] += 32;
        Layer12Synthesis(_V[ch],sbSamples[1][ch],sblimit,_pcmSamples[ch]);
        _pcmSamples[ch] += 32;
        Layer12Synthesis(_V[ch],sbSamples[2][ch],sblimit,_pcmSamples[ch]);
        _pcmSamples[ch] += 32;
    }
    _samplesRemaining += 96;
```

Layer 2 Requantization

The contents of the `Layer2QuantClass` structure should make sense now. The structure specifies how many bits to read for each subband, and whether those bits represent a single sample or a group of three samples.

LISTING 14.30   Layer 2 Quantization Class Tables

```
struct Layer2QuantClass {
   long _levels;  // Number of levels
   char _bits;    // bits to read
   bool _grouping;// Yes->decompose into three samples
};
```

The quantization class is also used by the `Layer2Requant` function to requantize each sample. The formula is the same one used by `Layer1Requant`.

LISTING 14.30 (CONTINUED)   Layer 2 Quantization Class Tables

```
// return 2.16 requantized and scaled value
inline long Layer2Requant(long sample,
                  Layer2QuantClass *quantClass,
                  int scaleIndex) {
   long levels = quantClass->_levels;
   return (layer1ScaleFactors[scaleIndex]  *
           (((sample+sample+1 - levels)<<15)/levels)
          ) >> 14;

}
```

In the following code, note that the number of levels is always one less than a power of 2 (except for the grouped classes); the all-ones value is forbidden to avoid false syncwords.

LISTING 14.30 (CONTINUED)   Layer 2 Quantization Class Tables

```
static Layer2QuantClass l2qc3 = {3,5,true};
static Layer2QuantClass l2qc5 = {5,7,true};
static Layer2QuantClass l2qc7 = {7,3,false};
static Layer2QuantClass l2qc9 = {9,10,true};
static Layer2QuantClass l2qc15 = {15,4,false};
static Layer2QuantClass l2qc31 = {31,5,false};
static Layer2QuantClass l2qc63 = {63,6,false};
static Layer2QuantClass l2qc127 = {127,7,false};
static Layer2QuantClass l2qc255 = {255,8,false};
static Layer2QuantClass l2qc511 = {511,9,false};
static Layer2QuantClass l2qc1023 = {1023,10,false};
static Layer2QuantClass l2qc2047 = {2047,11,false};
static Layer2QuantClass l2qc4095 = {4095,12,false};
static Layer2QuantClass l2qc8191 = {8191,13,false};
static Layer2QuantClass l2qc16383 = {16383,14,false};
static Layer2QuantClass l2qc32767 = {32767,15,false};
static Layer2QuantClass l2qc65535 = {65535,16,false};
```

Layer 3

Layer 3 compression is significantly more complex than Layer 2.

- Layer 3 allows the frame data to vary in size. Although the headers are always evenly spaced, the associated data is not limited to fit between two frame headers. This allows the Layer 3 compressor to vary the frame data size depending on the data to be compressed.

- Layer 3 stores scale factors in a more complex fashion: The scale factor selection bits can apply to groups of scale factors; scale factor codes have different lengths for different subbands.

- Samples are stored using Huffman codes, which allows common values to use fewer bits than less common values.

- The Layer 3 synthesis process uses two stages: Each Layer 2 subband is further subdivided into 18 *frequency lines*, and the samples can be grouped differently for different subbands.

Taken together, these considerations make Layer 3 decompressors much more complex than Layer 2 decompressors. The Layer 3 format is sufficiently complex that very few encoders take advantage of all its capabilities. In particular, the ability to vary the amount of data for each frame requires balancing compression requirements for several frames at once.

LISTING 14.31   Layer 3 Decompression Variables

```
private:
   void Layer3Decode();
```

LISTING 14.32   Layer 3 Frame Decoding

```
void DecompressMpeg::Layer3Decode() {
   cerr << "I don't support MPEG Layer 3 decompression.\n";
   exit(1);
}
```

A Reader for MPEG Files

MPEG audio files usually consist of an MPEG audio stream, although many other file formats (including WAVE) can contain MPEG data. In order to read a file, I need two things; a function that can test the file type and an audio class whose constructor accepts an `istream`.

LISTING 14.33   MPEG File Reader

```
bool IsMpegFile(istream &file);

class MpegRead:  public AudioAbstract {
private:
   istream &_stream;
   AbstractDecompressor *_decoder;
public:
   MpegRead(istream &input = cin);
   ~MpegRead();
   size_t GetSamples(AudioSample *buffer, size_t numSamples);
   size_t ReadBytes(AudioByte *buffer, size_t length);
   void MinMaxSamplingRate(long *min, long *max, long *preferred);
   void MinMaxChannels(int *min, int *max, int *preferred);
};
```

The `MpegRead` class is a simple example of the file format classes I'll discuss in the following chapters. The constructor accepts a C++ `istream`, the `GetSamples` method forwards requests to the `_decoder` object, and the `ReadBytes` method pulls data from the file.

LISTING 14.3 (CONTINUED)   mpeg.cpp

```cpp
bool IsMpegFile(istream &file) {
   file.seekg(0);  // Seek to beginning
   long magic = ReadIntMsb(file,2);
   if ((magic & 0xFFF0) == 0xFFF0) return true;
   else return false;
}

MpegRead::MpegRead(istream &input):AudioAbstract(),_stream(input) {
   cerr << "File Format:  MPEG\n";
   _decoder = new DecompressMpeg(*this);
}

MpegRead::~MpegRead() {
   if (_decoder) delete _decoder;
}

size_t MpegRead::GetSamples(AudioSample *buffer, size_t numSamples) {
   return _decoder->GetSamples(buffer,numSamples);
}

size_t MpegRead::ReadBytes(AudioByte *buffer, size_t length) {
   _stream.read(reinterpret_cast<char *>(buffer),length);
   return _stream.gcount();
}

void MpegRead::MinMaxChannels(int *min, int *max, int *preferred) {
   _decoder->MinMaxChannels(min, max, preferred);
}

void MpegRead::MinMaxSamplingRate(long *min, long *max, long *preferred) {
   _decoder->MinMaxSamplingRate(min, max, preferred);
}
```

More Information

The full ISO standard is available from several sources. In the United States, contact Global Engineering Documents (http://global.ihs.com).

Unfortunately, most of the currently available books on MPEG only cover the video encoding. However, *MPEG Video Compression Standard* by Joan Mitchell, William Pennebaker, Chad Fogg, and Didier LeGall provides some good historical information about the MPEG standards. The authors have also indicated that a future volume will specifically address audio encoding.

The Web site http://www.mpeg.org contains MPEG players and other information.

Part Four
General File Formats

AU File Format

15

The AU file format is simple and widely used on the Internet today. It originated on Sun computers as a dump of μ-Law sound data. Later, a basic header was added to make it easier to identify these files and to specify the sound format explicitly. The format is known as SND on NeXT computers.

The primary advantage of AU is simplicity. The header identifies all the important parameters, and the sound data is stored as a simple dump. The only disadvantage is that the header includes the total length of the sound data, which is often not known ahead of time. The easiest way around this is for programs writing AU files to set the length artificially high, and for programs reading AU files to stop when they hit the end of the file or when they've read the appropriate length. You should *not* set the sound data length to zero.

Table 15.1 shows the format of an AU header. All of these values are stored starting with the most significant byte. Although the offset is exactly 28 for most AU files, some people store additional data in the header; you should always be careful to obey the actual length. Also, as mentioned earlier, the number of bytes of sound data should be treated as an upper limit, not as a guarantee.

TABLE 15.1   AU Header

Length	Description
4	Magic string: `.snd`
4	Offset of the sound data from the beginning of the file (at least 28)
4	Number of bytes of sound data
4	Sound format, see Table 15.2
4	Sampling rate in samples per second
4	Number of channels
n	Optional text description (at least 4 bytes)
n	Sound data

TABLE 15.2   AU Format Codes

Code	Description
1	8-bit μ-Law G.711
2	8-bit linear
3	16-bit linear
4	24-bit linear
5	32-bit linear
6	Floating-point samples
7	Double-precision float samples
8	Fragmented sampled data
10	DSP program
11	8-bit fixed-point samples
12	16-bit fixed-point samples
13	24-bit fixed-point samples
14	32-bit fixed-point samples
18	16-bit linear with emphasis
19	16-bit linear compressed
20	16-bit linear with emphasis and compression
21	Music kit DSP commands
23	ADPCM G.721
24	ADPCM G.722
25	ADPCM G.723.3
26	ADPCM G.723.5
27	8-bit A-Law G.711

Table 15.2 lists some of the format codes used with AU format files. Despite the variety shown in this table, only three data formats are widely used: 8-bit μ-Law (usually sampled at 8,000 Hz), 8-bit linear, and 16-bit linear. The remainder are used almost exclusively on NeXT or Sun systems. In particular, the DSP formats are special NeXT formats, and the floating-point versions should generally be avoided, because they are rarely portable between systems. (Of course, G.711 μ-Law format is very portable and, as pointed out on page 111, it's essentially an 8-bit floating point format.)

Because AU format is so simple, I use it often. I generally convert files into AU format and then use it as a basis for further processing.

In the remainder of this chapter, I'll define two classes. `AuRead` is an `AudioAbstract` object that reads data from an AU file; `AuWrite` is an audio player that writes data to an AU file.

LISTING 15.1   au.h

```
Copyright © 1998, Tim Kientzle (Listing E.1)
#ifndef AU_H_INCLUDED
#define AU_H_INCLUDED
#include "audio.h"
#include "compress.h"
#include "aplayer.h"
#include <iostream>

bool IsAuFile(istream &file);

class AuRead:  public AudioAbstract {
    AuRead Members (Listing 15.4)
};

class AuWrite:  public AbstractPlayer {
    AuWrite Members (Listing 15.6)
};
#endif
```

LISTING 15.2   au.cpp

```
Copyright © 1998, Tim Kientzle (Listing E.1)
#include "au.h"
#include "g711.h"

Identify AU File (Listing 15.3)

AuRead Implementation (Listing 15.5)

AuWrite Implementation (Listing 15.7)
```

Identifying AU Files

Most recent AU files contain the header indicated in Table 15.1. In particular, the first 4 bytes are .snd. There are many older files that identify themselves as AU format (they use the .au extension), but they don't have this header. Such files are usually straight dumps of μ-Law sound data sampled at 8,000 Hz.

LISTING 15.3   Identify AU File

```
bool IsAuFile(istream &file) {
    file.seekg(0);  // Seek to beginning
    long magic = ReadIntMsb(file,4);
    return (magic == 0x2E736E64); // Should be '.snd'
}
```

Reading AU Files

All the classes I'll build for reading audio files have a similar skeleton. As illustrated in Figure 10.1 on page 101, when you ask the file class for samples, it forwards the request to the decoder object.

LISTING 15.4   AuRead Members

```
private:
    istream &_stream;
    AbstractDecompressor *_decoder;
public:
    AuRead(istream &input = cin):AudioAbstract(),_stream(input) {
        cerr << "File Format:  Sun AU (also known as NeXT SND)\n";
        _headerRead = false; // Haven't read header yet
        _decoder = 0;
    }
    ~AuRead() {
        if (_decoder) delete _decoder;
    }
    size_t GetSamples(AudioSample *buffer, size_t numSamples) {
        return _decoder->GetSamples(buffer,numSamples);
    }
```

The decoder object will, in turn, call `ReadBytes` to get raw bytes from the file. For AU files, `ReadBytes` is simple: It asks the stream for data and keeps a count to ensure that it doesn't read past the end of the data.

LISTING 15.4 (CONTINUED)   AuRead Members

```
private:
    size_t _dataLength;
public:
    size_t ReadBytes(AudioByte *buffer, size_t length);
```

LISTING 15.5   AuRead Implementation

```
size_t AuRead::ReadBytes(AudioByte *buffer, size_t length) {
   if (length > _dataLength) { length = _dataLength; }
   _stream.read(reinterpret_cast<char *>(buffer),length);
   size_t lengthRead = _stream.gcount();
   _dataLength -= lengthRead;
   return lengthRead;
}
```

The only part that remains is to read the file header and force the negotiation to match the file parameters.

LISTING 15.4 (CONTINUED)   AuRead Members

```
private:
   bool _headerRead; // true if header has already been read
   int _headerChannels; // channels from header
   int _headerRate; // sampling rate from header
   void ReadHeader(void);
```

When the objects negotiate the appropriate data format, I force the parameters to match the file being read.

LISTING 15.4 (CONTINUED)   AuRead Members

```
protected:
   void MinMaxSamplingRate(long *min, long *max, long *preferred) {
      ReadHeader();
      *min = *max = *preferred = _headerRate;
   }
   void MinMaxChannels(int *min, int *max, int *preferred) {
      ReadHeader();
      *min = *max = *preferred = _headerChannels;
   }
```

In addition to reading the appropriate data from the header, it's important to skip any remaining data that might follow the standard information. AU has been used as the basis for several other formats. These other formats simply add their own special data to the end of the standard AU header. You can't safely assume the header will be exactly 28 bytes.

LISTING 15.5 (CONTINUED)   AuRead Implementation

```
void AuRead::ReadHeader(void) {
    if (_headerRead) return;
    _headerRead = true;

    char header[24];
    _stream.read(header,24);

    long magic = BytesToIntMsb(header+0,4);
    if (magic != 0x2E736E64) { // '.snd'
        cerr << "Input file is not an AU file.\n";
        exit(1);
    }

    long headerLength = BytesToIntMsb(header+4,4);
    _dataLength = BytesToIntMsb(header+8,4);
    int format = BytesToIntMsb(header+12,4);
    _headerRate = BytesToIntMsb(header+16,4);
    _headerChannels = BytesToIntMsb(header+20,4);
    SkipBytes(_stream,headerLength - 24); // Junk rest of header

    // Create an appropriate decompression object
    switch(format) {
    case 1:  // ITU G.711 mu-Law
        _decoder = new DecompressG711MuLaw(*this);
        break;
    case 2:  // 8-bit linear
        _decoder = new DecompressPcm8Unsigned(*this);
        break;
    case 3:  // 16-bit linear
        _decoder = new DecompressPcm16MsbSigned(*this);
        break;
    default:
        cerr << "AU format " << format << " not supported.\n";
        exit(1);
    }

    cerr << "Sampling Rate:  " << _headerRate;
    cerr << " Channels:  " << _headerChannels;
    cerr << "\n";
}
```

Writing AU Files

Writing AU files is similar. An AU file writer is essentially a player object, so it inherits from `AbstractPlayer`, and implements the `Play` method to save the data.

The constructor accepts and stores the output stream.

LISTING 15.6   AuWrite Members

```
private:
   ostream &_stream;
public:
   AuWrite(AudioAbstract *audio, ostream &output = cout)
      :AbstractPlayer(audio),_stream(output) {
   };
```

Since `AuWrite` is a player class, it needs a `Play` member function to do the actual work. Because AU files can accept a variety of formats, the default format negotiation will work acceptably.

LISTING 15.6 (CONTINUED)   AuWrite Members

```
public:
   void Play(void);
```

This version writes only 16-bit linear files. It would be simple to add options to support 8-bit μ-Law or other output formats.

`WriteBuffer` manually converts a buffer of samples into a buffer of bytes. Each sample becomes 2 bytes, representing a 16-bit MSB format signed value.

LISTING 15.7   AuWrite Implementation

```
static void WriteBuffer
         (ostream &out, AudioSample *buffer, int length) {
   AudioSample *sampleBuff = buffer;
   AudioByte *byteBuff =
         reinterpret_cast<AudioByte *>(buffer);
   int i = length;
   while (i-->0) {
      int sample = *sampleBuff++;
      *byteBuff++ = sample >> 8;
      *byteBuff++ = sample;
   }
   out.write(reinterpret_cast<char *>(buffer),length*2);
};

void AuWrite::Play(void) {
   int samplingRate = SamplingRate();
   int channels = Channels();

   // Write AU header
   _stream.write(".snd",4); // Magic
   WriteIntMsb(_stream,28L,4); // Length of header
   WriteIntMsb(_stream,0x7FFFFFFFL,4); // length of data
   WriteIntMsb(_stream,3L,4); // 16-bit linear
```

```
        WriteIntMsb(_stream,samplingRate,4); // Sampling rate
        WriteIntMsb(_stream,channels,4); // number of channels
        WriteIntMsb(_stream,0,4); // padding

        // Read sound data and write it to the file
        long length;
        do {
           const int BuffSize = 10240;
           AudioSample buff[BuffSize];
           length = Previous()->GetSamples(buff,BuffSize);
           WriteBuffer(_stream,buff,length);
        } while (length > 0);
    }
```

A Simple AU Filter

Here's the simplest program that uses the above classes, for testing purposes. Although it simply reads and writes the same audio data in the same format, note that it will expand μ-Law data into 16-bit linear PCM as a consequence.

LISTING 15.8   autoau.cpp

```
Copyright © 1998, Tim Kientzle (Listing E.1)
#include "au.h"
int main(int, char **) {
   AuRead auIn;    // Read from 'cin'
   AuWrite auOut(&auIn); // Write to 'cout'
   auOut.Play();
   return 0;
}
```

VOC File Format

16

The VOC file format was developed by Creative Labs to demonstrate its sound cards. Although it has a few peculiarities (reflecting idiosyncracies of these sound cards), it has become fairly popular among MS-DOS and Windows users.

A VOC file consists of a header followed by data blocks. Some data blocks contain actual sound data; others contain format information or other auxiliary data. Originally designed for Intel-family processors, all multi-byte numbers are stored starting with the least significant byte.

Identifying VOC Files

Every VOC file begins with a 20-byte signature, containing the words *Creative Voice File* and the Control-Z character. The Control-Z is an end-of-file marker for MS-DOS; its presence ensures that the entire file can't accidentally be printed or edited on that system.

LISTING 16.1   Identify VOC File

```
bool IsVocFile(istream &file) {
   file.seekg(0);  // Seek to beginning
   char id[21];
   file.read(id,20);
   return (!strncmp(id,"Creative Voice File\x1a",20));
}
```

VOC Header

The header is shown in Table 16.1. It contains a signature value and a file version. Note the value 26 (hex 1A), which is an end-of-file on MS-DOS systems. The file version code is usually 266 (version 1.10) or 276 (version 1.20).

From Table 16.1, it's easy to write the code to read the VOC header.

TABLE 16.1   VOC File Header

Length	Description
19	String identifier: *Creative Voice File*
1	Byte value 26 (MS-DOS end-of-file)
2	Total size of header, usually 26
2	File version code: major * 256 + minor
2	Check value: 4,659 - file version

LISTING 16.2   VocRead Members

```
private:
    void ReadHeader(void);
```

LISTING 16.3   VocRead Implementation

```
void VocRead::ReadHeader(void) {
    char id[21];
    int headerSize, fileVersionCode, fileVersionCheck;

    _stream.read(id,20);
    if (strncmp(id,"Creative Voice File\x1a",20)) {
        cerr << "This is not a VOC file.\n";
        exit(1);
    }
    headerSize = ReadIntLsb(_stream,2);
    if (headerSize < 26) {
        cerr << "This VOC file is corrupted.\n";
        exit(1);
    }

    fileVersionCode = ReadIntLsb(_stream,2);
    fileVersionCheck = ReadIntLsb(_stream,2);

    if (fileVersionCode + fileVersionCheck != 0x1233)
        cerr << "This VOC file may be corrupted.\n";

    // Is header larger than 26 bytes?
    if (headerSize > 26)
        SkipBytes(_stream,26-headerSize); // Skip rest
}
```

Because the header may someday be extended, it's important to skip any data that might follow the standard information.

Data Blocks

To process a VOC file, you read and process data blocks in the order they appear in the file. There are a few cases in which different blocks can specify the same data; the first specification always overrides later ones. The format of a block is shown in Table 16.2.

TABLE 16.2   VOC Data-Block Format

Length	Description
1	Block type
3	Data length: n
n	Data

LISTING 16.2 (CONTINUED)   VocRead Members

```
private:
    void GetBlock(void);
    int _blockType;  // Type of current block
```

LISTING 16.3 (CONTINUED)   VocRead Implementation

```
void VocRead::GetBlock(void) {
    long blockLength = 0;
    _blockType = ReadIntLsb(_stream,1);
    if(_stream.eof()) _blockType = 0;
    if (_blockType != 0)
        blockLength = ReadIntLsb(_stream,3);

    switch(_blockType) {

        Handle VOC Block Types (Listing 16.4)

    }
}
```

The most important block types are the terminator block (type 0), the extension blocks (types 8 and 9), and the sound data block (type 1).

Terminator Block (Type 0)

The terminator block is the one exception to the block format shown in Table 16.2. It consists of a single zero byte, without the associated length field. This block marks the end of the VOC file.

LISTING 16.4   Handle VOC Block Types

```
case 0:  // End of data
   break;
```

Sound Data Block (Type 1)

The sound data block (type 1) starts with 2 bytes indicating the sample rate and compression. This is followed by the actual sound data. The sample rate code is computed from the sample rate as $256 - (1,000,000/\text{sample rate})$. Conversely, once you have the code, the sample rate is $1,000,000/(256 - \text{code})$. The compression codes are given in Table 16.3. Note that a VOC file can contain only one sound data block. Additional sound data can be stored in a sound continuation block.

TABLE 16.3   Compression Codes

Code	Description
0	PCM unsigned 8-bit data
1	Compressed, 4 bits per sample
2	Compressed, 2.6 bits per sample
3	Compressed, 2 bits per sample
4	PCM signed 16-bit data
6	CCITT A-Law
7	CCITT μ-Law
512	Creative Labs 16-bit to 4-bit ADPCM

Note that values above 3 are for use only in type 9 extension blocks.

The ReadData method, responsible for pulling raw sound data from the file, needs to know how many bytes of raw data remain in the current block. To support this, blocks that contain sound data will set bytesRemaining appropriately.

LISTING 16.2 (CONTINUED)   VocRead Members

```
private:
   unsigned long  bytesRemaining;  // bytes left in this block
   void ReadBlock1(long blockLength);
```

In order to keep GetBlock from growing too large (some compilers balk at too-large functions), I'll separate the work into a separate ReadBlock1 method.

LISTING 16.4 (CONTINUED)   Handle VOC Block Types

```
case 1:  // Sound Data Block
   ReadBlock1(blockLength);
   break;
```

The VOC format has evolved by adding new block types that specify the sound format in different ways. These blocks (types 8 and 9) will always precede the sound data block, so I need to be careful here not to overwrite any parameter that might have already been set by an earlier block.

LISTING 16.3 (CONTINUED)   VocRead Implementation

```
void VocRead::ReadBlock1(long blockLength) {
   // Read and interpret first two bytes...
   int sampleRateCode = ReadIntLsb(_stream,1);
   int compressionCode = ReadIntLsb(_stream,1);
   if (_fileSampleRate == -1)
      _fileSampleRate = 1000000L/(256-sampleRateCode);
   if (_fileCompression == -1)
      _fileCompression = compressionCode;
   if (_fileChannels == -1)
      _fileChannels = 1;
   if (_fileWidth == -1)
      _fileWidth = 8;
   if (_decoder == 0) { // No decoder object yet?
      switch(_fileCompression) {
      case 0:  // Unsigned 8-bit PCM
         _decoder = new DecompressPcm8Unsigned(*this);
         break;
      case 4:  // Signed 16-bit PCM
         _decoder = new DecompressPcm16LsbSigned(*this);
         break;
      case 1:  // Creative Labs 8-bit to 4-bit ADPCM
      case 2:  // Creative Labs 8-bit to 2.6-bit ADPCM
      case 3:  // Creative Labs 8-bit to 2-bit ADPCM
      case 6:  // CCITT A-Law
      case 7:  // CCITT mu-Law
      case 512:  // Creative Labs 16-bit to 4-bit ADPCM
      default:
         cerr << "I don't support VOC compression type ";
         cerr << _fileCompression << ".\n";
         exit(1);
      }
   }
   bytesRemaining = blockLength - 2;
}
```

Sound Continuation Block (Type 2)

A VOC file can have only one type 1 sound data block. However, the sound data might need to be broken across multiple blocks. This usually occurs because you want to insert some other type of block (such as a repeat marker) in the middle of the sound data. Subsequent sound data is stored in type 2 sound continuation blocks. The sound continuation block contains only sound sample data. It does not repeat any of the sound format information from the preceding type 1 block.

LISTING 16.4 (CONTINUED)   Handle VOC Block Types

```
case 2:    // Sound Data Continued
   bytesRemaining = blockLength;
   break;
```

Silence Block (Type 3)

In order to reduce the total size of the data, quiet sections can be replaced with silence blocks, indicating a period of silence. The data for this block contains a 2-byte number indicating the number of samples of silence to use and a 1-byte sample rate code. In theory, this allows the silence period to use a different sample rate than the sound. In practice, the sample rate used here should be the same as the preceding sound.

LISTING 16.4 (CONTINUED)   Handle VOC Block Types

```
case 3:  // Silence
{
   if (blockLength != 3) {
      cerr << "VOC Silence Block has length " << blockLength;
      cerr << "(should be 3)\n";
   }
   bytesRemaining = ReadIntLsb(_stream,2) + 1;
   int sampleRateCode = ReadIntLsb(_stream,1);
   if (_fileSampleRate == -1)
      _fileSampleRate = 1000000/(256-sampleRateCode);
   bytesRemaining = blockLength - 3;
   break;
}
```

Marker Block (Type 4)

The data for the marker block is a 2-byte number. This number can be used by multimedia applications to synchronize events. For example, a slide-show application might change the display each time it sees a marker block so that the slide matches the audio narration. Values 0 and 65,536 are reserved and should not be used.

LISTING 16.4 (CONTINUED)   Handle VOC Block Types

```
case 4:  // Marker block
    if (blockLength != 2) {
        cerr << "VOC Marker Block has length " << blockLength;
        cerr << "(should be 2)\n";
    }
    cerr << "VOC Marker:  ";
    cerr << ReadIntLsb(_stream,blockLength);
    cerr << "\n";
    bytesRemaining = blockLength - 2;
    break;
```

Text Block (Type 5)

The data is a null-terminated string of ASCII data. This can be used to store copyright information or other useful text data. Writers should be careful to include the trailing null; readers should be tolerant if the null is omitted.

LISTING 16.4 (CONTINUED)   Handle VOC Block Types

```
case 5:  // ASCII text block
{
    char *text = new char[blockLength+1];
    _stream.read(text,blockLength);
    text[blockLength] = 0;
    cerr << "Comment:  " << text << "\n";
    delete [] text;
    bytesRemaining = 0;
    break;
}
```

Repeat Loops (Types 6 and 7)

Block types 6 and 7 are used to implement looping within a VOC file. A block of type 6 is placed at the beginning of the section to be repeated, and a block of type 7 marks the end. The data for the start marker contains a 2-byte number indicating how many additional times this section should be repeated (a zero count means the data should be played only once). The end block has no data.

Because repeats can be nested, I need to provide a stack for repeat information. For each repeat, I store the remaining number of times to repeat this section and the file position at which the repeat begins.

LISTING 16.2 (CONTINUED)   VocRead Members

```
private:
   int repeatDepth;  // Number of nested repeats
#define maxRepeat 5
   int repeatCounts[maxRepeat];
   streampos repeatPosition[maxRepeat];
```

LISTING 16.5   Initialize VOC Data

```
repeatDepth = -1;
```

LISTING 16.4 (CONTINUED)   Handle VOC Block Types

```
case 6:  // Repeat loop
{
   if (blockLength != 2) {
      cerr << "VOC Repeat Loop Block has length " << blockLength;
      cerr << "(should be 2)\n";
   }
   cerr << "Start of VOC Repeat Block.\n";
   int repeatCount = ReadIntLsb(_stream,2);
   repeatDepth++;
   if (repeatDepth > maxRepeat) {
      cerr << "Too many nested repeats.\n";
      exit(1);
   }
   repeatCounts[repeatDepth] = repeatCount;
   repeatPosition[repeatDepth] = _stream.tellg();
   bytesRemaining = blockLength - 2;
   break;
}
case 7:  // Repeat end
{
   bytesRemaining = blockLength;
   if (blockLength != 0) {
      cerr << "VOC 'End Repeat' block has length " << blockLength;
      cerr << "(should be 0)\n";
   }
   if (repeatDepth < 0) {
      cerr << "Improper VOC 'End Repeat' block.\n";
      break;
   }

   cerr << "End of VOC Repeat Block(";
   cerr << repeatCounts[repeatDepth] << ")\n";
   if (repeatCounts[repeatDepth] <= 0) { // End of repeat?
      repeatDepth--;
   } else { // Position for next iteration
```

```
        _stream.seekg(repeatPosition[repeatDepth]);
        repeatCounts[repeatDepth]--;
    }
    break;
}
```

Extension Block (Type 8)

The type 8 extension block did not appear in early versions of the VOC format. It was added to support stereo sound files. When it appears, it always precedes the type 1 sound data block, and it overrides the sampling rate and compression information in the sound data block.

TABLE 16.4   Type 8 Extension Block Data

Length	Description
2	High-precision sample-rate code
1	Compression code
1	Mode (0 for mono, 1 for stereo)

The data in this block, outlined in Table 16.4, largely duplicates the information in the sound data block. In particular, the sample-rate code is a higher-precision version of the code used in the sound data block, and the compression code is identical. The only truly new information is the number of channels. For stereo data, the sound data in the type 1 and 2 blocks will alternate left and right samples.

The sample rate code is handled somewhat unusually for stereo sounds. The 2-byte code is normally computed as $65,536 - 256(1,000,000/\text{sample rate})$. For stereo sounds, however, you double the sample rate before using this formula. One result of this modification is that programs that don't understand this extension end up playing the interleaved samples at a rate that most closely preserves the sound. For full backward compatibility, the sample-rate code in the type 1 sound data block should always be set to the high-order byte of this sample-rate code.

LISTING 16.2 (CONTINUED)   VocRead Members

```
private:
    void ReadBlock8(long blockLength);
```

Again, to keep `GetBlock` from getting too large, I've split the handling of type 8 blocks out into a separate function.

LISTING 16.4 (CONTINUED) Handle VOC Block Types

```
case 8:  // Extension
   ReadBlock8(blockLength);
   break;
```

LISTING 16.3 (CONTINUED) VocRead Implementation

```
void VocRead::ReadBlock8(long blockLength) {
   if (blockLength != 4) {
      cerr << "VOC Extension Block 8 has length " << blockLength;
      cerr << "(should be 4)\n";
   }
   int sampleRateCode = ReadIntLsb(_stream,2);
   if (_fileSampleRate == -1)
      _fileSampleRate = 256000000L/(65536L-sampleRateCode);
   int compressionCode = ReadIntLsb(_stream,1);
   if (_fileCompression == -1)
      _fileCompression = compressionCode;
   int channels = ReadIntLsb(_stream,1);
   if (_fileChannels == -1) {
      _fileChannels = channels + 1;
      _fileSampleRate /= _fileChannels;
   }
   if (_fileWidth == -1)
      _fileWidth = 8;
   bytesRemaining = blockLength - 4;
}
```

Extension Block (Type 9)

Like the type 8 extension block, the type 9 block was introduced to add new capabilities. In particular, the type 9 block supports additional compression methods and stores sound format information in a more direct fashion. When it appears, it precedes block types 1 or 8 and the information in it overrides the information in those blocks.

The type 9 block, outlined in Table 16.5, stores sound information in a fashion that's dramatically different from the type 1 or type 8 blocks. In particular, the sample rate is stored directly rather than being encoded. In addition, the sample rate is not adjusted for the number of channels. The bits-per-sample field will range from 2 (for compressed data) to 16 (for 16-bit PCM data). The final 4 bytes are reserved for future extension.

For backward compatibility, a writer that creates type 9 blocks should follow it with a type 8 block, if possible. However, because the type 9 block introduces several new compression codes (including 16-bit PCM; see Table 16.3), this will not always be possible.

TABLE 16.5   Type 9 Extension Block Data

Length	Description
4	Sample rate
1	Bits used for each sample
1	Number of channels (1 for mono, 2 for stereo)
2	Compression code
4	Future extension

LISTING 16.2 (CONTINUED)   VocRead Members

```
private:
    void ReadBlock9(long blockLength);
```

LISTING 16.4 (CONTINUED)   Handle VOC Block Types

```
case 9:  // Extension
    ReadBlock9(blockLength);
    break;
```

LISTING 16.3 (CONTINUED)   VocRead Implementation

```
void VocRead::ReadBlock9(long blockLength) {
    if (blockLength != 12) {
        cerr << "VOC Extension Block 9 has length " << blockLength;
        cerr << "(should be 12)\n";
    }
    long sampleRate = ReadIntLsb(_stream,4);
    if (_fileSampleRate == -1)
        _fileSampleRate = sampleRate;
    int bitsPerSample = ReadIntLsb(_stream,1);
    if (_fileWidth == -1)
        _fileWidth = bitsPerSample;
    int channels = ReadIntLsb(_stream,1);
    if (_fileChannels == -1)
        _fileChannels = channels;
    int compressionCode = ReadIntLsb(_stream,2);
    if (_fileCompression == -1)
        _fileCompression = compressionCode;
    SkipBytes(_stream,blockLength - 8);
}
```

Other Blocks

Currently, only block values 0 through 9 are defined. Any unrecognized block type should be ignored.

LISTING 16.4 (CONTINUED)   Handle VOC Block Types

```
default:  // Skip any other type of block
   cerr << "Ignoring unrecognized VOC block type " << _blockType << "\n";
   SkipBytes(_stream,blockLength);
   break;
```

Reading VOC Files

Given the machinery already developed to process the VOC header and digest individual blocks, the rest of the `VocRead` class is reasonably straightforward.

LISTING 16.6   voc.h

```
Copyright © 1998, Tim Kientzle (Listing E.1)
#ifndef VOC_H_INCLUDED
#define VOC_H_INCLUDED
#include "audio.h"
#include "compress.h"
#include <iostream>

bool IsVocFile(istream &file);

class VocRead:  public AudioAbstract {
    VocRead Members (Listing 16.2)
};
#endif
```

LISTING 16.7   voc.cpp

```
Copyright © 1998, Tim Kientzle (Listing E.1)
#include <cstring>
#include "voc.h"

Identify VOC File (Listing 16.1)

VocRead Implementation (Listing 16.3)
```

LISTING 16.2 (CONTINUED)   VocRead Members

```
private:
   istream &_stream;
public:
   VocRead(istream &input = cin);
   ~VocRead() {
      if (_decoder) delete _decoder;
   };
```

The constructor's one important chore is scanning the first data blocks so that any sound format information is parsed and ready. This just means reading successive blocks until you find a sound data block or terminator block.

LISTING 16.3 (CONTINUED)   VocRead Implementation

```
VocRead::VocRead(istream &input):AudioAbstract(),_stream(input) {
   cerr << "File Format:  Creative Labs VOC\n";
```
   | Initialize VOC Data (Listing 16.5) | .
```
   ReadHeader();
   do {   // Find sound data block or terminator block
      GetBlock();
   } while ((_blockType != 1) && (_blockType != 0));
}
```

Because there are several block types that can specify the sound parameters, it is important to keep track of whether these values have already been set. Here, I initialize the basic sound parameters to an illegal value (-1).

LISTING 16.5 (CONTINUED)   Initialize VOC Data

```
   _fileChannels = -1;
   _fileSampleRate = -1;
   _fileCompression = -1;
   _fileWidth = -1;
   _decoder = 0;
```

The VocRead class has the same data as most of the other file reading classes. It needs to store basic information about the file and responds to requests based on that information.

LISTING 16.2 (CONTINUED)   VocRead Members

```
private:
    int _fileChannels;
    int _fileSampleRate;
    int _fileWidth;
    int _fileCompression;
    AbstractDecompressor *_decoder;
protected:
    void MinMaxSamplingRate(long *min, long *max, long *preferred) {
        *min = *max = *preferred = _fileSampleRate;
    };
    void MinMaxChannels(int *min, int *max, int *preferred) {
        *min = *max = *preferred = _fileChannels;
    };
    size_t GetSamples(AudioSample *buffer, size_t numSamples);
```

The GetSamples method is complicated by the potential for interleaving silence blocks (which aren't compressed) with normal sound data to be decoded. This isn't much of an issue for the most common VOC files, which contain only PCM data. Unfortunately, Creative Labs has not specified what this means for compressed audio data. (It's unclear whether the compressor is reset after a silence block or whether silence blocks are simply forbidden in compressed data.)

The GetSamples method looks at the current block type and decides whether to ignore it (it doesn't contain sound data), fill the buffer with zero samples (it is a silence block), or request data from the decompressor.

LISTING 16.3 (CONTINUED)   VocRead Implementation

```
size_t VocRead::GetSamples(AudioSample *buffer, size_t numSamples) {
    size_t samplesReturned = 0;
    while (numSamples > 0) {
        switch(_blockType) {
        case 0:  // End of file
            return samplesReturned;
        case 1:  // Encoded sound data
        case 2:  {
                size_t samplesRead = _decoder->GetSamples(buffer,numSamples);
                buffer += samplesRead;
                numSamples -= samplesRead;
                samplesReturned += samplesRead;
                if (bytesRemaining == 0) GetBlock();
                break;
            }
        case 3:  // Silence block
            while ((numSamples > 0) && (bytesRemaining > 0)) {
                *buffer++ = 0;
                samplesReturned++;
                numSamples--;
```

```
            bytesRemaining--;
        }
        if (bytesRemaining == 0) GetBlock();
        break;
      default:
        GetBlock();
        break;
      }
   }
   return samplesReturned;
}
```

The decoder object (invoked by GetSamples) will call ReadBytes to obtain raw sound data. Because GetSamples ensures that ReadBytes is invoked only when a type 1 or 2 block is currently being read, ReadBytes can be simple.

Note that this version of ReadBytes can return fewer than the requested number of bytes, even if this isn't the end of the file. The GetSamples method above is careful to call the decoder repeatedly (possibly resulting in multiple calls to ReadBytes) until it can satisfy the request.

LISTING 16.2 (CONTINUED)   VocRead Members

```
public:
    size_t ReadBytes(AudioByte *buffer, size_t length);
```

LISTING 16.3 (CONTINUED)   VocRead Implementation

```
size_t VocRead::ReadBytes(AudioByte *buffer, size_t length) {
   if (length > bytesRemaining) length = bytesRemaining;
   _stream.read(reinterpret_cast<char *>(buffer), length);
   size_t bytesRead = _stream.gcount();
   if (bytesRead < length) {
      cerr << "Error:    VOC file ended prematurely.";
      exit(1);
   }
   bytesRemaining -= bytesRead; // Amount left in block
   return bytesRead;
}
```

WAVE File Format 17

Because WAVE is the native sound format used by Microsoft Windows, it is naturally one of the most popular sound formats around. The overall structure is based on the *Interchange File Format* (IFF) originally developed by Electronic Arts for use on the Amiga (see Chapter 19). IFF also formed the basis of Apple's AIFF audio format, which I'll discuss in the next chapter.

Following IFF, Microsoft defined a general file format called the *Resource Interchange File Format* (RIFF). RIFF files are organized as a collection of nested chunks. Tags within the RIFF file identify the contents. Two common variations are WAVE (or WAV) files that hold audio and AVI files that hold video.

Identifying WAVE Files

A WAVE file is a particular kind of RIFF file, and every RIFF file begins with the characters RIFF. Following that are a 4-byte length and the type code. In this case, I'm interested only in the type WAVE.

LISTING 17.1   Identify WAVE Files

```
bool IsWaveFile(istream &file) {
    file.seekg(0); // Seek to beginning of file
    unsigned long form = ReadIntMsb(file,4);
    if (form != ChunkName('R','I','F','F'))
        return false; // Not RIFF file
    SkipBytes(file,4);  // Skip chunk size
    unsigned long type = ReadIntMsb(file,4);
    if (type == ChunkName('W','A','V','E'))
        return true;
    return false; // RIFF file, but not WAVE file
}
```

About RIFF and Other IFF Files

Because WAVE files are a special type of RIFF file, I'll start by discussing the basics of RIFF. Much of this discussion also applies to other IFF variants, including AIFF and IFF/8SVX.

A RIFF file consists of a collection of nested chunks, as illustrated in Figure 17.1. Each chunk contains a four-character code (such as RIFF, fmt, or LIST; shorter codes are padded with spaces). This code indicates the type of chunk. For example, an fmt chunk contains information about the format of a sound. Following the chunk type is a 4-byte size value, indicating the size of the data carried by the chunk. Note, for instance, that the entire file illustrated in Figure 17.1 is a single RIFF chunk. The size field in the RIFF chunk is exactly 8 bytes less than the total file size because the chunk type and size are not included in the count.

FIGURE 17.1   Nesting of Chunks in a RIFF File

Size of RIFF chunk

Certain types of chunks—such as the RIFF and LIST chunks in Figure 17.1—are *container chunks* that hold other chunks. The data of a container chunk starts with a four-character code indicating the type of data contained within that chunk. For example, the RIFF chunk in Figure 17.1 has the code WAVE, indicating that it contains audio data. The internal chunk names may mean different things, depending on the surrounding container. Because this fmt chunk is contained within a RIFF WAVE container, you know that it specifies the format of sound data. In a different type of container, it might contain different information.

An Overview of WAVE

WAVE files are RIFF files in which the outermost chunk is a RIFF container with a WAVE container type. Most WAVE files contain both an fmt chunk and a data chunk, as shown in Figure 17.2.

FIGURE 17.2   RIFF Chunk Format

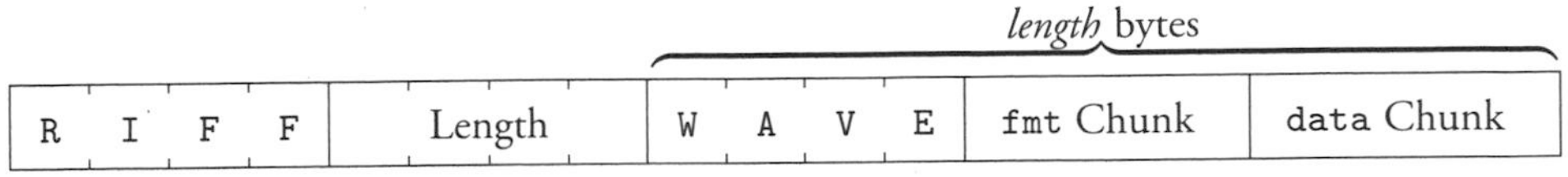

Because so many WAVE files have this same basic structure, many naive programs treat WAVE files as having a fixed header with the format shown in Table 17.1. This is fine for writing WAVE files as long as the writer writes only PCM data and properly sets the various size fields. Readers, however, need to be more robust.

TABLE 17.1   Naive WAVE File Format

Size	Description
4	Chunk type: RIFF
4	Total file size minus 8
4	RIFF container type: WAVE
4	Chunk type: fmt␣
4	Format chunk data length: usually 16
16	Format chunk data
4	Chunk type: data
4	Length of sound data
n	Actual sound samples

WAVE files can have other chunks in them. In particular, the single data chunk is sometimes replaced by a LIST container which contains slnt chunks (indicating silent intervals) and data chunks with sound data.

The WaveRead Class

As with other file formats, I'll define a single WaveRead class. To use it, open a file and initialize a new WaveRead object with the open file.

Like most file classes, WaveRead has to keep track of the current stream and the current decoder object. In addition, I keep a copy of the sound format data. Because the amount of format data varies depending on the compression method used, I need to dynamically allocate storage for it when I encounter it.

LISTING 17.2   wav.h

```
Copyright © 1998, Tim Kientzle (Listing E.1)
#include "audio.h"
#include "compress.h"

bool IsWaveFile(istream &file);

class WaveRead:  public AudioAbstract {
private:
   istream & _stream;
   AbstractDecompressor *_decoder; // Current decompressor
   unsigned char *_formatData; // Contents of fmt chunk
   unsigned long _formatDataLength; // length of fmt chunk
public:
   WaveRead(istream & s) ;
   ~WaveRead() ;
   WaveRead Members (Listing 17.4)
};
```

The verbose macro `ChunkName` converts four characters into a single 32-bit code. These codes are used extensively throughout this code. Also, the constructor and destructor need to initialize and clean up the pointer variables.

LISTING 17.3   wav.cpp

```
Copyright © 1998, Tim Kientzle (Listing E.1)
#include "wav.h"
#include "compress.h"
#include "imaadpcm.h"
#include "g711.h"
#include <cstdlib>

#define ChunkName(a,b,c,d) (                       \
    ((static_cast<unsigned long>(a)&255)<<24)      \
  + ((static_cast<unsigned long>(b)&255)<<16)      \
  + ((static_cast<unsigned long>(c)&255)<<8)       \
  + ((static_cast<unsigned long>(d)&255)))

Identify WAVE Files (Listing 17.1)

WaveRead Implementation (Listing 17.5)

WaveRead::WaveRead(istream & s): _stream(s) {
   cerr << "File Format:  Microsoft WAVE\n";
```

```
    _decoder = 0;
    _formatData = 0;
    _formatDataLength = 0;
    ┌─────────────────────────────────────┐
    │ WaveRead Initialization (Listing 17.8) │
    └─────────────────────────────────────┘
}

WaveRead::~WaveRead() {
    if (_decoder) delete _decoder;
    if(_formatData) { delete [] _formatData; }
}
```

Reading WAVE Files

In the original IFF specification, the authors are careful to emphasize that the various chunks may appear in any order. It's therefore possible that some WAVE files might, for instance, have the sound data chunk before the format chunk that specifies how that data is stored.

One way to accomodate such files is to skim the entire file (seeking past large chunks) and create a map in memory with the location and type of each chunk. You could then locate individual chunks as you needed them.

This approach, although robust, has a serious drawback: it requires that you have the entire file available immediately. In particular, if you're interested in streaming a WAVE file over a network and playing it as the data is received, you can't skim the entire file and locate the chunks before you begin playing.

I've taken a different approach with my WaveRead class, partly to allow for streaming and partly for simplicity. Instead of mapping the location of every chunk, I read the file from beginning to end, handling each chunk as I encounter it. There may be WAVE files that are unplayable with this code, however.

Containers

Remember that the significance of any chunk depends on both the type of chunk and the type of the enclosing container. To keep track of this information, I keep a stack of chunk information. For example, when reading an fmt chunk located within a RIFF WAVE container, the stack would contain two entries, one for the outer container and one for the fmt chunk. The _currentChunk variable identifies the current top of the stack, -1 indicates the stack is empty.

LISTING 17.4 WaveRead Members

```
private:
  // WAVE chunk stack
  struct {
    unsigned long type; // Type of chunk
    unsigned long size; // Size of chunk
    unsigned long remaining; // Bytes left to read
    bool isContainer;   // true if this is a container
    unsigned long containerType; // type of container
  } _chunk[5];

  int _currentChunk; // top of stack

  void NextChunk(void);
```

The NextChunk method is the core of this class, and it's lengthy. This method first skips the remains of the current chunk and updates the stack accordingly. It then reads the header of the next chunk and figures out what to do with it.

Because this is the primary place that data is read from the file, I need to be careful about checking for the end of file. If I reach the end of the file, I empty the stack. Other functions should check to ensure the stack isn't empty before they try to process the current chunk.

LISTING 17.5 WaveRead Implementation

```
void WaveRead::NextChunk(void) {
  ┌─────────────────────────────────────────────┐
  │ Skip Remainder of Current Chunk (Listing 17.6) │
  └─────────────────────────────────────────────┘
  ┌─────────────────────────────────────────┐
  │ Flush Finished Containers (Listing 17.7) │
  └─────────────────────────────────────────┘
  // Read the next chunk
  if (_stream.eof()) {
    _currentChunk = -1; // empty the stack
    return;
  }
  unsigned long type = ReadIntMsb(_stream,4);
  unsigned long size = ReadIntLsb(_stream,4);
  if (_stream.eof()) {
    _currentChunk = -1; // empty the stack
    return;
  }

  //, Put this chunk on the stack
  _currentChunk++;
  _chunk[_currentChunk].type = type;
  _chunk[_currentChunk].size = size;
  _chunk[_currentChunk].remaining = size;
  _chunk[_currentChunk].isContainer = false;
```

```
      _chunk[_currentChunk].containerType = 0;
```

> Process Specific WAVE Chunk and return (Listing 17.9)

> Process Generic RIFF Chunk and return (Listing 17.11)

```
      char code[5] = "CODE";
      code[0] = (type>>24)&255;   code[1] = (type>>16)&255;
      code[2] = (type>>8 )&255;   code[3] = (type    )&255;
      cerr << "Ignoring unrecognized '" << code << "' chunk\n";
  }
```

One general principle of RIFF and similar formats is that you should be able to skip any chunk you don't recognize. In this case, an unrecognized chunk won't be read anywhere else, so I have to be careful to skip the remains of the current chunk before I try to read the next. After skipping the chunk, I also need to be careful to make sure I properly track the remaining size of the enclosing container.

There's one important minor detail. In RIFF files (as in all IFF-derived file formats), every chunk occupies an even number of bytes in the file. If the actual size of the chunk is odd, there's an extra byte of padding that needs to be skipped.

LISTING 17.6   Skip Remainder of Current Chunk

```
  if ((_currentChunk >= 0) && (!_chunk[_currentChunk].isContainer)) {
      unsigned long lastChunkSize = _chunk[_currentChunk].size;
      if (lastChunkSize & 1) {  // Is there padding?
         _chunk[_currentChunk].remaining++;
         lastChunkSize++; // Account for padding in the container update
      }
      SkipBytes(_stream,_chunk[_currentChunk].remaining); // Flush the chunk
      _currentChunk--;  // Drop chunk from the stack
      // Sanity check:  containing chunk must be container
      if ((_currentChunk < 0) || (!_chunk[_currentChunk].isContainer)) {
         cerr << "Chunk contained in non-Container?!?!\n";
         exit(1);
      }
      // Reduce size of container
      if (_currentChunk >= 0) {
         // Sanity check:  make sure container is big enough.
         // Also, avoid a really nasty underflow situation.
         if ((lastChunkSize+8) > _chunk[_currentChunk].remaining) {
            cerr << "Error:  Chunk is too large to fit in container!?!?\n";
            _chunk[_currentChunk].remaining = 0; // container is empty
         } else
            _chunk[_currentChunk].remaining -= lastChunkSize + 8;
      }
  }
```

The chunk we just cleaned up might have been the last chunk in its container, which might in turn have been the last chunk in its container, and so on. Note that any container with fewer than 8 bytes left must be finished because a chunk header requires at least 8 bytes. Except for that detail, the following block of code looks a lot like the previous block of code.

LISTING 17.7   Flush Finished Containers

```
// There may be forms that are finished, drop them too
while (  (_currentChunk >= 0)  // there is a chunk
     &&  (_chunk[_currentChunk].remaining < 8)
     )
{
   SkipBytes(_stream,_chunk[_currentChunk].remaining); // Flush it
   unsigned long lastChunkSize = _chunk[_currentChunk].size;
   _currentChunk--;  // Drop container chunk
   // Sanity check, containing chunk must be container
   if (!_chunk[_currentChunk].isContainer) {
      cerr << "Chunk contained in non-container?!?!\n";
      exit(1);
   }
   // Reduce size of container
   if (_currentChunk >= 0) {
      if ((lastChunkSize+8) > _chunk[_currentChunk].remaining) {
         cerr << "Error in WAVE file:  Chunk is too large to fit!?!?\n";
         lastChunkSize = _chunk[_currentChunk].remaining;
      }
      _chunk[_currentChunk].remaining -= lastChunkSize + 8;
   }
}
```

The `NextChunk` method is also responsible for handling the data within a recognized chunk. I'll present those details in the following sections.

The RIFF WAVE Container

A WAVE file contains a single `RIFF` container, which in turn contains all other chunks in the file. I've chosen to read the outer-most chunk during the initialization.

LISTING 17.8   WaveRead Initialization

```
_currentChunk = -1; // Empty the stack
NextChunk();
// Ensure first chunk is RIFF/WAVE container
if (  (_currentChunk != 0)
   || (_chunk[0].type != ChunkName('R','I','F','F'))
   || (_chunk[0].isContainer != true)
   || (_chunk[0].containerType != ChunkName('W','A','V','E')) )
```

```
    {
        cerr << "Outermost chunk in WAVE file isn't RIFF!!";
        exit(1);
    }
```

Even if the current chunk isn't a RIFF chunk, you know that the outer-most chunk will always be a RIFF chunk.

LISTING 17.9   Process Specific WAVE Chunk and return

```
    if ((_currentChunk >= 0) &&
        (_chunk[0].type != ChunkName('R','I','F','F'))){
        cerr << "Outermost chunk is not RIFF ?!?!\n";
        _currentChunk = -1;
        return;
    }
```

Within the NextChunk method, a RIFF chunk is easy to handle. I need only to mark it as a container and read in the container type.

LISTING 17.9 (CONTINUED)   Process Specific WAVE Chunk and return

```
    if (type == ChunkName('R','I','F','F')) {
        _chunk[_currentChunk].isContainer = true;
        // Need to check size of container first.
        _chunk[_currentChunk].containerType = ReadIntMsb(_stream,4);
        _chunk[_currentChunk].remaining -= 4;
        if (_currentChunk > 0) {
            cerr << "RIFF chunk seen at inner level?!?!\n";
        }
        return;
    }
```

The fmt Chunk

The fmt chunk contains the actual sound format information. The precise contents of the fmt chunk vary depending on the compression method. Table 17.2 shows the format used for plain PCM data. Other compression techniques extend this with additional information.

I've taken a lazy approach to handling the format information. When I encounter the fmt chunk, I read it and store its contents in memory but don't try to use any of that information until it is actually needed.

TABLE 17.2   Contents of fmt Chunk for PCM Data

Size	Description
2	Compression code (see Table 17.3)
2	Number of channels
4	Samples per second
4	Average number of bytes per second
2	Block alignment
2	Significant bits per sample
2	Number of bytes of additional information
n	Additional compressor-specific information

LISTING 17.9 (CONTINUED)   Process Specific WAVE Chunk and return

```
if (type == ChunkName('f','m','t',' ')) {
   if (_currentChunk != 1) {
      cerr << "FMT chunk seen at wrong level?!?!\n";
   }
   _formatData = new unsigned char[size+2];
   _stream.read(reinterpret_cast<char *>(_formatData),size);
   _formatDataLength = _stream.gcount();
   _chunk[_currentChunk].remaining = 0;
   return;
}
```

I don't need to parse the format information until someone asks me about the file. For example, when someone asks me for the sampling rate or number of channels, I can read the appropriate bytes directly from the stored format information. Similarly, if someone asks me for samples, I need to first ensure that the decompression object has been set up. The `InitializeDecompression` method ensures that the `fmt` chunk has been read, and it sets up a decompressor.

LISTING 17.4 (CONTINUED)   WaveRead Members

```
private:
   void MinMaxSamplingRate(long *min, long *max, long *preferred);
   void MinMaxChannels(int *min, int *max, int *preferred);
   size_t GetSamples(AudioSample *buffer, size_t numSamples);
   void InitializeDecompression();
```

LISTING 17.5 (CONTINUED)   WaveRead Implementation

LISTING 17.5 (CONTINUED)   WaveRead Implementation

```
void WaveRead::MinMaxSamplingRate(long *min, long *max, long *preferred) {
    InitializeDecompression();
    unsigned long samplingRate = BytesToIntLsb(_formatData+4,4);
    *max = *min = *preferred = samplingRate;
}

void WaveRead::MinMaxChannels(int *min, int *max, int *preferred) {
    InitializeDecompression();
    unsigned long channels = BytesToIntLsb(_formatData+2,2);
    *min = *max = *preferred = channels;
}

size_t WaveRead::GetSamples(AudioSample *buffer, size_t numSamples) {
    if (!_decoder) InitializeDecompression();
    return _decoder->GetSamples(buffer,numSamples);
}
```

Creating a Decompression Object

Nearly 100 compression codes have been registered with Microsoft for use in WAVE files. The list of codes is defined in the mmreg.h header file included with the current version of Microsoft's development tools. Table 17.3 lists some of the more important ones.

To select a decoder, I first make sure the fmt chunk has been read. I then use the compression code to try to create a suitable decompression object.

TABLE 17.3   Selected WAVE Format Codes

Code	Description
0	Unknown/Illegal
1	PCM
2	Microsoft ADPCM
6	ITU G.711 A-Law
7	ITU G.711 μ-Law
17	IMA ADPCM
20	ITU G.723 ADPCM
49	GSM 6.10
64	ITU G.721 ADPCM
80	MPEG
65535	Experimental

LISTING 17.5 (CONTINUED)   WaveRead Implementation

```
void WaveRead::InitializeDecompression() {
  if (_decoder) return;

  // Make sure we've read the fmt chunk
  while (!_formatData) {
    NextChunk();
    if (_currentChunk < 0) {
      cerr << "No 'fmt' chunk found?!?!\n";
      exit(1);
    }
  }

  // Select decompressor based on compression type
  unsigned long type = BytesToIntLsb(_formatData+0 , 2);

    ┌─────────────────────────────────────────────────────────────┐
    │ Create Decompressor for WAVE File Based on type (Listing 17.10) │
    └─────────────────────────────────────────────────────────────┘

  if (!_decoder) {
    cerr << "I don't support WAVE compression type " << type << "\n";
    exit(1);
  }
}
```

PCM Data

Most WAVE files use plain PCM sound data. Samples of 8 bits or less are stored as unsigned data. Longer samples are stored as signed data.

LISTING 17.10   Create Decompressor for WAVE File Based on type

```
if (type == 1) {  // PCM format
  unsigned long bitsPerSample = BytesToIntLsb(_formatData+14, 2);
  if (bitsPerSample <= 8) // Wave stores 8-bit data as unsigned
    _decoder = new DecompressPcm8Unsigned(*this);
  else if (bitsPerSample <= 16) // 16 bit data is signed
    _decoder = new DecompressPcm16LsbSigned(*this);
}
```

IMA ADPCM Data

Microsoft uses its own variant of IMA ADPCM compression. It adds 2 bytes to the data outlined in Table 17.2 to indicate the length of each sound data packet.

LISTING 17.10 (CONTINUED)   Create Decompressor for WAVE File Based on type

```
if (type == 17) {  // IMA ADPCM format
   unsigned long bitsPerSample = BytesToIntLsb(_formatData+14, 2);
   if (bitsPerSample != 4) {
      cerr << "IMA ADPCM requires 4 bits per sample, not ";
      cerr << bitsPerSample << "\n";
      exit(1);
   }
   if (_formatDataLength < 20) {
      cerr << "IMA ADPCM requires additional decompression data.\n";
      exit(1);
   }
   int packetLength = BytesToIntLsb(_formatData+18,2);
   int channels = BytesToIntLsb(_formatData+2,2);
   _decoder = new DecompressImaAdpcmMs(*this,packetLength,channels);
}
```

μ-Law and A-Law

WAVE files can use μ-Law or A-Law compression.

LISTING 17.10 (CONTINUED)   Create Decompressor for WAVE File Based on type

```
if (type == 6) {
   _decoder = new DecompressG711ALaw(*this);
}
if (type == 7) {
   _decoder = new DecompressG711MuLaw(*this);
}
```

Other Compression Methods

It's more useful to get a text message than to get a cryptic number. Here I notice one of the more popular compression methods that I don't support.

LISTING 17.10 (CONTINUED)   Create Decompressor for WAVE File Based on type

```
if (type == 2) {
   cerr << "I don't support MS ADPCM compression.\n";
}
```

The data Chunk

The data chunk stores the actual compressed sound data. I don't need to do anything with it within NextChunk.

LISTING 17.9 (CONTINUED) Process Specific WAVE Chunk and return

```
if (type == ChunkName('d','a','t','a')) {
  return;
}
```

The important method here is ReadBytes. When someone requests sound data, I first need to make sure I'm reading from the data chunk, then simply grab the appropriate number of bytes and return.

LISTING 17.4 (CONTINUED) WaveRead Members

```
public:
    size_t ReadBytes(AudioByte *buffer, size_t numSamples);
```

LISTING 17.5 (CONTINUED) WaveRead Implementation

```
size_t WaveRead::ReadBytes(AudioByte *buffer, size_t numBytes) {
    while (_chunk[_currentChunk].type != ChunkName('d','a','t','a')) {
        NextChunk();
        if (_currentChunk < 0) {
            cerr << "I didn't find any sound data!?!?\n";
            return 0;
        }
    }
    if (numBytes > _chunk[_currentChunk].remaining)
        numBytes = _chunk[_currentChunk].remaining;
    _stream.read(reinterpret_cast<char *>(buffer), numBytes);
    numBytes = _stream.gcount();
    _chunk[_currentChunk].remaining -= numBytes;
    return numBytes;
}
```

Text Chunks

A variety of chunks carry textual annotations. These chunks can appear in any type of RIFF file, not just WAVE. Their names all start with an uppercase I to indicate that they are for informational purposes.

LISTING 17.11   Process Generic RIFF Chunk and return

```
if ((type & 0xFF000000) == ChunkName('I',0,0,0)) { // First letter 'I'??
  char *text = new char[size+2];
  _stream.read(text,size);
  long length = _stream.gcount();
  _chunk[_currentChunk].remaining -= length;
  text[length] = 0;
  if (type == ChunkName('I','C','M','T')) // Comment
     cerr << "Comment:  ";
  else if (type == ChunkName('I','C','O','P')) // Copyright notice
     cerr << "Copyright:  ";
  else if (type == ChunkName('I','N','A','M')) // Name of work
     cerr << "Title:  ";
  else if (type == ChunkName('I','A','R','T')) // Name of artist
     cerr << "Artist:  ";
  else
     cerr << "Text:  "; // Other Informational chunk
  cerr << text << "\n";
  return;
}
```

AIFF and AIFF-C File Formats

18

Apple adopted Electronic Arts' IFF format (see next chapter, page 231) for use on the Macintosh but made a few changes. The result is a similar file format called *Audio Interchange File Format* (AIFF). The original AIFF did not support compressed audio, so another variation—*Audio Interchange File Format Extension for Compression* (AIFF-C or AIFC)—was developed. AIFF and AIFF-C files are nearly identical, so I'll discuss them together. When I refer to AIFF, those comments will apply equally to AIFF-C. Where there's a difference, I'll make that clear.

The structure of an AIFF file is the same as a RIFF file and is outlined starting on page 204. However, AIFF files store multi-byte numbers in MSB form and use different chunk names.

AIFF files consist of a single, outer-most FORM chunk. The form type is AIFF or AIFC. That form may contain any or all of the chunks in Table 18.1. The most important are the COMM and SSND chunks, which are present in all AIFF and AIFF-C files, and the FVER chunk, which appears in all AIFF-C files.

Because AIFF and AIFF-C are nearly identical, it's interesting to explore why AIFF-C exists at all. In AIFF files, as in most IFF variants, the reader is expected to ignore any data it doesn't recognize. In particular, if you add new chunk types or add new information to the end of an existing chunk type, that new data will be ignored by older readers. The original AIFF format did not specify the compression method. In order to add that, you would have to add a new chunk type or extend the existing COMM chunk (which contains information about the sound format). In either case, older readers would ignore this information and try to play the sound data without the correct decompressor. The results would probably be horrible.

To avoid this, Apple engineers were forced to define a new container type, FORM/AIFC. Since the container type is different, older players that looked for FORM/AIFF would (correctly) not play the file. Newer players that understand both container types would know to look for the compression type code added to the COMM chunk and, as a result, can treat the two container types almost identically.

The engineers who designed AIFF-C did learn from their earlier mistake; they added an FVER chunk to the specification. This chunk contains a code based on the date of the

TABLE 18.1   AIFF Chunks

Chunk Type	Description
FVER	Version of AIFF-C file
COMM	Information about sound storage format
SSND	Sound data
MARK	Marker
COMT	Comment
INST	Instrument
MIDI	MIDI data
AESD	Recording information
APPL	Application-specific chunk
NAME	Name
AUTH	Author
(c)	Copyright information
ANNO	Annotation

relevant specification. If the file reader does not recognize this code, it should not play the file because new data must be understood to play this file. Changes to the FVER code should be uncommon; in the seven years since the introduction of AIFF-C, there has so far been no need to change it at all.

Identifying AIFF Files

AIFF files are IFF files, and every IFF file begins with the four characters FORM. Following that are a 4-byte length and a type code. In this case, I'm interested in the types AIFF and AIFC.

LISTING 18.1   Identify AIFF Files

```
bool IsAiffFile(istream &file) {
    file.seekg(0); // Seek to beginning of file
    unsigned long form = ReadIntMsb(file,4);
    if (form != ChunkName('F','O','R','M')) return false; // Not IFF file
    SkipBytes(file,4);  // Skip chunk size
    unsigned long type = ReadIntMsb(file,4);
    if (type == ChunkName('A','I','F','F')) return true;
    if (type == ChunkName('A','I','F','C')) return true;
    return false; // IFF file, but not AIFF or AIFF-C file
}
```

The AiffRead Class

I'll define one `AiffRead` class to handle AIFF and AIFF-C files. To use it, open a file and initialize a new `AiffRead` object with the open file.

The `AiffRead` class is similar to the `WaveRead` class I presented in the previous chapter.

LISTING 18.2   aiff.h

```
Copyright © 1998, Tim Kientzle (Listing E.1)
#include "audio.h"
#include "compress.h"

bool IsAiffFile(istream &file);

class AiffRead:  public AudioAbstract {
private:
   istream & _stream;
   AbstractDecompressor *_decoder; // current decompressor object
   void InitializeDecompression();
   unsigned char *_formatData; // contents of COMM chunk
   unsigned long _formatDataLength; // length of COMM chunk contents
   void MinMaxSamplingRate(long *min, long *max, long *preferred);
   void MinMaxChannels(int *min, int *max, int *preferred);
public:
   AiffRead(istream & s);
   ~AiffRead();
   size_t GetSamples(AudioSample *buffer, size_t numSamples);
   size_t ReadBytes(AudioByte *buffer, size_t numSamples);

   AiffRead Chunk Storage Interface (Listing 18.4)
};
```

The somewhat verbose `ChunkName` macro converts four characters into a single 32-bit code. These codes are used extensively.

LISTING 18.3   aiff.cpp

```
Copyright © 1998, Tim Kientzle (Listing E.1)
#include "aiff.h"
#include "compress.h"
#include "g711.h"
#include "imaadpcm.h"
#include <cstdlib>

#define ChunkName(a,b,c,d) (                          \
    ((static_cast<unsigned long>(a)&255)<<24)          \
```

```
    + ((static_cast<unsigned long>(b)&255)<<16)          \
    + ((static_cast<unsigned long>(c)&255)<<8)           \
    + ((static_cast<unsigned long>(d)&255)))
```

```
┌─────────────────────────────────────┐
│ Identify AIFF Files (Listing 18.1)   │
└─────────────────────────────────────┘
```

```
AiffRead::AiffRead(istream & s):  _stream(s) {
   cerr << "File Format:  Apple AIFF/AIFF-C\n";
   _decoder = 0;
   _formatData = 0;
   _formatDataLength = 0;
```

```
┌──────────────────────────────────────────────┐
│ AiffRead Chunk Stack Initialization (Listing 18.6) │
└──────────────────────────────────────────────┘
```

```
}

AiffRead::~AiffRead() {
   if(_decoder) delete _decoder;
   if(_formatData) { delete [] _formatData; }
}
```

```
┌──────────────────────────────────────┐
│ AiffRead Implementation (Listing 18.5) │
└──────────────────────────────────────┘
```

Reading AIFF Files

In the original IFF specification, the authors are careful to emphasize that the various chunks may appear in any order. It's therefore possible that some AIFF files might, for instance, have the sound data chunk before the format chunk that specifies how that data is stored.

One way to accommodate such files is to skim the entire file (seeking past large chunks) and create a map in memory with the locations and types of each chunk. You could then use this map to pull in specific chunks.

Although robust, this approach has a serious drawback: It requires that you have the entire file available immediately. If you're interested in streaming an AIFF file over a network and playing it as the data is received, you can't skim the entire file and locate the chunks before you begin playing.

I've taken a different approach with my `AiffRead` class, partly to allow for streaming, and partly for simplicity. Instead of mapping the location of every chunk, I read the file from beginning to end, handling each chunk as I encounter it. Although there can in theory be AIFF files that are unplayable with this code, I've never encountered one.

Containers

Remember that the significance of any chunk depends on the type of chunk and the type of the enclosing container. To keep track of this information, I keep a stack of chunk information. For example, when reading an `ssnd` chunk located within a `FORM AIFF` container, the stack contains two entries. The `_currentChunk` variable identifies the current top of the stack; `-1` indicates the stack is empty.

LISTING 18.4   AiffRead Chunk Storage Interface

```
private:
  // chunk stack
  struct {
     unsigned long type; // Type of chunk
     unsigned long size; // Size of chunk
     unsigned long remaining; // Bytes left to read
     bool isContainer;   // true if this is a container
     unsigned long containerType; // type of container
  } _chunk[5];

  int _currentChunk; // top of stack

  void PopStack();
  bool ReadAiffSpecificChunk(unsigned long type, unsigned long size);
  void DumpTextChunk(unsigned long size, const char *);
  bool ReadIffGenericChunk(unsigned long type, unsigned long size);
  void NextChunk(void);
```

The `NextChunk` method is the core of this class. This method first skips the remains of the current chunk and updates the stack accordingly. It then reads the header of the next chunk and figures out what to do with it.

Because this is the primary place that data is read from the file, I need to be careful about checking for the end of file. If I reach the end of the file, I empty the stack; other functions should check to ensure the stack isn't empty before they try to process the current chunk.

LISTING 18.5   AiffRead Implementation

```
void AiffRead::PopStack(void) {
```
> Skip Remainder of Current Chunk (Listing 17.6)

> Flush Finished Containers (Listing 17.7)
```
}

bool AiffRead::ReadAiffSpecificChunk(unsigned long type, unsigned long size) {
```
> Process Specific AIFF Chunk and return true (Listing 18.7)
```
   return false;
}

bool AiffRead::ReadIffGenericChunk(unsigned long type, unsigned long size) {
```
> Process Generic IFF Chunk and return true (Listing 19.9)

```
      return false;
   }

   // Dump text chunk see page 241
   void AiffRead::DumpTextChunk(unsigned long size, const char *name) {
      char *text = new char[size+2];
      _stream.read(text,size);
      long length = _stream.gcount();
      _chunk[_currentChunk].remaining -= length;
      text[length] = 0;
      cerr << name << " " << text << "\n";
      delete [] text;
   }

   void AiffRead::NextChunk(void) {
      PopStack();

      // Read the next chunk
      if (_stream.eof()) {
         _currentChunk = -1; // empty the stack
         return;
      }
      unsigned long type = ReadIntMsb(_stream,4);
      unsigned long size = ReadIntMsb(_stream,4);
      if (_stream.eof()) {
         _currentChunk = -1; // empty the stack
         return;
      }

      _currentChunk++;
      _chunk[_currentChunk].type = type;
      _chunk[_currentChunk].size = size;
      _chunk[_currentChunk].remaining = size;
      _chunk[_currentChunk].isContainer = false;
      _chunk[_currentChunk].containerType = 0;

      if (ReadAiffSpecificChunk(type,size)) return;
      if (ReadIffGenericChunk(type,size)) return;

      char code[5] = "CODE";
      code[0] = (type>>24)&255;   code[1] = (type>>16)&255;
      code[2] = (type>>8 )&255;   code[3] = (type    )&255;
      cerr << "Ignoring unrecognized '" << code << "' chunk\n";
   }
```

The ReadAiffSpecificChunk and ReadIffGenericChunk methods are responsible for handling the data within any recognized chunk. I'll present those details in the following sections.

A number of chunk types are common between AIFF and IFF/8SVX. I'll discuss these in the next chapter.

The FORM AIFF Container

An AIFF file contains a single FORM container, which in turn contains all other chunks in the file. I've chosen to read the outer-most chunk during the initialization.

LISTING 18.6   AiffRead Chunk Stack Initialization

```
_currentChunk = -1; // Empty the stack
NextChunk();
// Ensure first chunk is a FORM/AIFF container
if (   (_currentChunk != 0)
    || (_chunk[0].type != ChunkName('F','O','R','M'))
    || (_chunk[0].isContainer != true)
    || (   (_chunk[0].containerType != ChunkName('A','I','F','F'))
        &&(_chunk[0].containerType != ChunkName('A','I','F','C')))
    )
{
    cerr << "Outermost chunk in AIFF file isn't FORM/AIF?!!";
    exit(1);
}
```

Within the NextChunk method, a FORM chunk is easy to handle. I need only to mark it as a container and read in the container type.

LISTING 18.7   Process Specific AIFF Chunk and return true

```
if (type == ChunkName('F','O','R','M')) {
_chunk[_currentChunk].isContainer = true;
// Need to check size of container first.
_chunk[_currentChunk].containerType = ReadIntMsb(_stream,4);
_chunk[_currentChunk].remaining -= 4;
if (_currentChunk > 0) {
    cerr << "FORM chunk seen at inner level?!?!\n";
}
return true;
}
```

Even if the current chunk isn't a FORM chunk, you do know that the outer-most chunk will always be a FORM chunk.

LISTING 18.7 (CONTINUED)   Process Specific AIFF Chunk and return true

```
if ((_currentChunk >= 0) && (_chunk[0].type != ChunkName('F','O','R','M'))){
cerr << "Outermost chunk is not FORM ?!?!\n";
_currentChunk = -1;
return true;
}
```

The FVER Chunk

To avoid problems in case AIFF-C needs to be updated again in the future, a new FVER chunk was created. This chunk contains a time stamp indicating the date of the AIFF-C standard. When significant changes occur in the standard, this time stamp will change. As I'm writing this, the most recent revision of the AIFF-C standard was on May 23, 1990, at 2:40 p.m. Using the standard Macintosh time format (seconds since zero hours, January 1, 1904), the time stamp is 2726318400 (hexadecimal A2805140).

LISTING 18.7 (CONTINUED)   Process Specific AIFF Chunk and return true

```
if (type == ChunkName('F','V','E','R')) {
    unsigned long version = ReadIntMsb(_stream,4);
    if (version != 2726318400) {
        cerr << "Unrecognized AIFC file format.\n";
        exit(1);
    }
    _chunk[_currentChunk].remaining -= 4;
    return true;
}
```

The COMM Chunk

The COMM chunk stores information about the sound format.

LISTING 18.7 (CONTINUED)   Process Specific AIFF Chunk and return true

```
if (type == ChunkName('C','O','M','M')) {
    if (_currentChunk != 1) {
        cerr << "COMM chunk seen at wrong level?!?!\n";
    }
    _formatData = new unsigned char[size+2];
    _stream.read(reinterpret_cast<char *>(_formatData),size);
    _formatDataLength = _stream.gcount();
    _chunk[_currentChunk].remaining = 0;
    return true;
}
```

Most audio formats store values such as the sampling rate as integers. For additional precision, Apple decided to use a floating-point format. This makes sense for high-precision applications such as movie or video production, but it does make it more complex to read and write the format. The precise format used by Apple is an 80-bit floating-point format. The first 16 bits are used for a sign bit and a 15-bit base-2 exponent. It's reasonable to assume the number is normalized, which means I can safely ignore the least significant 32 bits and just use this quick integer conversion.

LISTING 18.5 (CONTINUED)   AiffRead Implementation

```
void AiffRead::MinMaxSamplingRate(long *min, long *max, long *preferred) {
   InitializeDecompression();

   unsigned ieeeExponent = BytesToIntMsb(_formatData+8,2);
   unsigned long ieeeMantissaHi = BytesToIntMsb(_formatData+10,4);
   ieeeExponent &= 0x7FFF; // Remove sign bit (rate can't be < 0)
   long samplingRate = ieeeMantissaHi >> (16414 - ieeeExponent);

   *min = *max = *preferred = samplingRate;
}

void AiffRead::MinMaxChannels(int *min, int *max, int *preferred) {
   InitializeDecompression();
   unsigned long channels = BytesToIntMsb(_formatData+0,2);
   *min = *max = *preferred = channels;
}
```

The precise contents of the COMM chunk vary depending on the compression method. Table 18.2 shows the format used for plain PCM data. Other compression techniques extend this with additional information.

TABLE 18.2   Contents of COMM Chunk

Size	Description
2	Number of channels
4	Total number of sample frames
2	Bits per sample
10	Sample frames per second (80-bit IEEE floating-point number)
4	Compression code (Table 18.3)
n	Name of compression

Throughout Apple's system software, 4-byte codes codes are used to identify data types and other important information. In the case of AIFF-C, these codes identify the compression method. The Macintosh multimedia software can look up a sound codec based on this 4-byte code, allowing new codecs to be installed dynamically. Note that the compression name is purely for human consumption; it can vary depending on the writing program.

When I get a request for sound samples, I first need to figure out what decoder to use by calling InitializeDecompression.

TABLE 18.3   Selected AIFF-C Format Codes

Code	Description
NONE	PCM
ACE2	ACE 2:1 compression
ACE8	ACE 8:3 compression
MAC3	MACE 3:1 compression
MAC6	MACE 6:1 compression
ulaw	ITU G.711 μ-Law
ima4	IMA ADPCM

LISTING 18.5 (CONTINUED)   AiffRead Implementation

```
size_t AiffRead::GetSamples(AudioSample *buffer, size_t numSamples) {
   if (!_decoder) InitializeDecompression();
   return _decoder->GetSamples(buffer,numSamples);
}
```

To select a decoder, I just pull the codec name from the file and compare it to the names I support.

LISTING 18.5 (CONTINUED)   AiffRead Implementation

```
void AiffRead::InitializeDecompression() {
   if (_decoder) return;

   // Make sure we've read the COMM chunk
   while (!_formatData) {
      NextChunk();
      if (_currentChunk < 0) {
         cerr << "No 'COMM' chunk found?!?!\n";
         exit(1);
      }
   }

   // Select decompressor based on compression type
   unsigned long type = ChunkName('N','O','N','E'); // Default is none
   if (_formatDataLength >= 22)
      type = BytesToIntMsb(_formatData+18 , 4);

   Create Decompressor for AIFF File Based on type (Listing 18.8)

   if (!_decoder) {
      char code[5] = "CODE";
      code[0] = (type>>24)&255;    code[1] = (type>>16)&255;
```

```
        code[2] = (type>>8 )&255;   code[3] = (type    )&255;
        cerr << "I don't support AIFF-C compression type " << code << "\n";
        exit(1);
    }
}
```

PCM Data

A file written with PCM sound data should be written as an AIFF file (not AIFC) for backward compatibility. Most AIFF/AIFC files are stored this way. PCM samples are stored in signed format; multi-byte samples are stored MSB first.

LISTING 18.8   Create Decompressor for AIFF File Based on type

```
if (type == ChunkName('N','O','N','E')) {  // PCM format
   unsigned long bitsPerSample = BytesToIntMsb(_formatData+6, 2);
   if (bitsPerSample <= 8) // Aiff stores 8-bit data as signed
      _decoder = new DecompressPcm8Signed(*this);
   else if (bitsPerSample <= 16) // 16 bit data is signed
      _decoder = new DecompressPcm16MsbSigned(*this);
}
```

μ-Law Data

AIFF-C files support μ-Law compression.

LISTING 18.8 (CONTINUED)   Create Decompressor for AIFF File Based on type

```
if (type == ChunkName('u','l','a','w')) {  // u-Law format
  _decoder = new DecompressG711MuLaw(*this);
}
```

IMA ADPCM Data

Apple uses its own variant of IMA ADPCM compression. See page 130.

LISTING 18.8 (CONTINUED)   Create Decompressor for AIFF File Based on type

```
if (type == ChunkName('i','m','a','4')) {  // IMA ADPCM format
   int channels = BytesToIntMsb(_formatData+0,2);
   _decoder = new DecompressImaAdpcmApple(*this,channels);
}
```

The SSND Chunk

The SSND chunk stores the actual compressed sound data. It starts with 8 bytes of information that are usually unused.

LISTING 18.7 (CONTINUED)   Process Specific AIFF Chunk and return true

```
if (type == ChunkName('S','S','N','D')) {
   SkipBytes(_stream,8);
   _chunk[_currentChunk].remaining -= 8;
   return true;
}
```

The important method here is ReadBytes. Whenever someone requests sound data, I first need to make sure I'm reading from the SSND chunk, then grab the appropriate number of bytes and return.

LISTING 18.5 (CONTINUED)   AiffRead Implementation

```
size_t AiffRead::ReadBytes(AudioByte *buffer, size_t numBytes) {
   while (_chunk[_currentChunk].type != ChunkName('S','S','N','D')) {
      NextChunk();
      if (_currentChunk < 0) { // stack empty?
         cerr << "I didn't find any sound data!?!?\n";
         return 0;
      }
   }
   if (numBytes > _chunk[_currentChunk].remaining)
      numBytes = _chunk[_currentChunk].remaining;
   _stream.read(reinterpret_cast<char *>(buffer), numBytes);
   numBytes = _stream.gcount();
   _chunk[_currentChunk].remaining -= numBytes;
   return numBytes;
}
```

IFF/8SVX File Format 19

The basic ideas of interchange file formats were developed by Electronic Arts for use on the Commodore Amiga. They developed a flexible file format called *IFF* (Interchange File Format) for storing a variety of types of data. IFF files can contain a single image, formatted text, animation, sound, or any combination of types of data. Developers are free to create new chunk types to store their own types of data.

The structure of an IFF file is the same as RIFF or AIFF files and is outlined starting on page 204. IFF files do, however, store multi-byte numbers in MSB form, and have different chunk names. Although IFF is used only occasionally today, it predates RIFF and AIFF. Much of the original IFF documentation is still applicable to all three file formats.

Usually, an IFF file consists of a single FORM chunk whose type indicates the type of data within the file. Less commonly, the outer-most chunk is a CAT chunk or a LIST chunk with several nested FORM chunks. In this chapter, I'll deal only with files containing a single FORM chunk.

Identifying IFF/8SVX Files

The files I support have a single outer-most FORM container with type 8SVX (an abbreviation for "8-bit sampled voice"). There are other ways of structuring IFF files; however, they are rarely used.

LISTING 19.1   Identify IFF/8SVX Files

```
bool IsIffFile(istream &file) {
    file.seekg(0); // Seek to beginning of file
    unsigned long form = ReadIntMsb(file,4);
    if (form != ChunkName('F','O','R','M')) return false; // Not IFF file
    SkipBytes(file,4);  // Skip chunk size
    unsigned long type = ReadIntMsb(file,4);
    if (type == ChunkName('8','S','V','X')) return true;
    return false; // IFF file, but not 8SVX file
}
```

An Overview of IFF/8SVX

The most common audio format on the Amiga is an IFF file consisting of a FORM container with type 8SVX. This is frequently referred to as IFF/8SVX. The 8SVX form was designed to hold digitized musical instruments.

The 8SVX form can contain a variety of chunks. Some of these chunks are listed in Table 19.1.

TABLE 19.1   IFF/8SVX Chunks

Name	Description
VHDR	Sound format information
NAME	Name of this sound
(c)	Copyright information
AUTH	Author
ANNO	Additional comment
BODY	Sound data
ATAK	Attack
RLSE	Release

Reading IFF/8SVX Files

As with other file formats, I'll define a single IffRead class. To use it, open a file and initialize a new IffRead object with the open file.

LISTING 19.2   iff.h

```
Copyright © 1998, Tim Kientzle (Listing E.1)
#include "audio.h"
#include "compress.h"

bool IsIffFile(istream &file);

class IffRead:  public AudioAbstract {
private:
    istream & _stream;
    AbstractDecompressor *_decoder;
    void InitializeDecompression();
    void DumpTextChunk(unsigned long, const char *);
    unsigned char *_formatData;
    unsigned long _formatDataLength;
```

```
    void MinMaxSamplingRate(long *min, long *max, long *preferred);
    void MinMaxChannels(int *min, int *max, int *preferred);
```

IffRead Chunk Storage Interface (Listing 19.4)

```
public:
    IffRead(istream & s);
    ~IffRead();
    size_t GetSamples(AudioSample *buffer, size_t numSamples);
    size_t ReadBytes(AudioByte *buffer, size_t numSamples);
};
```

The `ChunkName` macro converts four characters into a single 32-bit code.

LISTING 19.3 iff.cpp

Copyright © 1998, Tim Kientzle (Listing E.1)

```
#include "iff.h"
#include "compress.h"
#include "dpcm.h"
#include <cstdlib>

#define ChunkName(a,b,c,d) (                         \
    ((static_cast<unsigned long>(a)&255)<<24)        \
  + ((static_cast<unsigned long>(b)&255)<<16)        \
  + ((static_cast<unsigned long>(c)&255)<<8)         \
  + ((static_cast<unsigned long>(d)&255)))
```

Identify IFF/8SVX Files (Listing 19.1)

```
IffRead::IffRead(istream & s): _stream(s) {
    cerr << "File Format:  Electronic Arts' IFF/8SVX\n";
    _decoder = 0;
    _formatData = 0;
    _formatDataLength = 0;
```

IffRead Chunk Stack Initialization (Listing 19.6)

```
}

IffRead::~IffRead() {
    if(_formatData) { delete [] _formatData; }
    if(_decoder) delete _decoder;
}
```

IffRead Implementation (Listing 19.5)

Overview

In theory, the chunks within a given container can occur in almost any order. This makes it complex to robustly read an arbitrary IFF file. I always need to read the sound format information (VHDR chunk) before the sound data (BODY chunk). Although searching through the file to locate individual chunks isn't complex, it is somewhat tedious and makes it difficult to stream audio files.

In practice, everyone writes the sound format information (VHDR chunk) before the sound data (BODY chunk). This means that I can simplify things by reading directly through the file and processing chunks as I encounter them. The chunk nesting is important, so I do need to keep track of which chunks are contained in other chunks.

Containers

The significance of any chunk depends on the type of chunk and the type of the enclosing container. To track these, I keep a stack of chunk information. For example, when reading a BODY chunk located within a FORM 8SVX container, the stack would contain two entries. The _currentChunk variable identifies the current top of the stack. A value of -1 indicates the stack is empty.

LISTING 19.4   IffRead Chunk Storage Interface

```
private:
  // chunk stack
  struct {
    unsigned long type; // Type of chunk
    unsigned long size; // Size of chunk
    unsigned long remaining; // Bytes left to read
    bool isContainer;   // true if this is a container
    unsigned long containerType; // type of container
  } _chunk[5];

  int _currentChunk; // top of stack

  void PopStack();
  bool ReadIff8svxChunk(unsigned long type, unsigned long size);
  bool ReadIffGenericChunk(unsigned long type, unsigned long size);
  void NextChunk(void);
```

The NextChunk method is the core of this class. This method first skips the remains of the current chunk and updates the stack accordingly. It then reads the header of the next chunk and figures out what to do with it.

Because this is the primary place that data is read from the file, I need to be careful about checking for the end of file. If I reach the end of the file, I empty the stack; other functions should check to ensure the stack isn't empty before they try to process the current chunk.

LISTING 19.5   IffRead Implementation

```
void IffRead::PopStack(void) {

    Skip Remainder of Current Chunk (Listing 17.6)

    Flush Finished Containers (Listing 17.7)

}

bool IffRead::ReadIff8svxChunk(unsigned long type, unsigned long size) {

    Process Specific IFF/8SVX Chunk and return true (Listing 19.7)

    return false;
}

bool IffRead::ReadIffGenericChunk(unsigned long type, unsigned long size) {

    Process Generic IFF Chunk and return true (Listing 19.9)

    return false;
}

void IffRead::NextChunk(void) {
    PopStack();

    // Read the next chunk
    if (_stream.eof()) {
        _currentChunk = -1; // empty the stack
        return;
    }
    unsigned long type = ReadIntMsb(_stream,4);
    unsigned long size = ReadIntMsb(_stream,4);
    if (_stream.eof()) {
        _currentChunk = -1; // empty the stack
        return;
    }

    _currentChunk++;
    _chunk[_currentChunk].type = type;
    _chunk[_currentChunk].size = size;
    _chunk[_currentChunk].remaining = size;
    _chunk[_currentChunk].isContainer = false;
    _chunk[_currentChunk].containerType = 0;

    if (ReadIff8svxChunk(type,size)) return;
    if (ReadIffGenericChunk(type,size)) return;

    char code[5] = "CODE";
    code[0] = (type>>24)&255;   code[1] = (type>>16)&255;
    code[2] = (type>>8 )&255;   code[3] = (type    )&255;
    cerr << "Ignoring unrecognized '" << code << "' chunk\n";
}
```

The NextChunk method is also responsible for handling the data within a recognized chunk. I'll present those details in the following sections.

The FORM 8SVX Container

An IFF file contains a single FORM container, which in turn contains all other chunks in the file. I've chosen to read the outer-most chunk during the initialization.

LISTING 19.6   IffRead Chunk Stack Initialization

```
_currentChunk = -1; // Empty the stack
NextChunk(); // Read first chunk
// Ensure first chunk is a FORM/8SVX container
if ( (_currentChunk != 0)
   || (_chunk[0].type != ChunkName('F','O','R','M'))
   || (_chunk[0].isContainer != true)
   || (_chunk[0].containerType != ChunkName('8','S','V','X')) )
{
    cerr << "Outermost chunk in IFF file isn't FORM/8SVX!!";
    exit(1);
}
```

Even if the current chunk isn't a FORM chunk, you do know that the outer-most chunk will always be a FORM chunk.

LISTING 19.7   Process Specific IFF/8SVX Chunk and return true

```
if ((_currentChunk >= 0) && (_chunk[0].type != ChunkName('F','O','R','M'))){
    cerr << "Outermost chunk is not FORM ?!?!\n";
    _currentChunk = -1;
    return false;
}
```

Within the NextChunk method, a FORM chunk is easy to handle. I just need to mark it as a container and read in the container type.

LISTING 19.7 (CONTINUED)   Process Specific IFF/8SVX Chunk and return true

```
if (type == ChunkName('F','O','R','M')) {
    _chunk[_currentChunk].isContainer = true;
    // Need to check size of container first.
    _chunk[_currentChunk].containerType = ReadIntMsb(_stream,4);
    _chunk[_currentChunk].remaining -= 4;
    if (_currentChunk > 0)
        cerr << "FORM chunk seen at inner level?!?!\n";
    return true;
}
```

The VHDR Chunk

The VHDR chunk contains basic information about the format of the sound data. IFF/8SVX was originally designed as an instrument format for playing music. A single IFF/8SVX file contains a recording of a single instrument. The sound data shown in Table 19.2 illustrates several features designed to facilitate that usage.

An IFF/8SVX sound consists of an initial "one-shot" portion followed by a "repeat" section. When played as an instrument, the repeat section can be repeated until the end of the note. When IFF/8SVX is used for a simple recording rather than as an instrument, the repeat section length is set to zero.

TABLE 19.2   Contents of VHDR Chunk

Bytes	Description
4	One-shot samples for highest note
4	Repeat samples for highest note
4	Samples per cycle for highest note
2	Samples per second
1	Octaves in BODY chunk
1	Coding (0=PCM, 1=Fibonacci coding, 2=Exponential coding)
4	Volume (65,536=full volume)

Playing a digital instrument requires varying the sound to create different notes. In the case of IFF/8SVX, two techniques are used. The basic tool is to play the sound at different speeds. If you know the pitch of the recorded note and the pitch of the note you want, you can adjust the playback rate to achieve any desired pitch. This works well enough for many applications, but to get higher quality, you need to compensate for the fact that most instruments do subtly change their sound depending on the note. IFF/8SVX files allow you to store several recordings of the same instrument at different pitches so that you can choose the recording closest to the desired pitch, minimizing this error. The third field in Table 19.2 is the pitch of the highest recorded note. The BODY chunk stores the recorded notes one after the other, starting with the highest pitch. Each successive note is one octave lower in pitch than the previous one and is recorded at a different sampling rate. Note that the samples per second field is ignored for instrument recordings because the pitch information is what is relevant.

For simple recorded sounds, much of the VHDR information is not needed or used. In this case, the number of repeat samples, samples per cycle, and octave fields are set to zero.

LISTING 19.7 (CONTINUED)   Process Specific IFF/8SVX Chunk and return true

---

```
    if (type == ChunkName('V','H','D','R')) {
      if (_currentChunk != 1) {
         cerr << "VHDR chunk seen at wrong level?!?!\n";
      }
      _formatData = new unsigned char[size+2];
      _stream.read(reinterpret_cast<char *>(_formatData),size);
      _formatDataLength = _stream.gcount();
      _chunk[_currentChunk].remaining = 0;
      return true;
    }
```

InitializeDecompression ensures that the format information (from the VHDR chunk) has been read and stored in the _formatData variable. Both GetSamples and MinMaxSamplingRate need this information to be available.

LISTING 19.5 (CONTINUED)   IffRead Implementation

```
    size_t IffRead::GetSamples(AudioSample *buffer, size_t numSamples) {
      if (!_decoder) InitializeDecompression();
      return _decoder->GetSamples(buffer,numSamples);
    }

    void IffRead::MinMaxSamplingRate(long *min, long *max, long *preferred) {
      if (!_decoder) InitializeDecompression();
      long samplingRate = BytesToIntMsb(_formatData+12,2);
      *min = *max = *preferred = samplingRate;
    }
```

IFF/8SVX files are always mono.

LISTING 19.5 (CONTINUED)   IffRead Implementation

```
    void IffRead::MinMaxChannels(int *min, int *max, int *preferred) {
      *min = *max = *preferred = 1;
    }
```

To select a decoder, you need first to ensure that the VHDR chunk has been read, then use the type code.

LISTING 19.5 (CONTINUED)   IffRead Implementation

```
    void IffRead::InitializeDecompression() {
      if (_decoder) return;

      while (!_formatData) {    // Read the VHDR chunk
```

```
        NextChunk();
        if (_currentChunk < 0) {
            cerr << "No 'VHDR' chunk found?!?!\n";
            exit(1);
        }
    }

    // Select decompressor based on compression type
    unsigned long type = BytesToIntMsb(_formatData+15 , 1);
```

Create Decompressor for IFF/8SVX File Based on type (Listing 19.8)

```
    if (!_decoder) {
        cerr << "I don't support IFF/8SVX compression type " << type << "\n";
        exit(1);
    }
}
```

PCM Data

Essentially all IFF/8SVX files use 8-bit PCM sound data.

LISTING 19.8   Create Decompressor for IFF/8SVX File Based on type

```
if (type == 0) {  // PCM format
    _decoder = new DecompressPcm8Signed(*this);
}
```

Fibonacci DPCM Encoding

This encoding is often referred to as *Fibonacci delta* encoding. Unfortunately, the term *delta encoding* is well-established in hardware circles; it refers to a single-bit encoding technique. For that reason, I prefer the term *Fibonacci DPCM*.

LISTING 19.8 (CONTINUED)   Create Decompressor for IFF/8SVX File Based on type

```
if (type == 1) {  // Fibonacci DPCM
    _decoder = new DecompressDpcmFibonacci(*this);
}
```

Exponential DPCM Encoding

Exponential DPCM (or *exponential delta*) is less common, but it's easy to support.

LISTING 19.8 (CONTINUED)   Create Decompressor for IFF/8SVX File Based on type

```
if (type == 2) {  // Exponential
   _decoder = new DecompressDpcmExponential(*this);
}
```

The BODY Chunk

The BODY chunk stores the actual compressed sound data. I don't need to do anything with it within NextChunk. The important method here is ReadBytes. When someone requests sound data, I first need to make sure I'm reading from the BODY chunk, then grab the appropriate number of bytes and return.

LISTING 19.5 (CONTINUED)   IffRead Implementation

```
size_t IffRead::ReadBytes(AudioByte *buffer, size_t numBytes) {
   while (_chunk[_currentChunk].type != ChunkName('B','O','D','Y')) {
      NextChunk();
      if (_currentChunk < 0) {
         cerr << "I didn't find any sound data!?!?\n";
         return 0;
      }
   }
   if (numBytes > _chunk[_currentChunk].remaining)
      numBytes = _chunk[_currentChunk].remaining;
   _stream.read(reinterpret_cast<char *>(buffer), numBytes);
   numBytes = _stream.gcount();
   _chunk[_currentChunk].remaining -= numBytes;
   return numBytes;
}
```

IFF/8SVX Errata

Unfortunately, when dealing with established file formats, you need to make a serious effort to recognize and compensate for the most common errors made when creating such files. In the case of IFF files (including AIFF and WAVE), it's common for writers to append the audio data to a fixed header. This often results in the different size parameters being set inconsistently. (An IFF/8SVX header includes three size fields: the FORM chunk size, the BODY chunk size, and the number of samples stored in the VHDR chunk.) In the worst case, all of these size fields will be erroneously set to zero.

The following block of code compares the number of samples, as stored in the VHDR chunk, to the length of the BODY chunk. If these don't make sense, I just force some reasonable values and see what happens.

LISTING 19.7 (CONTINUED) Process Specific IFF/8SVX Chunk and return true

```
if (type == ChunkName('B','O','D','Y')) {
    if (_formatData) {
        unsigned long vhdrSamples = BytesToIntMsb(_formatData+0,4);
        unsigned long bodyLength = _chunk[_currentChunk].size;

        // Do they make any sense?
        if ((bodyLength == 0) && (vhdrSamples == 0)) {
            cerr << "IFF/8SVX file says it has no data!?\n";
            cerr << "I'll try to play something anyway, here goes...\n";
            _chunk[_currentChunk].size = 1000000L;
        } else if (bodyLength == 0) {
            cerr << "IFF/8SVX file has samples, but the body has no data!?\n";
            cerr << "Maybe the body is damaged, I'll try anyway...\n";
            _chunk[_currentChunk].size = vhdrSamples;
        } else if (vhdrSamples == 0) {
            cerr << "IFF/8SVX file has data in the body, but no samples?!\n";
            cerr << "Maybe the header is damaged, I'll try anyway...\n";
        }
    }
    return true;
}
```

Text Chunks

A variety of chunks carry textual annotations. These chunks can appear in any type of IFF file (including AIFF and AIFF-C).

LISTING 19.5 (CONTINUED) IffRead Implementation

```
void IffRead::DumpTextChunk(unsigned long size, const char *name) {
    char *text = new char[size+2];
    _stream.read(text,size);
    long length = _stream.gcount();
    _chunk[_currentChunk].remaining -= length;
    text[length] = 0;
    cerr << name << " " << text << "\n";
    delete [] text;
}
```

All these chunks have the same basic format; they contain a null-terminated ASCII string. DumpTextChunk simply reads the text and prints it preceded by a suitable keyword.

LISTING 19.9 Process Generic IFF Chunk and return true

```
if (type == ChunkName('A','N','N','O')) { // Comment
   DumpTextChunk(size,"Annotation:");
   return true;
}
if (type == ChunkName('(','c',')',' ')) { // Copyright
   DumpTextChunk(size,"Copyright:");
   return true;
}
if (type == ChunkName('N','A','M','E')) { // Name of work
   DumpTextChunk(size,"Name:");
   return true;
}
if (type == ChunkName('A','U','T','H')) { // Author
   DumpTextChunk(size,"Author:");
   return true;
}
```

Part Five
Music File Formats

Programming Music 20

The past century has witnessed some dramatic changes in the way we think about music. For example, in the late 19th century, most music was performed live. The Edison phonograph had just been invented and the only widely available "recorded music" was in the form of player piano rolls. Today, most music is heard in recorded form, from radios, tape players, compact discs, or over the Internet.

Computers are an integral part of almost every aspect of modern music production. Music is composed on a computer, scores are distributed electronically, performers use computerized instruments, and the result is recorded and processed digitally. Larger radio stations create playlists days in advance and use computer-driven jukeboxes to play the music you hear while driving home from work.

Although it's possible to store a song as a WAVE or AU recording, there are two reasons why specialized music formats are important. The first is size. It's more compact to store a list of notes to be played than to store a recording of the entire song. The second reason is ease of change. If you have a recording of a symphony, it's hard to isolate and change a single instrument. However, if your symphony is stored as a list of notes, then it's relatively easy to edit it.

Interestingly, these two concerns are especially important in computer game design. Because current computer games are designed to be played for many hours, storage space is a major concern. It's also important that the background music change as the game progresses. Note-based music storage is compact and makes it easier for the composer and game producer to specify how the music progresses throughout the game.

Note-based music formats do have limits. For example, both music formats in this part of the book assume you're working with the Western 12-tone scale. In addition, you may be limited in your instrument choices. The *General MIDI* standard (see page 291) specifies 175 instruments, but if you want to add a bullhorn or some other custom instrument sound, you may be out of luck. MOD is somewhat more versatile because it includes digitized instrument sounds, but it's limited in both the number and quality of those instrument sounds. Neither allows you to include long recorded vocals.

These issues are slowly being addressed. New MIDI standards allow for arbitrary tunings and digitized instrument samples. Similarly, other storage formats, such as

Apple's QuickTime multimedia framework, provide the ability to combine and synchronize note-based music with recorded audio and other types of data.

Instruments

It's tempting to think of an *instrument* as something that produces sound, but that's a bit misleading. The problem, which arises in many object-oriented designs, is that the same instrument might produce many different sounds simultaneously, and it's tricky to design an instrument object that supports this in a natural way. A better approach is to make an instrument something that produces *note* objects and have the notes produce the sound.

Implementing this in C++ requires defining two interrelated classes. The `AbstractInstrument` and `AbstractNote` classes will define the basic capabilities of instrument and note objects. Later, I'll define types of instruments and notes that can be used in practice.

LISTING 20.1   instrumt.h

```
#ifndef INST_H_INCLUDED
#define INST_H_INCLUDED
#include "audio.h"
```

AbstractNote Class Definition (Listing 20.2)

```
class AbstractInstrument {
private:
   long _samplingRate;
public:
   virtual void SamplingRate(long samplingRate) {
      _samplingRate = samplingRate;
   }
   virtual long SamplingRate() { return _samplingRate; }
public:
   virtual ~AbstractInstrument() {};
   virtual AbstractNote * NewNote(float pitch, float volume) = 0;
};
#endif
```

The `AbstractInstrument` class I've defined above has only one nontrivial member function, `NewNote`. This shouldn't be surprising. Just as there's little practical similarity between a violin and a harmonica, digital instruments will also generate their sounds in different ways. The most common ones will be *sampled instruments*, which store a recording of the instrument that can be played back at will. But it's also possible for instruments to use complex mathematical simulations to generate their sounds.

The one similarity among all instrument types is that they generate notes, possibly several at one time. As a result, every instrument class contains a `NewNote` method that can be used to create a suitable note object. The idiom is that you ask a particular instrument for a note, then ask the note to play itself into a buffer. A single instrument may have many notes playing at the same time.

Notes

All notes share certain capabilities, which are expressed in the base class `AbstractNote`. The most important capability is that a note can play itself into a buffer you provide. Because you typically play several notes at a time and add the results, I've adopted the convention that notes play by adding their output to the provided buffer. This reduces the amount of copying needed. You'll need to ensure that the total volume of all notes playing into a buffer is less than 1, or else you'll get overflow and distortion.

By default, repeated calls to the same note continue to play the note; the `Restart` method can be used to re-start the note. The `Pitch` method sets the desired output frequency, such as `Pitch(440)` to play a 440-Hz A. The `Volume` method takes a value between 0 and 1 to set the relative volume.

LISTING 20.2   AbstractNote Class Definition

```
class AbstractNote {
protected:
    AbstractNote() {}; // Limit who can create AbstractNote objects
public:
    virtual ~AbstractNote() {}; // Anyone can delete one
    virtual size_t AddSamples(AudioSample *buffer, size_t samples) =0;
    virtual void Restart() = 0; // restart this note
    virtual void EndNote(float) = 0; // stop playing this note
    virtual void Pitch(float) = 0; // set pitch in Hz
    virtual float Pitch() = 0;  // get pitch
    virtual void Volume(float) = 0; // set volume (0.0--1.0)
    virtual float Volume() = 0; // get current volume
};
```

Declaring the default constructor `AbstractNote()` as `protected` means that you can't create an `AbstractNote` object directly. Specifically, it means that only derived classes can call the constructor. Again, the idiom is that you ask the instrument to create a note for you. In practice, note classes rely extensively on data stored in the instrument class; only the instrument class itself is able to correctly initialize a note.

For simplicity, I've used floating point for the pitch and volume. Even on slow machines, this isn't much of a performance penalty, because the floating-point arithmetic is typically used only when the note is created. A handful of floating-point operations to set up a new note is a fairly modest requirement. Most of the running time of music programs is spent inside the `AddSamples` routine, which usually relies on faster fixed-point and integer arithmetic.

Synthesizing Instruments

21

Just as a bagpipe, harpsichord, and tambourine produce sound in different ways, people have also experimented with different ways to produce sounds digitally. In this chapter, I'll look at some of the approaches that have been used.

As you evaluate these approaches, keep in mind that there are two distinct goals that motivate these techniques. One goal is to duplicate the sound of an existing instrument. For example, many synthesizer manufacturers go to great effort to ensure that their piano sound is a precise match for the sound of a physical piano.

Another goal is to create sounds that have musical qualities, even if they have no physical counterparts.

Sampled Instruments

One obvious approach for duplicating the sound of another instrument is to start with a recording of the instrument you want to mimic. A *sampled instrument* contains one or more recordings of a sound and uses them to create the desired note. The obvious difficulty is that one recording cannot represent all possible notes. You must either record every possible note (which requires a lot of storage) or somehow pitch-shift the recording you do have. To save space, many music formats provide a single recording, and you must pitch-shift to produce all possible notes from that recording.

True pitch-shifting is time-consuming, so my music players make a common simplification: They merely vary the playback rate, skipping samples to approximate the pitch variation. This isn't ideal. Varying the playback rate does change the frequency spectrum, but it also changes the rate at which the spectrum changes. For real instruments, different notes tend to evolve at similar rates. Although crude, varying the playback rate is the best you can do on many systems.

Another problem with using a single recording is that most real-world instruments don't make precisely the same sound for different notes. For this reason, many of the more sophisticated music formats store several recordings, as many as one per octave, so that the amount of pitch-shifting is kept to a minimum.

The basic `SampledInstrument` class is really just a container for the sample data. Most of the work is done in the `SampledNote` class. The `_basePitch` and `_baseSampleRate` hold a critical piece of information about the sample: the apparent pitch when the sample is played at a particular rate. The `SampledNote` class will use this to determine how to resample the data to provide different pitches.

LISTING 21.1   sampled.h

```
Copyright © 1998, Tim Kientzle (Listing E.1)

#ifndef SAMPLED_H_INCLUDED
#define SAMPLED_H_INCLUDED
#include "audio.h"
#include "instrumt.h"

class SampledNote :  public AbstractNote {
   friend class SampledInstrument;

   SampledNote Members (Listing 21.3)

};

class SampledInstrument :  public AbstractInstrument {
private:
   AudioSample *_samples;
   int _sampleLength;
   int _repeatStart;
   int _repeatEnd;
   float _basePitch;
   float _baseSampleRate;

public:
   SampledInstrument();
   SampledInstrument(AudioSample * samples, int length,
                     int repeatStart, int repeatEnd);
   virtual ~SampledInstrument();
   void BasePitch(float basePitch, float baseSampleRate);
   friend class SampledNote;
   AbstractNote * NewNote(float pitch, float volume) {
      return new SampledNote(this,pitch,volume);
   };
};

   Sine Wave Instrument Definition (Listing 21.4)

#endif
```

When you create a `SampledInstrument`, you give it the recording to use as a template. One important fact about this recording is its pitch at some sampling rate. Essentially, the `SampledInstrument` object will vary the sampling rate in order to adjust the pitch.

LISTING 21.2   sampled.cpp

```cpp
#include <cmath>
#include "instrumt.h"
#include "sampled.h"

SampledInstrument::SampledInstrument() {
   _basePitch = 440;
   _baseSampleRate = 8000;
   _samples = 0;
   _sampleLength = 0;
   _repeatStart = _repeatEnd = 0;
}

SampledInstrument::SampledInstrument(AudioSample * samples,
      int length, int repeatStart, int repeatEnd) {
   _basePitch = 440;
   _baseSampleRate = 8000;
   _samples = 0;

   if (length > 0) { // Copy samples into local buffer
      _samples = new AudioSample[length];
      for(int i=0; i<length; i++)
         _samples[i] = samples[i];
   }
   _repeatStart = repeatStart;
   _repeatEnd = repeatEnd;
   _sampleLength = length;
}

SampledInstrument::~SampledInstrument() {
   if (_samples) delete [] _samples;
}

void SampledInstrument::BasePitch(float basePitch, float baseSampleRate) {
   _basePitch=basePitch;  _baseSampleRate=baseSampleRate;
}
```

The `SampledInstrument` class is really just a container for the instrument recording. When you ask it for a note, it creates a `SampledNote` object that does most of the real work.

First, `SampledNote` needs a handful of private variables. Clearly, the note needs a pointer to the instrument object. It will also need to have pointers to the raw sample data and various key places within that.

LISTING 21.3   SampledNote Members

```
private:
   SampledInstrument *_instrument;
   AudioSample *_currentSample;
   AudioSample *_endData;
   AudioSample *_startLoop;
   AudioSample *_endLoop;
   bool _repeating; // Should I loop?
public:
   // To end a note, just stop repeating
   void EndNote(float) { _repeating = false; }
```

The constructor is minimal. Because I need to be able to re-trigger the note and set the pitch and volume, I place those more involved operations in separate member functions.

LISTING 21.3 (CONTINUED)   SampledNote Members

```
protected:
   SampledNote(SampledInstrument *instr);
   SampledNote(SampledInstrument *instr, float pitch, float volume);
```

LISTING 21.2 (CONTINUED)   sampled.cpp

```
SampledNote::SampledNote(SampledInstrument *instr) {
   _instrument = instr;
   _requestPitch = instr->_basePitch;
   _requestSampleRate = instr->_baseSampleRate;
};

SampledNote::SampledNote(SampledInstrument *instr,
                         float pitch, float volume) {
   _instrument = instr;
   _requestPitch = instr->_basePitch;
   _requestSampleRate = instr->_baseSampleRate;
   Pitch(pitch);
   Volume(volume);
   Restart();
};
```

The easiest of these operations is restarting, which simply requires resetting the various pointers. I'll explain the `_fraction` variable in a minute.

LISTING 21.3 (CONTINUED)   SampledNote Members

```
public:
    void Restart();
```

LISTING 21.2 (CONTINUED)   sampled.cpp

```
void SampledNote::Restart() {
    _repeating = true;
    _currentSample = _instrument->_samples;
    _endData = _instrument->_samples + _instrument->_sampleLength;
    _startLoop = _instrument->_samples + _instrument->_repeatStart;
    _endLoop = _instrument->_samples + _instrument->_repeatEnd;
    _fraction = 0;
}
```

For efficiency, volume will be handled in fixed-point arithmetic. During playback, each sample will be multiplied by a constant and then divided by 8,192.

LISTING 21.3 (CONTINUED)   SampledNote Members

```
private:
    int _volume;
    enum {volumeBits = 13}; // _volume is 1/8192
public:
    void Volume(float volume) {
        _volume = int(volume * (1<<volumeBits));
    }
    float Volume() {
        return static_cast<float>(_volume) / (1<<volumeBits);
    }
```

I'll describe the actual playback logic now, and then get into the more involved `Pitch` calculations.

The `AddSamples` function varies the playback rate by changing the rate at which it steps through the sample buffer. A change in pitch requires simply changing the increment.

The increment won't necessarily be an integer. My `_increment` value is a fixed-point number that I use to step the sample pointer. The `_fraction` variable keeps the fractional part of the pointer. For each sample, I add `_increment` to `_fraction`, then move the pointer by the whole part of `_fraction`. The rest of the `AddSamples` method is simple bookkeeping.

Rather than pick the closest sample in time (which does introduce some distortion), you could use a variety of mathematical techniques to estimate an in-between sample.

LISTING 21.3 (CONTINUED)   SampledNote Members

```
private:
    enum {fractionBits = 10};
public:
    size_t AddSamples(AudioSample *buffer, size_t samples);
```

LISTING 21.2 (CONTINUED)   sampled.cpp

```
size_t SampledNote::AddSamples(AudioSample *buffer, size_t samplesRequested) {
    int samplesRemaining = samplesRequested;
    if (!_currentSample) return 0;  // No data?
    while(samplesRemaining) {
        if (_repeating && (_currentSample >= _endLoop)) {
            if (_startLoop == _endLoop) // No loop
                _repeating = false;  // Don't repeat
            else
                _currentSample -= _endLoop - _startLoop;
        }

        if (!_repeating && (_currentSample >= _endData))
                return samplesRequested - samplesRemaining;

        // This assumes that 'long' is larger than the
        // largest sample * (1<<volumeBits)
        long newSample = (*_currentSample) * static_cast<long>(_volume);
        newSample >>= volumeBits;

        *buffer++ += newSample;
        _fraction += _increment;
        _currentSample += _fraction >> fractionBits; // 8-bit fraction
        _fraction &= (1<<fractionBits)-1;
        samplesRemaining--;
    }
    return samplesRequested - samplesRemaining;
};
```

Now for that pitch calculation. As you can see from the above, the critical value is _increment, which controls how fast the _currentSample pointer steps through the data. The proper setting for the increment will depend on the desired output pitch, the desired output sampling rate, and the pitch that would result from using an increment of 1 at some assumed sampling rate. The _basePitch and _baseSampleRate variables in the SampledInstrument object hold the default pitch at the default sampling rate. So setting the correct increment requires computing the ratio of the desired pitch to the base pitch and scaling to produce a fixed-point value.

LISTING 21.3 (CONTINUED)   SampledNote Members

```
private:
   int _increment, _fraction;
   float _requestPitch;
   float _requestSampleRate;
   void SetIncrement();
public:
   void Pitch(float pitch) {
      _requestPitch = pitch;
      SetIncrement();
   };
   float Pitch() { return _requestPitch; };
```

LISTING 21.2 (CONTINUED)   sampled.cpp

```
void SampledNote::SetIncrement() {
   _increment = int(_requestPitch/_instrument->_basePitch
            * _instrument->_baseSampleRate/_instrument->SamplingRate()
            * (1<<fractionBits));
}
```

Some clients of this class will require more detailed manipulation of the playback. In particular, some clients need to force the instrument to begin playing at a particular point in the sample.

LISTING 21.3 (CONTINUED)   SampledNote Members

```
public:
   void SetSampleOffset(int offset);
```

LISTING 21.2 (CONTINUED)   sampled.cpp

```
void SampledNote::SetSampleOffset(int offset) {
   _currentSample = _instrument->_samples + offset;
   while (_currentSample >= _endData) {
      if (_startLoop == _endLoop) {
         _currentSample = 0;
         return;
      }
      _currentSample = _startLoop + (_currentSample - _endData);
      _endData = _endLoop;
   }
};
```

A Sine Wave Generator

There are many ways to use the `SampledInstrument` class I've just developed. One way is to read the instrument samples from an external file. Another is to create new instrument classes that use `SampledInstrument`. As an example of the latter, here's an instrument that just plays a sine wave. It creates a short sine wave sample and then uses `SampledInstrument` to play that sample.

In some object-oriented languages, you could subclass `SampledInstrument`, overriding its constructor with one that creates the sampled sine and then invokes the regular `SampledInstrument` constructor. However, that approach doesn't work with C++. Instead, I've created a new `AbstractInstrument` class that creates a `SampledInstrument` class and manipulates it.

LISTING 21.4   Sine Wave Instrument Definition

```
class SineWaveInstrument:  public AbstractInstrument {
private:
   SampledInstrument *_sampledInstrument;
   void CreateInstrument();
public:
   SineWaveInstrument() { _sampledInstrument = 0; };
   ~SineWaveInstrument() {
      if (_sampledInstrument)
         delete _sampledInstrument;
   }
   AbstractNote *NewNote(float pitch, float volume) {
      CreateInstrument();
      return _sampledInstrument->NewNote(pitch,volume);
   }
   void SamplingRate(long samplingRate) {
      AbstractInstrument::SamplingRate(samplingRate);
      CreateInstrument();
      _sampledInstrument->SamplingRate(samplingRate);
   }
   long SamplingRate() {
       return AbstractInstrument::SamplingRate();
   }
};
```

Object-oriented programmers refer to this type of object as a *proxy* object. In essence, it's no more than a substitute for another object; the underlying `_sampledInstrument` object actually does all the work. The only nontrivial part of this class is the part that creates the template instrument and initializes a `SampledInstrument` object from it. I'll defer the bulk of this until the next section, after I explain some modifications that make this sound more natural.

LISTING 21.2 (CONTINUED)   sampled.cpp

```
void SineWaveInstrument::CreateInstrument() {
   if(_sampledInstrument) return;
      Create Template and Initialize Sampled Instrument (Listing 21.5)
}
```

Amplitude Control

If you listen carefully to a plucked guitar string, a piano, or almost any real instrument, you'll notice that the volume changes in a fairly predictable way through the note. Most instruments have a loud initial segment, then hold a fairly steady volume for a period, and finally fade away. This variation in amplitude is called the *envelope*.

To make your own digital instruments sound more lifelike, you need to pay careful attention to envelope control. The simplest and most common form of envelope control is called *ADSR*, which stands for *attack*, *decay*, *sustain*, and *release*. Figure 21.1 illustrates a typical ADSR envelope.

FIGURE 21.1   ADSR Envelope

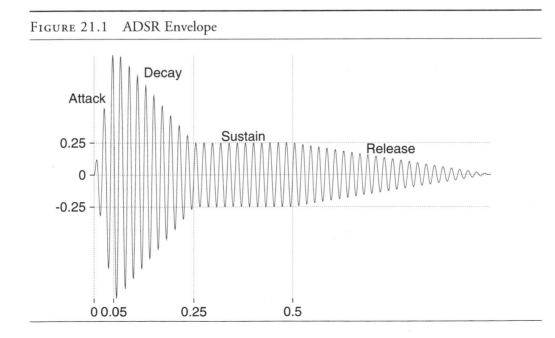

ADSR envelope control is handled in a variety of ways. In hardware synthesizers, there is often a separate volume control that is adjusted as the note plays. With sampled instruments, ADSR envelope control can be built directly into the sample. For other types of digital instruments, envelope control is an inherent part of the instrument. The *plucked string* algorithm I'll discuss later in this chapter is an example.

Envelope Control with Sampled Instruments

Many people take a variety of recorded sounds and create sampled instruments from them. This requires identifying three portions of the sound: an initial portion that includes the attack and decay, a sustain portion that will be looped, and a release portion. The most critical part of this is to ensure that the sustain portion loops correctly; the end of the sustain must properly match the beginning of the sustain.

To demonstrate how to build a sampled instrument, I'll create a template wave form from scratch. I'll use a 440-Hz sine wave, sampled at 44,000 samples per second, as my basic sound. I'll then impose the ADSR envelope shown in Figure 21.1. This envelope has a short attack (1/20 second) that carries it up to the maximum amplitude, then decays down to a sustain level of 1/4 amplitude. It finishes with a 1/2 second release. The beginning and end of the sustain portion have been carefully selected so that the sound will loop correctly.

Note that sampled instruments like this are usually constructed manually. You first record the instrument in question, then carefully manipulate the recording to build something suitable for playback.

LISTING 21.5   Create Template and Initialize Sampled Instrument

---

```
const float maxAmplitude
  = static_cast<float>((1L<<(8*sizeof(AudioSample)-1))-1);
const int numSamples = 44000;
AudioSample *buffer= new AudioSample[numSamples];
for(int i=0;i<numSamples;i++) {
   float amplitude = 0.0; // default
   float time = i / static_cast<float>(numSamples);
   if(time < 0.05) // Attack is 0.05 second
      amplitude = time / 0.05; // increase to one
   else if(time < 0.25) // Decay is 0.2 second
      amplitude = 1.0 - ((time-0.05) / 0.2 * 0.75); // Decay to 0.25
   else if(time < 0.5) // Sustain period (0.25 second in template)
      amplitude = 0.25;
   else if(time < 1.0) // decay for 0.5 second
      amplitude = 0.25 - ((time-0.5) / 0.5 * 0.25);

   buffer[i] = static_cast<AudioSample>(maxAmplitude * amplitude
      * sin(time * ( 440.0 * 2.0 * 3.14159265358979 ) ) );
}
```

```
_sampledInstrument
   = new SampledInstrument(buffer,numSamples,numSamples/4,numSamples/2);
_sampledInstrument->BasePitch(440.0,static_cast<float>(numSamples));
delete [] buffer;
```

This approach has one serious drawback; when you change the playback rate, you also change how quickly the envelope changes. More sophisticated methods track the envelope separately to avoid this problem.

Other Types of Envelope Control

Although straight-line ADSR envelopes are common, other types of envelope control are used as well. In particular, a steady sustain level is appropriate only for instruments such as violins and trumpets in which a continual excitation (the violinist's bow or the trumpeter's breath) keeps the sound steady for as long as desired. Contrast this with a guitar or piano. In these, after the initial attack, the sound continues to decay; there is no steady sustain.

Another popular effect is *tremolo*, in which the amplitude cycles steadily. Hardware synthesis uses a *low-frequency oscillator* (LFO), which feeds into the amplitude control. Using sampled instruments, you can use your looping section to store an entire cycle of the amplitude. Alternatively, you can rapidly adjust the volume by multiplying each sample by a number that changes steadily.

FM and Wavetable Synthesis

Sound card marketers wax eloquent about the relative merits of *FM synthesis* and *Wavetable synthesis*. In reality, these two approaches are more alike than different.

If you look carefully at the `AddSamples` method, the core part is often referred to as a *digital oscillator*. A digital oscillator has three inputs: a sampled waveform, an increment (pitch), and a volume. From these, it produces a sequence of output samples. In my `SampledNote` class, all three inputs are fixed.

To produce richer sounds, you can vary the increment and volume as the note plays. The most natural way to do this is to have two more digital oscillators that step through their own waveforms. As a result, the master oscillator plays with a varying pitch and volume. By selecting the waveform, speed, and level of the pitch and volume oscillators, you can produce a variety of effects, including envelope control, vibrato, and tremolo.

The simplest use of this is called *FM synthesis*. FM synthesis is characterized by a small collection of waveforms, often just a sine and square wave. The digital oscillators are referred to as *units* or *operators*. Hardware FM synthesis chips allow you to combine the operators in various ways.

Wavetable synthesis is exactly the same, except the waveforms are stored in memory and can be changed. In some systems, you can program the volume and pitch waveforms as well.

Plucked Strings

Sampled instruments have some interesting problems. The first is that their output tends to sound somewhat mechanical. This occurs because real instruments don't make precisely the same sound each time they're played. Slight differences in tone and texture occur naturally with physical instruments.

The second problem is that the sound of a sampled instrument doesn't continue to evolve over the entire life of the note. To save space, the bulk of the note is played from a single short loop of sound. On many real instruments, the precise sound continues to evolve for as long as the note is held.

Fortunately, a simple algorithm addresses both of these issues. This algorithm is called the *plucked string algorithm*, because it was first developed to mimic the evolving sound of a string. With minor alterations, however, it can be used to synthesize a variety of musical sounds. I'll describe the general ideas and then present a simple implementation of the algorithm.

The plucked string algorithm rests on three basic ideas.

- Because noise contains a broad range of frequencies, you can start with random values and slowly adjust them to produce an evolving sound.

- If you repeat a short section of sound, you'll get a musical tone. For example, if you take a 1/100 second loop and repeat it 100 times a second, you'll get a fairly strong 100-Hz tone, in addition to whatever else is present in the sound.

- It's easy to gradually remove high or low frequencies.

To see how these ideas work together, suppose you're working at a 44,100-Hz sampling rate. Fill a table with 441 random values and play that table in an endless repeat. Although you may not think the result is very musical, it does have a clear 100-Hz pitch.

Now you want to modify that table as you play it. The usual version of this algorithm simply replaces each sample with the average of that sample and the previous sample. This simple modification tends to smooth out sharp transitions. The result is that high frequencies are attenuated while low frequencies are left relatively unchanged. (This averaging is a simple example of a *low-pass filter*, so named because it leaves low frequencies relatively unchanged while diminishing higher frequencies.)

This simple algorithm requires very little memory. A 100-Hz tone at a 44,100-Hz sampling rate requires a modest 441 samples. It's also relatively fast. Practical implementations do more than just average pairs of samples, but not much more. Finally, it's quite flexible. Minor changes to the way you update the buffer can produce different effects.

Combining the ideas so far, you get the basic plucked-string algorithm:

```
while(samplesRemaining > 0) {
    *buffer++ += _buffer[_pos];
    samplesRemaining--;
    AudioSample thisSample = _buffer[_pos]
    _buffer[_pos] = (_buffer[_pos] + lastSample)/2;
    lastSample = thisSample;
    if(++_pos >= _bufferSize) _pos = 0;
}
```

After playing each sample into the provided `buffer`, you update that sample, temporarily storing the previous value in `lastSample`.

This basic algorithm requires some refinements. One obvious problem is that, as the note fades, it's difficult to tell when it is finished. Although the entire buffer will eventually be averaged down to the same value, there's no inherent reason for that value to be zero. The buffer might decay to a non-zero value because the original random samples may not have had a zero average. Another reason is that the buffer update itself may cause the average to drift over time (usually due to round-off).

A non-zero average is called *DC bias* by electrical engineers. In essence, it amounts to an unwanted zero-frequency component. Fortunately, it's relatively simple to remove this. You just keep a decaying average of the samples (measuring the DC bias) and then subtract that bias from each sample.

```
/* After updating _buffer[_pos] */
_dcBias = (_dcBias * 32767 +
            _buffer[_pos]*32768)/32768;
_buffer[_pos] -= _dcBias/32768;
```

I'm using a fixed-point calculation of `_dcBias` here (with 15 bits after the decimal point) for accuracy. This calculation is a simple *high-pass filter*, which suppresses low frequencies more than high frequencies. In particular, it will suppress the zero-frequency DC bias, with the result that the signal will eventually decay to zero.

The other problem with the basic plucked-string filter is more difficult to address. Remember that I want to use this as an instrument, to produce a variety of pitches. To produce a higher pitch, I will use a smaller buffer, which means that each location in the buffer will be averaged more frequently. In addition, high pitches are attenuated more quickly by the low-pass filter. The result is that high-pitched notes decay more quickly than low-pitched notes. When I experimented with one simple implementation, a 100-Hz note lasted for more than 15 seconds, while a 1,000-Hz note faded away in less than a second.

One way to address this is to change the way you update the samples. By using a weighted average instead of a simple average, you can cause the buffer contents to change more slowly, counteracting this rapid fade-out. However, if you change the weights too much, the sound changes dramatically (rather than a soft, guitar-like sound, you get a brittle, metallic sound). Adjusting the weights correctly requires a good understanding of the mathematics of filter design. You can find more complete details of this approach in F. Richard Moore's *Elements of Computer Music* (Prentice-Hall, 1990). In the next sections, I'll present a slightly different approach that requires less mathematics to understand.

Implementing the Plucked-String Algorithm

Like all of my instrument classes, two objects are involved. You create a `PluckedStringInstrument` and then ask it to give you corresponding `PluckedStringNote` objects.

LISTING 21.6   plucked.h

```
Copyright © 1998, Tim Kientzle (Listing E.1)

#ifndef PLUCKED_H_INCLUDED
#define PLUCKED_H_INCLUDED
#include "audio.h"
#include "instrumt.h"

PluckedStringNote Definition (Listing 21.9)

PluckedStringInstrument Definition (Listing 21.7)

#endif
```

However, unlike the `SampledInstrument` class, there's little for `PluckedStringInstrument` to do. Other than creating `PluckedStringNote` objects, it only stores the current sampling rate (a capability it inherits from `AbstractInstrument`).

LISTING 21.7   PluckedStringInstrument Definition

```
class PluckedStringInstrument :  public AbstractInstrument {
public:  // Do-nothing constructor and destructor
    PluckedStringInstrument() {};
    virtual ~PluckedStringInstrument() {};
```

```
public:
   AbstractNote * NewNote(float pitch, float volume) {
      return new PluckedStringNote(this,pitch,volume);
   };
};
```

LISTING 21.8   plucked.cpp

Copyright © 1998, Tim Kientzle (Listing E.1)

```
#include "instrumt.h"
#include "plucked.h"

#include <cstdlib> // rand, srand
#include <ctime> // time(), for seeding srand
#include <cmath> // sqrt
```

PluckedStringNote Implementation (Listing 21.10)

LISTING 21.9   PluckedStringNote Definition

```
class PluckedStringNote : public AbstractNote {
   friend class PluckedStringInstrument;
private: // Only a friend can create a PluckedStringNote
   PluckedStringInstrument *_instr;
   PluckedStringNote(PluckedStringInstrument *instr,
         float pitch, float volume);
public: // But anyone can delete one
   virtual ~PluckedStringNote();
private:
   float _pitch;
   float _volume;
public:
   void Pitch(float pitch) { _pitch = pitch; };
   float Pitch() { return _pitch; }
   void Volume(float volume) { _volume = volume; };
   float Volume() { return _volume; };
   void Restart();
   size_t AddSamples(AudioSample *buffer, size_t samples);
   void EndNote(float rate) { _decayRate = rate; }
private:
   float _decayRate; // Decay factor
   int _bufferSize; // Size of buffers
   long *_buffer;  // Most recent data
   long *_future; // Next filtered data
   int _pos; // Current position in buffer
   int _iterations; // How often to filter the buffer
   int _remaining; // When next to filter the buffer
};
```

The constructor simply sets the pitch and volume, then calls `Restart` to set everything up. The destructor just cleans up the two buffers.

LISTING 21.10   PluckedStringNote Implementation

```
PluckedStringNote::PluckedStringNote(PluckedStringInstrument *instr,
    float pitch, float volume) {
  _instr = instr;
  Pitch(pitch);
  Volume(volume);
  Restart();
}

PluckedStringNote::~PluckedStringNote() {
  delete [] _buffer;
  delete [] _future;
}
```

As I mentioned earlier, rather than adjust the low-pass filter to get a constant note duration, I took a less mathematical approach. Now I'll explain that approach.

There are two reasons why higher notes decay more quickly than low notes. One is that higher notes have more high-frequency energy and are, therefore, suppressed more rapidly by the low-pass filter. The other reason is that the smaller buffer means each sample is filtered more often. You can address both of these by arranging to update the buffer data less often.

The `_iterations` and `_remaining` variables control how often the buffer is updated. The `_iterations` variable specifies how many times the buffer should be played between each update; the `_remaining` variable specifies how many times the buffer should be played before the next update. Note that setting `_iterations` to 1 results in the usual behavior of this algorithm, in which the buffer contents are updated just as often as they are played.

LISTING 21.10 (CONTINUED)   PluckedStringNote Implementation

```
// Only invoke srand() once
static bool randomInitialized = false;

void PluckedStringNote::Restart() {
  if (!randomInitialized) {
    srand(time(0)); // Seed the random number generator
    randomInitialized = true; // Don't do it again
  }

  _bufferSize = static_cast<long>(_instr->SamplingRate() / _pitch);
```

```
      // Can only play up to half the sampling rate!
      if (_bufferSize < 2) {
        _bufferSize = 1;
        _iterations = 1;
      } else {
        // First approximation:  Update buffer every 1/100 second
        _iterations = _instr->SamplingRate()/100/_bufferSize;
        // Second approximation:  Square that
        _iterations *= _iterations;
      }

      if (_iterations < 1) _iterations = 1;
      _remaining = 1;
      _pos = 0;
      _decayRate = 0.0;
```

> Create the Buffer and Fill It with Random Values (Listing 21.11)

> Pre-Filter the Buffer (Listing 21.12)

> Scale the Buffer Contents (Listing 21.13)

> Normalize the Buffer Contents (Listing 21.14)

> Initialize Future Samples (Listing 21.15)

```
    }
```

An important fact about random-number generators is that the high-order bits are almost always more random than the low-order bits. The ANSI C constant RAND_MAX specifies the range of the rand() function.

LISTING 21.11   Create the Buffer and Fill It with Random Values

```
    {  // Create and fill the buffer with random values
      _buffer = new long[_bufferSize];
      for(int i=0;i<_bufferSize;i++) {
        AudioSample s = (rand() - (RAND_MAX/2) - 1)
              >> (sizeof(RAND_MAX)*8-sizeof(AudioSample)*8);
        _buffer[i] = s;
      }
    }
```

With physical instruments, soft notes tend to have less high-frequency energy, so it makes sense to pre-filter the buffer contents based on the volume. I've used a weighted average for this filtering; if the volume is 1, the data is unchanged; otherwise, it receives a varying degree of low-pass filtering.

LISTING 21.12   Pre-Filter the Buffer

```
long maxSample = 0;
{  // Use volume to pre-filter data.
   float s1 = 0.5 + _volume/2.0;
   float s2 = 0.5 - _volume/2.0;
   long lastSample = _buffer[_bufferSize-1];
   for(int i=0;i<_bufferSize;i++) {
      long thisSample = _buffer[i];
      _buffer[i] = static_cast<long>(thisSample * s1 + lastSample * s2);
      lastSample = thisSample;
      if (labs(_buffer[i])>maxSample) maxSample = labs(_buffer[i]);
   }
}
```

With the `SampledInstrument` class, I adjusted the volume by scaling each sample as I played the sound. I can avoid that by pre-scaling the buffer contents. I simply adjust the buffer so that the maximum sample has the desired amplitude.

LISTING 21.13   Scale the Buffer Contents

```
long average = 0;
{
   float volumeScale = _volume * ((1<<(sizeof(AudioSample)*8-1))-1)
                       /maxSample;
   for(int i=0;i<_bufferSize;i++) {
      _buffer[i] = static_cast<long>(_buffer[i] * volumeScale);
      average += _buffer[i];
   }
   average /= _bufferSize;
}
```

While scaling the buffer contents above, I added up all the buffer values to compute an average. I want this average to be zero, which I can enforce by adjusting the values one more time.

LISTING 21.14   Normalize the Buffer Contents

```
{
   for(int i=0;i<_bufferSize;i++)
      _buffer[i] -= average;
}
```

In the basic algorithm, only one buffer is used and the values are modified in place. In my modified version, the values are updated only infrequently. To improve the output, I gradually blend the values before and after each update so that the sound evolves smoothly even though the buffer may be filtered only once in 16 or more cycles.

To perform this blending, I need to know the buffer contents before and after each filtering. I keep the contents after filtering in _future. When it's time to update the buffer contents, I move _future to _buffer and then update _future.

LISTING 21.15   Initialize Future Samples

```
{
    _future = new long[_bufferSize];
    for(int i=0;i<_bufferSize;i++)
        _future[i] = _buffer[i];
}
```

Another advantage of this approach over the traditional version is speed; on most samples, I compute only a single weighted average (two integer multiplications and one integer division). Only infrequently do I go through a more involved filter operation. This is especially nice because the filtering must also renormalize the buffer (remove any DC bias that may have crept in) and detect if the note is finished. On a slower system, you could remove the blending and make the usual case even faster.

LISTING 21.10 (CONTINUED)   PluckedStringNote Implementation

```
size_t PluckedStringNote::AddSamples(AudioSample *buffer,
      size_t samplesRequested) {
   int samplesRemaining = samplesRequested;
   while(samplesRemaining > 0) {
      // Blend smoothly between _buffer and _future
      long blendedSample =
            (_buffer[_pos] * _remaining
            + _future[_pos] * (_iterations - _remaining)
            )/_iterations;

      *buffer++ += blendedSample; // Play the sample
      samplesRemaining--;

      if(++_pos>=_bufferSize) { // Reached end of _buffer
         _pos = 0;   // reset to beginning
         if (--_remaining == 0) { // Time to re-process our data?
            long *t = _buffer;  // Swap buffers
            _buffer = _future;
            _future = t;

            // Filter _buffer into _future
            long lastSample = _buffer[_bufferSize-1];
            long average = 0;
            // Make divisor larger to decay faster
            long divisor = 1024 * (1 << static_cast<int>(10 * _decayRate));
            int i;
            for (i=0;i<_bufferSize;i++) {
                _future[i] = (_buffer[i]*512 + lastSample*512)/divisor;
                lastSample = _buffer[i];
```

```
                average += _future[i];
        }

        // Re-normalize _future and see if the note has faded out yet
        average /= _bufferSize;
        long total = 0;
        for(i=0;i<_bufferSize;i++) {
            _future[i] -= average;
            total += labs(_future[i]); // Accumulate total amplitude
        }

        // If nothing left, return now
        if (total == 0) return (samplesRequested - samplesRemaining);

        _remaining = _iterations; // Reset delay until next update
        }
    }
    }
    return (samplesRequested - samplesRemaining);
}
```

Testing Notes

The following short program tests the instrument and note classes I've developed in this chapter. It first defines a simple `AudioAbstract` class that plays some notes. The `main` function creates an instrument object and asks the `PlayInstrument` class to play one or more notes on that instrument. You can easily adapt this to test other instruments.

Note how `PlayInstrument` works with multiple notes. It zeroes the buffer before asking the various notes to add their samples to it. It also watches the return value from `AddSamples` to see if that note is finished; when a note is finished, it deletes the note object. Finally, it returns the maximum amount of buffer used. It does this to indicate when all the notes are finished.

Remember that few instruments stop playing immediately; most will have a brief decay period. It's important to continue to play each note even after calling `EndNote`.

Listing 21.16   playnote.cpp

```
#include "audio.h"
#include "aplayer.h"

// Try to select appropriate player for Win32, Macintosh, or UNIX/NAS
#if defined(_WIN32)
#include "winplayr.h"
typedef WinPlayer Player;
```

```
#elif defined(macintosh)
#include "macplayr.h"
typedef MacPlayer Player;
#else
#include "nasplayr.h"
typedef NasPlayer Player;
#endif

#include "instrumt.h"
#include "sampled.h"
#include "au.h"
#include "plucked.h"
#include <cstdlib>
#include <fstream>

class PlayInstrument:  public AudioAbstract {
private:
    long _samplesRemaining;
    AbstractInstrument *_instr;
    AbstractNote *_notes[5];
    float _pitches[5];
    float _volumes[5];
protected:
    void MinMaxChannels(int *min, int *max, int *preferred) {
        *min = *max = *preferred = 1;
    };
public:
    void Init() {
        _samplesRemaining = 44100 * 5; // Play for five seconds
        for(int i=0;i<5;i++) {
            _notes[i] = 0;
            _pitches[i] = _volumes[i] = 0;
        }
    }
    PlayInstrument(AbstractInstrument *instr) {
        Init(); _instr = instr;
    }
    void AddNote(float pitch, float volume) {
        int i=0;
        while(_pitches[i] != 0)
            i++;
        _pitches[i] = pitch;
        _volumes[i] = volume;
    }
    ~PlayInstrument() {
        for(int i=0;i<5;i++)
            if (_notes[i]) delete _notes[i];
    }
    size_t GetSamples(AudioSample *buffer, size_t numSamples) {
        for(size_t s=0; s<numSamples; s++) // Zero the buffer
            buffer[s] = 0;
        size_t maxSamples = 0;
        int i;
        for(i=0;i<5;i++) { // Create notes if necessary
            if(_pitches[i] && !_notes[i]) // Create note if necessary
                _notes[i] = _instr->NewNote(_pitches[i],_volumes[i]);
```

```
            }

        for(i=0;i<5;i++) { // Play each note into buffer
            if(_notes[i]) { // If this note exists, play it
                size_t samplesRead = 0;
                // If it's time for note to start decaying...
                if((_samplesRemaining >= 0)
                    && (static_cast<long>(numSamples) > _samplesRemaining)) {
                    _notes[i]->AddSamples(buffer,_samplesRemaining);
                    _notes[i]->EndNote(0.5); // Tell note to start decaying
                    samplesRead
                        = _samplesRemaining + _notes[i]->AddSamples(
                        buffer+_samplesRemaining,numSamples-_samplesRemaining);
                } else {
                    samplesRead = _notes[i]->AddSamples(buffer,numSamples);
                }
                if (samplesRead < numSamples) { // This note done
                    delete _notes[i]; // Delete it
                    _notes[i] = 0;
                    _pitches[i] = 0; // Don't recreate it!
                    _volumes[i] = 0; // Don't recreate it!
                }
                if (samplesRead > maxSamples)
                    maxSamples = samplesRead;
            }
        }
        _samplesRemaining -= numSamples;
        return maxSamples;
    };
    void SamplingRate(long rate) {
        AudioAbstract::SamplingRate(rate);
        _instr->SamplingRate(rate);
    };
};

int main(int argc, char **argv) {
    bool saveOutput = false;
    AbstractInstrument *instr = 0;
    argv++;  argc--; // Skip program name

    // Process command-line options
    while ((argc>0) && (**argv == '-')) {
        char *p=*argv;
        switch(p[1]) {
        case '0':  // Select instrument 0
            instr = new SineWaveInstrument;
            break;
        case '1':  // Select instrument 1
            instr = new PluckedStringInstrument;
            break;
        case 'p':  // Play output
            saveOutput = false;
            break;
        case 'a':  // Record output in AU file
            saveOutput = true;
            break;
```

```
        }
        argv++; argc--;
    }

    if(instr == 0) {instr = new SineWaveInstrument; }
    PlayInstrument pi(instr);

    if (argc == 0) { // Default is a just major triad
        pi.AddNote(330.0F, 0.3F);
        pi.AddNote(440.0F, 0.3F);
        pi.AddNote(550.0F, 0.3F);
    } else { // Pick notes/volumes from command line
        while (argc>0) {
            float volume = 1.0/((argc+1)/2);
            if(argc>1) {
                volume = atof(argv[1]);
                argc--;
            }
            pi.AddNote(atof(argv[0]),volume);
            argc--;
            argv+= 2;
        }
    }

    AbstractPlayer *player;
    if (saveOutput) { // Play output into AU file
        ofstream out("playnote.au");
        player = new AuWrite(&pi, out);
        player->Play();
        delete player;
    } else { // Play output to speaker
        player = new Player(&pi);
        player->Play();
        delete player;
    }
    delete instr;
    return 0;
}
```

MIDI

22

One of the gems of downtown Oakland, California, is the beautifully restored Paramount Theater, an Art Deco vaudeville and movie theater that first opened in 1931. The theater's Wurlitzer organ boasts a huge assortment of pipes, cymbals, gongs, and other sound-producing machines, discreetly hidden behind two large grates at the front of the theater. The most impressive aspect of this massive machinery may be that it's all controlled by one person sitting at a single keyboard console. Rows of small levers allow the organist to select and change sounds to match the mood of the song, whether it's a 17th-century canon or a 20th-century show tune.

Now picture the plight of a pop musician of the late 1970s. New electronic synthesizers are a marvel, providing instrument sounds and capabilities that were unavailable just a few years before. However, musicians who need a large variety of sounds encounter an obstacle—it's hard to use several keyboards at once. What was needed was some way to connect a single physical keyboard to a variety of different sound generators, much as a 1931 organist could play dozens of instruments from a single console.

One answer to this was the *Musical Instrument Digital Interface* (MIDI). MIDI provides a relatively simple way for a single keyboard to control a variety of instruments. You simply "daisy-chain" your instruments, connecting each instrument to the next one in the chain. When you press or release a key, a *MIDI event* is relayed from box to box. These events specify a *channel*, and only boxes programmed to respond to that channel will obey. By configuring your master keyboard to specify different channels for different ranges of notes, you can effectively play several instruments at once.

MIDI is a simple digital protocol and was rapidly incorporated into computer music applications. By connecting a computer to a keyboard through a MIDI connection, you get the musical equivalent of word processing. You can play the keyboard to enter music into the computer, edit it on the computer (using traditional music notation), and then play it back through the keyboard. The increasing popularity of MIDI in many areas of computer music has driven several important extensions.

In 1988, the *Standard MIDI File Format* was adopted by the members of the *MIDI Manufacturer's Association* (MMA; www.midi.org). This specified a way to store MIDI events, with appropriate timing information, in a computer file. Because many programs already supported MIDI for communicating with synthesizers, MIDI files rapidly became a common means for exchanging computer music.

MIDI files do not specify precise instrument sounds. MIDI was originally a wire protocol; the sound depended on which boxes you plugged in. But the use of MIDI files for exchanging music makes compatibility more important. If the same file sounds like a flute on your synthesizer and a piano on mine, then meaningful exchange of MIDI files is somewhat limited. As a result, the MMA also standardized *General MIDI*. General MIDI specifies 175 standard instrument sounds, as well as other common capabilities.

Today, Standard MIDI Files authored for General MIDI are a common way to store and distribute music. In Europe, floppy disks containing MIDI files are sold in music stores, along with cassette tapes and compact discs.

MIDI is continuing to evolve. By the end of 1997, the MMA will be publishing the *Downloadable Samples* standard (DLS-1). This provides a mechanism for creating new sounds and including them in a MIDI composition. MIDI is also used as the foundation for Internet music playback and other new kinds of music publishing.

Standard MIDI Files

A MIDI file is a sequence of chunks. These chunks have the same general format as the chunks used by AIFF, IFF, and WAVE; each chunk has a four-character type, a 4-byte length code (in MSB format), and some data. Unlike those other formats, however, MIDI chunks do not nest.

Currently, there are only two types of chunks. The `MThd` chunk contains general header information; an `MTrk` chunk contains a single track.

Identifying MIDI Files

The `MThd` chunk, which appears at the beginning of every MIDI file, is the best way to identify a Standard MIDI File.

LISTING 22.1   Identify MIDI File

```
#define ChunkName(a,b,c,d) (                       \
    ((static_cast<unsigned long>(a)&255)<<24)      \
  + ((static_cast<unsigned long>(b)&255)<<16)      \
  + ((static_cast<unsigned long>(c)&255)<<8)       \
  + ((static_cast<unsigned long>(d)&255)))

bool IsMidiFile(istream &file) {
  file.seekg(0); // Seek to beginning of file
```

```
        unsigned long form = ReadIntMsb(file,4);
        return (form == ChunkName('M','T','h','d'));
    }
```

MIDI Header Chunk

The `MThd` chunk contains a few basic facts about the MIDI file, as outlined in Table 22.1. All of these values are stored in MSB format.

TABLE 22.1   Contents of MIDI MThd Chunk

Bytes	Description
2	File type
2	Number of tracks
2	Time format

The musical information in a MIDI file is organized as several *tracks*. For example, a MIDI file might store the piano, trumpet, and flute parts as separate tracks. Although this complicates playback slightly, it makes it easier to use MIDI files to exchange musical scores.

There are three types of MIDI files, distinguished by how they deal with tracks. *Type zero* files contain only one track. These are clearly the easiest to play, and are preferred when you want to make sure your MIDI files are easy for other people to play. *Type one* files contain multiple tracks that are played simultaneously. A program to play type one files must somehow "flatten" the data into a single event stream before playing. Finally, *type two* files contain multiple tracks but without assuming any relation among the tracks. Type two files are relatively uncommon.

I'll explain the time format information in a little while, when I explore the broader issue of MIDI timing.

LISTING 22.2   Read MIDI Header Chunk

```
void MidiRead::ReadHeader(void) {
    unsigned long chunkType = ReadIntMsb(_stream,4);
    unsigned long bytesRemaining = ReadIntMsb(_stream,4);
    if (chunkType != ChunkName('M','T','h','d')) {
        cerr << "First chunk must be 'MThd' chunk\n";
        exit(1);
    }

    _fileType = ReadIntMsb(_stream,2);
    _numberTracks = ReadIntMsb(_stream,2);
    _timeFormat = ReadIntMsb(_stream,2);
```

```
      bytesRemaining -= 6;

      // Sanity check the file type and number of tracks
      switch(_fileType) {
      case 0:
         cerr << "Tracks:  1\n";
         if (_numberTracks != 1)
            cerr << "But it has " << _numberTracks << " tracks?!?!\n";
         break;
      case 1:
         cerr << "Tracks:  " << _numberTracks << " simultaneous.\n";
         break;
      case 2:
         cerr << "Tracks:  " << _numberTracks << " independent.\n";
         break;
      default:
         cerr << "Unknown file type:  " << _fileType << "\n";
      }

      // Dump time format
      if (_timeFormat < 0) { // SMPTE time code
         cerr << "Time Format:  " << _timeFormat << " (SMPTE)\n";
      } else { // duration time code
         cerr << "Time Format:  " << _timeFormat << " ticks/quarter note\n";
      }

      SkipBytes(_stream,bytesRemaining);
   }
```

MIDI Tracks

Note that a track is different from a MIDI channel. Although it's common for a
multi-track file to play each track on a different channel, composers are free to use as
many tracks as they want and to have tracks play instruments on different channels in
any fashion.

The format of a track is a simple list of MIDI events, each preceded by a *delta time*
value.

Variable-Length Integers

To conserve space, MIDI files use *variable-length integers* to store delta times and other
critical values. This allows common small values (such as zero) to be stored in a single
byte while allowing values of up to 32 bits.

The format stores 7 bits in each byte; the most significant bit indicates whether this
is the last byte (most significant bit is zero) or there are more bytes following (most

significant bit is 1). The following short piece of code reads a variable-length integer from an `istream`. It stores the number of bytes read in `*size`.

LISTING 22.3   Read Variable-Length Integers

```
static unsigned long ReadVarInt(istream &in, int *size) {
    *size = 0;
    unsigned long l, retVal = 0;
    do {
        l = static_cast<unsigned long>(in.get()) & 255;
        (*size)++;
        if (*size > 6) {
            cerr << "Unterminated variable integer\n";
            exit(1);
        }
        retVal = (retVal << 7) + (l & 0x7F);
    } while (l & 0x80);
    return retVal;
}
```

Delta Times

MIDI events occur at certain points in time. There are two ways to mark such information. You could store the absolute time at which each event occurs, or you could store the time intervals between events. MIDI files use the latter approach. Every event is preceded by a number indicating the number of *ticks* that separate it from the previous event. (See page 287 for more information about MIDI timing, including how to determine the duration of a tick.)

The precise duration of a tick depends on the time format specified in the header and may be changed by special events within the file.

Reading MIDI Tracks

As I've discussed, a MIDI track is a list of MIDI events, each preceded by a delta time. Each chunk in a MIDI file has a specified length, so you need to carefully track the number of bytes read so that you know when the track data is finished. If this is not the first track, you need to ensure that new events are properly inserted into the in-memory event list.

LISTING 22.4   Read MIDI Track Chunks

```
void MidiRead::ReadTracks() {
    int tracksRead = 0;
    // Read rest of chunks
    while (!_stream.eof() && (tracksRead < _numberTracks)) {
```

```
unsigned long chunkType = ReadIntMsb(_stream,4);
long bytesRemaining = ReadIntMsb(_stream,4);
if (_stream.eof()) continue; // Skip rest of loop

// If this isn't an MTrk chunk, skip it
if (chunkType != ChunkName('M','T','r','k')) {
   char name[5];
   name[0] = chunkType >> 24;      name[1] = chunkType >> 16;
   name[2] = chunkType >> 8;       name[3] = chunkType;
   name[4] = 0;
   cerr << "Unrecognized chunk '" << name << "'\n";
   SkipBytes(_stream,bytesRemaining);
   continue; // Back to top of while loop
}

tracksRead++;

// Only read first track in a Type 2 file
if ((_fileType == 2) & (tracksRead > 1)) {
   SkipBytes(_stream,bytesRemaining);
   continue;
}

MidiEvent *pLastEvent = 0;

while((bytesRemaining > 0)&&(!_stream.eof())) {
   MidiEvent *pEvent = new MidiEvent;
   pEvent->track = tracksRead;
```
```
   ┌─────────────────────────────────────────┐
   │ Read MIDI Event (Listing 22.8)          │
   └─────────────────────────────────────────┘
   ┌─────────────────────────────────────────┐
   │ Read System-Exclusive Event (Listing 22.9) │
   └─────────────────────────────────────────┘
   ┌─────────────────────────────────────────┐
   │ Read Meta Event (Listing 22.10)         │
   └─────────────────────────────────────────┘
   ┌─────────────────────────────────────────┐
   │ Insert MIDI Event into List (Listing 22.5) │
   └─────────────────────────────────────────┘
```
```
   if(bytesRemaining < 0) {
      cerr << "Contents of track chunk were too long.\n";
   }
   }
}
}
}
```

As with any list insertion code, inserting a MIDI event into the event list requires two cases; one if the event goes at the beginning of the list (in which case, you need to update the list head), and another if the event goes in the middle of the list (in which case, another next pointer gets updated).

This is complicated by the need to insert it at the correct temporal position and to adjust the delays appropriately.

LISTING 22.5   Insert MIDI Event into List

```
if (   !_events
       || (!pLastEvent && (_events->delay > pEvent->delay))) {
    // this event goes at front of list
    pEvent->next = _events;
    _events = pLastEvent = pEvent;
} else { // Doesn't go at beginning of list.
    if (!pLastEvent) { // Skip past first event in list
        pLastEvent = _events;
        pEvent->delay -= _events->delay;
    }
    // Skip earlier events
    while( pLastEvent->next
           && pLastEvent->next->delay <= pEvent->delay ) {
        pEvent->delay -= pLastEvent->next->delay;
        pLastEvent = pLastEvent->next;
    }
    // Splice into list
    pEvent->next = pLastEvent->next;
    pLastEvent->next = pEvent;
}
if (pEvent->next) // Reduce delay of next item, if any
    pEvent->next->delay -= pEvent->delay;
pLastEvent = pEvent; // Last event in this track
```

MIDI Events

A MIDI event is a packet of data that specifies some musical action, such as a key press or key release. The first byte of a packet is a *status byte*, which specifies the type of event and, when appropriate, the channel. Status bytes always have the high bit set. The remaining bytes are *data bytes*, which never have the high bit set. This distinction is important.

Table 22.2 summarizes the MIDI messages used in Standard MIDI Files. Note that events 0x80 through 0xEF use the least significant 4 bits to indicate the channel. Events 0xF0, 0xF7, and 0xFF have special meanings that I'll discuss later. Also note that these events are not identical to the events used by the MIDI wire protocol. In particular, the wire protocol uses 0xF7 and 0xFF differently, and defines a number of other status bytes above 0xF0.

Numbering Conventions

Traditionally, MIDI channels are numbered from 1 to 16, and MIDI instruments are numbered from 1 to 128. However, the numeric codes range from 0 to 15 and 0 to 127,

TABLE 22.2   MIDI Events as Used in Standard MIDI Files

Code (hex)	Description
8c nn vv	Note *nn* off with velocity *vv* on channel *c*
9c nn vv	Note *nn* on with velocity *vv* on channel *c*
Ac nn vv	*Polyphonic key pressure aftertouch*
	Change the pressure (usually vibrato) of note *nn* (that's already playing) on channel *c* to *vv*
Bc mm ss	Change mode *mm* on channel *c* to *ss*
Cc ii	*Program change*
	Select instrument sound *ii* for channel *c*
Dc vv	*Channel pressure aftertouch*
	Change the pressure of all notes playing on channel *c* to *vv*
Ec ff cc	*Pitch wheel change*
	Change the pitch of all notes playing on channel *c* by a certain proportion; *ff* holds the least significant 7 bits, *cc* the most significant
F0 length data	*System exclusive* (SOX)
	The *length* is a variable-length integer indicating the length of the following *data*.
F7 length data	*Special system exclusive*
	The *length* is a variable-length integer indicating the length of the following *data*.
FF tt length data	*Meta event of type* tt
	The *length* is a variable-length integer indicating the length of the following *data*.

respectively. You'll need to add or subtract 1 when converting between numeric codes and conventional MIDI language.

As a concrete example, the MIDI event 0xC0 0x00 selects instrument 1 (not 0) on channel 1 (not 0). Similarly, to select instrument 128 on channel 16, you send 0xCF 0xFF.

Running Status

To make the wire protocol more efficient, MIDI uses a technique called *running status*, which omits repeated status bytes. When reading MIDI files, if you see a data byte where you expect to see a status byte, you reuse the previous status.

As a concrete example, the hexadecimal values 0x90 0x3C 0x40 form a note-on event for note 0x3C (middle C) with average velocity. If the next event starts with 0x40, then because that is a data byte, you reuse the previous status 0x90; this must be another note-on event. By omitting the common status, chords can be transferred more quickly. It's heavily used in Standard MIDI Files because it saves disk space.

To make running status even more useful, there is a convention that a note-on event with a velocity of zero is the same as a note-off event with a default velocity of 64. As a result, a long chain of notes on a single channel can be controlled with just 2 bytes per event.

Managing MIDI Events

The fact that MIDI data is inherently time-based influences how I read that data. In particular, MIDI files are often stored as separate tracks. Although the events in each track are stored in temporal order, the event stream that gets played is the combination of all these tracks. Also, events in one track (such as tempo changes) affect the playback of events in other tracks.

As a result, for type one files, you must read all the events into memory before you play them. To accomplish this, I store a single linked list of MIDI events.

LISTING 22.6   MIDI Event List Variables

```
private:
    MidiEvent *_events; // List of all MIDI events in song
    MidiEvent *_currentEvent; // Current event being processed
```

Most events consist of a status byte and a couple of data bytes. I must also store the delay value and the track number on which this event occurred.

Some special MIDI events can contain arbitrary amounts of data, so I provide an additional structure to hold that data when it is needed.

LISTING 22.7   MIDI Event Structure

```
struct MidiExtendedEventData {
    long length;
    AudioByte *data;
    // Constructor and destructor
    MidiExtendedEventData() { data = 0; }
    ~MidiExtendedEventData() { if (data) delete [] data; }
};

struct MidiEvent {
    MidiEvent *next;
    unsigned long delay; // Delay since previous event
```

```
      unsigned char track; // Number of track for this event
      unsigned char status; // Event status byte
      unsigned char data[2]; // Data for MIDI event
      MidiExtendedEventData *metaData; // Long data for system messages, etc.

      MidiEvent() { // Constructor
         next = 0;
         metaData = 0;
         delay = track = status = 0;
      }
      ~MidiEvent() { // Destructor
         if(metaData) delete metaData;
      }
   };
```

Reading MIDI Events

Most MIDI events have a fixed length. For example, a note-on event always has 2 data bytes following the status. I use a short table to simplify reading most events. To handle running status, I keep a pointer pLastEvent that points to the last event read from this track.

LISTING 22.8   Read MIDI Event

```
   {  static const char eventLength[] = {
      2, 2, 2, 2, 2, 2, 2, 2, 2, 2, 2, 2, 2, 2, 2, 2,   // 0x80 - 0x8F
      2, 2, 2, 2, 2, 2, 2, 2, 2, 2, 2, 2, 2, 2, 2, 2,   // 0x90 - 0x9F
      2, 2, 2, 2, 2, 2, 2, 2, 2, 2, 2, 2, 2, 2, 2, 2,   // 0xA0 - 0xAF
      2, 2, 2, 2, 2, 2, 2, 2, 2, 2, 2, 2, 2, 2, 2, 2,   // 0xB0 - 0xBF
      1, 1, 1, 1, 1, 1, 1, 1, 1, 1, 1, 1, 1, 1, 1, 1,   // 0xC0 - 0xCF
      1, 1, 1, 1, 1, 1, 1, 1, 1, 1, 1, 1, 1, 1, 1, 1,   // 0xD0 - 0xDF
      2, 2, 2, 2, 2, 2, 2, 2, 2, 2, 2, 2, 2, 2, 2, 2,   // 0xE0 - 0xEF
      0, 0, 2, 1, 0, 0, 0, 0, 0, 0, 0, 0, 0, 0, 0, 0,   // 0xF0 - 0xFF
      };

      int sizeRead;
      pEvent->delay = ReadVarInt(_stream,&sizeRead);
      bytesRemaining -= sizeRead; // Count the delta time
      int dataRead = 0;    // Number of bytes of data read so far
      int byte = _stream.get();
      bytesRemaining--;   // Count this byte
      if (byte >= 0x80) { // this is a new status
         pEvent->status = byte;
      } else { // running status
         pEvent->status = pLastEvent->status; // re-use last status
         pEvent->data[dataRead++] = byte; // this is first data byte
      }
      while(dataRead < eventLength[pEvent->status - 0x80]) {
         pEvent->data[dataRead++] = _stream.get();
         bytesRemaining--;
      }
   }
```

Sysex Events

The 0xF0 event is used to transfer a variety of special commands, referred to as *System-Exclusive messages* or *sysex events*. The general format is given in Table 22.3.

These events are handled differently in Standard MIDI Files than they are in the wire protocol. In a Standard MIDI File, as shown in Table 22.2, the 0xF0 status value is followed by a length value and a corresponding amount of data. As a result, a sysex event can contain any byte value.

In the wire protocol, there is no length value. The end of the data is found only by detecting the next status value. Every data byte of a sysex event will have the high bit cleared. Also, note that running status cannot be used with sysex events.

In a MIDI file, 0xF7 events provide an escape mechanism to allow arbitrary binary data to be included. The format is similar to that of a 0xF0 sysex event. If you send a MIDI file out to a MIDI synthesizer, the data portion of a 0xF7 event should be dumped to the synthesizer, but the 0xF7 status byte itself is not sent. This is useful for synthesizers that place timing requirements on sysex events. With such synthesizers, you can use a single 0xF0 event to store the first part of the sysex and then use successive 0xF7 events to store successive portions, with suitable delays between the parts. Because of the system-specific nature of 0xF7 events, they're fairly uncommon in Standard MIDI Files.

TABLE 22.3   Format of System-Exclusive Message

Bytes	Description
1	Status byte 0xF0 (start of system exclusive—SOX)
m	Length of following data (only in MIDI file), stored as a variable-length integer
1–3	Manufacturer ID If the first byte is zero, this is a 3-byte ID; otherwise, it's a single-byte ID. 0x7D is reserved for experimental use, 0x7E is used for standard non-real-time messages, 0x7F is used for standard real-time messages.
n	Data bytes Like all MIDI events, all data bytes in a sysex message (including the manufacturer ID, above) have the upper bit set to zero.
1	Status byte 0xF7 (end of system exclusive—EOX) Although any status byte, except real-time events, marks the end of a SOX message, it's recommended that 0xF7 be included after such a message.

In the wire protocol, the 0xF7 status value has no data and performs no action. It is conventionally used to mark the end of a sysex event, although any status value could serve the same purpose. It's conventional in MIDI files to include a 0xF7 byte as the last data byte in a 0xF0 sysex event. If a sysex event is broken across multiple MIDI file events using the 0xF7 escape mechanism, this trailing 0xF7 byte is included only in the last event.

LISTING 22.9   Read System-Exclusive Event

```
// Read a sysex event from _stream:
//  * store event into pEvent structure
//  * decrease bytesRemaining appropriately
if (   (pEvent->status == 0xF0)
    || (pEvent->status == 0xF7) ) {
  int sizeRead;
  unsigned long msgLength = ReadVarInt(_stream,&sizeRead);
  bytesRemaining-= sizeRead;
  pEvent->metaData = new MidiExtendedEventData;
  pEvent->metaData->length = msgLength;
  pEvent->metaData->data = new AudioByte[msgLength];
  _stream.read(reinterpret_cast<char *>(pEvent->metaData->data),
               msgLength);
  bytesRemaining-= msgLength;
}
```

Meta Events

A musical score is more than a list of timed notes. MIDI files must also somehow carry information such as key signatures and copyright notices. Standard MIDI files use special *meta events* to specify this information. Many meta events occur at the beginning of a track, although they can appear anywhere. For example, many compositions change key signature in the middle of the piece, so there might be many key signature meta events scattered through the file.

By convention, in a type one file, the first track is reserved exclusively for certain meta events. For example, key signatures, time signatures, and tempo information are stored only in the first track. Many other meta events—including track name and track sequence number—should occur only at the beginning of their tracks. Meta events do not exist in the MIDI wire protocol (although sysex events have been added to the wire protocol to duplicate many of these functions).

Within the file, meta events are stored much like sysex events. Instead of a single 0xF0 or 0xF7 byte, a meta event begins with 0xFF and a type byte, followed by the length and data.

LISTING 22.10   Read Meta Event

```
// Read a meta event from _stream:
//   * store event into pEvent structure
//   * decrease bytesRemaining appropriately
if (pEvent->status == 0xFF) {
    pEvent->data[0] = _stream.get(); // Meta event type
    bytesRemaining -= 1;
    int sizeRead;
    unsigned long msgLength = ReadVarInt(_stream,&sizeRead);
    bytesRemaining -= sizeRead;
    pEvent->metaData = new MidiExtendedEventData;
    pEvent->metaData->length = msgLength;
    pEvent->metaData->data = new AudioByte[msgLength+1];
    _stream.read(reinterpret_cast<char *>(pEvent->metaData->data),
                msgLength);
    bytesRemaining -= msgLength;
    pEvent->metaData->data[msgLength] = 0; // Add null terminator

    Dump Meta Event (Listing 22.11)

}
```

Track Sequence Number Meta Event (Type 0)

This meta event contains a 2-byte (16-bit) value, which is used by some systems to identify and select musical sequences. In a type zero or type one file, this always appears at the beginning of the first track. In a type two file, which can contain multiple independent sequences, it may appear at the beginning of any track.

Text Meta Events (Types 1 through 15)

Meta event types 1 through 15 are used to store text comments. Like any meta event, they are stored in the file as 0xFF *type len data*. Table 22.4 lists the currently defined text meta events.

LISTING 22.11   Dump Meta Event

```
if(pEvent->data[0] == 3) {
    cerr << "Track " << static_cast<int>(pEvent->track) << ": ";
    cerr << reinterpret_cast<char *>(pEvent->metaData->data) << "\n";
} else if (pEvent->data[0] < 16) {
    const char *textPrefix[] = { "",
        "Comment: ", "Copyright: ", "Track Name: ",
        "Instrument Name ", "Lyric: ", "Marker: ",
        "Cue Point: ", "Text: ", "Text: ", "Text: ",
        "Text: ", "Text: ", "Text: ", "Text: ", "Text: "};
    cerr << textPrefix[ pEvent->data[0] ];
    cerr << reinterpret_cast<char *>(pEvent->metaData->data) << "\n";
}
```

TABLE 22.4   Text Meta Events

Meta Event	Description
1	Comment
2	Copyright notice
3	Track name
4	Instrument name
5	Lyric
6	Marker
7	Cue point
8–15	Undefined

End of Track Meta Event (Type 47)

Meta event type 47 marks the end of a MIDI track; it contains no data.

It may not be immediately obvious why you need a special event to mark the end of the MIDI stream. The real purpose of the end-of-track event is to hold a delay value. Some MIDI files, especially those that are meant to be played repeatedly, require a pause after the end of the piece. The only way to ensure a silent interval after the last note finishes is to add another event. Although the actual event used doesn't matter (it could just as easily be a meaningless program or mode change), the end-of-track meta event is provided for this purpose.

Tempo Meta Event (Type 81)

Meta event type 81 sets the playback speed. The MIDI header specifies the duration of a tick in terms of the length of a *MIDI quarter note*. The data is 3 bytes that specify the number of microseconds per MIDI quarter note. (See below for more information on MIDI timing.)

Time Signature (Type 88)

A time signature meta event contains 4 bytes of data. The first 2 indicate the musical time signature, such as 3/4 or 6/8. The numerator is stored directly, the second indicates the power of 2. For example, 6/8 time is represented by the two bytes 6 and 3 ($2^3 = 8$). The third byte specifies the number of *MIDI clocks* per metronome click. A MIDI clock is 1/24 of a MIDI quarter note, and the duration of a MIDI quarter note is specified by tempo meta events. The fourth byte specifies how the music should be written. A MIDI quarter note may not correspond to a quarter note in sheet music; this value represents the number of notated 32nd notes in one MIDI quarter note.

Key Signature Meta Event (Type 89)

The first byte indicates the number of sharps (if positive) or flats (if negative), the second indicates whether this is a major (0) or minor (1) key. C Major, for instance, is represented as 0 0.

Sequencer-Specific Meta Events (Type 127)

A sequencer-specific meta event allows MIDI manufacturers to add custom data to a MIDI file. To avoid confusion, the first byte identifies the manufacturer (if the first byte is zero, the first 3 bytes identify the manufacturer). Microsoft, for example, uses a sequencer-specific meta event to mark MPC-compatible MIDI files with manufacturer ID 0 0 65.

MIDI Timing

The first step in playing a MIDI file is to translate the delta time tick counts into something more useful. MIDI files use two techniques to specify the duration of a tick. If the time format code in the header chunk is negative, the MIDI file specifies the tick rate using *SMPTE* conventions. If the time format code is positive, it uses musical tempo to specify the tick rate.

LISTING 22.12   Compute Default Samples Per Tick

```
if (_timeFormat < 0) {          // SMPTE Time format
    Compute Default Samples Per Tick Using SMPTE Conventions (Listing 22.13)
} else {                        // Musical Time Format
    Compute Default Samples Per Tick Using Musical Conventions (Listing 22.14)
}
```

SMPTE-Based Timing

The Society of Motion Picture and Television Engineers (SMPTE) uses a standard technique for precisely specifying times. This technique counts the passage of hours, minutes, seconds, and *frames*. A frame is the duration of a single frame in a motion picture or television display and ranges from 1/24 to 1/30 of a second. This technique is widely used by video and audio engineers and is an important tool for precisely synchronizing the playback of video and audio sources.

To use SMPTE timing, you first need to specify the number of frames per second. SMPTE times are then expressed as four values, usually written as 01:23:43:21 (1 hour, 23 minutes, 43 seconds, 21 frames), expressing an elapsed time.

Intuitively, there are three primary SMPTE formats: 24 frames per second is used by motion picture equipment, 25 frames per second is used by PAL and SECAM television equipment (used in Europe and Asia), and 30 frames per second is used by black-and-white NTSC television equipment (used in North America and Japan). The odd one is NTSC color television. When the National Television Systems Committee (NTSC) adopted a color television standard, it was necessary for technical reasons to slightly change the frame rate. The value they chose was 29.97 frames per second. Because this is not an integer, you can't specify hour:minute:second:frame unless you fudge some. SMPTE has adopted a standard fudge factor for NTSC color synchronization: There are 30 frames in every second—but the first second of a minute has only 28 frames and the first second of every tenth minute has 30 frames. As a result, 1:03:58:29 is immediately followed by 1:03:59:00, but 1:03:59:29 is immediately followed by 1:03:00:02 (drop two frames at the beginning of every minute). This method of counting time is referred to as *drop-frame* format. (Technically, the length of a frame is always the same. The SMPTE drop-frame time format varies the lengths of seconds and minutes so that, on average, the SMPTE time agrees with "wall-clock time.")

You specify SMPTE timing in a MIDI file by putting an appropriate 16-bit time format code into the header. The upper 8 bits are a negative number (to indicate SMPTE conventions). The precise value indicates the format, with the convention that 29 refers to drop-frame format. The lower 8 bits indicate the number of ticks per frame.

LISTING 22.13   Compute Default Samples Per Tick Using SMPTE Conventions

```
int frameCode = (-_timeFormat) >> 8;
float framesPerSecond;
switch(frameCode) {
case 24:  framesPerSecond = 24.0; break;
case 25:  framesPerSecond = 25.0; break;
case 29:  framesPerSecond = 29.97F; break; // "drop-frame" format
case 30:  framesPerSecond = 30.0; break;
default:
   cerr << "Illegal SMPTE frame code.\n";
   framesPerSecond = 30.0;
   break;
}
int ticksPerFrame = _timeFormat & 0xFF;
samplesPerTick =
     SamplingRate()         // samples per second
   / framesPerSecond
   / ticksPerFrame;
```

Tempo-Based Timing

While SMPTE timing is convenient for motion picture and television synchronization, most musicians prefer to specify a *tempo*, usually in *beats per minute* (bpm). A beat often corresponds to a quarter note. The tempo typically varies from 80 bpm to 200 bpm; the MIDI default is 120 bpm.

With this format, the MIDI header specifies a positive number indicating the number of ticks per beat.

LISTING 22.14   Compute Default Samples Per Tick Using Musical Conventions

```
samplesPerTick =
   60.0 / 120  // Default is 120 quarter notes per minute
   * SamplingRate()     // samples per second
   / _timeFormat;       // Ticks/quarter note
```

The advantage of this format for musicians is that the tempo can be varied during the piece by inserting tempo meta events. The data for the tempo meta event is a 3-byte number specifying the number of microseconds (millionths of a second) per beat.

LISTING 22.15   Process Tempo Meta Events

```
if (   (pEvent->status == 0xFF)     // meta event
   && (pEvent->data[0] == 0x51)) { // Tempo meta event
   // argument is microseconds per beat
   float beatsPerSecond =  1.0E6
        / BytesToIntMsb(pEvent->metaData->data,3);
   if (_timeFormat > 0) { // ''musical'' time specification
      samplesPerTick =
         SamplingRate()   // samples per second
         / beatsPerSecond
         / _timeFormat;   // ticks per beat
   }
}
```

One of the most confusing aspects of MIDI timing is the large number of different terms used.

MIDI tick The delta-time values within a Standard MIDI file are specified in *ticks*.

MIDI clock A *MIDI clock* is 1/24 of a MIDI quarter note.

MIDI quarter note The duration of a MIDI quarter note (in milliseconds) is specified by a tempo meta event (see page 286). The Standard MIDI file header relates MIDI quarter notes to MIDI ticks.

Musical quarter note A MIDI quarter note is purely a timing convention; usually it corresponds to a quarter note as written in sheet music, but not always. A time signature meta event (see page 286) specifies the correct relationship.

Tempo Musical *tempo* is traditionally measured in beats per minute. Typically, a beat corresponds to a musical quarter note.

Metronome The appropriate metronome rate for this piece is specified by a time signature meta event (see page 286).

TABLE 22.5   General MIDI Melody Instruments

Piano		*Bass*		*Reed*		*Synth Effects*	
1	Acoustic grand piano	33	Acoustic bass	65	Soprano sax	97	FX 1 (rain)
2	Bright acoustic piano	34	Electric bass (finger)	66	Alto sax	98	FX 2 (soundtrack)
3	Electric grand piano	35	Electric bass (pick)	67	Tenor sax	99	FX 3 (crystal)
4	Honky-tonk piano	36	Fretless bass	68	Baritone sax	100	FX 4 (atmosphere)
5	Electric piano 1	37	Slap bass 1	69	Oboe	101	FX 5 (brightness)
6	Electric piano 2	38	Slap bass 2	70	English horn	102	FX 6 (goblins)
7	Harpsichord	39	Synth bass 1	71	Bassoon	103	FX 7 (echoes)
8	Clavinet	40	Synth bass 2	72	Clarinet	104	FX 8 (sci-fi)
Chromatic Percussion		*Strings*		*Pipe*		*Ethnic*	
9	Celesta	41	Violin	73	Piccolo	105	Sitar
10	Glockenspiel	42	Viola	74	Flute	106	Banjo
11	Music box	43	Cello	75	Recorder	107	Shamisen
12	Vibraphone	44	Contrabass	76	Pan flute	108	Koto
13	Marimba	45	Tremolo strings	77	Blown bottle	109	Kalimba
14	Xylophone	46	Pizzicato strings	78	Shakuhachi	110	Bagpipe
15	Tubular bells	47	Orchestral harp	79	Whistle	111	Fiddle
16	Dulcimer	48	Timpani	80	Ocarina	112	Shanai
Organ		*Ensemble*		*Synth Lead*		*Percussive*	
17	Drawbar organ	49	String ensemble 1	81	Lead 1 (square)	113	Tinkle bell
18	Percussive organ	50	String ensemble 2	82	Lead 2 (sawtooth)	114	Agogo
19	Rock organ	51	SynthStrings 1	83	Lead 3 (calliope)	115	Steel drums
20	Church organ	52	SynthStrings 2	84	Lead 4 (chiff)	116	Woodblock
21	Reed organ	53	Choir aahs	85	Lead 5 (charang)	117	Taiko drum
22	Accordion	54	Voice oohs	86	Lead 6 (voice)	118	Melodic tom
23	Harmonica	55	Synth voice	87	Lead 7 (fifths)	119	Synth drum
24	Tango accordion	56	Orchestra hit	88	Lead 8 (bass+lead)	120	Reverse cymbal
Guitar		*Brass*		*Synth Pad*		*Sound Effects*	
25	Acoustic guitar (nylon)	57	Trumpet	89	Pad 1 (new age)	121	Guitar fret noise
26	Acoustic guitar (steel)	58	Trombone	90	Pad 2 (warm)	122	Breath noise
27	Electric guitar (jazz)	59	Tuba	91	Pad 3 (polysynth)	123	Seashore
28	Electric guitar (clean)	60	Muted trumpet	92	Pad 4 (choir)	124	Bird tweet
29	Electric guitar (mute)	61	French horn	93	Pad 5 (bowed)	125	Telephone ring
30	Overdriven guitar	62	Brass section	94	Pad 6 (metallic)	126	Helicopter
31	Distortion guitar	63	SynthBrass 1	95	Pad 7 (halo)	127	Applause
32	Guitar harmonics	64	SynthBrass 2	96	Pad 8 (sweep)	128	Gunshot

General MIDI

You can't generally expect different synthesizers to react identically to commands. Although this does allow vendors to distinguish their instruments (one vendor might have a distinctive piano sound, for instance), it leads to some frustration for musicians.

General MIDI is an attempt to deal with some of the fundamental incompatibilities. MIDI products (software and hardware) that claim to be compliant with General MIDI must satisfy certain requirements.

- Channels 1 through 9 and 11 through 16 are the General MIDI *melody channels*. These channels must respond to a program-change event by selecting one of the 128 instruments given in Table 22.5.

- Channel 10 (the *rhythm channel*) must support the 47 instrument sounds specified in Table 22.6. These sounds are all the result of a program change to instrument 1.

- The product must support 16 simultaneous notes on the melody channels and 8 simultaneous notes on the rhythm channel.

- General MIDI products must support a collection of other capabilities, including certain controllers (modulation, volume, pan, expression, sustain, reset all

TABLE 22.6   General MIDI Rhythm Instruments

Note	Description	Note	Description	Note	Description
35	Acoustic bass drum	51	Ride cymbal 1	67	High agogo
36	Bass drum 1	52	Chinese cymbal	68	Low agogo
37	Side stick	53	Ride bell	69	Cabasa
38	Acoustic snare	54	Tambourine	70	Maracas
39	Hand clap	55	Splash cymbal	71	Short whistle
40	Electric snare	56	Cowbell	72	Long whistle
41	Low floor tom	57	Crash cymbal 2	73	Short guiro
42	Closed hi-hat	58	Vibraslap	74	Long guiro
43	High floor tom	59	Ride cymbal 2	75	Claves
44	Pedal hi-hat	60	Hi bongo	76	Hi wood block
45	Low tom	61	Low bongo	77	Low wood block
46	Open hi-hat	62	Mute hi conga	78	Mute cuica
47	Low-mid tom	63	Open hi conga	79	Open cuica
48	Hi-mid tom	64	Low conga	80	Mute triangle
49	Crash cymbal 1	65	High timbale	81	Open triangle
50	High tom	66	Low timbale		

controllers, and all notes off), parameters (pitch bend sensitivity, fine and coarse tuning), channel aftertouch, and pitch bend.

Note that the melody and rhythm channels support fundamentally different kinds of instrument selections. To select an instrument on a melody channel, you send a MIDI program-change event to select the instrument and then send note-on and note-off events to play notes on that instrument. However, this approach makes little sense with percussion instruments that have only a single note. To play a percussion instrument, you select the first instrument on the rhythm channel and play the corresponding note.

There has been interest in further standardizing the General MIDI requirements. For example, General MIDI only names the 175 standard instruments; it makes no attempt to give a more precise characterization. It also does not specify how instruments should handle note or channel velocity information. For example, one synthesizer could interpret channel velocity linearly while another might interpret it logarithmically. However, the MMA has produced a *General MIDI Developer Guidelines and Survey* that surveys common practice and gives many recommendations for people interested in implementing the General MIDI specification.

Downloadable Samples

The new *Downloadable Samples Standard Level 1.0* (DLS-1) specifies a way to store MIDI instrument sounds in a file. This file, called a *DLS file*, stores one or more instrument samples together with a variety of information about how these samples should be played. The detailed file format is based on WAVE.

One part of the DLS-1 standard deserves special attention. The DLS file format specifies a number of parameters detailing how this instrument sample should be played. This implicitly defines a detailed model for playing sampled instruments. The core idea is the same as I used for my SampledInstrument class in the previous chapter, but the DLS model adds several refinements:

- A pan response for left-right stereo positioning of the output;

- A *low-frequency oscillator* that provides vibrato and tremolo control;

- An envelope generator that varies the amplitude over time;

- A second envelope generator that varies the pitch over time;

- Support for fine tune, sustain, pitch bending, modulation wheel, volume, and expression controls.

A MIDI Player

In a sense, all the classes I've presented for reading audio files are interpreters. The `WaveRead` class, for instance, interprets the header and compression information to produce a stream of `AudioSample` values.

The instructions that a MIDI player must interpret are more complex, and the `MidiRead` class in this chapter reflects that complexity.

My code works in three passes. The first pass reads the tracks into memory. You've already seen most of that code. The second pass post-processes the event stream to simplify the playback. The third pass is the actual playback.

The playback process involves a number of objects. The most obvious is the `MidiRead` object, which is used by other parts of the program. It satisfies requests for `GetSamples`.

To satisfy those requests, the `MidiRead` object scans the event list and passes requests to the channel objects—the real heart of the playback. My MIDI player consists of 16 synthesizers, one for each channel. The `MidiRead` object stores the MIDI score and uses it to drive the channels, which are responsible for creating and managing the note objects that actually create sound. Each channel adds together the output of the notes, and the `MidiRead` object adds together the output of the channels to obtain the final sound.

The channels share some resources. Channel objects must eventually obtain instrument objects (see Chapter 21) and use them to create the notes. I've created a single `MidiInstrumentMap` object that keeps track of the various instrument objects, and a `MidiTuningMap` object that knows how to translate MIDI note values into absolute pitches.

LISTING 22.16 midi.h

Copyright © 1998, Tim Kientzle (Listing E.1)

```
#ifndef MIDI_H_INCLUDED
#define MIDI_H_INCLUDED
#include "audio.h"
#include "instrumt.h"
#include "sampled.h"
#include "plucked.h"
#include <iostream>
#include <cmath>

bool IsMidiFile(istream &file);

class MidiRead;
```

MIDI Instrument Map (Listing 22.26)

MIDI Tuning Map (Listing 22.25)

MIDI Channel Object (Listing 22.23)

MIDI Event Structure (Listing 22.7)

```
class MidiRead: public AudioAbstract {
private:
   // Information about song being played
   MidiInstrumentMap *_instrumentMap;
   MidiTuningMap *_tuningMap;
   MidiChannelAbstract *_channel[16];
public:
   MidiInstrumentMap *InstrumentMap() { return _instrumentMap; }
   MidiTuningMap *TuningMap() { return _tuningMap; }

private:
   int _fileType; // Standard MIDI file type
   int _numberTracks; // Number of tracks
   int _timeFormat; // Time Format code

   unsigned long _samplesRemaining; // Samples remaining until next event
```

MIDI Event List Variables (Listing 22.6)

```
private:
   // General information
   void ReadTracks(); // Read File into memory
   void ReadHeader(); // Read File into memory
   void PostProcess(); // Post-process event stream
   istream &_stream; // File being read
public:
   MidiRead(istream &input = cin);
   ~MidiRead();
protected:
   void MinMaxSamplingRate(long *min, long *max, long *preferred) {
      *min = *max = *preferred = 11025;
   }
   void MinMaxChannels(int *min, int *max, int *preferred) {
      *min = *max = *preferred = 1;
   }
   size_t GetSamples(AudioSample *buffer, size_t numSamples);
};
#endif
```

LISTING 22.17   midi.cpp

Copyright © 1998, Tim Kientzle (Listing E.1)

```
#include <cstring>
```

```
#include <istream>
#include <cstdio>
#include <cmath>

#include "audio.h"
#include "instrumt.h"
#include "sampled.h"
#include "plucked.h"
#include "midi.h"
```

> Identify MIDI File (Listing 22.1)

> MIDI Instrument Map Methods (Listing 22.27)

> Read Variable-Length Integers (Listing 22.3)

> MIDI Channels (Listing 22.24)

> Read MIDI Header Chunk (Listing 22.2)

> Read MIDI Track Chunks (Listing 22.4)

> Post-Process MIDI Event Stream (Listing 22.18)

> Play MIDI Events (Listing 22.21)

```
// Read file
MidiRead::MidiRead(istream &s):AudioAbstract(), _stream(s) {
   cerr << "File Format:  MIDI\n";
   _currentEvent = _events = 0;
   for(int i=0;i<16;i++) _channel[i] = 0;
   _instrumentMap = new MidiInstrumentMap;
   _tuningMap = new MidiTuningMap;
}

MidiRead::~MidiRead() {
   MidiEvent *pEvent, *pNext = _events;
   while (pNext) { // Delete event list
      pEvent = pNext;
      pNext = pEvent->next;
      delete pEvent;
   }
   for(int i=0; i< 16; i++) { // Delete channel objects
      if (_channel[i])
         delete _channel[i];
   }
   delete _instrumentMap; // Delete instrument map
   delete _tuningMap; // Delete tuning map
};
```

Post-Processing the MIDI Event Stream

Once you've read the MIDI file and appropriately interleaved all of the events from the tracks, it is worthwhile to make one quick pass over the event stream to simplify the upcoming playback. This can't be done during the file read because I need to process the event stream in temporal order.

Rather than juggle the MIDI timing information during playback, I take this opportunity to convert all the delays to sample counts. This change simplifies the bookkeeping in `GetSamples`. A given event delay is unlikely to translate into an exact number of audio samples. I'm careful here to carry over fractional samples so that the overall timing remains accurate.

I also use this opportunity to collect some statistics about the MIDI event stream. I keep track of note volumes and identify the maximum total volume in the piece. With this information, I can scale the playback amplitude to avoid overflow. To simplify things, I'm not tracking Master Volume, Channel Volume, or Expression here. (*Expression* is a temporary change of channel volume used for emphasis.)

LISTING 22.18   Post-Process MIDI Event Stream

```
void MidiRead::PostProcess() {
  cerr << "Analyzing MIDI file . . . ";
  double samplesPerTick; // Samples to play for each MIDI tick
  double samplesRemainingFraction; // fractional samples left over

  ┌─────────────────────────────────────────────────────┐
  │ Compute Default Samples Per Tick (Listing 22.12)      │
  └─────────────────────────────────────────────────────┘

  samplesRemainingFraction = 0.0;

  // For finding the maximum volume
  long currentVolume = 0;
  long maxTotalVolume = 0;
  long simultaneousNotes = 0;
  long maxSimultaneousNotes = 0;
  char volume[16][128]; // Volume of each playing note
  for(int i=0;i<16;i++)
    for(int j=0;j<128;j++)
      volume[i][j] = 0;

  // For finding out which channels are being used
  bool possible[16];
  bool active[16];
  for(int j=0;j<16;j++) {
    active[j] = false;
    possible[j] = true;
  }

  MidiEvent *pEvent = _events;
  MidiEvent *pLastEvent = 0;
```

```
while(pEvent) {
    // Convert delay from ticks to audio samples
    if (pEvent->delay > 0) {
        float samples = pEvent->delay * samplesPerTick
            + samplesRemainingFraction;
        pEvent->delay = static_cast<unsigned long>(samples);
        samplesRemainingFraction = samples - pEvent->delay;
    }

    // Track maximum volume
    int ch = pEvent->status & 0x0F;
    switch(pEvent->status & 0xF0) {
    case 0x90:
        if ((pEvent->data[1] != 0) && possible[ch]) {
            active[ch] = true; // This channel is used
            if (volume[ch][ pEvent->data[0] ]) { // Note already on?!?!
                // Turn it off before starting over...
                currentVolume -= volume[ch][ pEvent->data[0] ];
                simultaneousNotes--;
            }
            volume[ch][ pEvent->data[0] ] = pEvent->data[1];
            currentVolume += volume[ch][ pEvent->data[0] ];
            if (currentVolume > maxTotalVolume)
                maxTotalVolume = currentVolume;
            simultaneousNotes++;
            if (simultaneousNotes > maxSimultaneousNotes)
                maxSimultaneousNotes = simultaneousNotes;
            break;
        }
        // Note on with zero velocity is really a note off
        // Convert it into a real note off
        pEvent->status = 0x80 | ch;
        pEvent->data[1] = 64; // With average velocity
        // Fall through and process it as a Note Off
    case 0x80:
        currentVolume -= volume[ch][ pEvent->data[0] ];
        simultaneousNotes--;
        volume[ch][ pEvent->data[0] ] = 0;
        break;
    }
```

> Check for MPC MIDI (Listing 22.20)

> Process Tempo Meta Events (Listing 22.15)

```
    pLastEvent = pEvent;
    pEvent = pEvent->next;
}
cerr << ". . done.\n";
cerr << "Maximum Simultaneous Notes:  " << maxSimultaneousNotes << "\n";
cerr << "Maximum Total volume:  " << maxTotalVolume << "\n";
cerr << "\n";
```

> Initialize Channels (Listing 22.19)

```
    // Set sampling rate on the instrument map
    _instrumentMap->SamplingRate(SamplingRate());
}
```

The configuration of channels depends on the file. To speed up playback, I set any unused channels to use a special `MidiChannelSilent` object, which does no playback but is very fast. Channels that are used but have not already been initialized are set to use the General MIDI defaults.

LISTING 22.19   Initialize Channels

```
{
    // Fill up empty channels
    for(int ch=0; ch< 16; ch++) {
        if (_channel[ch]) continue; // Already there!
        if (!active[ch])
            _channel[ch] = new MidiChannelSilent();
        else {
            int instrumentSet;
            if (ch==10) instrumentSet = MidiInstrumentMap::gmRhythmBank;
            else        instrumentSet = MidiInstrumentMap::gmMelodyBank;
            _channel[ch] = new MidiChannelStandard(
                                this,
                                instrumentSet,
                                1.0/maxTotalVolume);
        }
    }
}
```

Although this post-processing step does simplify some things, it has one serious drawback. Many people are now experimenting with MIDI as a way to stream music data over the Internet. This works well because MIDI streams are pretty compact, which reduces bandwidth problems. The approach I've used here doesn't allow such streaming because it requires you to read the entire event stream before you start playing.

Base and Extended MIDI

To simplify things for PC hardware vendors, the Multimedia PC (MPC) specification originally published by Microsoft defines two levels of MIDI capability. The idea is that low-cost systems can provide minimal *Base Multitimbral Synthesizer* support while higher-end systems can provide *Extended Multitimbral Synthesizer* support. These two levels are known as *Base MIDI* and *Extended MIDI*. Support for these standards is fading as General MIDI support becomes more common, but a large number of files on Internet archives still use these MPC conventions.

These standards are significantly less capable than the General MIDI standard. In particular, Base MIDI requires only 6 simultaneous melody notes on 3 instruments, and 3 simultaneous rhythm notes on 3 instruments. Extended MIDI requires 16 simultaneous melody notes on 9 instruments and 16 simultaneous rhythm notes on 8 instruments. For comparison, recall that General MIDI requires the playback device to support 16 simultaneous melody notes on 16 instruments and 8 simultaneous rhythm notes on 8 instruments.

Part of the goal for these standards is to allow a single MIDI file to include a simplified version playable on a Base MIDI synthesizer and a more complete version playable on an Extended MIDI synthesizer. The standard accomplishes this by partitioning the MIDI channels. Channels 1 through 10 are used by Extended MIDI; 13 through 16 are used by Base MIDI. The instrument definitions match those of General MIDI except that Base MIDI uses channel 16 for key-based percussion. Channels 11 and 12 are not used. The MPC standard encourages MIDI authors to include both Base MIDI and Extended MIDI versions within the same file. A Base MIDI system will play only channels 13 through 16, and an Extended MIDI system will play only channels 1 through 10.

The Base MIDI/Extended MIDI definitions are troublesome because they contradict the General MIDI specification in two ways. First, the MPC standard encourages MIDI authors to put two versions of a song in the same MIDI file and asserts that a given system will play only one of the versions. With General MIDI, all channels are active. As a result, a General MIDI synthesizer plays both the Base MIDI and Extended MIDI versions simultaneously.

More problematic is that MPC puts key-based percussion on channels 10 and 16. With General MIDI, channel 16 is a melody channel.

Fortunately, Microsoft has standardized a way to mark MPC MIDI files. According to the *Microsoft Win32 Programmer's Reference*, MIDI files authored to the MPC standards should be marked accordingly. This mark consists of a sequencer-specific meta event (discussed later) with the 3-byte manufacturer ID 00 00 65. If Windows sees this meta event, it plays the file according to MPC standards; otherwise, it asks the user to configure the MIDI playback.

In my case, I can pretend to be an Extended MIDI device by blanking out channels 11 through 16.

LISTING 22.20 Check for MPC MIDI

```
if(   (pEvent->status == 0xFF) // Meta event
   && (pEvent->data[0] == 127) // Sequencer-specific
   && (pEvent->metaData->length >= 3)
   && (pEvent->metaData->data[0] == 0)  // three-byte manufacturer ID
   && (pEvent->metaData->data[1] == 0)  // 0 0 65 = Microsoft
```

```
            && (pEvent->metaData->data[2] == 65)
        ) {
            cerr << "This is an MPC MIDI file.\n";
            // Blank out channels 11 through 16 (we're an Extended MIDI device)
            for (int i=10;i<16;i++)
                if(!_channel[i]) {
                    _channel[i] = new MidiChannelSilent();
                    possible[i] = false; // Don't count notes on these channels
                }
    }
}
```

Playing a MIDI Event Stream

Now that the MIDI events have been read into memory and the deltas have been
converted into sample counts, it's reasonably straightforward to play the events. The
GetSamples method skims the event stream; each delta time is handled by playing all
channels for that duration; and each event is dispatched to the appropriate channel.

LISTING 22.21   Play MIDI Events

```
size_t MidiRead::GetSamples(AudioSample *buffer, size_t numSamples) {
    if (_events == 0) { // If I haven't yet read the file, do so.
        ReadHeader(); // Slurp in MIDI events from file
        ReadTracks();
        PostProcess(); // Convert to sample-based timing
        _currentEvent = _events; // Start with first event
        _samplesRemaining = 0;
    }
    for(size_t i=0; i<numSamples; i++)
        buffer[i]=0;
    size_t samplesReturned = 0;
    while (_currentEvent && (numSamples>0)) {
        if (_samplesRemaining > 0) {
            size_t samplesToPlay = numSamples;
            if (samplesToPlay > _samplesRemaining)
                samplesToPlay = _samplesRemaining;
            for (int i=0;i<16;i++)
                _channel[i]->AddSamples(buffer,samplesToPlay);
            buffer += samplesToPlay;
            samplesReturned += samplesToPlay;
            _samplesRemaining -= samplesToPlay;
            numSamples -= samplesToPlay;
            if (numSamples == 0)
                return samplesReturned;
        }

        _samplesRemaining += _currentEvent->delay;
```

```
Play a Single MIDI Event (Listing 22.22)
```

```
        _currentEvent = _currentEvent->next;
    }

    return samplesReturned;
}
```

Most of the channel messages are dispatched directly to the individual channel.

LISTING 22.22   Play a Single MIDI Event

```
int ch = _currentEvent->status & 0xF;
switch(_currentEvent->status & 0xF0) {
case 0x80:  // Note-off event
    _channel[ch]->EndNote(_currentEvent->data[0],_currentEvent->data[1]);
    break;
case 0x90:  // Note-on event
    if (_currentEvent->data[1] == 0)
        _channel[ch]->EndNote(_currentEvent->data[0], 64);
    else
        _channel[ch]->StartNote(_currentEvent->data[0],
                                _currentEvent->data[1]);
    break;
case 0xA0:  // Key Aftertouch
    _channel[ch]->KeyAftertouch(_currentEvent->data[0],
                                _currentEvent->data[1]);
    break;
case 0xB0:  // Mode change
    _channel[ch]->Mode(_currentEvent->data[0],
                       _currentEvent->data[1]);
    break;
case 0xC0:  // Program channel
    _channel[ch]->Program(_currentEvent->data[0]);
    break;
case 0xD0:  // Channel Aftertouch
    _channel[ch]->ChannelAftertouch(_currentEvent->data[0]);
    break;
case 0xE0:  // Pitch Wheel
    _channel[ch]->PitchBend(_currentEvent->data[1]*128
                            + _currentEvent->data[0]);
    break;
case 0xF0:  // Special
    if(_currentEvent->status == 0xFF) { // Meta event
        switch(_currentEvent->data[0]) {
        case 0:  break; // Track Sequence Number
        case 1:  case 2:  case 3:  case 4:  case 5:
        case 6:  case 7:  case 8:  case 9:  case 10:
        case 11:  case 12:  case 13:  case 14:  case 15:
           break; // Text Comments
        case 47:  break; // End of Track
        case 81:  break; // Tempo
        case 88:  break; // Time Signature
        case 89:  break; // Key Signature
        case 127:  break; // Sequencer-Specific
        default:  fprintf(stderr,"Track %2d:  (Meta 0x%02x)\n",
```

```
                          _currentEvent->track,
                          _currentEvent->data[0]);
        }
    } else if(_currentEvent->status == 0xF0) { // sysex event
      fprintf(stderr,"Track %2d:  (Sysex Event)\n",
                      _currentEvent->track);
    } else if(_currentEvent->status == 0xF7) { // special sysex event
      fprintf(stderr,"Track %2d:  (Special Sysex Event)\n",
                      _currentEvent->track);
    } else {
      fprintf(stderr,"Track %2d:  ",_currentEvent->track);
      fprintf(stderr, "Status:  0x%02x\n", _currentEvent->status);
    }
    break;
default:  // Some event not covered above??
    fprintf(stderr,"Track %2d, Bad Status:  0x%x\n",
            _currentEvent->track,_currentEvent->status);
    break;
}
```

MIDI Channels

As you can see from the previous section, the `MidiRead` object converts events into requests to the channel objects. Now it's time to look at what the channel objects need to do to support those requests.

Most of the playback code doesn't care what kind of channel object is available on a channel, as long as the channel object responds to certain messages. The `MidiChannelAbstract` class defines the capabilities of a MIDI channel object. Most of these methods support a single type of MIDI event.

LISTING 22.23   MIDI Channel Object

```
// A channel keeps track of currently playing notes
class MidiChannelAbstract {
public:
   virtual ~MidiChannelAbstract() {};
   virtual void StartNote(int pitch, int velocity) = 0;
   virtual void EndNote(int pitch, int velocity) = 0;
   virtual void Program(int instrument) = 0;
   virtual void ChannelAftertouch(int velocity) = 0;
   virtual void KeyAftertouch(int note, int velocity) = 0;
   virtual void Mode(int mode, int value) = 0;
   virtual void PitchBend(int value) = 0;
   virtual size_t AddSamples(AudioSample *buffer, size_t numberSamples) = 0;
};
```

To play Base MIDI or Extended MIDI files, it's convenient to be able to "silence" one or more channels. This simple placeholder provides an efficient silent channel.

LISTING 22.23 (CONTINUED)   MIDI Channel Object

```cpp
// A placeholder that does nothing
class MidiChannelSilent: public MidiChannelAbstract {
public:
    ~MidiChannelSilent() {};
    void StartNote(int, int) {};
    void EndNote(int, int) {};
    void Program(int) {};
    void ChannelAftertouch(int) {};
    void KeyAftertouch(int, int) {};
    void Mode(int, int) {};
    void PitchBend(int) {};
    size_t AddSamples(AudioSample *, size_t) { return 0; };
};
```

Of course, silent channels are the exception. The typical channel has to track which notes are playing and juggle a variety of instruments. To simplify the instrument juggling, I've put all the instrument management into a single "instrument map" object, which I'll discuss later.

LISTING 22.23 (CONTINUED)   MIDI Channel Object

```cpp
// A channel keeps track of currently playing notes
class MidiChannelStandard: public MidiChannelAbstract {
private:
    float _masterVolume;
    float _channelVolume;

    MidiRead *_midiRead;
    int _defaultInstrumentBank;
    int _currentInstrumentBank;
    int _currentInstrumentNumber;
    int _currentTuning;

    AbstractNote *_note[128]; // Current notes

    int _controllerLong[32]; // 14-bit controllers
    int _controllerShort[32]; // 7-bit controllers
    int _currentRegisteredParameter;
    int _registeredParameter[8]; // Registered parameters
    void AllNotesOff();
    void ResetControllers();
public:
    MidiChannelStandard(MidiRead *midiObject,
                        int instrumentBank,
                        float masterVolume);
    ~MidiChannelStandard();
    void StartNote(int pitch, int velocity);
    void EndNote(int pitch, int velocity);
    void Program(int instrument);
```

```
      void ChannelAftertouch(int velocity);
      void KeyAftertouch(int note, int velocity);
      void Mode(int mode, int value);
      void PitchBend(int value);
      size_t AddSamples(AudioSample *buffer, size_t numberSamples);
};
```

LISTING 22.24   MIDI Channels

```
MidiChannelStandard::
MidiChannelStandard(MidiRead *midiRead,
                    int currentBank,
                    float masterVolume) {
    _masterVolume = masterVolume;
    _midiRead = midiRead;
    _defaultInstrumentBank = currentBank;
    _currentInstrumentBank = currentBank;
    _currentInstrumentNumber = 0;
    _currentTuning = 0;
    for (int i=0; i<128;i++)
       _note[i] = 0;
    ResetControllers();
}


MidiChannelStandard::~MidiChannelStandard() { // Clean up
    for (int i=0; i<128; i++)
       if(_note[i]) {
          delete _note[i];
          _note[i] = 0;
       }
}
```

One difference between a simple electronic synthesizer and a piano is that a piano produces different sounds depending on how quickly you depress the key. The MIDI protocol allows for such behavior through *velocity*, which is how quickly you press or release a key. For note-on events, a higher velocity translates into a louder note (there is often a change in the overall sound, as well). For a note-off event, a higher velocity is a faster release and hence a shorter duration.

LISTING 22.24 (CONTINUED)   MIDI Channels

```
void MidiChannelStandard::Program(int instrument) {
    _currentInstrumentNumber = instrument;
    _currentInstrumentBank = _controllerLong[0];
}

void MidiChannelStandard::StartNote(int note, int velocity) {
    if (_note[note]) delete _note[note];
```

```
        // Select the correct instrument
        AbstractInstrument *instr =
            _midiRead->InstrumentMap()->Instrument(_currentInstrumentBank,
                                    _currentInstrumentNumber,note);

        // Get the tuning for this note
        float pitch = _midiRead->TuningMap()->Tuning(_currentTuning,note);

        _note[note] = instr->NewNote(pitch,
                            velocity*_channelVolume*_masterVolume);
    }

    void MidiChannelStandard::EndNote(int note, int velocity) {
        if(_note[note])
            _note[note]->EndNote(velocity/127.0);
    }

    void MidiChannelStandard::AllNotesOff() {
        for (int i=0; i<128;i++)
            if(_note[i])
                _note[i]->EndNote(0.0);
    }
```

Aftertouch and Pitch Wheel

MIDI's keyboard-centric heritage is especially obvious here. Sophisticated keyboards allow you to control the playback of a note that is already being played. This is handled through a pressure sensor under the key; by varying the pressure, called *aftertouch*, you vary the sound. Usually this varies the vibrato parameters, but depending on the keyboard, this can also vary other sound characteristics. Similarly, many electronic keyboards support a large *pitch wheel* which allows you to "bend" the pitch of all notes. The pitch wheel applies to a complete channel, not just to a single note. Similarly, there are two aftertouch messages—one for an individual note, the other for a complete channel.

LISTING 22.24 (CONTINUED)   MIDI Channels

```
    // I don't yet support aftertouch or pitch wheel
    void MidiChannelStandard::KeyAftertouch(int note, int velocity) {
        cerr << "Key Aftertouch:  " << note << " velocity:  " << velocity << "\n";
    }

    void MidiChannelStandard::ChannelAftertouch(int velocity) {
        cerr << "Channel Aftertouch:  velocity:  " << velocity << "\n";
    }

    void MidiChannelStandard::PitchBend(int) {
    }
```

A channel plays by playing all the currently active notes.

LISTING 22.24 (CONTINUED)   MIDI Channels

```
size_t MidiChannelStandard::AddSamples(AudioSample *buffer,
                                       size_t numberSamples) {
    for(int i=0; i< 128; i++) {
        if (_note[i]) {
            size_t samplesRead =
                _note[i]->AddSamples(buffer,numberSamples);
            if (samplesRead < numberSamples) { // Note finished?
                delete _note[i];
                _note[i] = 0;
            }
        }
    }
    return numberSamples;
}
```

Controllers and Modes

Events 0xB0 through 0xBF are used to change a variety of parameters. These parameters are arranged into four groups: 7-bit continuous controllers, 14-bit continuous controllers, parameters, and channel modes.

7-Bit Controllers

A control change message has 2 data bytes. The first specifies what is to be changed (*controller number*); the second specifies the new value. As with all data bytes, the values are limited to 7 bits, which is more than adequate for many purposes. The MIDI standard reserves controllers 64 through 95 (0x40 through 0x5F) for this purpose.

Table 22.7 summarizes the 7-bit controllers. Note that some have fewer than 128 values. For example, the legato foot switch and portamento controllers turn some effect on or off. For such controllers, values less than 64 are "off" and values 64 and above are interpreted as "on." This extends to any controller with a small range; 0 should always mean the least value, 127 the largest, with other values interpolated appropriately.

14-Bit Controllers

Seven bits is insufficient for some purposes, so the MIDI standard also defines 32 14-bit controllers. Such a controller requires two controller numbers, one for the upper 7 bits,

TABLE 22.7   7-Bit Controllers

Message (hex)	Description
Bc 40 *vv*	Damper pedal (on/off)
Bc 41 *vv*	Portamento (on/off)
Bc 42 *vv*	Sostenuto
Bc 43 *vv*	Soft pedal
Bc 44 *vv*	Legato foot switch (on/off)
Bc 45 *vv*	Hold 2
Bc 46 *vv*	Sound controller 1 (sound variation)
Bc 47 *vv*	Sound controller 2 (timbre/harmonic intensity)
Bc 48 *vv*	Sound controller 3 (release time)
Bc 49 *vv*	Sound controller 4 (attack time)
Bc 4A *vv*	Sound controller 5 (brightness)
Bc 4B *vv*	Sound controller 6 (no default)
Bc 4C *vv*	Sound controller 7 (no default)
Bc 4D *vv*	Sound controller 8 (no default)
Bc 4E *vv*	Sound controller 9 (no default)
Bc 4F *vv*	Sound controller 10 (no default)
Bc 50 *vv*	General purpose controller 5
Bc 51 *vv*	General purpose controller 6
Bc 52 *vv*	General purpose controller 7
Bc 53 *vv*	General purpose controller 8
Bc 54 *vv*	Portamento control
Bc 5B *vv*	Effects 1 depth
Bc 5C *vv*	Effects 2 depth
Bc 5D *vv*	Effects 3 depth
Bc 5E *vv*	Effects 4 depth
Bc 5F *vv*	Effects 5 depth

and one for the lower 7 bits. Controller numbers 0 through 31 (0x00 through 0x1F) are used for the most significant 7 bits of 14-bit controllers, and controller numbers 32 through 63 (0x20 through 0x3F) are used for the least significant 7 bits. Table 22.8 lists the currently defined 14-bit controllers. Because the two halves are set independently, you need to pay attention to the interaction between them—in particular, whenever the upper 7 bits are changed, the lower 7 bits are implicitly set to zero. When creating MIDI files, you should always set the upper 7 bits first.

TABLE 22.8   14-Bit Controllers

Controller for Upper 7 Bits	Controller for Lower 7 Bits	Description
0 (0x00)	32 (0x20)	Bank select
1 (0x01)	33 (0x21)	Modulation wheel or lever
2 (0x02)	34 (0x22)	Breath controller
3 (0x03)	35 (0x23)	Undefined
4 (0x04)	36 (0x24)	Foot controller
5 (0x05)	37 (0x25)	Portamento time
6 (0x06)	38 (0x26)	Data entry
7 (0x07)	39 (0x27)	Channel volume
8 (0x08)	40 (0x28)	Balance
9 (0x09)	41 (0x29)	Undefined
10 (0x0A)	42 (0x2A)	Pan
11 (0x0B)	43 (0x2B)	Expression controller
12 (0x0C)	44 (0x2C)	Effect control 1
13 (0x0D)	45 (0x2D)	Effect control 2
14 (0x0E)	46 (0x2E)	Undefined
15 (0x0F)	47 (0x2F)	Undefined
16 (0x10)	48 (0x30)	General purpose controller 1
17 (0x11)	49 (0x31)	General purpose controller 2
18 (0x12)	50 (0x32)	General purpose controller 3
19 (0x13)	51 (0x33)	General purpose controller 4
20–31	52–63	Undefined

Parameters

Some controllers are handled through the slightly different *parameter* mechanism. Rather than set the controller directly, you first select the corresponding parameter by sending its 14-bit code (using two messages to convey the upper and lower 7 bits), and then modify that parameter. Note that all parameters are 14-bit values. The standard provides for up to 16,384 *registered* parameters and another 16,384 *non-registered* parameters. Registered parameters are official parts of the standard; non-registered parameters may be used by anyone for any purpose. As you can see from Table 22.9, the parameter mechanism requires only eight controller numbers. Table 22.10 lists the current registered parameters. Note that parameters 1 and 2 together represent a 28-bit tuning value.

TABLE 22.9   Controller Messages for Changing Parameters

Message (hex)	Description
Bc 06 vv	Data entry: Set most significant 7 bits of current parameter
Bc 26 vv	Data entry: Set least significant 7 bits of current parameter
Bc 60 vv	Data increment: Add 1 to current parameter
Bc 61 vv	Data decrement: Subtract 1 from current parameter
Bc 62 vv	Select non-registered parameter (upper 7 bits, lower 7 bits are zero)
Bc 63 vv	Select non-registered parameter (lower 7 bits)
Bc 64 vv	Select registered parameter (upper 7 bits, lower 7 bits are zero)
Bc 65 vv	Select registered parameter (lower 7 bits)

TABLE 22.10   Registered Parameters

Parameter	Description
0	Pitch bend sensitivity
1	Fine tuning
2	Coarse tuning
3	Tuning program select
4	Tuning bank select

To demonstrate how this mechanism works, you can set parameter 2 (coarse tuning) on channel 3 to 0x12BC with the following sequence of bytes:

- 0xB2 0x64 0x00 – Select registered parameter whose upper 7 bits are 0.

- 0x65 0x02 – Complete selection of registered parameter 2. (Note running status; the 0xB2 is implied.)

- 0x06 0x25 – Send upper 7 bits of new coarse tuning value.

- 0x06 0x3C – Send lower 7 bits of new coarse tuning value.

Channel Modes

In addition to controllers, there are eight *channel mode* messages. The channel number in this case has a distinctly different meaning. Recall that a typical MIDI environment has many boxes wired together. Each separate box might respond to any subset of the 16 channels. To simplify certain tasks, each box also has a *basic channel*. Channel mode messages sent to this basic channel change the operation of the entire box. If a single synthesizer responds to all channels, the basic channel will generally be channel 1.

In the case of a software synthesizer, such as the one I'll develop in this chapter, it's unclear how to interpret the basic channel. You can think of a software synthesizer as one box that responds to all 16 channels, or as 16 virtual boxes, each responding to a single channel. I've used the latter interpretation in the code in this chapter. Table 22.11 summarizes the channel mode messages.

TABLE 22.11   Channel Mode Messages

Message (hex)	Description
B*c* F8 00	All sound off: Turn off all notes, silence reverb, and so on
B*c* F9 00	Reset all controllers (ignored in omni mode)
B*c* FA *vv*	Local control
B*c* FB 00	All notes off
B*c* FC 00	Omni off (also all notes off)
B*c* FD 00	Omni on (also all notes off)
B*c* FE *vv*	Mono on/Poly off (also all notes off): *vv* is the number of channels—starting with the basic channel—that should use mono mode
B*c* FF 00	Poly on/Mono off (also all notes off)

Omni mode specifies whether a given box responds to all channels (omni on) or only its basic channel (omni off). *Mono mode* and *poly mode* specify how a single channel handles multiple notes. In mono mode, each channel plays only one note at a time; if a note-on event is received before the previous note is turned off, the currently playing note is changed to the new pitch. This is a form of legato. Note that the sender must still send a note-off event for the previous note; it's a general rule in MIDI that every note-on event must eventually be followed by a matching note-off event. In poly mode, each channel may play as many notes as it can.

Implementation

LISTING 22.24 (CONTINUED)   MIDI Channels

```
void MidiChannelStandard::Mode(int mode, int value) {
    // 14-bit controllers
    if (mode < 32) // 0--31 are most-significant bits
        _controllerLong[mode] = value << 7;
    if ((mode >= 32) && (mode < 64)) // least-significant bits
```

```
      _controllerLong[mode-32] =
            (_controllerLong[mode-32] & 0x3F80) + value;

   // 7-bit controllers
   if ((mode >= 64) && (mode < 96)) // single-byte controllers
      _controllerShort[mode-64] = value;

   // Parameter settings
   if (mode == 96) {     // 96 is Data Increment
      _registeredParameter[_currentRegisteredParameter]++;
      _controllerLong[6] = _registeredParameter[_currentRegisteredParameter];
   }
   if (mode == 97) {     // 97 is Data Decrement
      _registeredParameter[_currentRegisteredParameter]--;
      _controllerLong[6] = _registeredParameter[_currentRegisteredParameter];
   }
   // 98 is Non-Registered Parameter LSB
   // 99 is Non-Registered Parameter MSB
   if (mode == 100) {  // Registered Parameter LSB
      _currentRegisteredParameter =
         (_currentRegisteredParameter & 0x3F80)+(value);
      _controllerLong[6] = _registeredParameter[_currentRegisteredParameter];
   }
   if (mode == 101) {  // Registered Parameter MSB
      _currentRegisteredParameter = value<<7;
      _controllerLong[6] = _registeredParameter[_currentRegisteredParameter];
   }


   /***********************************/
   /* Channel mode messages (120--127) */
   /***********************************/
   // 120 is All Sound Off
   // 121 is Reset All Controllers
   if (mode == 121) ResetControllers();
   // 123 is All Notes Off (so are 124--127)
   if (mode >= 123) AllNotesOff();
   // 124 is Omni Mode Off
   // 125 is Omni Mode on
   // 126 is Mono Mode On (one note per channel)
   // 127 is Poly Mode On (multiple notes per channel)
}

void MidiChannelStandard::ResetControllers() {
   int i;
   for(i=0;i<32;i++) {
      _controllerLong[i] = 0;
      _controllerShort[i] = 0;
   }

   for(i=0;i<8;i++) {
      _registeredParameter[i] = 0;
   }
   _controllerLong[0] = _defaultInstrumentBank;
   _controllerLong[7] = 100 << 7; // Default volume
   _controllerLong[8] = 0x2000; // Balance control:  1/2 = equal output
   _controllerLong[10] = 0x2000; // Pan control:  1/2 = centered
```

```
_controllerLong[11] = 0x2000; // Average expression

_currentRegisteredParameter = 0;
_registeredParameter[0] = 0; // Pitch bend default:  +-2 semitones
_registeredParameter[1] = 0x2000; // Default fine tuning
_registeredParameter[2] = 0x2000; // Default coarse tuning

// Update some miscellaneous variables
_channelVolume = _controllerLong[7]/16384.0;
}
```

MIDI Tuning

A recent addition to the MIDI standard is the ability to redefine what pitch values are assigned to the MIDI note values. To support this, my MIDI player has a single *tuning map* which translates note values into frequencies.

In this initial version, the tuning map uses equal tempering and A440 is note 69. (The General MIDI specification calls for Middle C to be note 60, which is equivalent.)

LISTING 22.25   MIDI Tuning Map

```
class MidiTuningMap {
public:
   float Tuning(int, int note) {
      return 440.0*pow(2.0,(note-69)/12.0);
   }
};
```

MIDI Instruments

All channels share a common "instrument map" object, responsible for managing the collection of instruments used by a particular song.

Before playing each note, the channel requests an appropriate instrument from the instrument map by using the Instrument method, which takes three parameters.

Bank The General MIDI standard defines only two instrument banks, one for melody instruments and one for rhythm (percussion) instruments. Extensions (such as Yamaha XG) define additional banks. The bank is selected by controllers 0x00 (most significant 7 bits) and 0x20 (least significant 7 bits). Following the Yamaha XG standard, I define the General MIDI melody bank as zero, and the General MIDI rhythm bank as 0x3F80 (most significant 7 bits are 0x7F; least significant 7 bits are zero). (The Roland GS standard also uses controller zero to specify additional instruments, but in a slightly different fashion.) Note that, according to the General MIDI standard, a synthesizer in General MIDI mode should ignore bank-selection commands.

Program A program is not necessarily synonymous with an instrument. For example, the General MIDI rhythm bank defines only a single program, but that program contains 47 instruments. The General MIDI melody bank contains 128 programs, each corresponding to a different instrument.

Note For some programs, a different instrument is used for each key. This is especially common for percussion (such as the General MIDI rhythm program) and special effects programs.

A full General MIDI implementation would require 175 distinct instrument descriptions. For simplicity, my `MidiInstrumentMap` class currently maintains only one instrument, the `SineWaveInstrument`. (See page 256.)

A more complete implementation would keep a list of current instrument objects, creating new ones only as necessary.

LISTING 22.26   MIDI Instrument Map

```
class MidiInstrumentMap {
private:
   AbstractInstrument *_instr;
public:
   enum {gmMelodyBank = 0, gmRhythmBank = (0x7f<<7)};

   MidiInstrumentMap() {
//       _instr = new PluckedStringInstrument;
       _instr = new SineWaveInstrument;
   };
   ~MidiInstrumentMap() { delete _instr;  };
   AbstractInstrument *Instrument(int bank, int program, int note);
   void SamplingRate(long s) {
      _instr->SamplingRate(s);
   }
};
```

In a full implementation, the `Instrument` method would be fairly complex. It would need to select the appropriate instrument based on the current bank, program, and note value. This will require some tricky memory management. High-quality sampled instrument definitions require a lot of memory, and it makes sense to economize by storing only those instruments that are actually needed. If you want to work with a hardware sound card, memory management is even trickier since most sound cards have only enough storage for a handful of instrument definitions at a time.

LISTING 22.27   MIDI Instrument Map Methods

```
AbstractInstrument *MidiInstrumentMap::Instrument(
              int bank, int program, int note) {
    ┌─────────────────────────────────────────┐
    │ Dump Instrument Name (Listing 22.28)     │
    └─────────────────────────────────────────┘
    return _instr;
};
```

It's convenient to be able to see what instruments are being used by a particular piece. This short code just dumps the instrument name the first time that instrument is selected. Note that there are two different instrument tables here: one for the General MIDI rhythm instruments, the other for the General MIDI melody instruments.

LISTING 22.28   Dump Instrument Name

```
{
    if((bank == gmRhythmBank)&&(program==0)) {
        static bool instrumentPrinted[128];
        const struct {
            int note;
            const char *name;
        } instruments[] = {
         {35,"Acoustic Bass Drum"}, {36,"Bass Drum 1"},
         {37,"Side Stick"}, {38,"Acoustic Snare"}, {39,"Hand Clap"},
         {40,"Electric Snare"}, {41,"Low Floor Tom"},
         {42,"Closed Hi-Hat"}, {43,"High Floor Tom"},
         {44,"Pedal Hi-Hat"}, {45,"Low Tom"}, {46,"Open Hi-Hat"},
             :
             :
         {74,"Long Guiro"}, {75,"Claves"}, {76,"Hi Wood Block"},
         {77,"Low Wood Block"}, {78,"Mute Cuica"}, {79,"Open Cuica"},
         {80,"Mute Triangle"}, {81,"Open Triangle"}, {0,0}
        };

        if (!instrumentPrinted[note]) {
            cerr << "Instrument:  ";
            int i=0;
            while( (instruments[i].note != 0)
                   && (instruments[i].note != note+1)) {
                i++;
            }

            if ((instruments[i].note == 0))
                cerr << "Unknown Percussion.\n";
            else
                cerr << instruments[i].name << " (Note " << note << ")\n";
            instrumentPrinted[note] = true;
        }
    }
```

```
    if (bank == gmMelodyBank) {
        static bool instrumentPrinted[128];
        const char *instruments[] = {
            "Acoustic Grand Piano", "Bright Acoustic Piano",
            "Electric Grand Piano", "Honky-tonk Piano", "Electric Piano 1",
            "Electric Piano 2", "Harpsichord", "Clavinet", "Celesta",
                 .
                 .
                 .
        };
        if(!instrumentPrinted[program]) {
            cerr << "Instrument:  " << instruments[program];
            cerr << " (Program " << program << ")\n";
            instrumentPrinted[program] = true;
        }
    }
}
```

Caveats

The player program developed in this chapter will read any Standard MIDI file and produce sound from it. My goal, however, has not been to develop a complete MIDI synthesizer, but to survey the breadth of the MIDI standard. There's a lot of work to be done before this code can claim to be a useful MIDI playback engine, much less claim General MIDI compliance.

The most obvious deficiency is that it lacks the full range of General MIDI instruments. Adding additional instruments requires augmenting the `MidiInstrumentMap` object. One approach would be to develop a collection of sampled instrument sounds, store them in files, and have the instrument map load them as they're needed. A more ambitious plan would survey the extensive literature on instrument synthesis and develop custom instrument code for each instrument.

There are also many minor details: The code presented in this chapter does not support mono/poly mode, nor does it support pitch bending, fine tuning, or the many controllers routinely used by MIDI composers.

MIDI Wire Protocol

When sent over a wire, MIDI looks different from the way it does in a Standard MIDI file. In particular, there are a number of *system events* that are not used in MIDI files. Table 22.12 summarizes them. Note that 0xF7 and 0xFF have noticably different meanings in MIDI files than they do in the wire protocol.

TABLE 22.12   MIDI Protocol System Events

Code (hex)	Description
F0	System exclusive
F1 *nd*	MIDI time code quarter frame
	Communicates one nybble *d* of a 4-byte time specification; *n* selects the nybble.
F2 *aa bb*	Song pointer
F3 *cc*	Song select
F4	Undefined
F5	Undefined
F6	Tune
F7	End of system exclusive
F8	Timer
F9	Undefined
FA	Start
FB	Continue
FC	Stop
FD	Undefined
FE	Active sensing
FF	System reset

Real-Time Commands

Several groups of MIDI events are divided into real-time and non-real-time. Generally, real-time messages are messages that are time critical; they must be processed at a particular time in order to have the desired effect. For example, a note-on or a pitch-bend event must occur at a particular time. Not all messages are real-time. For example, events such as instrument changes affect how later events are interpreted, but the exact timing of that event is not critical.

The single-byte events from 0xF8 to 0xFF are all real-time events. These are used for timing synchronization and, therefore, must be sent over the wire at precise times even if they interrupt another event. For example, a MIDI device might receive 0x90 0x48 0xF8 0x40 and should know that this is two events; a 3-byte note-on event with a 1-byte timer event in the middle. Fortunately, these real-time events are prohibited in Standard MIDI Files, so I don't need to worry about parsing MIDI events punctuated with real-time commands.

Other MIDI File Formats

Many file formats have adopted the basic ideas of the Standard MIDI file format. Microsoft's RMID format is a simple wrapper that bundles a Standard MIDI file inside a Microsoft RIFF structure. Similarly, Apple's AIFF audio format has a special chunk that can contain MIDI note information. Apple's QuickTime multimedia framework also supports MIDI events. Creative Labs' Creative Music Format (CMF) starts with a series of FM synthesizer programs to define various instruments and follows it with a stream of MIDI events.

Because MIDI was originally developed for sending music information over a wire, it's well-suited for networked music applications. With some work, the engine I've developed in this chapter could be modified to play type zero MIDI files as they are read, supporting streaming Internet playback. A more ambitious scheme is being marketed by Headspace, Inc. Its Rich Music Format (RMF), which provides interactive music for games and the Internet, is based on MIDI.

MIDI Standards

MIDI is a large standard and if you want to fully exploit it, expect to spend time studying the official standards. Even if you're already familiar with the standard, you might want to order the most recent version from the MMA. (See www.midi.org for information.) The official standard is an evolving document, with new sections and clarifications added at regular intervals. Among other additions, the official standard defines the following.

Notation Information are MIDI system-exclusive messages that provide time signature, tempo, key signature, and other related information. They're similar to the Standard MIDI File meta events.

MIDI Time Code is a standard way to precisely synchronize MIDI playback devices by broadcasting SMPTE time signals.

Standard MIDI Files as I've discussed them in this chapter.

General MIDI System as I've discussed in this chapter.

MIDI Show Control allows lighting and other intelligent equipment to be controlled using MIDI messages.

MIDI Machine Control allows MIDI messages to control a variety of audio recording and production systems, such as tape recorders.

MIDI Sample Dump provides a way for MIDI hardware devices to request and send sampled instrument definitions.

File Dump allows MIDI devices to transfer arbitrary data.

During 1997, the Downloadable Samples standard (DLS-1) should be finalized, which will allow Standard MIDI Files to include definitions of sampled instruments, providing complete control over the instrument sounds.

MOD 23

MIDI is a good way to store music, but it has some drawbacks. The most obvious is that MIDI was originally designed to connect a variety of music hardware. A synthesizer will typically support only a fixed set of instrument sounds, and each synthesizer is different. Even instruments with the same names often sound slightly different, so many MIDI files sound right only on certain synthesizers.

One way around this problem is to use sampled instruments. In this approach, the music file contains digital recordings of one representative note from each instrument. The synthesizer uses this recorded note as a template, pitch-shifting the sound to produce different notes. This approach is taken by the MOD file format. These files, also called *player modules* or *tracker modules*, contain a collection of recorded sounds and a set of note information. By including the recorded instrument sounds, MOD files are independent of the capabilities of any synthesizer or sound card. As a result, MOD files should sound the same on all systems.

Another major difference is that MIDI files are *event based*; they store a sequence of events and specify the times at which each event occurs. A MIDI player reads the next event from the file and waits until the appropriate time to use that event. A MIDI file can specify any number of note starts without specifying that a note ends. There's no inherent limit to the number of simultaneous notes.

In contrast, MOD files are structured around *beats*. (This is completely different from the musical notion. Some people prefer the term *division* to emphasize this distinction.) Each beat corresponds to a time interval and completely describes what happens during that interval. One consequence is that MOD files, unlike MIDI, can play only a limited number of simultaneous notes. Although this may be a drawback for musicians, it's an asset for programmers, who can exploit those limits to provide more reliable playback.

Even the four channel limit of the original MOD format isn't as restrictive as it may seem. For example, if a song makes heavy use of piano chords, it's reasonable to store a chord as a single instrument and play it as if it were a single note. This is similar to such General MIDI instruments as "string section." Later MOD variants support 6, 8, 16, and even 32 channels.

The biggest drawback of MOD files is that they were developed as an ad hoc format used by a single program, and many minor variants were developed by other programmers. As a result, there is no easy way to discern these variants, which leads to a lot of confusion. I'll explain the popular *ProTracker* format, with occasional notes indicating where variants differ.

Identifying MOD Files

Unfortunately, MOD files cannot be identified as reliably as files in some other formats. The popular ProTracker variant contains a 4-byte signature, but doesn't put it at the beginning of the file. Other MOD variants not only use different signatures, but place those signatures at other points in the file.

The basic 31-voice ProTracker format can be identified by the M.K. or M!K! signature that follows the lengthy header information.

LISTING 23.1   Identify MOD File

```
bool IsModFile(istream &file) {
   file.seekg(20+30*31+1+1+128);
   char marker[4];
   file.read(marker,4);
   if (memcmp(marker,"M.K.",4)==0) return true;
   if (memcmp(marker,"M!K!",4)==0) return true;
   return false;
}
```

Amiga Sound Hardware

MOD files originated on the Amiga and were carefully tailored to the Amiga sound hardware. I'll briefly describe this sound hardware, which will make it easier to understand the file format. Not surprisingly, later formats are not strictly modeled on the Amiga sound hardware. But, rather than becoming more hardware-independent, many later variants adopted the peculiarities of specific PC sound cards.

The Amiga sound hardware provides four independent channels, identified as zero through three. Channels zero and three are connected to the left speaker; channels one and two are connected to the right speaker. Each channel is programmed independently. To obtain a centered sound, you have to use two of the four channels. Later formats have diverged from the Amiga hardware model to allow stereo samples or to provide separate left and right volume control on a per-channel or per-instrument basis.

FIGURE 23.1   A Sound with a Repeating Section

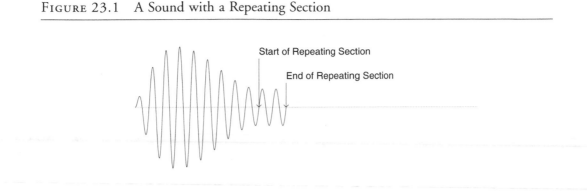

Start of Repeating Section

End of Repeating Section

The Amiga sound hardware was designed to support music playback. One interesting aspect of instrument sounds is that they can be continued indefinitely. If you turn on a synthesizer and press a key, the synthesizer will continue to make a sound for as long as you hold the key. When configuring the Amiga sound hardware, you provide it with the start and end point of the sound sample and the start and end point of the *repeat section*. Figure 23.1 shows a simple instrument sound with a repeat section. As the hardware plays this sound, it will continue to output samples until it reaches the end, then start over at the reset point. It continues to repeat the indicated section until that channel is explicitly reprogrammed. The resulting sound is shown in Figure 23.2.

The hardware can output the samples at a variable rate. The precise rate is controlled by a hardware divider. The Amiga has a master clock that runs at 3.575872 MHz. If you set the divider to 447, the sound hardware will emit $3,575,872/447 \approx 8,000$ samples

FIGURE 23.2   The Reconstructed Sound

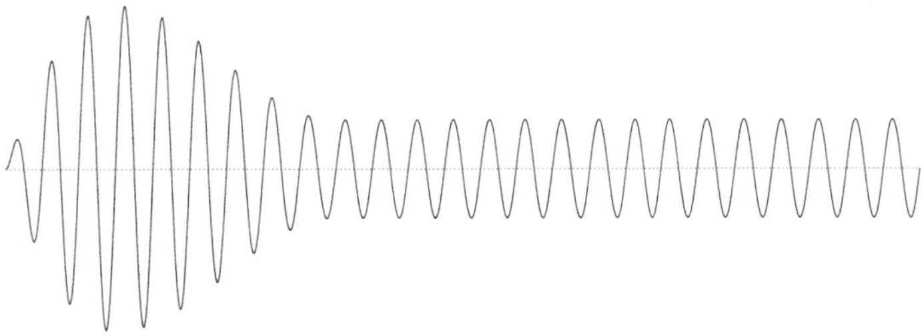

per second. Each channel can have a different divider. If you change the divider rate for a sound, you change the playback rate and, therefore, the pitch. This hardware support for variable-rate output does not introduce resampling distortion, unlike the software approach I use in this chapter.

Each channel also has a separate volume control. A filter can be enabled on the output to filter out the sampling harmonics. The filter attenuates frequencies above 4,000 Hz.

MOD Format Overview

The MOD file format can be viewed as a compression approach. It attempts to identify a variety of repeating patterns in the music to be stored so that the result is more compact. For example, it stores one recorded note for each instrument, which is expanded into a variety of sounds during playback. It also stores *patterns*, short sections of music that can be repeated or played in different orders to take advantage of repeated sequences of notes.

Instruments

The most common MOD file format allows up to 31 different instrument sounds. Each sound is characterized by a digitized sample with an optional repeated portion, together with a default volume and a *finetune* parameter.

The finetune parameter allows the precise playback rate (and hence, pitch) to be adjusted on a per-instrument basis.

Timing

Before explaining how notes are handled, I'll describe the timing model used by MOD files.

The fundamental timing unit in a MOD file is the *tick*, usually 1/50 second. (This rate corresponds to the vertical retrace rate on the European/PAL version of the Amiga. Some nonstandard MOD files assume a tick is 1/60 second, corresponding to the US/NTSC version of the Amiga. Many MOD players allow the tick rate to be adjusted.) The MOD file allows a variety of sound changes to occur on each tick. For example, a note played with *tremolo* will have its volume adjusted on each tick.

However, note changes can occur only at the start of each new *beat*. Typically, a beat is six ticks, although this is dynamically adjustable. Beats are also referred to as *rows*, because many MOD file editors display each beat on one row of a text display.

Notes

A complete set of notes is specified for each beat. Each note consists of an instrument number, a period (divider value), and an effect code. (Some variant formats also store a volume with each note.) The instrument number and period correspond directly to the Amiga sound hardware. If the instrument number and period are both zero, the previous note should continue playing. If only one of them is zero, a new note will begin, but the zero value will be replaced with the previous value.

The effect code is a 12-bit value that indicates a variety of note manipulations that can be applied. Table 23.1 summarizes some of the possible effects. Most of these effects apply to only one channel. Changes to the period or volume remain until the next note change. Ongoing changes, such as arpeggio or vibrato, must be explicitly continued.

The effects listed in Table 23.1 fall generally into four categories: those that affect the playback order (loop pattern, small jump), those that affect a note only at the beginning of the beat (set volume), those that affect a note on every tick (vibrato, volume slide), and those that affect global parameters (set tempo, set filter).

TABLE 23.1   Note Effects

Name	Description
Arpeggio	The period is varied with each tick to simulate a rapid cycle of three notes.
Portamento	The period is varied with each tick to create a smoothly increasing or decreasing pitch.
Vibrato	The period is varied with each tick according to a sine, square, or ramp waveform.
Set Volume	The volume is set to the indicated value.
Volume Slide	The volume is increased or decreased each tick.
Tremolo	The volume is varied with each tick according to a sine, square, or ramp waveform.
Far Jump	After this beat, play resumes with the first beat of the indicated pattern.
Small Jump	This pattern ends after this beat and the next pattern will begin at the specified beat.
Set Tempo	Sets the number of ticks per beat or the length of a tick.
Loop Pattern	Causes a section of a pattern to be repeated.
Retrigger	Restarts the note several times during the beat.

Beats

A beat consists of one note specification for each channel. Typically, there are four channels, but variant formats can have six or eight channels. As mentioned above, a beat has a definite duration, typically six ticks, although this is settable dynamically.

Patterns

MOD files were designed for storing music, which typically has repeated sections. A *pattern* stores up to 64 beats. At the normal playback rate, this is just over seven seconds of music. A MOD file can have up to 64 patterns. Some MOD variants don't use patterns; they store a continuous list of beats.

Playlist

A *playlist* is a list of up to 128 pattern numbers.

Format Details

Now that you know generally how a MOD file is constructed, I'll dive into the details of the file storage. This is also a good time to start developing the code to read and play MOD files.

A MOD file player is much more complex than a player for WAVE or AIFF formats (although arguably less complex than a MIDI player). In addition to the obvious ModRead class, I'll define a number of auxiliary classes.

- ModNoteData stores data for a single note (period, instrument code, and effect code).

- ModSong stores the entire song, including the patterns (which contain many ModNoteData objects) and the playlist. During playback, ModSong keeps track of the current pattern and beat within that pattern.

- ModInstrument inherits from AbstractInstrument. It uses a SampledInstrument object to manage playback.

- ModNote is a playback object, derived from AbstractNote.

- ModChannel stores per-channel information, including the currently playing note (both ModNoteData and ModNote) and default values for various effects.

LISTING 23.2   mod.h

```
#ifndef MOD_H_INCLUDED
#define MOD_H_INCLUDED
#include <cstdio>
#include "audio.h"
#include "instrumt.h"
#include "sampled.h"

bool IsModFile(istream &file);

// First, pre-declare some things
struct ModNoteData;
class ModInstrument;

class ModNote:  public AbstractNote {
```
    ModNote Members (Listing 23.4)
```
};

class ModInstrument:  public AbstractInstrument {
```
    ModInstrument Members (Listing 23.5)
```
};

struct ModNoteData {
```
    ModNoteData Members (Listing 23.6)
```
};

class ModSong {
```
    ModSong Members (Listing 23.8)
```
};

struct ModChannel {
```
    ModChannel Members (Listing 23.12)
```
};

class ModRead:  public AudioAbstract {
```
    ModRead Members (Listing 23.10)
```
};

#endif
```

LISTING 23.3   mod.cpp

```
Copyright © 1998, Tim Kientzle (Listing E.1)
#include <cstdio>
#include <cmath>
#include <cstdlib>
#include <cstring>
#include "mod.h"
#include "audio.h"
#include "instrumt.h"
#include "sampled.h"

MOD Vibrato and Tremolo Waveforms (Listing 23.17)

Identify MOD File (Listing 23.1)
```

Instruments

As described earlier, each instrument has sample data, with an optional repeat section, a default volume, and a finetune parameter. There's also a name of up to 22 characters.

Within the file, the instrument data is stored in two pieces. A 30-byte header is stored early in the file, containing the information shown in Table 23.2. The actual sample data (8-bit signed samples) is stored at the end of the file.

Several of the parameters in Table 23.2 require additional explanation. Note that the sample data length and repeat information is stored as a count of 16-bit words, even though the sample data itself is stored as 8-bit signed bytes. (Some variants store the start of the repeat section as a byte offset.) The repeating section usually extends to the end of the sample, but not always. Instruments that do not have a repeating section are often stored with a repeat start of zero, and a repeat length of one word. Because the first 2

TABLE 23.2   MOD File Instrument Data

Bytes	Description
22	Name of sample (not necessarily null-terminated!)
2	Length of sample data in words
1	Finetune
1	Volume
2	Start of repeating section in words
2	Length of repeating section in words

bytes of an instrument are usually zero, this simply plays zero bytes after the sound is finished.

The volume is always in the range 0 to 64. The instrument volume is the default used for all notes played on that instrument. Some files do contain values outside that range, and various effects may push the volume out of that range, but MOD players truncate out-of-range volume parameters.

The finetune is a slight pitch adjustment that applies to an instrument. Rather than resample the sound (with the associated inherent loss), music editors use this to adjust the playback pitch. The value codes a number from -8 to +7. Each finetune value is a step of 1/8 of a halftone.

The class names may be confusing. A `ModNoteData` compactly stores the basic note information and a `ModNote` is the actual playback object. During playback, there is one `ModNoteData` object for every note in the entire piece but only one `ModNote` for each channel.

`ModInstrument` doesn't explicitly provide sample storage; that's handled by the `SampledInstrument` class. It does provide alternative ways to set the pitch and volume, however. MOD files compute pitch in terms of the period (the Amiga hardware divider setting), and it's easier to embed the conversion from period to pitch within `ModNote`.

LISTING 23.4   ModNote Members

```
private:
   AbstractNote *_abstractNote;
public:
   void Restart() {
      if (_abstractNote) _abstractNote->Restart();
   }
   size_t AddSamples(AudioSample *buff, size_t length) {
      if (_abstractNote) return _abstractNote->AddSamples(buff,length);
      else return 0;
   }

   // This is the only place that assumes we're using a sampled note
   void SetSampleOffset(int offset) {
      // Should use dynamic_cast here
      if (_abstractNote)
         reinterpret_cast<SampledNote *>(_abstractNote)
            ->SetSampleOffset(offset);
   }
   void Pitch(float t) {
      if (_abstractNote)  _abstractNote->Pitch(t);
   }
   float Pitch() {
      if (_abstractNote)    return _abstractNote->Pitch();
      else                  return 440.0;
   }
   void EndNote(float v) {
      if (_abstractNote)    _abstractNote->EndNote(v);
```

```
    }
private:
    void Volume(float) {};
    float Volume() {return 1.0;}
public:
    void SetModVolume(int volume);
    void SetModPeriod(int period);
    ModNote(AbstractNote *,int period, int volume);
    ~ModNote();
```

LISTING 23.5   ModInstrument Members

```
private:
    SampledInstrument *_sampledInstrument;
private:
    char _name[23];  /* Null-terminated string */
public:
    const char *Name() { return _name; }
private:
    signed char _finetune; /* -8 to +7 */
    unsigned char _volume; /* 0 to 64 */
    long _length; /* Bytes */
    long _repeatStart; /* Bytes from beginning */
    long _repeatLength; /* length of repeat */
public:
    ModInstrument() { _sampledInstrument = 0; _name[0] = 0; }
    virtual ~ModInstrument(){
       if (_sampledInstrument)
          delete _sampledInstrument;
    };
    void ReadHeader(istream &modFile);
    void ReadSample(istream &modFile);
    ModNote *NewModNote(int period);
    void SamplingRate(long s) {
       AbstractInstrument::SamplingRate(s);
       if(_sampledInstrument)
          _sampledInstrument->SamplingRate(s);
    }
    long SamplingRate() {
        return AbstractInstrument::SamplingRate();
    }
private:
    AbstractNote *NewNote(float pitch, float volume);
```

Because an instrument is stored in two pieces, I need two methods to recover those pieces. The `ReadHeader` method pulls in the basic parameters; `ReadSample` reads the actual sample data. `ReadSample` also checks for several common special cases, such as a short repeat of zero bytes.

LISTING 23.3 (CONTINUED)   mod.cpp

```cpp
void ModInstrument::ReadHeader(istream &modFile){
   modFile.read(_name,22);
   _name[22]=0;
   _length = ReadIntMsb(modFile,2) * 2;
   _finetune = ReadIntMsb(modFile,1);
   if (_finetune > 7) _finetune -= 16;
   _volume = ReadIntMsb(modFile,1);
   if (_volume > 64) _volume = 64;
   _repeatStart = ReadIntMsb(modFile,2) * 2;
   _repeatLength = ReadIntMsb(modFile,2) * 2;
}

void ModInstrument::ReadSample(istream &modFile) {
   if (_length < 1) return;
   AudioSample *data
         = new AudioSample[_length+_repeatLength+1024];
   AudioByte *byteBuff
         = reinterpret_cast<AudioByte *>(data);
   modFile.read(reinterpret_cast<char *>(byteBuff),_length);

   for(long s = _length-1; s>=0; s--) {
      data[s] = static_cast<signed char>(byteBuff[s]) *
               (1<<(8*sizeof(AudioSample)-8));
   }

   // Adjust the repeat portion
   int repeatTest=0;
   for(int i=_repeatStart;i<_repeatLength;i++)
      repeatTest += data[i];
   // If entire repeat is zero, set to no repeat
   if(repeatTest==0) {
      _repeatLength = 0;
      _repeatStart = _length;
   }
   // MOD convention:  a two-byte repeat at the beginning means
   // no repeat
   if((_repeatLength<=2) && (_repeatStart == 0)) {
      _repeatLength = 0;
      _repeatStart = _length;
   }

   _sampledInstrument = new SampledInstrument(data,
            _length,_repeatStart,_repeatStart+_repeatLength);

   // The Pitch() parameters are determined by
   // the convention that A440 uses a divider of
   // 254, as modified by the finetune value
   _sampledInstrument
         ->BasePitch(440*pow(2.0,-_finetune/96.0),
                  3575872.0F/254.0F);

   delete [] data;
}
```

Because MOD files express volume using integer values from 0 to 64 and express pitch by means of a hardware divider value, it's convenient to set the volume and pitch directly using those values. The assumption that a divider of 254 corresponds to A440 is arbitrary; as long as you use the same assumptions consistently, you'll end up with the same result.

LISTING 23.3 (CONTINUED)   mod.cpp

```cpp
void ModNote::SetModVolume(int volume) {
   if (volume > 64) volume = 64;
   if (volume < 0) volume = 0;
   if (_abstractNote)
      _abstractNote->Volume(volume/64.0/4.0);
}

void ModNote::SetModPeriod(int period) {
   if (period < 113) period=113;
   if (period > 856) period=856;
   if (_abstractNote)
      _abstractNote->Pitch(440.0*254.0/period);
}
```

Likewise, it's convenient to create new notes using the MOD conventions. This `ModNote` constructor use MOD-style period and volume values. The corresponding `ModInstrument::NewModNote` method is similar, but it takes the volume setting from the instrument default.

LISTING 23.3 (CONTINUED)   mod.cpp

```cpp
ModNote::ModNote(AbstractNote *abstractNote, int period,
   int volume) {
   _abstractNote = abstractNote;
   SetModVolume(volume);
   SetModPeriod(period);
   Restart();
}

ModNote::~ModNote() {
   if (_abstractNote)  delete _abstractNote;
}

ModNote *
ModInstrument::NewModNote(int period) {
   AbstractNote *note = NewNote(440,0.5); // Generic note
   // ModNote constructor will reset pitch and volume
   return new ModNote(note,period,_volume);
}

AbstractNote *
ModInstrument::NewNote(float pitch, float volume) {
```

```
    if (_sampledInstrument)
       return _sampledInstrument->NewNote(pitch,volume);
    else
       return 0;
}
```

Notes

Each note contains an 8-bit instrument number, a 12-bit period, and a 12-bit effect value. In the file, this data is packed into 4 bytes, as shown in Table 23.3. It's easier to understand this arrangement if you keep in mind that an early version of this format supported only 15 instruments.

Technically, you could use an arbitrary period for any note. This would allow you to use different scales or do slow pitch slides by varying the period. In practice, the periods listed in Table 23.4 are the only ones used, and some MOD file players and editors

TABLE 23.3   Arrangement of Note Information

Field	Description
Instr1	Upper 4 bits of instrument number
Period	12-bit period
Instr2	Lower 4 bits of instrument number
Effect	12-bit effect

TABLE 23.4   Periods for Notes

Octave	C	C♯	D	D♯	E	F	F♯	G	G♯	A	A♯	B
0	1712	1616	1525	1440	1357	1281	1209	1141	1077	1017	961	907
1	856	808	762	720	678	640	604	570	538	508	480	453
2	428	404	381	360	339	320	302	285	269	254	240	226
3	214	202	190	180	170	160	151	143	135	127	120	113
4	107	101	95	90	85	80	76	71	67	64	60	57

Note that octaves 0 and 4 are not widely supported.

properly handle only these precise values. The relation between periods and note values assumes the instruments were sampled in a particular fashion. By appropriately sampling the instrument sounds, you can get significantly more than the three-octave range suggested here.

The effect value is treated as a single 4-bit effect code followed either by one 8-bit parameter or two 4-bit parameters. When I discuss the playing code, I'll explain the effects in more detail.

LISTING 23.6   ModNoteData Members

```
enum effectType { none=0, arpeggio, slideUp, slideDown,
   pitchSlide, vibrato, pitchSlidePlusVolumeSlide,
   vibratoPlusVolumeSlide, tremolo, setSampleOffset,
   volumeSlide, farJump, setVolume, smallJump, setTempo,
   setFilter, pitchUp, pitchDown, setGlissando, setVibrato,
   setFinetune, patternLoop, setTremolo, retrigger, volumeUp,
   volumeDown, cutNote, delayNote, delayPattern, invertLoop,
   effectCount
   };

unsigned char _instrument; // 8 bits for instrument
unsigned short _period; // 12 bits for period
ModNoteData::effectType _effect; // 4(8) bits for effect
unsigned char _parameter; // 8(4) bits for parameter

public:
   void ReadNote(istream &modFile); // HUH?
```

Nothing in the MOD format requires these particular note values. A gradual pitch slide could be handled with a gradual change in period rather than with an effect code. Similarly, you could experiment with 13-tone or other unusual scales. However, many MOD player programs translate periods into internal note codes for playback. These programs will not honor periods other than these standard ones.

The technique used to convert periods into note codes is useful for printing MOD files.

LISTING 23.7   Convert Periods into Note Names

```
void NoteName(int period, char *name) {
   static const int periods[] = // periods for octave 0
      {1712,1616,1525,1440,1357,1281,1209,1141,1077,1017,961,907};
   static const char *notenames[] =
      {"C-","C#","D-","D#","E-","F-","F#","G-","G#","A-","A#","B-"};
   int octave = 0;    // Move period into octave 0
   while (period < 870) { octave++; period *= 2; }
   int a,b,c; // Binary search table
   a=0;b=sizeof(periods)/sizeof(periods[0])-1;
   while((b-a) > 1) {
```

```
    c = (b+a)/2;
    if (period < periods[c]) a=c; else b=c;
}
// Pick the closest period
if (periods[a]-period > period-periods[b]) c = b;
else c = a;
// Format note name into buffer
sprintf(name,"%2s%1d",notenames[c],octave);
}
```

You may have noticed that the effect list given earlier had more than 16 effects listed. In fact, MOD uses the top-most nybble to specify the effect. If the top nybble is 14, however, the second nybble specifies the effect. The ReadNote method uses two look-up tables to convert MOD effect codes into internal effect codes.

LISTING 23.3 (CONTINUED)   mod.cpp

```cpp
void ModNoteData::ReadNote(istream &modFile) {

    static ModNoteData::effectType primaryEffects[] = {
        arpeggio, slideUp, slideDown, pitchSlide,
        vibrato, pitchSlidePlusVolumeSlide,
        vibratoPlusVolumeSlide, tremolo, none,
        setSampleOffset, volumeSlide, farJump, setVolume,
        smallJump, none, setTempo
    };

    static ModNoteData::effectType secondaryEffects[] = {
        setFilter, pitchUp, pitchDown, setGlissando,
        setVibrato, setFinetune, patternLoop, setTremolo,
        none, retrigger, volumeUp, volumeDown, cutNote,
        delayNote, delayPattern, invertLoop
    };

    unsigned char b[4];
    int effectValue;
    modFile.read(reinterpret_cast<char *>(b),4);
    _instrument = (b[0]&0xF0) | ((b[2]>>4) & 0x0F);
    _period = ((static_cast<int>(b[0])&0x0F)<<8)
            + (static_cast<int>(b[1]) & 0xFF);
    effectValue = static_cast<int>(b[2]) & 0x0F;
    _parameter = static_cast<int>(b[3]) & 0xFF;
    // Effect 14 is handled a bit differently...
    if (effectValue == 14) {
        _effect = secondaryEffects[(_parameter>>4)&0x0F];
        _parameter &= 0x0F;
    } else if ((effectValue == 0) && (_parameter == 0)){
        _effect = none;
    } else {
        _effect = primaryEffects[effectValue];
    }
}
```

Song Storage

As described earlier, a MOD file contains up to 64 patterns. Each pattern contains 64 beats, each with four notes. In addition, there is a *playlist* of 128 bytes. The playlist indicates the order in which the patterns should be played. One optimization is that the highest-numbered pattern used in the playlist is the last pattern stored in the file. As a result, you must first read the playlist, scan it to determine the highest pattern to load (patterns are stored in numerical order), and then load the patterns. (Older MOD variants used a single byte to store the number of patterns in the file. Some later variants used this byte for other purposes, which means you can't rely on it to determine the number of active patterns.)

LISTING 23.8   ModSong Members

```
private:
    unsigned char _playList[128];
    int _playListLength;
    int _maxPattern;
    typedef ModNoteData Beat[4]; // 4 notes in a beat
    typedef Beat *Pattern;   // Pattern is an array of beats
    Pattern *_patterns;
public:
    void ReadPlayList(istream &modFile);
    void ReadPatterns(istream &modFile);
    ModSong();
    ~ModSong();
```

ModSong is also responsible for keeping track of the current position within the song. The first complication is that various effects can alter the playback order. For example, the "delay pattern" effect causes the previous beat to be repeated, which requires us to remember the last beat played. Other effects determine which beat will be played next, so I've chosen to set up the next beat in advance and allow those effects to change the appropriate variables. Another complication is that the position in the song is determined by the current position in the playlist, which in turn selects a pattern and the beat within that pattern. The result is that six variables control the play order.

LISTING 23.8 (CONTINUED)   ModSong Members

```
private:
    // Information needed to play MOD file
    int _thisIndex; // current position in play list
    int _thisBeat; // current beat in corresponding pattern
    int _lastIndex; // previous index/beat
    int _lastBeat;
    int _nextIndex; // Next index/beat
    int _nextBeat;
```

```
public:
    bool Advance(); // Advance to next beat, true if end-of-song
    void Back(); // Backup to previous beat
    void AdvanceNextIndex(); // Skip to next pattern index
    void NextIndex(int i); // Set next pattern index
    void NextBeat(int b); // Set next beat
    void Stop(); // Next call to Advance() will return true
    ModNoteData &ThisNote(int ch) {
        return _patterns[ _playList[_thisIndex] ] [_thisBeat] [ch];
    }
```

LISTING 23.9   Initialize ModSong Variables

```
_lastIndex = _lastBeat = 0;
_thisIndex = _thisBeat = 0;
_nextIndex = _nextBeat = 0;
```

Advancing to the next beat is now easy. The `Advance` method also indicates whether this is the end of the song.

LISTING 23.3 (CONTINUED)   mod.cpp

```
void ModSong::Stop() {
    _nextIndex = _playListLength;
}

bool ModSong::Advance() { // Returns true if end-of-song
    _lastBeat = _thisBeat;
    _lastIndex = _thisIndex;
    _thisBeat = _nextBeat;
    _thisIndex = _nextIndex;
    _nextBeat++;
    if (_nextBeat >= 64) {  // Advance to next pattern?
        _nextBeat = 0;
        _nextIndex++;
    }
    if (_thisIndex >= _playListLength)  return true;
    else return false;
}

void ModSong::Back() {
    _nextBeat = _thisBeat;
    _nextIndex = _thisIndex;
    _thisBeat = _lastBeat;
    _thisIndex = _lastIndex;
}

void ModSong::NextBeat(int b) {
    _nextBeat = b;
}
```

```
void ModSong::NextIndex(int i) {
   _nextIndex = i;
}

void ModSong::AdvanceNextIndex() {
   _nextIndex++;
}
```

To save some memory for songs that have fewer patterns, I allocate memory for individual patterns as they are read. The destructor needs to free only patterns that have been allocated.

LISTING 23.3 (CONTINUED)   mod.cpp

```
ModSong::ModSong() {
   _maxPattern=0;
   _patterns = 0;
      Initialize ModSong Variables (Listing 23.9)
}

ModSong::~ModSong() { // Free patterns
   if (_patterns) {
      for(int p=0;p<=_maxPattern;p++)
         delete [] _patterns[p];
      delete [] _patterns;
   }
}
```

Reading the playlist and the patterns requires computing the highest-numbered pattern.

LISTING 23.3 (CONTINUED)   mod.cpp

```
void ModSong::ReadPlayList(istream &modFile) {
   _playListLength = ReadIntMsb(modFile,1);
   (void)ReadIntMsb(modFile,1); // Discard extra byte
   _maxPattern=0;
   for(int i=0;i<128;i++) {
      _playList[i] = ReadIntMsb(modFile,1);
      if (_playList[i] > _maxPattern)
         _maxPattern = _playList[i];
   }
}

void ModSong::ReadPatterns(istream &modFile) {
   _patterns = new Pattern[_maxPattern+1];
   for (int p=0;p<=_maxPattern;p++) {
      _patterns[p] = new Beat[64];
```

```
        for (int b=0;b<64;b++)
            for (int n=0;n<4;n++)
                _patterns[p][b][n].ReadNote(modFile);
    }
}
```

Overall File Structure

Now that you've seen how all the pieces are stored, Table 23.5 shows how those pieces fit together into the file.

TABLE 23.5   Overall Organization of a MOD File

Length	Description
20	Name of song
30 for each instrument	Instrument data
1	Length of playlist
1	Number of patterns (only in old files)
128	Playlist
4	Signature
1024 for each pattern	Patterns
	Instrument sample data follows

The signature is used to determine the precise format. Unfortunately, it doesn't appear at the same location in all MOD variants. Table 23.6 quickly summarizes some of the more common ones and how they vary from what's been discussed so far. If the signature doesn't match any of these, the file may be an older 15-instrument file, which has no particular signature.

TABLE 23.6   Common Signatures and Their Meanings

Signature	Description
M.K.	The most common signature. These files have the format described in this chapter.
M!K!	Like the above but with more than 64 patterns.
FLT4	Identical to M!K!
FLT8	Each beat has 8 channels.
6CHN	Each beat has 6 channels.
8CHN	Each beat has 8 channels.

The top-level class in this chapter is the `ModRead` class, which is derived from class `AudioAbstract`. `ModRead` uses an auxiliary `ModChannel` class to keep track of information about each channel during playback.

LISTING 23.10   ModRead Members

```
void MinMaxSamplingRate(long *min, long *max, long *preferred) {
   *min = 8000;
   *max = 44100;
   *preferred = 11025;
}
long SamplingRate() { return AudioAbstract::SamplingRate(); }
void SamplingRate(long s) {
   AudioAbstract::SamplingRate(s);
   for (int i=0;i<numInstruments;i++)
      if(_instrument[i])
         _instrument[i]->SamplingRate(s);
}
void MinMaxChannels(int *min, int *max, int *preferred) {
   *min = 1;
   *max = *preferred = 2;
}
```

The `ModRead` class needs a handful of variables to store the contents of the file.

LISTING 23.10 (CONTINUED)   ModRead Members

```
public:
   ModRead(istream &); // Constructor takes an open stream
   ~ModRead();

private:
   // Read MOD file data
   char _name[21];
   char _marker[4];
   enum {numInstruments = 32};
   ModInstrument *_instrument[numInstruments];
   ModSong _song;
   void ReadMod(istream &modFile);
```

The constructor calls `ReadMod` to read the file, which in turn creates the other objects and asks them to read themselves from the file. I'll add other variables to the `ModRead` class as I develop the playing code in the next section.

LISTING 23.3 (CONTINUED)   mod.cpp

```
ModRead::ModRead(istream &modFile) {
   cerr << "File Format:  ProTracker MOD\n";
```
   Initialize ModRead Variables (Listing 23.11)

```
        ReadMod(modFile);    // Slurp in the file
}

ModRead::~ModRead() {
    for (int i=1;i<numInstruments;i++)
        if (_instrument[i]) delete _instrument[i];
    if (_sampleBufferLeft) delete [] _sampleBufferLeft;
    if (_sampleBufferRight) delete [] _sampleBufferRight;

}

void ModRead::ReadMod(istream &modFile) {
    modFile.read(_name,20);
    _name[20] = 0;
    cerr << "Name:  " << _name << "\n";

    _instrument[0] = NULL;
    for (int i=1;i<numInstruments;i++) {
        _instrument[i] = new ModInstrument();
        _instrument[i]->ReadHeader(modFile);
    }

    { // Many composers provide comments in the instrument names area
      // so dump that to the user.
        char msg[80];
        cerr << "Instruments:  \n";
        int step = (numInstruments+2)/3; // Use three columns
        for (int i=1;i<=step;i++) {
            sprintf(msg,"%2d:%-22s  ",i,_instrument[i]->Name());
            cerr << msg;
            if (i+step < numInstruments) {
                sprintf(msg,"%2d:%-22s  ",i+step,
                        _instrument[i+step]->Name());
                cerr << msg;
            }
            if (i+step+step < numInstruments) {
                sprintf(msg,"%2d:%-22s",i+step+step,
                        _instrument[i+step+step]->Name());
                cerr << msg;
            }
            cerr << "\n";
        }
    }

    _song.ReadPlayList(modFile);
    modFile.read(_marker,4); // Read separator
    if (memcmp(_marker,"M.K.",4)==0) {
        // Protracker MOD with no more than 64 patterns
    } else if (memcmp(_marker,"M!K!",4)==0) {
        // Protracker MOD with more than 64 patterns
    } else {
        // I don't handle any other format
        cerr << "Unrecognized signature '"
             << _marker[0] << _marker[1]
             << _marker[2] << _marker[3]
             << "'\n";
```

```
        exit(1);
    }
    _song.ReadPatterns(modFile);
    for (int i1=1;i1<numInstruments;i1++)
        _instrument[i1]->ReadSample(modFile);
}
```

Playing MOD Files

Now that you can read files, it's time to think about how to play them. Because `ModRead` derives from class `AudioAbstract`, it needs to implement `GetSamples`. In this case, the fastest approach is to implement a `PlayBeat` method that plays a single beat into a buffer (or two buffers for stereo output). The `GetSamples` method then copies data from that buffer to satisfy the request, calling `PlayBeat` to refill the buffer as necessary.

LISTING 23.10 (CONTINUED)   ModRead Members

```
public:
    size_t GetSamples(AudioSample *buffer, size_t numSamples);
```

`PlayBeat` plays stereo samples into two buffers, and `GetSamples` has to properly interleave the samples.

LISTING 23.3 (CONTINUED)   mod.cpp

```
size_t ModRead::GetSamples(AudioSample *buff, size_t length) {
    int requestedLength = length;
    do {
        switch(Channels()) {
        case 1:  // Mono, just copy and convert
            while ((_sampleLength > 0)&&(length > 0)) {
                *buff++ = *_sampleStartLeft++;
                _sampleLength--;
                length--;
            }
            break;
        case 2:  // Stereo, interleave two channels
            while ((_sampleLength > 0)&&(length > 0)) {
                *buff++ = *_sampleStartLeft++;
                *buff++ = *_sampleStartRight++;
                _sampleLength--;
                length-=2;
            }
            break;
        default:  cerr << "Internal error\n";
            exit(1); // This can't happen!!
        }
        if (length > 0) // Need more data?
            PlayBeat(); // Generate next beat
```

```
        if (_sampleLength == 0) break; // No more data!!
    } while (length>0);
    return requestedLength-length;
}
```

The buffering is complicated by two factors. The first is that individual instrument samples are mono but need to be played into either the left or the right channel at various times. The second is that the size of a beat can vary during the playback; various effects change the duration of a beat.

To handle the stereo playback, I've defined two buffers, one for each channel. The playback routine selects the appropriate buffer, depending on the channel being played. For mono playback, these two are the same. There are also start and length variables to indicate how much data remains in the buffers.

LISTING 23.10 (CONTINUED)   ModRead Members

```
private:
    AudioSample *_sampleBufferLeft; // Left channel
    AudioSample *_sampleBufferRight; // Right channel
    int _sampleBufferSize;
    AudioSample *_sampleStartLeft; // position in sampleBufferLeft
    AudioSample *_sampleStartRight;
    int _sampleLength; // length of data in sample buffers
    void SetSampleBufferSize();
```

LISTING 23.11   Initialize ModRead Variables

```
    _sampleBufferLeft = 0;
    _sampleBufferRight = 0;
    _sampleBufferSize = 0;
    _sampleLength = 0;
```

The `SetSampleBufferSize` method is called whenever the beat duration might have changed; it's responsible for updating the buffers to ensure there is enough space. It can compute the required size from the current sampling rate and the two MOD timing parameters, `_ticksPerMinute` and `_ticksPerBeat`. Note that I'm counting ticks per minute rather than ticks per second for increased accuracy.

LISTING 23.10 (CONTINUED)   ModRead Members

```
private:
    int _ticksPerMinute; // tick rate
    int _ticksPerBeat;
    int _samplesPerBeat;
    int _samplesPerTick; // This is approximate!!
```

As I mentioned earlier, the defaults are 50 ticks per second, and 6 ticks to a beat.

LISTING 23.11 (CONTINUED)   Initialize ModRead Variables

```
    _ticksPerMinute = 50 * 60;
    _ticksPerBeat = 6;
```

To simplify things, `SetSampleBufferSize` assumes the left buffer is used for mono, then sets the right buffer if necessary. It recomputes `samplesPerBeat` and `samplesPerTick` for use throughout the class. Note that `samplesPerTick` may not precisely divide `samplesPerBeat`. This complicates code in which a complete beat needs to be played one tick at a time, but produces more accurate overall timing.

LISTING 23.3 (CONTINUED)   mod.cpp

```
// Make sure the sample buffer is large enough
void ModRead::SetSampleBufferSize() {
    _samplesPerBeat = SamplingRate() * _ticksPerBeat * 60
                  / _ticksPerMinute;
    _samplesPerTick = _samplesPerBeat / _ticksPerBeat;
    if (_sampleBufferLeft && (_sampleBufferSize >= _samplesPerBeat))
       return;
    if (_sampleBufferRight == _sampleBufferLeft)
       _sampleBufferRight = 0;
    if (_sampleBufferLeft)
       delete [] _sampleBufferLeft;
    _sampleBufferLeft = new AudioSample[_samplesPerBeat];
    switch(Channels()) {
    // If mono, both channels use same buffer
    case 1:  _sampleBufferRight = _sampleBufferLeft; break;
    case 2:
       if (_sampleBufferRight)
          delete [] _sampleBufferRight;
       _sampleBufferRight = new AudioSample[_samplesPerBeat];
       break;
    default:
       cerr << "Illegal number of channels:  "
            << Channels()
            << "\n";
       exit(1);
    }
    _sampleBufferSize = _samplesPerBeat;
    _sampleStartLeft = _sampleBufferLeft;
    _sampleStartRight = _sampleBufferRight;
    _sampleLength = 0; // Nothing in buffer now
}
```

The PlayBeat Method

The `PlayBeat` method is really the core of the entire class. It keeps track of the current beat, plays the various notes into the correct sample buffers, and processes all of the various note effects. Most of the rest of this chapter is devoted to explaining parts of this one large method.

PlayBeat is also responsible for playing notes in the appropriate channels. There is quite a bit of state associated with a single channel, which is why the `ModChannel` structure exists.

LISTING 23.10 (CONTINUED)   ModRead Members

```
private:
   // Current 'live' notes
   enum {numberChannels = 4};
   ModChannel _channel[numberChannels];

   void PlayBeat(); // play next beat into sampleBuffer
```

The state for each channel includes the basic note parameters (period, instrument, and volume), and the previous values for each effect. Within a MOD file, a zero instrument or period indicates that the previous instrument or period should be kept. Many effects use the same convention.

LISTING 23.12   ModChannel Members

```
public:
   ModNoteData _currentNote;
   int _currentVolume;
   ModNote *_liveNote;
   unsigned char _defaultParameter[ModNoteData::effectCount];
   ModChannel();
   ~ModChannel();
```

LISTING 23.3 (CONTINUED)   mod.cpp

```
ModChannel::ModChannel() {
   _liveNote = NULL;
   for(int i0=0;i0<ModNoteData::effectCount;i0++)
      _defaultParameter[i0]=0;

   │Initialize ModChannel Variables (Listing 23.15)│

};

ModChannel::~ModChannel() {
   if (_liveNote) delete _liveNote;
};
```

Here's how this works. The `PlayBeat` method first advances to the next beat, then looks at all the notes in this beat to process global effects (effects that alter global parameters, such as the play order and the tempo). It can then prepare the sample buffers and finally go through and play the notes into the buffers.

LISTING 23.3 (CONTINUED)   mod.cpp

```cpp
/* Play this Beat */
void ModRead::PlayBeat() {
  AudioSample *sampleBuffer;
  if (_song.Advance()) return;

  for(int ch0=0;ch0<numberChannels;ch0++) {
    ModNoteData currentNote = _song.ThisNote(ch0);
    switch(currentNote._effect) {
    default:  break;
```
┌───┐
│ Process Global Effect for currentNote (Listing 23.16) │
└───┘
```cpp
    }
  }

  SetSampleBufferSize();
  memset(_sampleBufferLeft, 0,
       sizeof(_sampleBufferLeft[0]) * _samplesPerBeat);
  if (Channels()==2)
    memset(_sampleBufferRight, 0,
       sizeof(_sampleBufferRight[0]) * _samplesPerBeat);

  // Set up and play each channel
  for(int ch=0;ch<numberChannels;ch++) {
    switch(ch) {
    case 0:  case 3:  case 4:  case 7:
      sampleBuffer = _sampleBufferLeft; break;
    case 1:  case 2:  case 5:  case 6:  default:
      sampleBuffer = _sampleBufferRight; break;
    }
    ModNoteData currentNote = _song.ThisNote(ch);
    // If either instrument or period is non-zero,
    // start a new note.
    if (   (currentNote._instrument != 0)
        || (currentNote._period != 0)) {
      // First, get defaults from the previous note
      if (currentNote._instrument == 0)
        currentNote._instrument = _channel[ch]._currentNote._instrument;
      if (currentNote._period == 0)
        currentNote._period = _channel[ch]._currentNote._period;
      if (currentNote._instrument >= numInstruments) {
        cerr << "Illegal instrument number "
             << int(currentNote._instrument) << ".\n";
        break;
      }
```
┌─────────────────────────────────┐
│ Set Up New Note (Listing 23.13) │
└─────────────────────────────────┘

```
      } else { // Otherwise, continue the previous note
         currentNote._instrument = _channel[ch]._currentNote._instrument;
         currentNote._period = _channel[ch]._currentNote._period;
      }

      if (_channel[ch]._liveNote) {
         ModNote &currentLiveNote = *_channel[ch]._liveNote;
         int defaultParameter
               = _channel[ch]._defaultParameter[currentNote._effect];
         int thisParameter = currentNote._parameter;
         switch(currentNote._effect) {
```

> Play currentLiveNote with Effects (Listing 23.14)

```
         default:
            cerr << "Internal error:  illegal effect code.\n";
            break;
         }
         // Save the current (updated) parameter as the new default.
         _channel[ch]._defaultParameter[currentNote._effect] =thisParameter;
      }
      // Save the defaults for next time
      _channel[ch]._currentNote = currentNote;
   }

   // Set variables for GetSamples
   _sampleLength = _samplesPerBeat;
   _sampleStartLeft = _sampleBufferLeft;
   _sampleStartRight = _sampleBufferRight;
}
```

Usually, setting up a new note means creating a new note for the appropriate instrument. Tremolo and vibrato need to be reset if either of those effects is used. The most important variation is for pitch slide, in which case I need to save the goal value and retrieve the instrument and period from the last note on this channel.

LISTING 23.13   Set Up New Note

```
if (currentNote._instrument != 0) {
   if ( (currentNote._effect == ModNoteData::tremolo)
      && ((_channel[ch]._defaultParameter[ModNoteData::tremolo] & 4)==0) )
         _channel[ch]._currentTremolo = 0;
   if ( (currentNote._effect == ModNoteData::vibrato)
      ||(currentNote._effect == ModNoteData::vibratoPlusVolumeSlide)) {
      if ((_channel[ch]._defaultParameter[ModNoteData::vibrato] & 4)==0)
         _channel[ch]._currentVibrato = 0;
   }
   if (currentNote._effect == ModNoteData::pitchSlide) {
      if (currentNote._period) {
         _channel[ch]._pitchGoal = currentNote._period;
      } else if (_channel[ch]._pitchGoal == 0) {
         // No applicable goal, so ignore this effect
         currentNote._effect = ModNoteData::none;
```

```
        currentNote._parameter = 0;
      }
      // Put actual period/instrument into currentNote
      currentNote._period = _channel[ch]._currentNote._period;
      currentNote._instrument = _channel[ch]._currentNote._instrument;
   }
   // Note:  this is not the same as 'else'
   if (currentNote._effect != ModNoteData::pitchSlide) {
      if (_channel[ch]._liveNote) delete _channel[ch]._liveNote;
      _channel[ch]._liveNote = _instrument[currentNote._instrument]->
                     NewModNote(currentNote._period);
   }
}
```

Playing Notes with Effects

The simplest case is when there is no effect. This common case is handled efficiently by the `SampledInstrument` class.

LISTING 23.14   Play currentLiveNote with Effects

```
case ModNoteData::none:
   currentLiveNote.AddSamples(sampleBuffer,_samplesPerBeat);
   break;
```

I'll go through the remaining effects in numerical order, as they appear in the MOD file.

Effect 0: Arpeggio

The arpeggio effect plays rapid triples of notes. The parameter is interpreted as two nybbles, x and y. The three notes played are the current note, the current note plus x halftones, and the current note plus y halftones. I've precomputed a simple table to shift notes up appropriately.

One minor point here is that because `samplesPerBeat` may not be precisely a multiple of `samplesPerTick`, you need to be careful about the last tick. I loop through counting up by `samplesPerTick` and fudge the ending condition so that I know the loop will end one tick early. I can then play `samplesPerBeat-i` ticks, which correctly accounts for the remainder of the beat.

Unlike many effects, an arpeggio effect with a zero parameter does *not* mean you should use the default. Rather, it means all three notes are the same; this is equivalent to "no effect."

LISTING 23.14 (CONTINUED) Play currentLiveNote with Effects

```
case ModNoteData::arpeggio:
  { const float halfTones[] = {
          0.0F,        1.05946309F, 1.12246205F, 1.18920712F,
          1.25992105F, 1.33483985F, 1.41421356F, 1.49830708F,
          1.58740105F, 1.68179283F, 1.78179744F, 1.88774863F,
          2.0F,        2.11892619F, 2.24492410F, 2.37841423F};

    AudioSample *currentSampleBuffer = sampleBuffer;
    float pitches[3];
    currentLiveNote.SetModPeriod(currentNote._period);
    pitches[0] = currentLiveNote.Pitch();
    pitches[1] = pitches[0] * halfTones[(thisParameter>>4)&0xF];
    pitches[2] = pitches[0] * halfTones[(thisParameter&0xF)];
    int currentPitch = 0;
    int i;
    for(i=0;i<_samplesPerBeat-_samplesPerTick*3/2;i+=_samplesPerTick) {
        currentLiveNote.AddSamples(currentSampleBuffer,_samplesPerTick);
        currentSampleBuffer += _samplesPerTick;
        if (++currentPitch > 2) currentPitch = 0;
        currentLiveNote.Pitch(pitches[currentPitch]);
    };
    currentLiveNote.AddSamples(currentSampleBuffer,_samplesPerBeat-i);
    currentLiveNote.Pitch(pitches[0]); // reset original pitch
  }
  break;
```

Effect 1: Slide Up

Slide up, also known as *portamento up*, increases the pitch after each tick but not at the beginning or end of the beat. The parameter is interpreted as a single 8-bit number to be subtracted from the period at each tick. Remember that decreasing the period corresponds to increasing the pitch.

LISTING 23.14 (CONTINUED) Play currentLiveNote with Effects

```
case ModNoteData::slideUp:
  { if (thisParameter == 0) thisParameter = defaultParameter;
    AudioSample *currentSampleBuffer = sampleBuffer;
    int i;
    for(i=0; i<_samplesPerBeat-_samplesPerTick*3/2; i+=_samplesPerTick) {
        currentLiveNote.AddSamples(currentSampleBuffer,_samplesPerTick);
        currentSampleBuffer += _samplesPerTick;
        currentNote._period -= thisParameter;
        currentLiveNote.SetModPeriod(currentNote._period);
    };
    currentLiveNote.AddSamples(currentSampleBuffer,_samplesPerBeat-i);
  }
  break;
```

Effect 2: Slide Down

This is exactly like slide up, except that the pitch is decreased (period is increased).

LISTING 23.14 (CONTINUED) Play currentLiveNote with Effects

```
case ModNoteData::slideDown:
   {
      if (thisParameter == 0) thisParameter = defaultParameter;
      AudioSample *currentSampleBuffer = sampleBuffer;
      int i = 0;
      for(;i<_samplesPerBeat-_samplesPerTick;i+=_samplesPerTick) {
         currentLiveNote.AddSamples(currentSampleBuffer,_samplesPerTick);
         currentSampleBuffer += _samplesPerTick;
         currentNote._period += thisParameter;
         currentLiveNote.SetModPeriod(currentNote._period);
      };
      currentLiveNote.AddSamples(currentSampleBuffer,_samplesPerBeat-i);
   }
   break;
```

Effect 3: Pitch Slide

Pitch slide, also known as *tone portamento*, treats the current note as a goal. The existing note is gradually changed until the specified note is reached. It's possible to continue a slide without specifying a new note or repeating the slide parameters; a zero parameter means that the previous value should be used.

The argument is treated as an 8-bit value that is added to or subtracted from the period. Once the period reaches the goal, the period stops changing and future slides *must* specify a new goal.

LISTING 23.12 (CONTINUED) ModChannel Members

```
public:
   int _pitchGoal; // current target period for Pitch Slide
```

LISTING 23.15 Initialize ModChannel Variables

```
_pitchGoal = 0;
```

LISTING 23.14 (CONTINUED) Play currentLiveNote with Effects

```
case ModNoteData::pitchSlide:
   {
```

```
            if (thisParameter == 0) thisParameter = defaultParameter;
            AudioSample *currentSampleBuffer = sampleBuffer;
            int i = 0;
            for(;i<_samplesPerBeat-_samplesPerTick;i+=_samplesPerTick) {
               currentLiveNote.AddSamples(currentSampleBuffer,_samplesPerTick);
               currentSampleBuffer += _samplesPerTick;
               if (_channel[ch]._pitchGoal == 0) {
                  // Do nothing
               } else if (currentNote._period > _channel[ch]._pitchGoal) {
                  currentNote._period -= thisParameter;
                  if (currentNote._period <= _channel[ch]._pitchGoal) {
                     currentNote._period = _channel[ch]._pitchGoal;
                     _channel[ch]._pitchGoal = 0;
                  }
               } else {
                  currentNote._period += thisParameter;
                  if (currentNote._period >= _channel[ch]._pitchGoal) {
                     currentNote._period = _channel[ch]._pitchGoal;
                     _channel[ch]._pitchGoal = 0;
                  }
               }
               currentLiveNote.SetModPeriod(currentNote._period);
            };
            currentLiveNote.AddSamples(currentSampleBuffer,_samplesPerBeat-i);
         }
         break;
```

Effect 4: Vibrato

Vibrato is a periodic change in the pitch. This is implemented by using a 64-element waveform to alter the period with each tick. The parameter is interpreted as two nybbles. The high-order nybble indicates how fast to step through the waveform; the low-order nybble specifies the amplitude of the variation.

You may have noticed that effects that modify the period first changed the currentNote._period variable, then used that to set the period. This was done so that period changes would be preserved across multiple beats. With vibrato, it's important to preserve the base period so that continuing vibrato will start from the same reference. As a result, this code does not update currentNote._period.

LISTING 23.12 (CONTINUED)   ModChannel Members

```
public:
   const float *_vibratoWaveform; // Current waveform
   int _currentVibrato; // position in waveform
```

LISTING 23.14 (CONTINUED)   Play currentLiveNote with Effects

```
case ModNoteData::vibrato:
    {
        if (thisParameter == 0)
            thisParameter = defaultParameter;
        int step = (thisParameter >> 4)&0xF;
        int amplitude = (thisParameter&0xF)*2;
        AudioSample *currentSampleBuffer = sampleBuffer;

        // Set vibrato
        currentLiveNote.SetModPeriod(currentNote._period
            +int(_channel[ch]._vibratoWaveform[_channel[ch]._currentVibrato]
                *amplitude));
        // Step vibrato
        _channel[ch]._currentVibrato += step;
        _channel[ch]._currentVibrato &= 63;

        int i=0;
        for(;i<_samplesPerBeat-_samplesPerTick;i+=_samplesPerTick) {
            currentLiveNote.AddSamples(currentSampleBuffer,_samplesPerTick);
            currentSampleBuffer += _samplesPerTick;
            // Set vibrato
            currentLiveNote.SetModPeriod(currentNote._period
                +int(_channel[ch]._vibratoWaveform[_channel[ch]._currentVibrato]
                    *amplitude));
            // Step vibrato
            _channel[ch]._currentVibrato += step;
            _channel[ch]._currentVibrato &= 63;
        };
        currentLiveNote.AddSamples(currentSampleBuffer,_samplesPerBeat-i);
    }
    break;
```

Effect 5: Pitch Slide plus Volume Slide

This effect combines a pitch slide (effect 3) with a gradual change in volume. The parameter for the pitch slide is taken from the current default for that effect while the parameter to this effect specifies the volume change.

The volume change is encoded in an unusual fashion. If the upper nybble is non-zero, it represents the amount to add to the volume on each tick. If the upper nybble is zero, then the lower nybble represents the amount to subtract from the volume on each tick. There is no default for the volume slide. A parameter of zero makes this equivalent to a pitch slide with a zero argument (that is, it merely continues the previous pitch slide without changing the volume).

LISTING 23.14 (CONTINUED)   Play currentLiveNote with Effects

```
case ModNoteData::pitchSlidePlusVolumeSlide:
    {
        int portParameter
            = _channel[ch]._defaultParameter[ModNoteData::pitchSlide];
        // No default for volume slide
        int volumeChange = (thisParameter & 0xF0)?
                            (thisParameter >> 4) & 0xF :
                            -(thisParameter & 0xF);
        AudioSample *currentSampleBuffer = sampleBuffer;
        int i=0;
        for(;i<_samplesPerBeat-_samplesPerTick;i+=_samplesPerTick) {
            currentLiveNote.AddSamples(currentSampleBuffer,_samplesPerTick);
            currentSampleBuffer += _samplesPerTick;
            // Adjust the volume
            currentLiveNote.SetModVolume(_channel[ch]._currentVolume
                                         +volumeChange);
            // Slide the pitch
            if (_channel[ch]._pitchGoal == 0) {
                // Do nothing
            } else if (currentNote._period > _channel[ch]._pitchGoal) {
                currentNote._period -= portParameter;
                if (currentNote._period <= _channel[ch]._pitchGoal) {
                    currentNote._period = _channel[ch]._pitchGoal;
                    _channel[ch]._pitchGoal = 0;
                }
            } else {
                currentNote._period += _channel[ch]._pitchGoal;
                if (currentNote._period >= _channel[ch]._pitchGoal) {
                    currentNote._period = _channel[ch]._pitchGoal;
                    _channel[ch]._pitchGoal = 0;
                }
            }
            currentLiveNote.SetModPeriod(currentNote._period);
        };
        currentLiveNote.AddSamples(currentSampleBuffer,_samplesPerBeat-i);
    }
    break;
```

Effect 6: Vibrato plus Volume Slide

As with effect 5, this continues the last vibrato while changing the volume.

LISTING 23.14 (CONTINUED)   Play currentLiveNote with Effects

```
case ModNoteData::vibratoPlusVolumeSlide:
    {
        // Pick up vibrato parameter from last vibrato
        int vibratoParameter
            = _channel[ch]._defaultParameter[ModNoteData::vibrato];
```

```
        int step = (vibratoParameter >> 4)&0xF;
        int amplitude = (vibratoParameter&0xF)*2;
        // No default for volume slide
        int volumeChange = (thisParameter & 0xF0)?
                        (thisParameter >> 4) & 0xF :
                        -(thisParameter & 0xF);
        AudioSample *currentSampleBuffer = sampleBuffer;
        // Set vibrato
        currentLiveNote.SetModPeriod(currentNote._period
           +int(_channel[ch]._vibratoWaveform[_channel[ch]._currentVibrato]
                *amplitude));
        // Step vibrato
        _channel[ch]._currentVibrato += step;
        _channel[ch]._currentVibrato &= 63;

        int i=0;
        for(;i<_samplesPerBeat-_samplesPerTick;i+=_samplesPerTick) {
            currentLiveNote.AddSamples(currentSampleBuffer,_samplesPerTick);
            currentSampleBuffer += _samplesPerTick;
            // Adjust the volume
            currentLiveNote.SetModVolume(_channel[ch]._currentVolume
                                        +volumeChange);
            // Set vibrato
            currentLiveNote.SetModPeriod(currentNote._period
               +int(_channel[ch]._vibratoWaveform[_channel[ch]._currentVibrato]
                    *amplitude));
            // Step vibrato
            _channel[ch]._currentVibrato += step;
            _channel[ch]._currentVibrato &= 63;
        };
        currentLiveNote.AddSamples(currentSampleBuffer,_samplesPerBeat-i);
    }
    break;
```

Effect 7: Tremolo

Tremolo is like vibrato except that the volume is varied rather than the period. One peculiarity is that the amplitude is multiplied by 4 rather than 2.

LISTING 23.12 (CONTINUED)   ModChannel Members

```
public:
    const float *_tremoloWaveform; // current waveform
    int _currentTremolo; // position in waveform
```

LISTING 23.14 (CONTINUED)   Play currentLiveNote with Effects

```
case ModNoteData::tremolo:
    cerr << "Effect tremolo exercised.\n";
    {
```

```
    if (thisParameter == 0)
        thisParameter = defaultParameter;
    int step = (thisParameter >> 4)&0xF;
    int amplitude = (thisParameter&0xF)*2*2;
    AudioSample *currentSampleBuffer = sampleBuffer;
    // Set volume
    currentLiveNote.SetModVolume(_channel[ch]._currentVolume
        +int(_channel[ch]._tremoloWaveform[_channel[ch]._currentTremolo]
            *amplitude));
    // Step tremolo
    _channel[ch]._currentTremolo += step;
    _channel[ch]._currentTremolo &= 63;

    int i=0;
    for(;i<_samplesPerBeat-_samplesPerTick;i+=_samplesPerTick) {
        currentLiveNote.AddSamples(currentSampleBuffer,_samplesPerTick);
        currentSampleBuffer += _samplesPerTick;
        // Set volume
        currentLiveNote.SetModVolume(_channel[ch]._currentVolume
            +int(_channel[ch]._tremoloWaveform[_channel[ch]._currentTremolo]
                *amplitude));
        // Step tremolo
        _channel[ch]._currentTremolo += step;
        _channel[ch]._currentTremolo &= 63;
    };
    currentLiveNote.AddSamples(currentSampleBuffer,_samplesPerBeat-i);
}
break;
```

Effect 8: Unused

There is no effect 8.

Effect 9: Set Sample Offset

This effect allows you to vary the point in the sample at which a note begins playing. This can be used to create a variety of useful effects. For example, you might store several drum sounds in a single sample and start from different locations to generate different sounds. Alternatively, you can soften an instrument by skipping the initial attack.

LISTING 23.14 (CONTINUED)   Play currentLiveNote with Effects

```
case ModNoteData::setSampleOffset:
    currentLiveNote.Restart();
    currentLiveNote.SetSampleOffset(thisParameter*512);
    currentLiveNote.AddSamples(sampleBuffer,_samplesPerBeat);
    break;
```

Effect 10: Volume Slide

As mentioned, the volume slide parameter is encoded in an unusual fashion. Like most of the per-tick effects, the volume change does not occur at the beginning or end of the beat.

LISTING 23.14 (CONTINUED)   Play currentLiveNote with Effects

```
case ModNoteData::volumeSlide:
  {
    AudioSample *currentSampleBuffer = sampleBuffer;
    int volumeChange = (thisParameter & 0xF0)?
                       (thisParameter >> 4) & 0xF :
                       -(thisParameter & 0xF);
    int i=0;
    for(;i<_samplesPerBeat-_samplesPerTick;i+=_samplesPerTick) {
      currentLiveNote.AddSamples(currentSampleBuffer,_samplesPerTick);
      currentSampleBuffer += _samplesPerTick;
      _channel[ch]._currentVolume += volumeChange;
      currentLiveNote.SetModVolume(_channel[ch]._currentVolume);
    };
    currentLiveNote.AddSamples(currentSampleBuffer,_samplesPerBeat-i);
  }
  break;
```

Effect 11: Far Jump

The far jump, also known as *position jump*, is used primarily to create endlessly looping songs. It can also be used to end the current pattern, but usually a small jump (effect 13) is used for this.

Far jump is handled at the beginning of `PlayBeat` because it has a global effect. It's played the same as `none`.

LISTING 23.16   Process Global Effect for currentNote

```
case ModNoteData::farJump:
  _song.NextIndex(currentNote._parameter); // Jump to this pattern
  _song.NextBeat(0); // at beat 0
  break;
```

LISTING 23.14 (CONTINUED)   Play currentLiveNote with Effects

```
case ModNoteData::farJump:
  currentLiveNote.AddSamples(sampleBuffer,_samplesPerBeat);
  break;
```

Effect 12: Set Volume

This effect simply sets the volume to the given value. Note that this overrides the default volume for that instrument.

LISTING 23.14 (CONTINUED)   Play currentLiveNote with Effects

```
case ModNoteData::setVolume:
    currentLiveNote.SetModVolume(thisParameter);
    _channel[ch]._currentVolume=thisParameter;
    currentLiveNote.AddSamples(sampleBuffer,_samplesPerBeat);
    break;
```

Effect 13: Pattern Break (Small Jump)

The small jump, also known as a *pattern break*, is used to end the current pattern prematurely. The parameter is interpreted in BCD to set the beat at which the next pattern should resume. Usually, the parameter is zero. Although the 64-beat pattern is convenient for music in 4:4 time, it's less convenient for 3:4, 6:8, or other time signatures. The small jump is useful for ending a pattern prematurely to get the effect of a different pattern length.

LISTING 23.16 (CONTINUED)   Process Global Effect for currentNote

```
case ModNoteData::smallJump:
    _song.AdvanceNextIndex();  // jump to next pattern
    _song.NextBeat((currentNote._parameter>>4)*10
           + (currentNote._parameter &0x0F)); // at this beat
    break;
```

LISTING 23.14 (CONTINUED)   Play currentLiveNote with Effects

```
case ModNoteData::smallJump:
    currentLiveNote.AddSamples(sampleBuffer,_samplesPerBeat);
    break;
```

Effect 14/0: Set Filter

If the first nybble of the 12-bit effect is 14, then the second nybble selects the effect, and the third nybble is the argument.

The set filter effect enables or disables the Amiga's 4,000-Hz low-pass filter on the output. Because this is time-consuming to simulate in software and not available on all sound cards, it's not widely used or implemented.

LISTING 23.14 (CONTINUED)   Play currentLiveNote with Effects

---

```
case ModNoteData::setFilter:
  cerr << "Effect setFilter not implemented.\n";
  currentLiveNote.AddSamples(sampleBuffer,_samplesPerBeat);
  break;
```

Effect 14/1: Fine Slide Up

This effect is used to make small adjustments to the period. Unlike the slide up effect, it adjusts the period only once, at the beginning of the beat. It is often used to create slow pitch slides, hence the name.

LISTING 23.14 (CONTINUED)   Play currentLiveNote with Effects

---

```
case ModNoteData::pitchUp:
  cerr << "Effect pitchUp exercised.\n";
  currentNote._period -= thisParameter;
  currentLiveNote.SetModPeriod(currentNote._period);
  currentLiveNote.AddSamples(sampleBuffer,_samplesPerBeat);
  break;
```

Effect 14/2: Fine Slide Down

This is just like fine slide up, but it decreases the pitch (increases the period).

LISTING 23.14 (CONTINUED)   Play currentLiveNote with Effects

---

```
case ModNoteData::pitchDown:
  cerr << "Effect pitchDown exercised.\n";
  currentNote._period += thisParameter;
  currentLiveNote.SetModPeriod(currentNote._period);
  currentLiveNote.AddSamples(sampleBuffer,_samplesPerBeat);
  break;
```

Effect 14/3: Set Glissando

This affects the operation of effect 3 (slide to note). If the parameter is non-zero, subsequent slides will always play the nearest note. If the parameter is zero, slides will adjust the period smoothly.

LISTING 23.14 (CONTINUED) Play currentLiveNote with Effects

```
case ModNoteData::setGlissando:
  cerr << "Effect setGlissando not implemented.\n";
  currentLiveNote.AddSamples(sampleBuffer,_samplesPerBeat);
  break;
```

Effect 14/4: Set Vibrato Waveform

The vibrato and tremolo effects rely on a 64-element waveform. There are three waveforms available: sine wave, square wave, and an increasing ramp. These three possibilities are selected as numbers 0, 1, and 2, respectively. In addition, an argument of 3 is supposed to select one of these at random. However, because this option is almost never used, I've made it equivalent to 0. If any of these are increased by 4, the same waveform is selected but the effect is not reset with each new note.

LISTING 23.12 (CONTINUED) ModChannel Members

```
public:
    static const float _waveform[3][64]; // waveform library
```

LISTING 23.17 MOD Vibrato and Tremolo Waveforms

```
// Waveforms for vibrato (varying pitch) and tremolo (varying volume)
static float vibratoTremoloWaveforms[3][64] = {
  // Sine waveform
  {0.0F,    .09802F, .19509F, .29028F, .38268F, .47140F, .55557F,
   .63439F, .70711F, .77301F, .83147F, .88192F, .92388F, .95694F,
   .98079F, .99518F,1.00000F, .99518F, .98079F, .95694F, .92388F,
   .88192F, .83147F, .77301F, .70711F, .63439F, .55557F, .47140F,
   .38268F, .29028F, .19509F, .09802F,-.00000F,-.09802F,-.19509F,
  -.29028F,-.38268F,-.47140F,-.55557F,-.63439F,-.70711F,-.77301F,
  -.83147F,-.88192F,-.92388F,-.95694F,-.98079F,-.99518F,-1.0F,
  -.99518F,-.98079F,-.95694F,-.92388F,-.88192F,-.83147F,-.77301F,
  -.70711F,-.63439F,-.55557F,-.47140F,-.38268F,-.29028F,-.19509F,
  -.09802F },
  // Square waveform:  32x1, then 32x-1
  {1.0F, 1.0F, 1.0F, 1.0F, 1.0F, 1.0F, 1.0F, 1.0F,
   1.0F, 1.0F, 1.0F, 1.0F, 1.0F, 1.0F, 1.0F, 1.0F,
   1.0F, 1.0F, 1.0F, 1.0F, 1.0F, 1.0F, 1.0F, 1.0F,
   1.0F, 1.0F, 1.0F, 1.0F, 1.0F, 1.0F, 1.0F, 1.0F,
  -1.0F,-1.0F,-1.0F,-1.0F,-1.0F,-1.0F,-1.0F,-1.0F,
  -1.0F,-1.0F,-1.0F,-1.0F,-1.0F,-1.0F,-1.0F,-1.0F,
  -1.0F,-1.0F,-1.0F,-1.0F,-1.0F,-1.0F,-1.0F,-1.0F,
  -1.0F,-1.0F,-1.0F,-1.0F,-1.0F,-1.0F,-1.0F,-1.0F },
  // Ramp waveform:  0->1, then -1->0
  {0.0F,    .03125F, .06250F, .09375F, .12500F, .15625F, .18750F,
```

```
    .21875F, .25000F, .28125F, .31250F, .34375F, .37500F, .40625F,
    .43750F, .46875F, .50000F, .53125F, .56250F, .59375F, .62500F,
    .65625F, .68750F, .71875F, .75000F, .78125F, .81250F, .84375F,
    .87500F, .90625F, .93750F, .96875F
 -1.0F,    -.96875F,-.93750F,-.90625F,-.87500F,-.84375F,-.81250F,
 -.78125F,-.75000F,-.71875F,-.68750F,-.65625F,-.62500F,-.59375F,
 -.56250F,-.53125F,-.50000F,-.46875F,-.43750F,-.40625F,-.37500F,
 -.34375F,-.31250F,-.28125F,-.25000F,-.21875F,-.18750F,-.15625F,
 -.12500F,-.09375F,-.06250F,-.03125F }
 };
```

LISTING 23.15 (CONTINUED)   Initialize ModChannel Variables

```
_vibratoWaveform = &(vibratoTremoloWaveforms[0][0]);
_currentVibrato = 0;
```

LISTING 23.14 (CONTINUED)   Play currentLiveNote with Effects

```
case ModNoteData::setVibrato:
  cerr << "Effect setVibrato exercised.\n";
  // Random selection always selects 0
  if ((thisParameter & 3) == 3) thisParameter &= 4;
  _channel[ch]._vibratoWaveform
     = &(vibratoTremoloWaveforms[thisParameter & 0x3][0]);
  currentLiveNote.AddSamples(sampleBuffer,_samplesPerBeat);
  break;
```

Effect 14/5: Set Finetune

This allows you to vary the finetune parameter on a per-note basis. It is rarely used.

LISTING 23.14 (CONTINUED)   Play currentLiveNote with Effects

```
case ModNoteData::setFinetune:
  cerr << "Effect setFinetune not implemented.\n";
  currentLiveNote.AddSamples(sampleBuffer,_samplesPerBeat);
  break;
```

Effect 14/6: Pattern Loop

If the parameter is zero, this marks the beginning of a loop. If the parameter is non-zero, this marks the end of the loop. The parameter in this case indicates how many times the loop should be repeated.

LISTING 23.16 (CONTINUED)   Process Global Effect for currentNote

```
case ModNoteData::patternLoop:
  cerr << "Loop pattern effect not implemented.\n";
  break;
```

LISTING 23.14 (CONTINUED)   Play currentLiveNote with Effects

```
case ModNoteData::patternLoop:
  currentLiveNote.AddSamples(sampleBuffer,_samplesPerBeat);
  break;
```

Effect 14/7: Set Tremolo Waveform

This effect is identical to set vibrato waveform (effect 14/4) but affects the tremolo waveform.

LISTING 23.15 (CONTINUED)   Initialize ModChannel Variables

```
_tremoloWaveform = &(vibratoTremoloWaveforms[0][0]);
_currentTremolo = 0;
```

LISTING 23.14 (CONTINUED)   Play currentLiveNote with Effects

```
case ModNoteData::setTremolo:
  cerr << "Effect setTremolo exercised.\n";
  // Random selection always selects 0
  if ((thisParameter & 3) == 3) thisParameter &= 4;
  _channel[ch]._tremoloWaveform
    = &(vibratoTremoloWaveforms[thisParameter & 0x3][0]);
  currentLiveNote.AddSamples(sampleBuffer,_samplesPerBeat);
  break;
```

Effect 14/8: Unused

There is no effect with this value.

Effect 14/9: Retrigger

Quick drum beats or stutters can be accomplished by restarting the note periodically during the beat. The retrigger effect accepts a parameter that specifies how often to restart the note (in ticks). In this implementation, I compute `samplesPerNote`, the number of samples to play before the next trigger.

LISTING 23.14 (CONTINUED)   Play currentLiveNote with Effects

```
case ModNoteData::retrigger:
  // Restart note several times
  {
    if (thisParameter == 0) thisParameter = defaultParameter;
    AudioSample *currentSampleBuffer = sampleBuffer;
    int samplesPerNote = _samplesPerTick * thisParameter;
    int i=0;
    for(;i<_samplesPerBeat-samplesPerNote-_samplesPerTick/2
        ;i+=samplesPerNote) {
      currentLiveNote.AddSamples(currentSampleBuffer,samplesPerNote);
      currentSampleBuffer += samplesPerNote;
      currentLiveNote.Restart();
    };
    currentLiveNote.AddSamples(currentSampleBuffer,_samplesPerBeat-i);
  }
  break;
```

Effect 14/10: Volume Up

This is similar to fine slide up (effect 14/1), but it changes the volume.

LISTING 23.14 (CONTINUED)   Play currentLiveNote with Effects

```
case ModNoteData::volumeUp:
  _channel[ch]._currentVolume += thisParameter;
  currentLiveNote.SetModVolume(_channel[ch]._currentVolume);
  currentLiveNote.AddSamples(sampleBuffer,_samplesPerBeat);
  break;
```

Effect 14/11: Volume Down

As above, except volume decreases.

LISTING 23.14 (CONTINUED)   Play currentLiveNote with Effects

```
case ModNoteData::volumeDown:
  cerr << "Effect volumeDown exercised.\n";
  currentLiveNote.SetModVolume(_channel[ch]._currentVolume-thisParameter);
  currentLiveNote.AddSamples(sampleBuffer,_samplesPerBeat);
  break;
```

Effect 14/12: Cut Note

The note volume is reduced to zero after the specified number of ticks. It is important to continue playing the note after the volume decreases because the next beat might increase the volume again. Although the difference is minor for instruments like pianos, this effect can also be used to drop a single drumbeat from a sample.

LISTING 23.14 (CONTINUED)   Play currentLiveNote with Effects

```
case ModNoteData::cutNote:
   // Play for 'parameter' ticks, then cut volume to zero
   // and continue playing
   cerr << "Effect cutNote exercised.\n";
   {
      if (thisParameter == 0) thisParameter = defaultParameter;
      int playSamples = _samplesPerTick * thisParameter;
      if (playSamples < _samplesPerBeat) {
         currentLiveNote.AddSamples(sampleBuffer, playSamples);
         _channel[ch]._currentVolume = 0;
         currentLiveNote.SetModVolume(_channel[ch]._currentVolume);
         currentLiveNote.AddSamples(sampleBuffer+playSamples,
                             _samplesPerBeat-playSamples);
      } else { // Play whole beat
         currentLiveNote.AddSamples(sampleBuffer,_samplesPerBeat);
      }
   }
   break;
```

Effect 14/13: Delay Note

The delay note effect doesn't begin playing the note until after the specified number of ticks has elapsed. Some later MOD formats have slightly redefined this effect to mean that the note change won't occur until that point. This would require continuing to play the previous note at the beginning of the beat.

LISTING 23.14 (CONTINUED)   Play currentLiveNote with Effects

```
case ModNoteData::delayNote:
   {
      if (thisParameter == 0) thisParameter = defaultParameter;
      int skipSamples = _samplesPerTick * thisParameter;
      if (skipSamples < _samplesPerBeat)
         currentLiveNote.AddSamples(sampleBuffer+skipSamples,
                             _samplesPerBeat-skipSamples);
   }
   break;
```

Effect 14/14: Delay Pattern

Delay pattern causes the previous beat to be repeated the indicated number of times before playing this beat. Note that global effects from the previous beat are not interpreted. It's not clear what should happen if there are multiple delay pattern effects in the same beat.

To implement this, I've added a `delayPatternCount` variable to the channel state. This variable is negative if there is no delay currently in effect. If it's positive, this indicates the remaining number of repetitions. If it's zero, the delay is complete and you can allow the current beat to play.

LISTING 23.12 (CONTINUED)   ModChannel Members

```
public:
    int _delayPatternCount; // >= 0 if delay pattern loop is in effect
```

LISTING 23.15 (CONTINUED)   Initialize ModChannel Variables

```
_delayPatternCount = -1;
```

LISTING 23.16 (CONTINUED)   Process Global Effect for currentNote

```
case ModNoteData::delayPattern:
    // Delay Pattern is essentially a one-beat loop
    if (_channel[ch0]._delayPatternCount < 0) { // Starting new delay
        _channel[ch0]._delayPatternCount = currentNote._parameter;
    }
    if (_channel[ch0]._delayPatternCount >0) { // Positive count,
        _song.Back();
        _channel[ch0]._delayPatternCount--; // Count delays
    } else {
        _channel[ch0]._delayPatternCount = -1; // no longer delaying
    }
    break;
```

LISTING 23.14 (CONTINUED)   Play currentLiveNote with Effects

```
case ModNoteData::delayPattern:
    currentLiveNote.AddSamples(sampleBuffer,_samplesPerBeat);
    break;
```

TABLE 23.7   Increments for Invert Loop Effect

Param	0	1	2	3	4	5	6	7	8	9	10	11	12	13	14	15
Step	0	5	6	7	8	10	11	13	16	19	22	26	32	43	64	128

Effect 14/15: Invert Loop

This effect is a good example of programmer ingenuity in producing interesting sound effects. The effect sets up two loops: The first loop is the regular play loop that selects samples and outputs them. The second loop sweeps through the sound data at a much slower rate, negating the samples as it goes. There are two interesting results: The sound data changes as it is played, and a section of the sound is negated. The precise effect varies according to the length of the sound's repeated section and the rate of the negate loop. Essentially, the sound is being combined with a variable square wave.

The parameter selects an increment from Table 23.7. On each tick, this increment is added to a counter. When the counter exceeds 128, the next sample in the repeat portion of the sound is negated. When the end of the repeat portion is reached, the loop continues at the beginning of the repeat portion. This procedure continues as long as the invert loop effect is used.

Because of its complexity, this effect is not often implemented.

LISTING 23.14 (CONTINUED)   Play currentLiveNote with Effects

```
case ModNoteData::invertLoop:
    cerr << "Effect invertLoop not implemented.\n";
    currentLiveNote.AddSamples(sampleBuffer,_samplesPerBeat);
    break;
```

Effect 15: Set Speed

MOD players use two speed parameters. The first is the tick rate; the second is the number of ticks per beat. The parameter has different effects, depending on its value.

- If the parameter is zero, the song is stopped.

- If the parameter is less than or equal to 32, it determines the number of ticks per beat.

- If the parameter is greater than 32, it sets the number of ticks per second, using a formula in which 125 represents the default tick rate of 50 per second.

LISTING 23.16 (CONTINUED)   Process Global Effect for currentNote

```
case ModNoteData::setTempo:
  if (currentNote._parameter == 0) { // stop song
    cerr << "Set tempo 0 exercised.\n";
    _song.Stop();
    _sampleLength = 0;
    return;
  } else if (currentNote._parameter <= 32) { // set ticks per beat
    _ticksPerBeat = currentNote._parameter;
  } else { // set tick rate
    _ticksPerMinute = 50L * 60 * currentNote._parameter/125;
  }
  break;
```

LISTING 23.14 (CONTINUED)   Play currentLiveNote with Effects

```
case ModNoteData::setTempo:
  currentLiveNote.AddSamples(sampleBuffer,_samplesPerBeat);
  break;
```

Part Six
Audio Processing

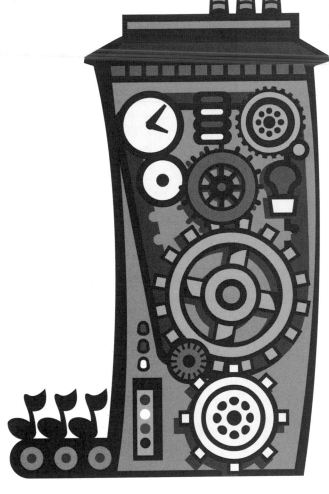

Fourier Transforms 24

By now, you've figured out that a critical part of sound manipulation is the ability to look at a sound as a series of samples or as a collection of frequencies. Each viewpoint allows you to do manipulations that are difficult in the other, so it's important to be able to convert between the two.

Engineers refer to these two viewpoints as *time domain* and *frequency domain*. In the time domain, a sound looks like a sequence of samples. When you look at a sound this way, it's very easy to adjust the amplitude of a sound (just scale each sample), mix several sounds together (add samples), or delay a sound. In the frequency domain, a sound looks like a collection of frequencies added together. From this view, it's easy to isolate specific components, such as treble and bass, and manipulate those components individually.

The basic tool used to convert between these two is called the *Fourier Transform* (pronounced "FOUR-ee-ay") after the French mathematician Jean-Baptiste Fourier (1768–1830). The Fourier Transform has its origins in some pretty heavy-duty mathematics. Fortunately, you can get a good working understanding of the Fourier Transform without worrying about the more esoteric mathematical details. In this chapter, I'll demonstrate some basic properties of sine waves and show how those ideas translate into a method for efficiently computing the frequency spectrum of a signal. Although I will present the Fourier equations in all of their glory, don't worry if your math is a bit rusty; the important ideas are pretty simple.

Fourier Transform Basics

Even if you skip most of this chapter, there are a few things you should know about Fourier Transforms and how they can be used. The purpose of a Fourier Transform is to allow you to manipulate frequency information. However, when you record or play a sound, you are always working with time-domain samples. As a result, Fourier Transforms always come in pairs: A *forward* version converts time-domain samples into a frequency-domain spectrum; an *inverse* version converts the spectrum back into samples.

One typical application is in sound compression. An MPEG compressor, for example, converts samples into frequency information because the latter is easier to compress. The MPEG decompressor uncompresses the frequency information, then uses the inverse transformation to convert the spectrum back into samples for playback.

Another application is in sound manipulation. For example, the pops and clicks that give character to old recordings consist primarily of high frequencies. By converting your sound samples into frequency information, you can more easily identify and remove those artifacts, then convert back into samples for further processing, storage, or playback.

The forward and inverse transforms are always exact. If you convert samples into a frequency spectrum with a forward transform and then convert the spectrum back into samples with the inverse transform, you will get exactly the same samples back (except for minor differences caused by numeric round-off). This means that you lose no information; the frequency domain and time domain are equivalent.

However useful the frequency domain is, it does have weaknesses. In real signals, the frequency spectrum varies from instant to instant. The spectrum computed by a Fourier Transform, however, does not obviously reflect this variation. As a result, people typically use the Fourier Transform to evaluate small blocks of samples, ranging from 32 to 1,024 samples at a time, depending on the application. Fewer samples give you less frequency resolution. If two signals are close together in frequency, you'll need to work with large blocks of samples to distinguish them. But larger blocks of samples obscure timing information. Removing pops and clicks from old recordings is a difficult process because you need both frequency and timing information.

The transform discovered by Jean-Baptiste Fourier is just one of many similar transforms used for audio processing. The original Fourier Transform describes continuous signals, such as those used in electronic audio applications. The *Discrete Fourier Transform* (DFT), which I'll describe in this chapter, is the same idea applied to sampled signals. Other widely-used frequency transforms include the *Cosine Transform* and the *Discrete Cosine Transform* (DCT).

You'll often hear about *Fast Fourier Transform* (FFT) algorithms. Keep in mind that these are not different transforms but simply a family of fast methods for computing the DFT. There are now many subtly different FFT algorithms.

Sine Waves

Figure 24.1 illustrates some of the important features of a sine wave. The *frequency* is the number of complete cycles that occur per second; it's related to the *duration*, which is the time required for one cycle. The height of the graph corresponds to the *amplitude*, which is the digital sample value, electrical voltage or current, or air pressure.

FIGURE 24.1   Frequency, Wavelength, and Amplitude

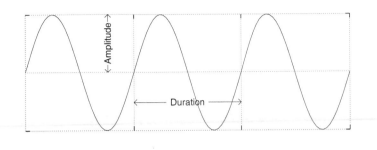

Mathematically, a sine wave is written using either the sin() or cos() functions familiar from trigonometry. The simple function $\sin(t)$ has an amplitude of 1, a duration of 2π seconds, and a corresponding frequency of $1/2\pi$ cycles per second. With a little care, you can massage this into a more useful form: $A\sin(2\pi f t)$ represents a sine wave with amplitude A and frequency f.

Of course, this assumes that t represents time (in seconds) and f is the frequency value. When you're working with a sampled signal, it's more convenient to let t be the *sample number*. In this case, $A\sin(2\pi f t)$ represents a sine wave with amplitude A and frequency fS, where S is the sampling rate. In the following, I'll work with groups of N samples at a time and only be interested in certain frequencies, so I'll use sine waves written as $\sin(2\pi t f/N)$ and $\cos(2\pi t f/N)$, which have an amplitude of one and a frequency of fS/N.

Amplitude and frequency don't give the whole story. Time delays can cause sine waves to be offset from one another, as shown in Figure 24.2. Although you can measure

FIGURE 24.2   Three Sine Waves with Different Phase

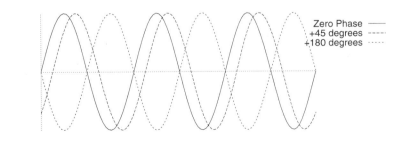

FIGURE 24.3 A Sine Wave Labeled with Degrees of Phase

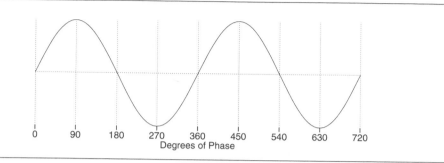

Degrees of Phase

such offsets as time delays, it's more useful to measure these differences as fractions of a cycle, referred to as *phase*.

Because sine waves are intimately related to circles, phase is conventionally measured in degrees. A single complete cycle is 360 degrees. Figure 24.3 shows another sine wave. This time, the horizontal axis is labeled in *degrees of phase*. Just as a rotation of 360 degrees leaves you where you started, a phase change of 360 degrees leaves you with the same signal.

Phase changes are often caused by time delays. For example, a 1,000-Hz signal takes 1/1,000 second for one cycle. If you delay it by 1/2,000 second (half a cycle), you get a 180-degree phase-shift. Note that this effect depends on the relation between the frequency and the time delay. If you delay a 250-Hz signal by that same 1/2,000 of a second, you get only a 45-degree phase-shift.

If you add together two sine waves with the same frequency, the result is a new sine wave with the same frequency. This is true even if the two original signals have different amplitudes and phases. For example, $A\sin(2\pi f t)$ and $B\cos(2\pi f t)$ are two sine waves with different amplitudes and different phases, but the same frequency.

Measuring One Frequency at a Time

If you have a beaker full of sea water, you might ask: "How much potassium chloride is in this beaker?" Similarly, if you have a sampled sound that is composed of many different sine waves, you might ask: "How loud a 1,000-Hz sine wave is in this sound?" The Discrete Fourier Transform (DFT) provides a way to answer this question. If you're interested in only a single frequency, you can use the DFT to measure how loud that frequency is as part of the total sound. By repeating this measurement for different frequencies, you can build up a fairly complete picture of the *spectrum* of the sound.

FIGURE 24.4   Multiplying Two Sine Waves with the Same Frequency

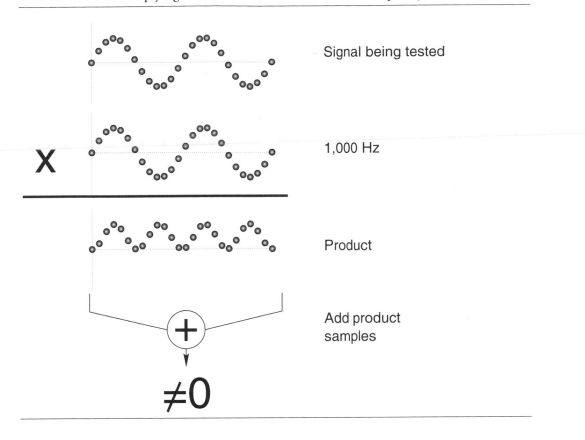

Although the DFT rests on some involved mathematics, the basic idea is simple: If you multiply two different sine waves, you get different results depending on whether the frequencies agree.

For example, suppose you want to test how much 1,000 Hz is in a certain signal. You first multiply the signal in question by a 1,000-Hz sine wave and then add together the product samples. Figure 24.4 illustrates this process if the signal you're testing happens to be a 1,000-Hz sine wave with the same phase. (This picture obviously changes depending on the phase; I'll discuss the details later.) Although it may not be obvious, in this case the final sum is proportional to the amplitude of the signal being tested.

In contrast, Figure 24.5 shows what happens when the signal being tested is a sine wave with a different frequency. Here the product includes both positive and negative values. If you add together the product samples in Figure 24.5, you'll end up with zero.

FIGURE 24.5 Multiplying Two Sine Waves with Different Frequencies

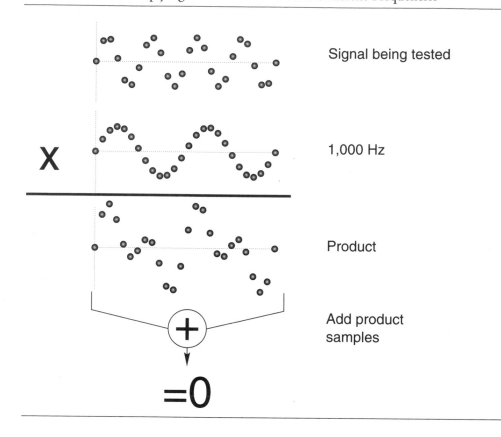

Signal being tested

X

1,000 Hz

Product

Add product
samples

=0

This observation suggests that to measure the amplitude of a single frequency, you multiply your signal by a sine wave of that frequency and add together the resulting samples.

To represent this symbolically, assume your samples are $s_0, s_1, \ldots, s_t, \ldots$. The variable t represents sample number (which is a stand-in for time). As a first approximation, you can measure the amplitude of a frequency f with the following summation:

$$\text{amplitude} = \sum_{t=0}^{N-1} s_t \cos(2\pi t f/N)$$

I'm glossing over many details here. For example, if you study the preceding discussion, you'll notice that the basic technique for measuring frequencies works only for certain frequencies. The values t and f here do not directly represent time and frequency. Rather, f is an integer, and the actual frequency being tested is f/N times the sampling frequency. Similarly, t is the integer sample number. Also, the result of this sum does not directly give you the amplitude but merely a number proportional to the amplitude. Despite these caveats, the intuition is still valid; multiplying your signal by a sine wave and then summing gives you a number proportional to the amplitude.

If you repeat this calculation for different values of f, you can measure the amplitude of all the frequencies in your signal. For every integer f less than N, you can define A_f to be the amplitude of the corresponding frequency as part of your signal. These values can be calculated using the same formula.

$$A_f = \sum_{t=0}^{N-1} s_t \cos(2\pi t f/N)$$

The next step is the part that mathematicians find so magical. If you know the A_f values, you can get your samples back. Remember that A_f is just the amplitude of the sine wave of frequency fS/N. To recover your signal, you need to add up all of those different frequencies. In symbols, this looks like

$$s_t = \sum_{f=0}^{N-1} A_f \cos(2\pi t f/N)$$

This *inverse* transform is similar to the *forward* transform I described above. If you work with Fourier Transforms extensively, this similarity becomes important.

Accounting for Phase

Amplitude and frequency are only part of the picture. In order to have a Fourier Transform that can be undone precisely, you also need to measure the phase of each frequency. I've already shown how you measure the amplitude for each frequency. But what about phase?

Complex numbers come to the rescue. With a little insight, the earlier calculation can be changed into one that gives a 2-dimensional result. A single complex number is essentially a 2-dimensional value, so it can simultaneously represent amplitude and phase.

It turns out that the phase part is obtained indirectly. Rather than measure amplitude and phase, you measure two amplitudes, each corresponding to a different phase. One of those phases is represented by cos() and the other by sin(). Using complex numbers, you can do both of these measurements at once, just multiply the sin() part by $-i$. (I use i to represent $\sqrt{-1}$; some people prefer the letter j.)

$$A_f = \sum_{t=0}^{N-1} \left(s_t \cos(2\pi t f/N) - i s_t \sin(2\pi t f/N) \right)$$

Each A_f is now a complex number; the real and imaginary parts give the amplitude of two sine waves at different phases. Recall that every complex number $a + ib$ has a magnitude $\sqrt{a^2 + b^2}$ and an angle $\tan^{-1}(a/b)$. The magnitude of A_f is the amplitude of a single sine wave whose phase is the angle of A_f.

For compactness, people typically replace $\cos(2\pi t f/N) - i \sin(2\pi t f/N)$ with the equivalent (but admittedly more cryptic) $e^{-2\pi i t f/N}$, which gives the version of the DFT usually used in textbooks:

$$A_f = \sum_{t=0}^{N-1} s_t e^{-2\pi i t f/N}$$

Not surprisingly, the full Inverse DFT looks quite similar. By now, you should understand that this formulation, for each frequency, combines a sine wave and a cosine wave to get a single wave with the correct frequency, amplitude, and phase. Adding these waves together yields the original signal:

$$s(t) = \sum_{f=0}^{N-1} A_f e^{2\pi i t f/N}$$

Implementing the DFT

The DFT is easy to translate into computer code. Using the `complex` package from the Standard C++ library, you could implement the Forward DFT as in Listing 24.1, taking advantage of the fact that `polar(1.0,x)` is the same as e^{ix}.

LISTING 24.1   Discrete Fourier Transform

```
void ForwardDft(complex <double> *samples,
                int length, complex<double>*result) {
   static const double
         twoPi = 2*3.1415926535897932384626;
   for(int f = 0; f<length; f++) {
      result[f] = 0.0;
      for(int t = 0; t < length; t++)
         result[f] += samples[t] * polar(1.0,-twoPi*f*t/length);
   }
}
```

This code is appealingly simple, and you should keep it handy if you do much work with Fourier Transforms. Because it is so simple, you can be reasonably certain that it's correct. By comparing other Fourier Transform programs with this one, you can verify that they're also working correctly.

However, this code is actually quite slow, much too slow for practical use. You can significantly speed it up by rearranging the above code (you can move the exponential calculation out of the inner loop), but it's possible to do much better.

The basic problem is that this formula computes each point of the spectrum separately. In practice, you almost always want to compute the entire spectrum at once, which allows you to combine the calculations for different frequencies.

Scaling

If you start with a set of samples, use the Forward DFT given earlier to obtain a spectrum and then use the Inverse DFT to get a set of samples, you won't get the exact samples you started with. The result will actually be N times larger than what you started with. To compensate, you have to introduce a factor of $1/N$ somewhere. There are at least three ways to do this.

One way to get the properly scaled answer is to divide the results from the Forward DFT by N. The Forward and Inverse DFTs then look like:

$$A_f = \frac{1}{N} \sum_{t=0}^{N-1} s_t e^{-2\pi i t f/N}$$

$$s_t = \sum_{f=0}^{N-1} A_f e^{2\pi i t f/N}$$

Now, if you take the Forward DFT of a set of samples and then the Inverse DFT of the resulting spectrum, you will get exactly the samples you started with.

But there are other ways to deal with this irregularity. Some people prefer to divide the output of the Forward and Inverse DFTs by $\sqrt{N}$, which gives you very symmetric formulas.

$$A_f = \frac{1}{\sqrt{N}} \sum_{t=0}^{N-1} s_t e^{-2\pi i t f/N}$$

$$s_t = \frac{1}{\sqrt{N}} \sum_{f=0}^{N-1} A_f e^{2\pi i t f/N}$$

Usually, however, people are most concerned with the time required to calculate the forward transform, so the most common correction is to divide the result of the Inverse DFT by N.

$$A_f = \sum_{t=0}^{N-1} s_t e^{-2\pi it f/N}$$

$$s_t = \frac{1}{N} \sum_{f=0}^{N-1} A_f e^{2\pi it f/N}$$

Although the first one has a slight claim to technical correctness, the important question in practice is the *relative* output. Any of these three scaling techniques will give you the same relative answers.

Measuring the Entire Spectrum at Once

In the 1960s, Cooley and Tukey discovered a more practical way to compute the DFT. Their Fast Fourier Transform (FFT) algorithm effectively computes the entire spectrum at once. Many people have studied the FFT, and there are now a large number of subtly different FFT algorithms. I'll focus on one widely used technique that rapidly computes the spectrum assuming the number of samples is a power of two. This isn't the fastest FFT algorithm; it is, however, relatively easy to understand and fast enough for most purposes.

Small FFTs

In the introduction to this chapter, I explained that you usually work with small numbers of samples at a time. To explain the FFT algorithm, I'll start by looking at small numbers of samples. The question I want to explore is: How much frequency information is there in a small number of samples?

As an extreme case, consider what happens if I have only one sample. Only one frequency is required to completely describe a single sample. The simplest frequency to use is the zero frequency. A zero-frequency signal has only an amplitude and is often referred to as *DC* by engineers.

The next step is to look at two samples. As you might guess, two samples can always be completely described by two frequencies, the zero frequency and one-half of the sampling rate $(S/2)$.

FIGURE 24.6   The Frequency Spectrum of Two Samples

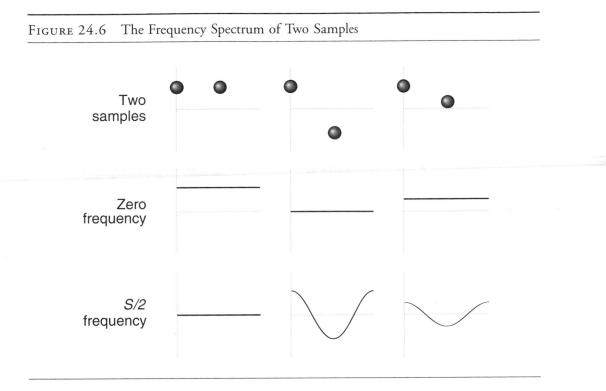

Figure 24.6 illustrates some of the possibilities with two samples. Each column shows two samples and how they can be described as a sum of a zero-frequency sine wave and an $S/2$-frequency sine wave.

Similarly, three samples can be described with three frequencies: zero, one-third the sampling rate, and two-thirds the sampling rate. Four samples are described with four frequencies ranging from zero to three-fourths the sampling rate.

The last two sentences should have gotten your attention. On page 26, I explained that one-half the sampling frequency is a magic limit; no sampled signal can have a frequency higher than this. So how can two-thirds or three-fourths the sampling rate be a component of a sound signal? The full answer rests on the fact that the DFT deals with complex-valued signals, for which the Nyquist limit works a little differently.

Fortunately, audio processing only requires you to work with real-valued signals, so things are simpler. Although the DFT requires you to work with a range of frequencies from 0 to S, the section from $S/2$ to S is always the mirror image of the part from 0 to $S/2$. People often find it easier to rearrange the DFT spectrum so that it extends from $-S/2$ to $S/2$, as shown in Figure 24.7.

FIGURE 24.7   Two Ways to Think of the Same Frequency Spectrum

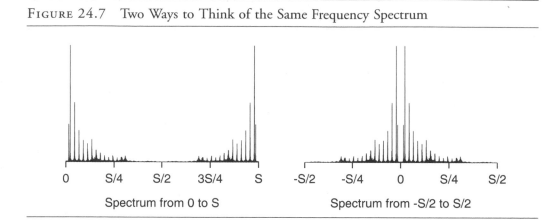

(Actually, it's not precisely a mirror image. One half is the complex conjugate of the other half; the real values are the same, the imaginary values are negated.)

Decomposing Long FFTs

Now suppose you have 1,024 samples and you want to compute the spectrum. From the above discussion, you know that the result will be 1,024 complex numbers representing the amplitude and phase for evenly spaced frequencies from 0 to 1,023/1,024 of the sampling rate.

You can think of your 1,024 samples as points on a continuous signal. You're simply picking 1,024 evenly spaced points and treating those as representative. It makes sense, then, to pick 512 evenly spaced points (every other sample) and consider the spectrum of those points. This smaller spectrum will describe evenly spaced frequencies from 0 to 511/512 of the sampling rate, which are half the frequencies of interest.

The FFT algorithm is based on this idea. A 1,024-sample DFT can be split into two 512-sample DFTs, one containing the even samples and the other the odd samples. They give you two 512-point spectrums that you must somehow combine to obtain the full 1,024-point spectrum.

To compute a 512-sample DFT, you decompose it into two 256-sample DFTs, and so on. In this way, you eventually find yourself computing DFTs of pairs of samples.

With this outline in hand, you need only understand how to compute 2-sample DFTs and how to combine two small spectrums into a single larger spectrum.

2-Point FFT

If you have two samples, it's easy to see that the zero-frequency part is simply the average of the two samples. Similarly, the $S/2$ part is one-half the difference. In symbols

$$A_0 = 1/2(s_0 + s_1)$$

$$A_1 = 1/2(s_0 - s_1)$$

This is precisely the 2-point FFT, and it forms the basis of the most common FFT algorithm. Note the pattern of adding and then subtracting.

4-Point FFTs

To show how you combine FFTs into larger FFTs, I'll look at a 4-point FFT of the samples s_0, s_1, s_2, and s_3. I want to compute the amplitude (and phase) of four frequencies: zero, $S/4$, $S/2$, and $3S/4$.

If I look just at s_0 and s_2, I have two samples with half the sampling rate. Using the formulas above for the 2-point FFT, I can compute a zero-frequency component $(s_0 + s_2)/2$ and another component $(s_0 - s_2)/2$ for a frequency that is half the sampling rate of this subsequence—that is, $S/4$.

I can do the same calculation with s_1 and s_3, giving me another pair of estimates for the zero-frequency component and the $S/4$ component. There's no reason for these second estimates to be the same as the first, so you need a way to reconcile them and to generate information about $S/2$ and $3S/4$.

The important fact is that the frequency information gleaned from s_0 and s_2 is at a different phase than the information provided by s_1 and s_3. You can reconcile that phase by multiplying the latter results by a *phase-shift coefficient* of $-i$. (The significance of the value $-i$ is that $(-i)^4 = 1$; so $-i$ represents a shift of one sample out of four.)

The final formulas for the 4-point FFT are

$$A_0 = 1/4((s_0 + s_2) + (s_1 + s_3))$$

$$A_1 = 1/4((s_0 - s_2) + (-i) * (s_1 - s_3))$$

$$A_2 = 1/4((s_0 + s_2) - (s_1 + s_3))$$

$$A_3 = 1/4((s_0 - s_2) - (-i) * (s_1 - s_3))$$

The pattern is clear; compute the two 2-point FFTs, multiply the second estimates by appropriate phase-shift coefficients, then combine the two sets of estimates by first taking corresponding sums, then corresponding differences.

For longer FFTs, you use the same structure. First, compute two half-size FFTs, then multiply the second by appropriate complex numbers, then combine them again by first taking sums, then differences. This suggests a recursive implementation, which I'll describe in detail in a moment.

Formal Derivation of the FFT

My description of the DFT and the FFT algorithm has, to this point, taken a deliberately intuitive approach. My goal is for you to have some gut-level understanding of the formulas. This means I sometimes take minor liberties with the mathematics in order to clarify an important point. But there are times when technical accuracy is paramount, so in this section I'll repeat the material from the previous section in a more rigorous manner.

I explained earlier that the intuition behind the FFT is that you can use every other sample to compute a half-resolution version of the spectrum. Formally, this means that the DFT formula can be rewritten as two summations. The first has all the even terms from the original; the second has all the odd terms.

$$A_f = \sum_{t=0}^{N-1} s_t e^{-2\pi i f t/N}$$

$$= \sum_{t=0}^{(N/2)-1} s_{2t} e^{-2\pi i f(2t)/N} + \sum_{t=0}^{(N/2)-1} s_{2t+1} e^{-2\pi i f(2t+1)/N}$$

With a little care, you can rewrite the two latter summations.

$$A_f = \sum_{t=0}^{N-1} s_t e^{-2\pi i f t/N}$$

$$= \sum_{t=0}^{(N/2)-1} s_{2t} e^{-2\pi i f t/(N/2)} + e^{-2\pi i f/N} \sum_{t=0}^{(N/2)-1} s_{2t+1} e^{-2\pi i f t/(N/2)}$$

Note that the two latter summations are exactly N/2-point DFTs: The first is the DFT of the even samples; the second is the DFT of the odd samples. The factor of $e^{-2\pi i f/N}$, which factors out of the second one, is precisely the "phase-shift coefficient" I referred to earlier. In the case of $N = 4$, there are four phase-shift coefficients, one for each frequency. From this formula, you can see they are 1, $-i$, $-1 = (-i)^2$, and $i = (-i)^3$. (Compare this with the formulas in the previous section.)

Note that the phase-shift coefficients come in pairs. If you list the phase-shift coefficients for a particular value of N, the second half of the list is the negative of the first half. This gives you the pattern of adding and subtracting that I mentioned in the previous section.

That's all the mathematics you need to derive the FFT algorithm. The formula above tells you how to combine two N/2-point DFTs to get the same result as a single N-point DFT. To develop the rest of the algorithm, you need to organize these combining operations.

Programming the FFT

From the ideas above, a little work will get you a recursive implementation similar to the following.

LISTING 24.2   Slow FFT Implementation

```
static void SlowFftRecursion(complex<double> *samples, int length,
                int start, int skip, complex<double> *result) {

    if (length == 1) {  // 1-point FFT is easy!
       *result = samples[start];
       return;
    }

    // Compute two half-size FFTs
    SlowFftRecursion(samples,length/2,start,skip*2,result);
    SlowFftRecursion(samples,length/2,start+skip,skip*2,result+length/2);

    // Compute sums and differences of pairs
    for(int j=0; j<length/2; j++) {
       // Multiply the second piece by a phase-shift coefficient
       complex<double> t = result[j+length/2] * polar(1.0,-2*PI*j/length);
       // subtract
       result[j + length/2] = result[j] - t;
       // add
       result[j] += t;
    }
}

void SlowForwardFft(complex<double> *samples, int length,
            complex<double>*result) {
    SlowFftRecursion(samples,length,0,1,result);
}
```

To test this, you should compare its output to the DFT implementation given earlier.

There are a number of ways to accelerate this code. The most obvious is to eliminate the repeated calls to polar in the inner loop. (polar(1,x) is the same as e^{ix}). The next step is to eliminate the recursion altogether, but this requires some additional work.

If you look carefully at the recursion in SlowFftRecursion, the lowest-level recursions (the 1-point FFTs) simply copy the data over in a particular order, while the remainder of the work is done in place. To eliminate the recursion, you need to first find another way to do this reordering.

Once the reordering is done, you can emulate the recursive steps in a slightly different order. First, do 2-point FFTs on successive pairs, then compute 4-point FFTs on each group of four samples, and so forth. The resulting nonrecursive implementation will look similar to the following.

LISTING 24.3   Skeleton of the Nonrecursive FFT Implementation

---

```
for(int halfSize=1; halfSize < length; halfSize *= 2)
    for(int fftStep = 0; fftStep < halfSize; fftStep++)
        for(int i=fftStep; i < length; i += 2*halfSize) {
            complex<double> t = currentPhaseShift * samples[i+halfSize];
            samples[i+halfSize] = samples[i] - t;
            samples[i] += t;
        }
```

The result of all of this work is the following module that exports only four functions, and two of those are slow versions provided only for comparison. The fastest version does all the work in place and hence requires only a single array.

LISTING 24.4   fft.h

Copyright © 1998, Tim Kientzle (Listing E.1)

```
#include <complex>

// Length must be a power of two
void ForwardFft(complex<double> *, int length);
void InverseFft(complex<double> *, int length);

// Slower versions are exported for comparison and experimentation
void ForwardDft(complex <double> *samples,
                int length, complex<double>*result);
void SlowForwardFft(complex<double> *samples, int length,
                    complex<double>*result);
```

If you've understood the previous discussion, this code is surprisingly simple. The only additional optimization is how I compute the phase-shift coefficients. Since each successive coefficient is just a power of the first one, I need to use only one multiplication in the inner loop to compute the next phase-shift coefficient.

LISTING 24.5   fft.cpp

```
Copyright © 1998, Tim Kientzle (Listing E.1)
#include "fft.h"
#include <cmath>
#include <iostream>

const double PI = 3.14159265358979323846264338;

Discrete Fourier Transform (Listing 24.1)

Slow FFT Implementation (Listing 24.2)

Rearrange Samples for Fast FFT (Listing 24.6)

void ForwardFft(complex<double> *samples, int length ) {
   Rearrange(samples,length);

   for(int halfSize=1; halfSize < length; halfSize *= 2) {
      complex<double> phaseShiftStep = polar(1.0,-PI/halfSize);
      complex<double> currentPhaseShift(1,0);
      for(int fftStep = 0; fftStep < halfSize; fftStep++) {
         for(int i=fftStep; i < length; i += 2*halfSize) {
            complex<double> t = currentPhaseShift * samples[i+halfSize];
            samples[i+halfSize] = samples[i] - t;
            samples[i] += t;
         }
         currentPhaseShift *= phaseShiftStep;
      }
   }
}


//
// Using some simple facts about complex numbers, you
// can compute the Inverse FFT by conjugating the samples
// before and after the Forward FFT computation.
// I also scale by 1/N here.
//
void InverseFft(complex<double> *samples, int length ) {
   for(int i=0; i<length; i++)
      samples[i] = conj(samples[i]);
   ForwardFft(samples,length);
   for(int i=0; i<length; i++)
      samples[i] = conj(samples[i]) / static_cast<double>(length);
}
```

Rearranging the samples is the tricky part. Each FFT is computed by taking first the even elements and then the odd elements. This division is then repeated within each half.

The trick is to look at the binary value of the array index for each element. Remember that an even number has a zero in the least significant bit and that the even elements will go into the first half, where there's a zero in the most significant bit. The first rearrangement step corresponds to moving the least significant bit of the array index into the most significant bit.

Repeating this at each level, you end up with each element moved to a location whose binary index is bit-reversed.

In this function, I store a list indicating how each element should be moved. I recompute this list whenever a different size is requested. Usually, a program will compute many same-size FFTs, so this will always be called with the same size.

LISTING 24.6   Rearrange Samples for Fast FFT

```
static void Rearrange(complex<double> *samples, int length) {
   static int rearrangeSize = 0; // size of rearrange table
   static int *rearrange = 0;

   if (rearrangeSize != length) {
      // Recompute whenever size changes
      if (rearrange) delete [] rearrange;
      rearrange = new int[length];

      // Fill in destination of each value
      rearrange[0] = 0;
      for(int limit=1, bit=length/2; limit<length; limit <<= 1, bit>>=1 )
         for(int i=0;i<limit;i++)
            rearrange[i+limit] = rearrange[i] + bit;

      // Put zero in any spot that stays the same
      // Also zero one side of each swap,
      // so each swap only happens once
      for(int i=0; i<length; i++) {
         if (rearrange[i] == i) rearrange[i] = 0;
         else rearrange[ rearrange[i] ] = 0;
      }
      rearrangeSize = length;
   }

   // Use the rearrange table to swap elements
   // zero indexes are simply skipped
   complex <double> t;
   for (int i=0; i<length; i++)
      if (rearrange[i]) { // Does this element get exchanged?
         t = samples[i];   // Yes, do the exchange
         samples[i] = samples[ rearrange[i] ];
         samples[ rearrange[i] ] = t;
      }
}
```

Speed

When designing complex audio processing systems, speed is critical. For example, if you need to use 1,024-point FFTs with CD-quality sound, you must calculate each FFT in less than 6 milliseconds to keep up with the data. This is a tough requirement to meet. The `ForwardFft` routine I showed above, for instance, requires 36 milliseconds for a 1,024-point FFT on a 486/66 processor. (For comparison, the `SlowForwardFft` routine requires 163 milliseconds on the 486/66, while the `ForwardDft` routine requires nearly 70 seconds!) A 200-MHz PowerPC 603e can perform the above FFT in 6 milliseconds, but that doesn't leave time for any additional processing you may require.

If real-time performance is important, you have several options. You could use faster hardware. In particular, modern DSP chips are optimized for very fast FFTs. You could also use smaller FFTs. Two 512-point FFTs take less time than one 1,024-point FFT. Finally, you could use fixed-point or integer arithmetic instead of floating point arithmetic.

Playing with FFTs

The following two short programs can be used to experiment with the FFT. Each one reads a text file containing numbers, performs the appropriate transformation, and outputs a similar text file.

Listing 24.7   fftmain.cpp

```
Copyright © 1998, Tim Kientzle (Listing E.1)

#include "fft.h"
#include <iostream>
#include <iomanip>
#include <cstdlib>

int main(int argc, char **argv) {
    int length = 8;
    if (argc > 1) length = atoi(argv[1]);
    if ((((~length+1)&length) != length) {
        cerr << "Length must be a power of two!\n";
        exit(1);
    }
    complex<double> *input = new complex<double>[length];
    for(int i=0; (i < length)&&(!cin.eof()); i++)
        cin >> input[i];

    complex<double> *output = new complex<double>[length];
    for(int i=0;i<length;i++) output[i] = input[i];
    ForwardFft(output,length);

    // Uncomment next section to test
```

```
#if 0
   complex<double> *compare = new complex<double>[length];
   ForwardDft(input,length,compare);
   double maxerr=0; int maxindex=0;
   for(int i=0;i<length;i++) {
      // Compute the relative error
      double error = abs(output[i] - compare[i]) / abs(compare[i]);
      if(error > maxerr) {
         maxindex=i; maxerr=error;
      }
   }
   cerr << "Maximum relative error:" << maxerr << "\n";
#endif

   for(int i=0;i<length;i++)
      cout << setprecision(20) << output[i] << "\n";
   return 0;
}
```

These two programs use the Standard C++ Library to read complex numbers from standard input. The Standard C++ Library accepts complex numbers in two formats. If the first character is a parenthesis, it expects a parenthesized pair of numbers containing the real and imaginary parts. Otherwise, it reads a single floating-point number for the real part and sets the imaginary part to zero. For example, both (1,0) and 1.0 will be accepted as the complex number 1+0i.

LISTING 24.8   ifftmain.cpp

```
#include "fft.h"
#include <iostream>
#include <iomanip>
#include <cstdlib>

int main(int argc, char **argv) {
   int length = 8;
   if (argc > 1) length = atoi(argv[1]);
   if (((~length+1)&length) != length) {
      cerr << "Length must be a power of two!\n";
      exit(1);
   }
   complex<double> *a = new complex<double>[length];
   for(int i=0; (i < length)&&(!cin.eof()); i++)
      cin >> a[i];
   InverseFft(a,length);
   for(int i=0;i<length;i++)
      cout << setprecision(20) << a[i] << "\n";
   return 0;
}
```

Using FFTs

Now that you can calculate FFTs, you're all set to plug in your favorite waveforms and see what happens. Figures 24.8 through 24.11 show a few common waveforms and their FFTs, computed with the ForwardFft routine shown earlier. All of these figures show a sampled waveform on the left and the FFT of that waveform on the right. The vertical axis on the FFT plots is in decibels; zero on that scale represents a magnitude of one.

An important fact about all Fourier Transforms is that they compute the spectrum of a *periodic* signal. They assume the 32 or 512 or 1,024 samples they're given are one part of an infinitely repeating signal. This assumption works nicely with Figure 24.8, for instance. If you look closely at the sine wave, it has an exact number of cycles. If you made many copies of this graph, you could line them up side-by-side and the curves would match exactly.

Figure 24.12, however, doesn't meet this assumption, and so the output of the FFT isn't quite so nice. The frequency spectrum is at least zero decibels at every point.

FIGURE 24.8   A Sine Wave and Its FFT

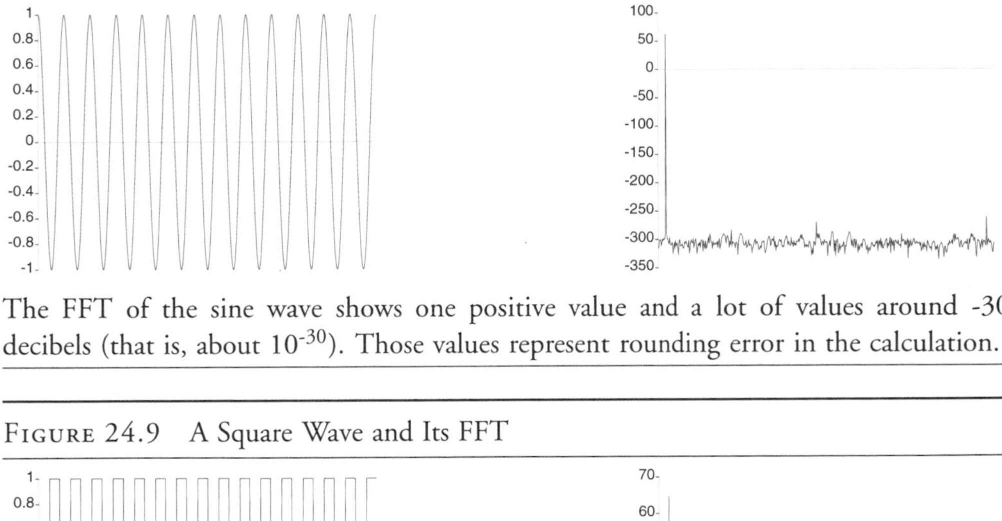

The FFT of the sine wave shows one positive value and a lot of values around -300 decibels (that is, about 10^{-30}). Those values represent rounding error in the calculation.

FIGURE 24.9   A Square Wave and Its FFT

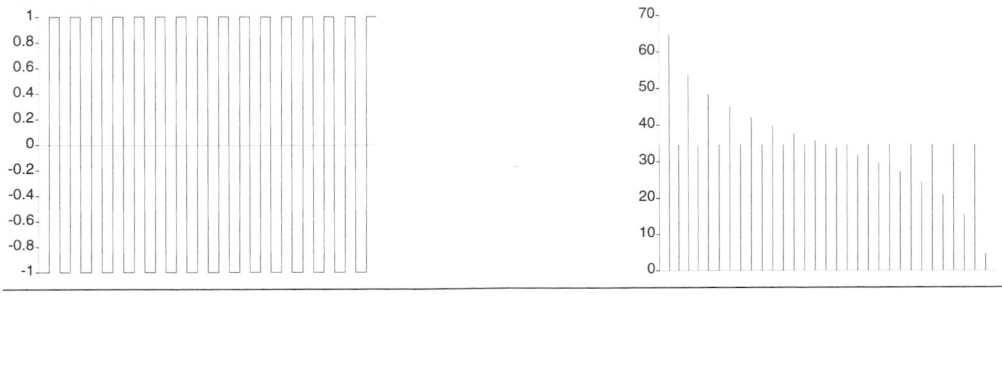

When presented with Figure 24.12, the FFT algorithm computes the spectrum assuming that the partial sine wave in the figure repeats, as shown in Figure 24.13. The sharp transitions in this figure are essentially pulses.

FIGURE 24.10   A Pulse and Its FFT

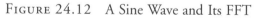

A pulse has equal energy at all frequencies. The FFT magnitude is one (zero decibels), coinciding with the x-axis. (The FFT magnitude would look the same regardless of when the pulse occurred; the FFT phase, however, would look different.)

FIGURE 24.11   Random Data and Its FFT

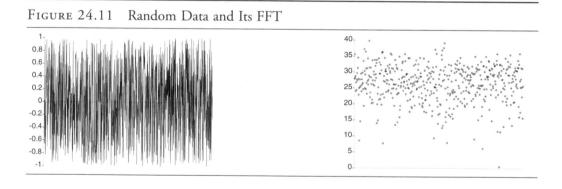

FIGURE 24.12   A Sine Wave and Its FFT

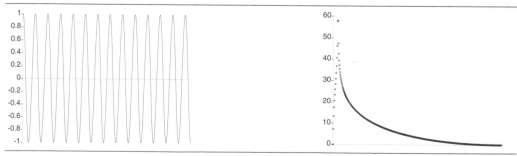

FIGURE 24.13   The Sine Wave from Figure 24.12 as Part of a Periodic Signal

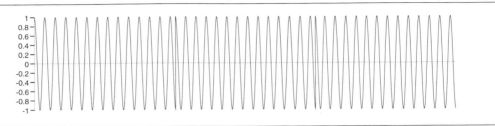

As Figure 24.10 suggests, any sharp jump in a signal is noise; it contains all frequencies. The problem with blindly applying the FFT to a piece of an arbitrary signal is that you're also measuring the implicit jumps from the end of the section back to the beginning. It's often important to smooth out those jumps so that the noise doesn't obscure the rest of your spectrum. Fortunately, this isn't hard to do.

Windowing

The trick is to *window* the signal. With proper windowing, Figure 24.12 becomes Figure 24.14. Note that the beginning and ending of the signal have been scaled down to reduce the sharp jump that obscured the spectrum we wanted.

FIGURE 24.14   Sine Wave from Figure 24.12 with a Hamming Window and Its FFT

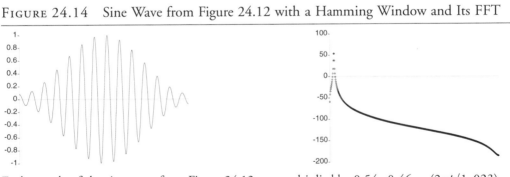

Each sample of the sine wave from Figure 24.12 was multiplied by $0.54 - 0.46\cos(2\pi t/1{,}023)$, where t is the corresponding sample number $(0\ldots 1{,}023)$.

Figure 24.14 also shows the FFT of the windowed sine wave. Note that most of the amplitudes are below -100 dB, which is a big improvement over Figure 24.11. This still doesn't look as clean as the spectrum in Figure 24.8. The FFT can measure only certain frequencies, and the sine wave of Figure 24.12 isn't one of them. In addition, the windowing process does change the spectrum slightly.

There are a number of windows in common use. The one I've used here is the *Hamming window*, which has a smooth, bell-shaped curve. One of the more subtle issues in properly using the FFT is selecting the correct windowing function.

Observations

Like many sophisticated mathematical concepts, the Fourier Transform has many facets. The longer you look, the more you'll see.

- The fact that the Forward and Inverse Fourier Transforms are essentially the same is important. From a purely practical viewpoint, it makes it simpler to implement algorithms such as the FFT, because the same code can serve both purposes. From a more theoretical viewpoint, it can give a lot of insight into the nature of different kinds of signals.

- The FFT is a fast way of computing a type of convolution. With a little work, you can use this technique to rapidly compute other types of convolutions. Because convolutions are common in many signal-processing algorithms, this is an important tool.

- The Forward and Inverse FFTs operate on complex values and give complex results. For the Inverse FFT, the complex inputs represent amplitude and phase, but it's not immediately clear what complex inputs mean for the Forward FFT. In audio engineering, the input to the Forward FFT is always real-valued samples, although other engineering disciplines do use complex values.

- The Inverse FFT computes the sum of many sine and cosine waves. If you look closely, you'll see that it uses the same ideas used by the popular CORDIC algorithms.

Filtering

25

Filters are used to modify the frequency content of a sound. The treble and bass controls on most stereo systems are simple examples of filters. Filtering is the basis for a variety of audio processing. For example, you can use filtering to isolate a person's voice by allowing only certain frequencies, or you can use it to remove the hiss from an old recording.

Adding Sine Waves

The last chapter discussed the importance of phase. One way to change the phase of a signal is to delay it. Consider, for example, adding a 500-Hz sine wave to itself, but with one copy delayed by 1/1,000 of a second. As shown in Figure 25.1, these two waves precisely cancel each other out.

If you keep that same 1/1,000 of a second delay, but use a 1,000-Hz sine wave, the amplitude will be doubled. So you see that the process diagramed in Figure 25.2 modifies sine waves in different ways depending on their frequency. If you feed a complex sound into this diagram, the output will have a different frequency content than the input.

FIGURE 25.1   Cancelling Out a 500-Hertz Sine Wave

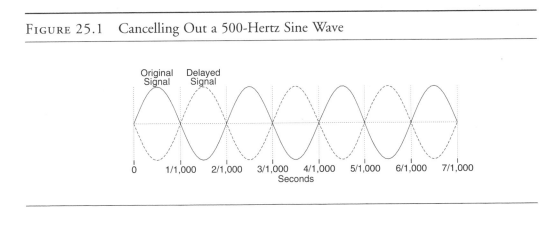

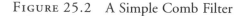

FIGURE 25.2 A Simple Comb Filter

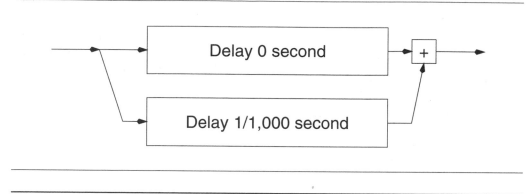

FIGURE 25.3 Frequency Response of a Comb Filter

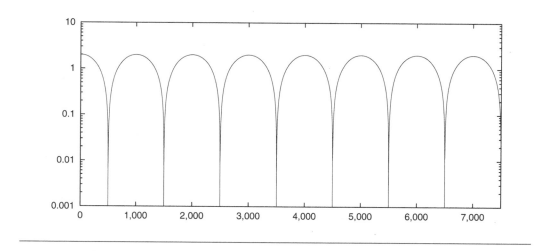

The simple filter in Figure 25.2 is called a *comb filter*. If you graph what it does to the amplitude of a sine wave, you end up with the graph in Figure 25.3. This graph shows that multiples of 1,000 Hz are doubled and other frequencies are selectively suppressed. The name of this filter comes from the distinctive shape of this graph.

You don't need sophisticated mathematics to understand comb filters. If $\sin(t)$ is one sine wave, then $\sin(t + p)$ is the same sine wave phase-shifted by p. By applying a few trigonometric identities, you can simplify the sum to $2 \cos(p/2) \sin(t + p/2)$. In this latter form, because p is fixed, you can see that the amplitude is $2 \cos(p/2)$. The graph in Figure 25.3 is just the graph of abs($\cos(x)$) on a logarithmic scale.

FIR Filters

As you might imagine, by using a more complex network of delays, you can selectively reinforce or suppress just about any frequency. Although a full mathematical analysis can get quite involved, you can design simple filters by playing with the FFT presented in the last chapter.

When analyzing filters, it is useful to see what happens when you feed the filter an impulse. If you look at the comb filter in Figure 25.2, you can see that if you put in an impulse, the output will be two copies of the same impulse, separated by 1/1,000 second. Because this output terminates, this filter is called a *finite impulse response* (FIR) filter.

Designing Simple FIR Filters

As an example, I'll show how to design a basic *low-pass filter*. An ideal low-pass filter has a cut-off frequency; it exactly blocks frequencies above that point and passes lower frequencies unaltered. Put slightly differently, it has the *frequency response* shown in Figure 25.4.

It is easy to quickly design usable filters, thanks to an important fact about Fourier Transforms. That fact is usually stated as: Multiplication in one domain is equivalent to convolution in the other domain. In the rest of this section, I'll explore what this statement means.

Imagine if your signal were stored as a collection of numbers such that each number was the amplitude of a different frequency. Low-pass filtering would then be easy; just multiply each high-frequency sample by zero and each low-frequency sample by 1. That's the multiplication part.

FIGURE 25.4   Frequency Response of an Ideal Low-Pass Filter

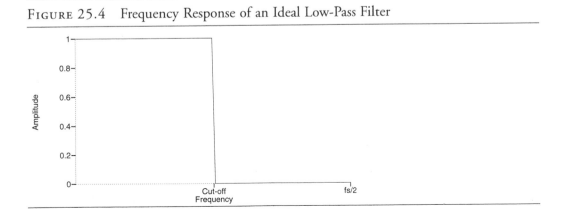

FIGURE 25.5   Filtering Is Convolution in the Time Domain

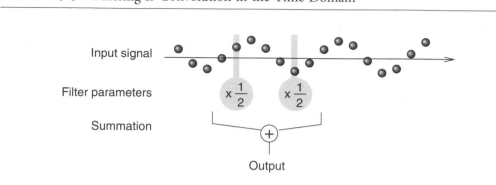

In fact, you can do filtering in just this way. You first use an FFT to convert your samples into a collection of frequency components, then modify the frequency components and use an Inverse FFT to convert back. There are some subtleties involved that make this more complex than it sounds, but many filtering techniques do exactly this.

More typically, you use a Fourier Transform to convert multiplication in the frequency domain into another operation in the time domain. Figure 25.5 shows the simple comb filter I showed earlier, but in a slightly different form. This filter picks out certain samples, multiplies the selected samples by weighting values, then sums them to get a single output sample. This pattern of weighting and summing is called *convolution*. As the input signal moves past the filter, successive output samples are generated.

FIGURE 25.6   The Frequency Response of a Low-Pass Filter

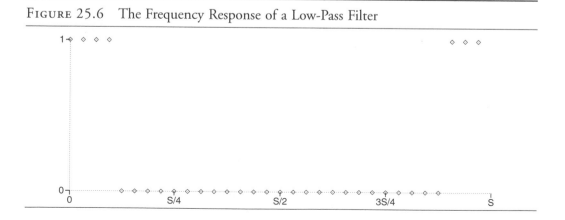

FIGURE 25.7   A 32-Element Low-Pass Filter

To design a digital filter, you start with a desired frequency response and figure out what weights to use in your convolution. To do so, just take the Inverse FFT of the frequency response.

In Figure 25.6, I've used 32 samples to specify the frequency response I want. I've arranged these samples to match the requirements of the Inverse FFT. The samples specify a frequency response from 0 to $S/2$, and then mirror that response from $S/2$ to S.

Taking the Inverse FFT of Figure 25.6 gives the weights in Figure 25.7. Note that these weights are just the real part of the Inverse FFT. Because my filter must have real inputs and real outputs, I have to discard the imaginary component.

My choice of 32 elements was completely arbitrary; you can use any number of elements when you design the filter. To get a detailed picture of the frequency response, I padded the 32-element filter with zeroes and used a 1,024-element Forward FFT. For

FIGURE 25.8   Frequency Response of Filters with Various Numbers of Elements

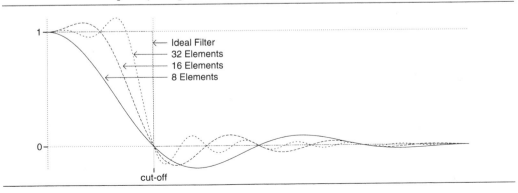

comparison, I've done the same with 16-element and 8-element low-pass filters. Figure 25.8 shows the results.

As you can see, this doesn't look very much like the ideal frequency response I started with. Figure 25.9 identifies some of the features of a frequency-response graph. A high-quality filter will have very little ripple in the pass band or in the stop band, and it will have a narrow transition band.

FIGURE 25.9   How to Read a Frequency Response Graph

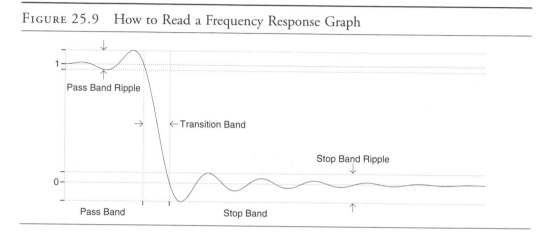

Implementing FIR Filters

The basic design technique I outlined above is simple. However, actually implementing the resulting filters is trickier than you might think. Listing 25.1 shows the obvious way to implement such a filter.

LISTING 25.1   Simple Implementation of 32-Element Filter

```
while(/* not at end of samples */) {
    float weights[32] = { ... };
    float *currentWeight = weights;
    float *currentSample = in;
    float result = 0;
    // Filter one sample (32 multiplies and 32 additions)
    for(int i=0;i<32;i++)
        result += *currentSample++ * *currentWeight++;
    *out++ = result;
    in++;
}
```

The problem with Listing 25.1 is that it requires 32 multiplications and 32 additions for *every sample*. At 44,100 samples per second, this is nearly 1.5 million multiplications per second.

You can cut this total in half by noticing that the weights are symmetric; once you've multiplied an input sample by a particular weight, you can store that product for later use. The next listing outlines one way to do this.

LISTING 25.2   Using Fewer Multiplications

```
// Array of 32 past samples, each pre-weighted by 16 different values
float *pastWeightedSamples[32];
for(int i=0;i<32;i++)
    pastWeightedSamples[i] = new float[16];

while(/* not at end of samples */) {
    // Shift down
    float *last = pastWeightedSamples[31];
    for(int i=0;i<31;i++) {
        float *t = pastWeightedSamples[i];
        pastWeightedSamples[i] = last;
        last = pastWeightedSamples[i];
    }

    // Add new element to array (16 multiplies)
    float weights[16] = { ... };
    for(int i=0; i<16; i++)
        pastWeightedSamples[i] = weights[i] * *in;

    // Sum to get output sample (32 additions)
    float result = 0;
    for(int i=0; i<16; i++)
        result += pastWeightedSamples[i][i];
    for(int i=16; i<32; i++)
        result += pastWeightedSamples[i][32-i];
}
```

To reduce the number of multiplications further, you can try fudging some of the weights. For instance, if you make two weights match, you can save a multiplication. If you change a weight to zero, you also save one multiplication.

Rounding the weights will change the frequency response. Good filter design is often iterative; you experiment with different approximations to speed the implementation and then use a Forward FFT to see what effect those changes have on the frequency response.

Phase Shift

One of the factors that affects good filter design is phase-shift. As you delay signals, you change their phase (that's why digital filters work), so it's inevitable that frequencies in the output will also be phase-shifted (the FFT of the filter parameters will tell you the phase shift). With careful design, it's possible to minimize (or even eliminate) this phase shift, but that requires techniques beyond the scope of this book.

IIR Filters

FIR filters have important design trade-offs. To get sharp cut-offs, you need to use a lot of terms, but more terms make the filter slower to compute.

One way to get a sharp cut-off without introducing a lot of terms is to use feedback. Figure 25.10 illustrates a simple example of such a filter. One important difference from the filters I've discussed so far is that if you feed an impulse into this filter, you'll continue to get an output forever. For this reason, filters that incorporate feedback are often called *infinite impulse response* (IIR) filters.

FIGURE 25.10   A Simple IIR Filter

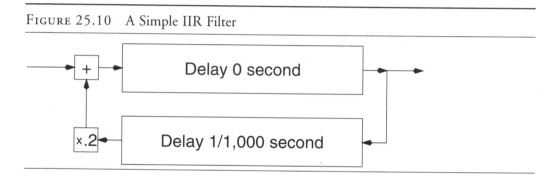

Music Synthesis with Filters

The shapes of musical instruments are carefully designed to produce certain sounds. One way they produce their characteristic sounds is by filtering: The reflections within the body of the instrument reinforce certain sounds and cancel others, much as a digital filter does. As a result, you can use digital filters to efficiently synthesize some instrument sounds. The plucked string algorithm I discussed on page 260 is a simple example of this idea in practice.

Part Seven
Appendices

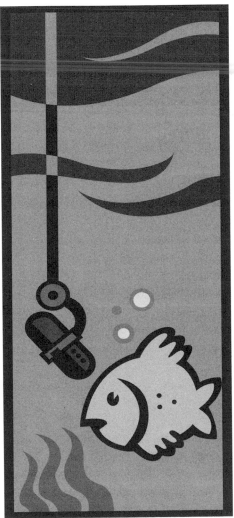

About the CD-ROM

The CD-ROM accompanying this book includes a variety of useful materials. The CD-ROM contains two independent partitions. One is in a modified ISO 9660 format that should be readable on all Windows and UNIX machines. The other is a Mac OS HFS format partition. Both partitions have the same overall structure, although they do not contain identical files.

Source Code

The *Source* directory contains all of the source code from the book (and a few files that do not appear in the printed book). The C++ source code files are all contained in the *Common* subdirectory.

Note that the source files all use UNIX end-of-line conventions: Each line ends with a single LF character (character 10). Most modern programming editors support all common end-of-line conventions, so this shouldn't be an issue in practice. However, some simpler text editors (including Windows Notepad and Mac OS SimpleText) do have trouble with such files.

Project Files

The *Source* directory also contains one subdirectory for each platform. The project files and makefiles refer to the source code in the *Common* directory.

Windows

I've included project files for Visual C++ 4.2 and Visual C++ 5.0. To compile the project, you'll need to copy the entire *Source* directory (including all subdirectories) to your hard disk. If you change the relative locations of the project files and the source files, you'll need to remove all the files from the project and re-add them all.

Mac OS

I've included project files for Metrowerks CodeWarrior Gold 11. After suitable conversion, these project files also work with the Mac OS version of CodeWarrior Pro 1.

- If you're only interested in compiling the code, you only need to copy the project and resource files to your hard disk.

- If you want to modify the code, you'll need to copy the entire *Source* folder.

By default, the project file checks in three places for source files: first in the same directory as the project file, then up two levels in the *Common* folder, and finally in the fixed directory on the CD-ROM. This allows the project to correctly compile in either of the above situations (although you may get a warning about one of the paths not existing).

UNIX

I've included a Makefile compatible with GNU gmake. It should be usable with other make programs with only minor changes. The Makefile assumes you're using the GCC 2.7.2 compiler.

- If you only want to compile the source, you may be able to simply cd to the directory containing the makefile and type make.

- If you need to edit the compiler options, you'll need to copy the makefile to your hard disk and make appropriate minor changes.

- If you need to change the source files, you will need to copy the contents of the *Common* directory to your hard disk and edit the makefile accordingly.

By default, the makefile looks up two levels in the *Common* directory for sources and stores all output files in /tmp. This should allow you to compile straight from the CD-ROM on many systems. If you change the relative locations of the makefile and source directory, you'll need to edit the SRCDIR macro in the makefile. Note that the makefile does not create the OBJDIR or BINDIR directories; you'll need to ensure they exist before you try compiling.

Note also that playsnd *will not compile* unless you have the NAS libraries and headers installed on your system. If they're not in the default search path for your compiler, you may need to edit the LIBS macro to tell the compiler where to find them. If you don't use NAS, try working with playtoau instead, which works identically to playsnd but outputs a 16-bit AU file to stdout instead of playing to a speaker. NAS support for several systems is available from ftp://ftp.x.org/contrib/audio/.

Others

If you have a system or compiler other than the ones listed above, you'll need to either convert the UNIX Makefile to one appropriate for your system, or create a new project from scratch. The files in the *Common* directory actually create several different programs. The following describes each program and lists the source code used to build it. (If you need to know the full dependencies, look in the UNIX Makefile.)

playsnd This is the primary demonstration program. It opens a file, determines if it is one of the supported file types, and then plays it. The files used to compile this are:

General `audio.cpp`, `audio.h`, `aplayer.cpp`, `aplayer.h`

Utility `open.cpp`, `open.h`

Compression `compress.cpp`, `compress.h`, `dpcm.cpp`, `dpcm.h`, `g711.cpp`, `g711.h`, `imaadpcm.cpp`, `imaadpcm.h`, `mpeg.cpp`, `mpeg.h`

File Formats `aiff.cpp`, `aiff.h`, `au.cpp`, `au.h` `iff.cpp`, `iff.h`, `voc.cpp`, `voc.h`, `wav.cpp`, `wav.h`

Music `instrumt.h`, `midi.cpp`, `midi.h`, `mod.cpp`, `mod.h` `plucked.cpp`, `plucked.h`, `sampled.cpp`, `sampled.h`

System-Specific If you're using Win32, you'll need `winmain.cpp`, `winplayr.h`, and `winplayr.cpp`. If you're using Mac OS, you'll need `macmain.cpp`, `macplayr.h`, `macplayr.cpp`, and the resource file `playsound.`μ`.rsrc` (which is located in the CW11 project directory). If you're using the Network Audio System on UNIX, you'll need `nasmain.cpp`, `nasplayr.h`, and `nasplayr.cpp`.

playtoau This is the same as `playsnd` above, but instead of playing to a speaker, it creates an AU-format file on stdout. This allows you to convert any file format to AU, which is useful if you have a separate utility that can play AU files, or if your system is too slow to play a particular format (such as MPEG) in real time. The output is always 16-bit PCM. It compiles from the same files as `playsnd`, except that it uses the `playtoau.cpp` file instead of one of the sets of system-specific files above.

playau This short example from page 37 reads an AU file from standard input and plays it to a speaker. To compile it, you'll need to use the general and system-specific files listed for `playsnd`, as well as `au.cpp`, `au.h`, `compress.cpp`, `compress.h`, `g711.cpp`, and `g711.h`.

autoau The short example from page 186. This reads an AU file on `cin` and outputs another AU file on `cout`. The output is always 16 bit PCM. To compile it, use the general files from `playsnd` and `autoau.cpp`, `au.h`, `au.cpp`, `compress.cpp`, `compress.h`, `g711.cpp`, and `g711.h`.

playnote The test program from page 268. To compile it, you'll need the general and system-specific files listed above for `playsnd` and `playnote.cpp`, `instrumt.h`, `sampled.cpp`, `sampled.h`, `plucked.cpp`, and `plucked.h`.

sinetoau The test program from page 38. To compile it, use the general files listed for `playsnd` and `sinetoau.cpp`, `sinewave.cpp`, `sinewave.h`, `au.cpp`, `au.h`, `g711.cpp`, and `g711.h`.

logtest The sample program from page 114 that computes the actual signal-to-noise ratio for different signals using G711 logarithmic and PCM encodings. This program was used to generate Figure 11.2 on page 115. To compile, use the files `logtest.cpp`, `audio.cpp`, `audio.h`, `g711.cpp`, `g711.h`, and `compress.h`.

testmatrix A program that demonstrates the speed difference between the different implementations of the MPEG matrixing operation, as described on page 159.

fftmain A short program that reads data from `cin`, performs an FFT on that data, then outputs the data to `cout`. To compile, use `fftmain.cpp`, `fft.cpp`, and `fft.h`.

ifftmain Like the above, but performs an Inverse FFT. To compile, use `ifftmain.cpp`, `fft.cpp`, and `fft.h`.

Note that all of these programs have simple text user interfaces. The `playsnd` and `testmatrix` programs have been tested and run on a variety of systems. The others were developed for demonstration purposes, and may require some experimentation to properly compile on your system.

Sample Files

The *Samples* directory contains some sample audio files in a variety of formats. I've used a number of audio tools to convert a short clip into different formats (not all of which are described in this book). The purpose of this directory is to provide you with a library of files in different formats that you can use for experimentation. For formats such as WAV that support a number of compression methods, I've tried to provide examples using a variety of compression methods in both mono and stereo formats.

Contributed Materials

The *Contrib* directory contains materials from a number of sources.

Computer Music Consultants (All Platforms)

Donald Griffin is a consultant who composes music for games, multimedia titles, and other purposes. He's provided two articles that discuss some of the issues involved in producing high-quality music for these purposes. Other articles by Donald Griffin can be found on http://www.computer-music.com.

Sonic Foundry (Windows)

Sonic Foundry produces a number of high-quality commercial audio tools used for professional audio production. Sound Forge 4.0 is their flagship audio production system. The CD-ROM includes demonstration versions of Sound Forge and several useful plug-ins, including a version of Qsound's 3D audio tool.

To install the demonstration versions, run `setup.exe` and select *Install*. The directory also contains a number of example WAVE files that were created with Sound Forge.

SoundApp (Mac OS)

Norman Franke's freeware SoundApp plays a variety of sound file formats on Mac OS. The CD-ROM includes a fat binary of SoundApp for both PowerPC and 680x0 Mac OS computers. Visit http://www-cs-students.stanford.edu/~franke/SoundApp/ for more information.

Syntrillium (Windows)

Syntrillium's Cool Edit 96 is a high-quality, easy-to-use sound editing application for Microsoft Windows 95 and Windows 3.1. It works with dozens of audio file formats and supports files up to 1 gigabyte in size. The CD-ROM includes the unregistered shareware version of Cool Edit, and information about developing custom plug-ins.

If you have Windows 95, you install Cool Edit 96 by running `c96setup.exe`. If you have Windows 3.1, you install Cool Edit 1.53 by running `cool153z.exe`. More information is available from http://www.syntrillium.com.

WHAM (Windows 3.1)

Andrew Bulhak's WHAM reads and writes a variety of sound formats on Windows 3.1.

XAudio (Windows, Linux, Solaris)

XAudio is a project to produce a high-quality multiplatform MPEG audio decoder. The core of the project is a portable, high-performance library which is currently in alpha test. To demonstrate the library, they've used it to develop MPEG audio players for a variety of platforms, including Windows 95 and NT, Linux, Solaris, SGI Irix, FreeBSD, and Be OS. Other versions should follow. The CD-ROM includes demonstration versions of their players and documentation for their library. Check http://www.mpeg.org for more information about the library or the player programs.

A Brief Introduction to C++

Although C++ is rapidly becoming the *lingua franca* for many professional developers, it's still generally less well-known than C. However, as I explained on page 37, object-oriented programming techniques are appropriate for this kind of project, so I've developed the code in this book in C++.

This appendix is intended to help fill the gap for people who are comfortable with C but may not be experienced with C++. My goal here is not to teach C++ but only to provide enough background for you to read and generally understand the code in this book.

If you need to go further, there are many excellent books on C++ that you may want to read. Stephen Blaha's *C++ For Professional Programmers* (International Thomson Computer Press, 1995) is targeted at people who already know C and includes coverage of most of the new ANSI C++ features. If you intend to work extensively with C++, you should read Scott Meyers' books *Effective C++* (Addison-Wesley, 1992) and *More Effective C++* (Addison-Wesley, 1996). These books contain a lot of practical advice about writing good C++ programs, and Scott's explanations will help you to better understand the intricacies of the language. Finally, if you plan to work with C++ or any other object-oriented language, you should read *Design Patterns* by Erich Gamma, Richard Helm, Ralph Johnson, and John Vlissides (Addison-Wesley, 1995). This book describes a number of standard ways that groups of objects interact and has ignited a feverish search to identify and document other common software design patterns.

Improving C: A Better struct

The most obvious new feature of C++ is the `class` construct. Curiously, a C++ `class` is almost the same as a C++ `struct`, so I'll ignore the new nomenclature for a while and explain how C++ made `struct` better.

Even if you don't care about object-oriented programming, you've probably used a C `struct` once or twice. They're handy because they give you a way to refer to some cluster of related data with a single name. For example, suppose you need to manage a buffer of characters. One buffer requires at least three pieces of data: You need pointers to the beginning and end of the data, and you need a block of memory to keep the data. Because a buffer is a single conceptual entity, it's nice to declare a single `struct` to hold it all, such as:

```
struct Buffer {
    char *_begin;
    char *_end;
    char _data[256];
};
```

(I've prefixed all the members of `Buffer` with an underscore; that's just my personal convention.)

Even at this basic level, C++ provides some new features to make life easier. The first is that C++ automatically makes the name `Buffer` a type name. Rather than declaring a variable as `struct Buffer myBuff` as you would in C, you can simply say `Buffer myBuff`. The second is that C++ makes it easier to create a new `Buffer` on the heap. Rather than messing with `malloc()`, `sizeof` and a couple of casts, C++ allows you to simply say `new Buffer`. The result is a pointer to a new `Buffer`. Similarly, when you're done, you can use `delete` to get rid of it. (One quick word of warning: Although `malloc/free` still work in C++, you should never mix them with `new/delete`.)

Here's a quick example to show how this works:

```
Buffer myBuff;              /* One on the stack */
myBuff._begin = myBuff._data;
myBuff._end = myBuff._data;

Buffer *pBuff = new Buffer;     /* One on the heap */
pBuff->_begin = pBuff->_data;
pBuff->_end = pBuff->_data;

/* Do some stuff with pBuff and myBuff */

delete pBuff;     /* Delete the one on the heap */
```

Note that `->` and `.` are used to access members just as in C. Also note that C++ allows you to declare new variables anywhere, not just at the beginning of a block.

In this example, the first thing I did with the new `Buffer` variables was to initialize them by setting `_begin` and `_end` to point to the relevant data. It's easy to see that I'll want to do this every time I create a new `Buffer`.

C++ makes this especially easy to do. Whenever you create a new `struct`, C++ automatically calls the *constructor* for that `struct`. Here's my `Buffer` declaration, this time with a constructor:

```
struct Buffer {
    char *_begin;
    char *_end;
    char _data[256];
    Buffer() { _begin = _data; _end = _data; };
};
```

The constructor is the part that looks like a function. Now whenever you declare a new variable with `Buffer myBuff` or allocate a new `Buffer` with `new Buffer`, the compiler will automatically call the constructor (which always has the same name as the `struct`). Typical C-style scoping rules apply. The name `_begin` is part of the `Buffer` struct. Because the constructor is declared inside the `struct`, it can see and use those names. I'll explore this idea a bit more carefully in a moment.

Now if you want to use a `Buffer`, you simply create one and use it:

```
Buffer myBuff;  // Create and initialize a buffer
*myBuff._end++ = 'a'; // Put an 'a' into the buffer
```

Note that `//` indicates a comment in C++. (The old-style `/* C comments */` still work, too.)

Toward Object-Oriented Programming

Object is really just a fancy word for `struct`. The important feature is that an object can have functions, as well as data. Here's the `Buffer` example again, but with two *member functions* (also called *methods*).

```
struct Buffer {
    char *_begin;
    char *_end;
    char _data[256];
    Buffer() { _begin = _data; _end = _data; }
    void Insert(char a) { *_end++ = a; }
    char Remove() { return *_begin++; }
};
```

You use these member functions just as you would any other member of the structure, using `->` and `..` For example

```
Buffer myBuff;
myBuff.Insert('a');
Buffer *pBuff = new Buffer;
pBuff->Insert('b');
```

Again, C++ allows you to declare new variables at any place, not just the beginning of a block. This makes most programs easier to read, because you can declare new variables close to where they are used. In particular, you can declare a new variable in the initialization of a `for` statement:

```
for(int i=0; i < 10; i++) { // Insert 10 a's
    myBuff.Insert('a');
}
```

If you also had a `Stack` structure that had an `Insert()` member function, you can call it, as well:

```
Buffer myBuff;
Stack myStack;
myBuff.Insert('a'); // Insert 'a' into the buffer
myStack.Insert('a'); // Insert 'a' onto the stack
```

This ability to reuse the same name (*polymorphism*) is a help in large programs. For example, in my audio toolkit, almost every object has a `GetSamples` member function. Because this accomplishes the same goal for each of them, it's nicer to reuse the same name than to have to needlessly invent new names.

C++ allows you to reuse names in another important way. Even within a single `struct`, you can have more than one method with the same name. For example, if you wanted to be able to give strings of characters to your buffer, you could define both `Insert(char a)` and `Insert(char *a)`. With those definitions, you could write `myBuff.Insert('a')` or `myBuff.Insert("abcdef")` and the compiler would check the types of the arguments and call the correct function. This ability to *overload* a function name applies to normal functions, as well, not just to member functions.

C++'s ability to select functions according to argument types is part of a general emphasis throughout the language on *type-safe* programming. One example of this difference between C and C++ lies in their treatment of the (typeless) `void *` pointer. Both languages allow you to assign any pointer to a `void *`. However, C also allows you to freely assign a `void *` to another pointer type, while C++ requires you to use an explicit cast. C++ also checks function argument and return types (even across multiple source files) and enforces a number of other restrictions that should help you to avoid some common programming errors.

Real OOP: Classes and Inheritance

I'm now ready to rewrite the `Buffer` example using common C++ notation.

```
class Buffer {
private:
    char *_begin;
    char *_end;
    char *_data;
public:
    Buffer() { _begin = _end = _data = new char[256]; }
    ~Buffer() { delete [] _data; }
    void Insert(char a) { *_end++ = a; }
    char Remove() { return *_begin++; }
};
```

I've changed a number of things here. First, I've used the word `class` instead of `struct`. Although the two are nearly interchangable in C++, it's traditional to use `class` for anything that has member functions.

I've also added visibility specifications. The terms `private:` and `public:` tell the compiler that certain parts of this class can be manipulated from outside and some can't. Note that I've hidden all of the data members. This is considered good style in most circles.

One of the reasons private data is considered good style is that it makes it easier to change the way your data is stored. For instance, even in this simple example, I've already changed `_data` from an array to a pointer and added code to allocate the buffer on the stack. Of course, if I allocate the buffer, I need to ensure the buffer is cleaned up, so I've added a *destructor*. The destructor has the same name as the class but starts with a tilde (`~Buffer`). The compiler calls the destructor automatically at the appropriate times (during `delete`, or at the end of a block for automatic variables).

Because the buffer itself is an array, I've also used the array forms of `new` and `delete`. The phrase `new char[256]` allocates a block of 256 chars; `delete [] _data` frees the block. If you allocate an array, you must use the array form of `delete` to release it. Few compilers enforce this, and you can trash your heap if you're careless.

Inheritance

Most programs are developed incrementally. You first develop a core of basic functionality, then adorn the program with myriads of smaller features. C++, like all other object-oriented languages, supports this explicitly through *inheritance*.

Inheritance is used in two ways. The first is to customize another class. For example, if you need a `Buffer` with some additional capabilities, you could create a new class `SpecialBuffer` that inherits from `Buffer`:

```
class SpecialBuffer :public Buffer {
    // new capabilities of a SpecialBuffer
}
```

The notation `:public Buffer` indicates that a `SpecialBuffer` does everything a `Buffer` does. In particular, `SpecialBuffer` automatically gains all the member variables and functions of a `Buffer`.

Inheritance is a remarkably useful software design tool. For example, when designing my player classes, I knew that different types of players would need to share certain capabilities. By defining those capabilities once, in a common *base class*, I was able to simplify the individual player classes. And because there was only one copy of the shared code, the entire program was easier to debug and maintain.

The other use of inheritance is to improve code abstraction. By defining a common interface in a base class, you can ensure that each derived class will be used identically. This often makes it useful to define a base class even if you have no code in it.

Virtual Functions

Usually, when you write `object.Foo()`, the compiler looks at the type of `object` and selects the correct `Foo()` function at compile time. However, this isn't always what you want.

Suppose you have several classes with a common interface. For example, my `WaveRead` and `MidiRead` classes both inherit from `AudioAbstract`, so you can call the `GetSamples` method on either one. In fact, if you look at my code, much of it cares only that an object inherits from `AudioAbstract`. In those cases, I work with pointers to `AudioAbstract`. Consider the following short example:

```
MidiRead audioObject; // create MidiRead object
AudioAbstract *audioPointer = &audioObject;
audioPointer->GetSamples(); // ask for samples
```

Normally, the compiler looks at the type of `audioPointer`. Based on that, it converts the last line into a call to the `GetSamples` method in `AudioAbstract`. This is clearly not right. The solution is to mark methods like `GetSamples` as `virtual`. The `virtual` declaration tells the compiler to check the type of the object at run-time and use that to select the `GetSamples` method to call. (Virtual methods are only slightly less efficient than nonvirtual methods. The compiler builds a table of function addresses for each class and does a single array look-up to locate the virtual function. The loss in efficiency is slight enough that many programmers develop a habit of defining every member function virtual.)

By suitable use of virtual functions and inheritance, you can build a family of classes that are largely interchangable but provide distinctly different functionality. For example, my MIDI code uses classes that inherit from `AbstractNote`. This allows it to use a variety of instrument synthesis methods without any of the MIDI code changing.

There are a few minor complications introduced by C++'s form of inheritance. One is that destructors should always be virtual. Otherwise, when an object is deleted, the wrong destructor might be called. (Fortunately, the `virtual` declaration is inherited, so it suffices to declare destructors in base classes as `virtual`.)

Because of the interaction of some of C++'s type rules, it is important to distinguish between *concrete* classes and *abstract* classes. In a nutshell, a concrete class is one that you create objects from; an abstract class is one that you never create objects from. For example, you'll never find me creating an object of class `AudioAbstract` (I do declare many pointers to `AudioAbstract`, but those always point to objects of derived classes.) Two important rules in C++ are *never inherit from a concrete class* and *never create an object of an abstract class.*

In my code, abstract classes include the word `Abstract` in the name. This makes it easy to ensure that I never create an object from an abstract class and that I always inherit from an abstract class.

There is a way, using virtual functions, to enforce this distinction. If a virtual function is declared with = 0, then the compiler will prevent you from creating an object of that class. These are called *pure virtual* functions, and many people define an abstract class to be a class with at least one pure virtual function. However, this definition seems unnecessarily restrictive to me, especially because abstract and concrete classes are useful design concepts in OO languages other than C++.

Real-World Considerations

Early OO languages were notorious for performance problems. Because C++ was designed, in part, to address these concerns, a lot of C++ details were included to allow more efficient code.

Constructor Initializations

In my earlier `Buffer` example, it's reasonable to think you might want to specify the size when you create the buffer. One way to do this is to add a new member function so that you can resize the buffer after creating the object. This would slow things down, so C++

goes further and allows you to have multiple constructors. In my buffer example, I would probably include both a *default constructor* (one that takes no arguments)

```
Buffer() { _data = new char[256]; }
```

and another constructor that does take an argument

```
Buffer(int i) { _data = new char[i]; }
```

With this addition, I have two ways to create a new `Buffer`. As before, I can create a default `Buffer` either on the stack or on the heap.

```
Buffer myBuff;

Buffer *pBuff = new Buffer;
```

I can also create a custom `Buffer` by specifying the size.

```
Buffer myBuff(1024);

Buffer *pBuff = new Buffer(1000);
```

Although this looks like a function call, it's really a special way to initialize a variable. You can also initialize built-in types using this notation:

```
int i=3; // Old-style initialization

int j(4); // New-style initialization
```

The new style initialization has a slight performance benefit in some situations. (If you use old-style, some compilers create a temporary object, then copy it into the variable, then delete the temporary; with new-style, it always initializes the object in the variable.)

Double-Colon Notation

Generally, you refer to a member function by starting with an object. Sometimes, however, you need to state explicitly which class contains the member function you want. This occurs when defining member functions (which I'll describe in a moment) and when you need to temporarily override the normal inheritance rules. Just as you write `object.Foo()` or `objectPointer->Foo()`, you can write `Class::Foo()` or even `object.Class::Foo()` (although this last form is unusual).

A typical example of this usage appears on page 270, in the definition of `PlayNote::SamplingRate` (that is, the `SamplingRate` member of the `PlayNote` class). In this case, the `PlayNote` class doesn't want to *replace* the definition of `AudioAbstract::SamplingRate`, but instead to *augment* it. It does so by first calling the parent's version, then it does any additional processing.

Defining Methods in Separate Files

C programmers have developed a convention of separating their code into modules. Each module consists of an *interface* stored in a .H (header) file, and an *implementation* stored in a .C (source) file. This is to speed up compilation; it's much faster for the compiler to read only the header files. In my Buffer example, I put all the member functions in the class definition, but this is clearly not how production code is written.

Usually, the class definition contains only declarations of the member functions, constructors, and destructors. In practice, my Buffer example would probably appear like this in a header .H file:

```
class Buffer {
private:
    char *_begin;
    char *_end;
    char *_data;
public:
    Buffer();
    ~Buffer();
    void Insert(char a);
    char Remove();
};
```

The source .CPP (implementation) file would contain the actual function bodies. Of course, there might be many classes with an Insert() member function, so you need to use the appropriate double-colon notation to specify the correct one. In this case, the functions would appear like this in the source file:

```
Buffer::Buffer() { _begin = _end = _data = new char[256]; }
Buffer::~Buffer() { delete [] _data; }
void Buffer::Insert(char a) { *_end++ = a; }
char Buffer::Remove() { return *_begin++; }
```

Note that constructors and destructors do not have return types.

This separation does introduce some minor maintenance headaches; you have to be careful to ensure that the declarations in your .H file and the definitions in your .CPP file are kept consistent. Fortunately, most compilers are happy to point out any inconsistencies that creep in.

C++ I/O

Operator Overloading

One of the principles of C++ is that you should be able to create new data types (classes) that can be used intuitively. For example, a mathematician who needs to work with some new kind of number might want to create a class to hold those numbers and redefine + and * so that he can use common arithmetic notation.

C++ allows you to redefine common operators. In effect, an expression such as a + b is translated into a.operator+(b) (or into operator+(a,b), depending on the context). By defining (or redefining) the operator+ member function, you can change how addition works. (You cannot, however, change the precedence or introduce new operators.)

This capability is dangerous, and you should use it infrequently. It's easy to create illegible programs by redefining common operators. I do not use it in my programs; I introduce it here because the Standard C++ Library redefines some operators.

I/O

The Standard C++ Library has redefined the << and >> operators. When used with numbers, they still mean "shift left" and "shift right." If the left-hand operand is a *stream class*, however, they perform I/O. For example, cout << "Hello\n" sends the string "Hello\n" to the cout stream. (cout is the C++ stream equivalent of the C stdout file handle.) Note that this mechanism is type-safe; the compiler chooses the correct definition of operator<< based on the types. In contrast, C's printf relies on you to provide a format specifier that matches your types.

There are four standard I/O streams, called cout, cin, cerr, and clog. The first three correspond to C's stdout, stdin, and stderr. C++ I/O is convenient if the output formatting is not critical. You can even use multiple << and >> operators in the obvious way.

```
cout << "The value of i is:  " << i << "\n";
```
However, I prefer C-style printf for most formatted output.

Miscellany

C++ Casts

Casts are a common part of C programming. Although slightly less common in C++, they're still essential. The common C notation of (int)var, unfortunately, is not very clear because it doesn't specify a reason for the cast. By clearly identifying the purpose of the cast, the compiler can help check your code. C++ provides a new syntax that identifies the purpose of the cast for better error checking and stands out better in source code.

- `reinterpret_cast<type>(expression)` This reinterprets the same bits as a new type. It's used primarily for casting pointers, as in `reinterpret_cast<int *>(buffer)`.

- `static_cast<type>(expression)` This forces the compiler to apply a standard conversion, such as `static_cast<int>(sin(x))`.

- `const_cast<type>(expression)` This changes the `const`-ness or `volatile`-ness of an expression. Note that this is the only new-style cast that can be used for this purpose.

- `dynamic_cast<type>(expression)` This converts a pointer to an object into a pointer to a compatible object. This conversion is dynamically tested at run-time. This is the least widely-supported of the new casts.

In this book, I use `reinterpret_cast` and `static_cast` regularly, and I occasionally use `const_cast`. I don't use `dynamic_cast` because not all compilers support it. However, there are several uses of `reinterpret_cast` in my code that should probably be changed into `dynamic_cast`.

References

C++ provides an alternative to C-style pointers that is safer and simpler in many circumstances. A declaration such as `int &i` makes i a *reference* to an integer. Internally, a reference is handled like a pointer. It's efficient to pass large objects to functions using references.

However, references are not pointers. A reference uses nonpointer syntax. You use the dot operator `.` to refer to elements of a class or structure, not the arrow operator `->`. A reference variable must be initialized when it is created. You cannot have a NULL reference. You also are not allowed to change what a reference refers to.

Note that the use of `&` to declare a reference does not interfere with the use of `&` as the address-of operator.

I do not use references much, but they are necessary with certain system classes.

this

When you call a member function with `object.Foo(a,b)`, the compiler essentially rewrites this to `Foo(&object,a,b)`. Likewise, when you declare a member function `Foo()` in a class, it gets essentially rewritten as `Foo(class *this)`. Every member function (except `static` class methods, which I'm not going to discuss) has a special variable called `this`. `this` is a pointer to the current object. Within a member function, you can call other member functions with `Bar()` or `this->Bar()`. `this` isn't often used directly. However, it is useful whenever an object needs to give another object a pointer to itself. (As in `SampledInstrument::NewNote`, on page 250. A sampled instrument object gives a sampled note object a pointer to itself so that the note object can access common data stored in the instrument object.)

Friends

Proper use of `private` and `public` can greatly simplify your life. By limiting how other people use your class, you make it easier to change the implementation at a future date. But exceptions occur. Occasionally, you'll have a pair of closely tied classes that need to access each other's intimate details or a special function that needs access to class data that otherwise needs to be private.

By declaring a function or class to be a `friend`, you tell the compiler to let that function or class access otherwise private data. For example, in the `WinPlayer` class on page 64, I needed to create a function that was not a member of the class (so that I could pass a pointer to that function to the system audio services) but still had access to private class data. Similarly, on page 250, I needed to ensure that a `SampledNote` object can access the shared note information stored in the associated `SampledInstrument` object.

Coding Style C

Every programmer has his or her own somewhat unique ideas about what constitutes good programming style. Usually, these ideas are culled from a variety of sources, including books, magazine articles, and other languages.

I've spent some time developing the coding style used in this book. My primary goal is to make the code easy to understand. This requires keeping individual classes simple, as well as making the class interfaces both consistent and opaque (you don't need to know what's inside a class to be able to use it). I've also avoided a number of C++ features in the interests of simplicity.

Efficiency is a secondary concern. Although I believe my code is reasonably efficient, I've avoided some complex coding that would make it more efficient. Flexibility is also secondary. It should be easy to use this code in a variety of situations, but I have omitted many details (such as conversion constructors and virtual member functions) that might make it even more flexible.

The following is a list of some of my conventions, in no particular order.

- I've liberally included visibility specifications (that is, "public," "protected," or "private") throughout the class definitions. You shouldn't have to search to find out the visibility of an item.

- I've simplified the error handling. Many errors result in a simple message to `cerr` and a call to `exit`. Although this makes the code less robust, it simplifies the code considerably. If you want to use my code in a commercial product, you'll probably need to augment the error handling.

- I do not use multiple inheritance.

- I do not use global variables.

- I use `static` (local to file) functions and variables where possible. This sometimes allows me to keep implementation details out of the header files.

- Multi-word identifiers are run together with uppercase letters indicating the start of words, such as `ClassName` or `variableName`.

- Class and function names start with uppercase letters.

- Variable names always begin with lowercase letters. Member variable names begin with underscores. (This differentiates function-local variables from member variables.)

- All member variables are declared `private`.

- Only the simplest methods are defined in header files.

- I use new-style casts extensively. Instead of writing `(double)i`, I write `static_cast<double>(i)`. I do not use `dynamic_cast`, however, because not all the compilers I use support it.

- To keep the code simple, I've avoided the use of templates, nested types, deep inheritance trees, namespaces, static class methods and variables, and many other C++ features.

- I use the new C++ `bool` data type, even though there are still compilers that don't support it. I use only the most basic facilities, so you should be able to get my code running by adding the following lines:

```
typedef int bool;

#define true (1)

#define false (0)
```

Systems Used D

The source code has been tested with a number of development tools. For the most part, building my code on different compilers revealed minor problems that earlier compilers did not catch. However, I also encountered library bugs, non-compliant compilers, and other frustrating problems. Most compilers now release new versions about every 6 months; it's likely that the problems I encountered have been addressed.

In most cases, the code compiles (or tests) with no warnings. However, with every system I used, certain options caused the tool to complain about problems with the system headers. In each case, I disabled such options.

Microsoft Visual C++ 4.2 under Windows 95 My use of the `bool` keyword triggered some compiler warnings, although the code does compile and run correctly. (The 4.2 compiler does not fully support `bool`.)

Microsoft Visual C++ 5.0 under Windows 95 The 5.0 compiler still complains about some uses of `bool`.

Metrowerks CodeWarrior Gold 11 under Mac OS 7.6 I've had some difficulties with CodeWarrior Gold 11, mostly with its support for C++ stream I/O. As a result, much of the text output is wrong (the library doesn't correctly print long integers using `cerr << i` syntax). These bugs seem purely cosmetic; apart from incorrect text output, the code works correctly.

As this book was going to press, I tried a newer version of the Metrowerks libraries, which seemed to fix some problems, but introduced others.

GNU GCC 2.7.2 under FreeBSD 2.1 This system was running Network Audio System 1.2 patchlevel 1. The current GNU implementation of the Standard C++ Library does not include a complete set of new-style headers. For example, you may need to create a `cstdio` file that simply includes `stdio.h`. (The current C++ Standard specifies that standard headers do not have any extension. It also provides the C headers by prefixing each name with the letter `c`.)

Parasoft CodeWizard under Windows 95 CodeWizard complained about my failure to `delete` certain pointer variables in destructors. In most of these cases, I have multiple pointers to a common block of memory (see `SampledNote`, for instance), and so it's correct to only `delete` one of these pointers. (In the case of `SampledNote`, the sample storage is actually owned by another object, so it's correct to delete none of them.)

NuMega BoundsChecker under Windows 95 BoundsChecker's *FinalCheck* complained about some uninitialized variables in the Windows libraries. It also pointed out some places where I allocated and initialized tables and then (deliberately) never freed that memory.

If you manage to get this code working with another compiler or operating system, please let me know.

Reusing My Source Code E

As I mentioned at the beginning of this book, I've designed the source code to demonstrate certain concepts and programming techniques. However, with appropriate modifications, it should be useful in a variety of software applications.

You are welcome to use this source code, subject to certain restrictions. These restrictions are spelled out in the following copyright notice, which appears at the top of each of my source code files. This notice is similar to the one used by the Berkeley BSD operating-system project. If you have any questions about your reuse of my source code, please contact me through the publisher.

LISTING E.1   Copyright © 1998, Tim Kientzle

```
/*
    Copyright 1998 Tim Kientzle.  All rights reserved.

Redistribution and use in source and binary forms, with or without
modification, are permitted provided that the following conditions are
met:

1. Redistributions of source code must retain the above copyright
   notice, this list of conditions and the following disclaimer.
2. Redistributions in binary form must reproduce the above copyright
   notice, this list of conditions and the following disclaimer in the
   documentation and/or other materials provided with the distribution.
3. All advertising materials mentioning features or use of this software
   must display the following acknowledgment:
       This product includes software developed by Tim Kientzle
       and published in ''The Programmer's Guide to Sound.''
4. Neither the names of Tim Kientzle nor Addison-Wesley
   may be used to endorse or promote products derived from this software
   without specific prior written permission.

THIS SOFTWARE IS PROVIDED ''AS IS'' AND ANY EXPRESS OR IMPLIED
WARRANTIES, INCLUDING, BUT NOT LIMITED TO, THE IMPLIED WARRANTIES OF
MERCHANTABILITY AND FITNESS FOR A PARTICULAR PURPOSE ARE DISCLAIMED.
IN NO EVENT SHALL TIM KIENTZLE OR ADDISON-WESLEY BE LIABLE FOR
ANY DIRECT, INDIRECT, INCIDENTAL, SPECIAL, EXEMPLARY, OR
CONSEQUENTIAL DAMAGES (INCLUDING, BUT NOT LIMITED TO, PROCUREMENT
OF SUBSTITUTE GOODS OR SERVICES; LOSS OF USE, DATA, OR PROFITS; OR
```

```
BUSINESS INTERRUPTION) HOWEVER CAUSED AND ON ANY THEORY OF LIABILITY,
WHETHER IN CONTRACT, STRICT LIABILITY, OR TORT (INCLUDING NEGLIGENCE
OR OTHERWISE) ARISING IN ANY WAY OUT OF THE USE OF THIS SOFTWARE,
EVEN IF ADVISED OF THE POSSIBILITY OF SUCH DAMAGE.
*/
```

Index

Disclaimer

Addison Wesley Longman warrants the enclosed disc to be free of defects in materials and faulty workmanship under normal use for a period of ninety days after purchase. If a defect is discovered in the disc during this warranty period, a replacement disc can be obtained at no charge by sending the defective disc, postage prepaid, with proof of purchase to:

Addison-Wesley Developers Press
Editorial Department
One Jacob Way
Reading, MA 01867

After the ninety-day period, a replacement will be sent upon receipt of the defective disc and a check or money order for $10.00, payable to Addison Wesley Longman, Inc.

Addison Wesley Longman makes no warranty or representation, either express or implied, with respect to this software, its quality, performance, merchantability, or fitness for a particular purpose. In no event will Addison Wesley Longman, its distributors, or dealers be liable for direct, indirect, special, incidental, or consequential damages arising out of the use or inability to use the software. The exclusion of implied warranties is not permitted in some states. Therefore, the above exclusion may not apply to you. This warranty provides you with specific legal rights. There may be other rights that you may have that vary from state to state.

Using the CD-ROM

The CD-ROM contains the full source code from the book, a collection of sample audio files, and a variety of useful tools and information from other sources. The CD-ROM is in a hybrid format that should be readable on any Windows, Mac OS, or UNIX system. For more information about the material on the CD-ROM, please refer to Appendix A, starting on page 401.

Overall Organization

The CD-ROM contains three top-level directories:

Source This directory contains the full source code from the book and project files so you can compile the sample programs in several popular development environments. Before you try to compile the sample code, please refer to page 401 for detailed instructions. If you wish to use the source in your projects, refer to page 423 for details.

Samples A collection of sample audio files for your reference and experimentation.

Contrib Material from other sources. This includes freely available software, shareware, demonstration versions of commercial software, and other useful material. More detailed information begins on page 405. Each directory has a README.TXT file that tells you what is in that directory, any restrictions on your use of those files, and how to contact the original source.

Any updates to the CD-ROM contents will be made available at:
http://www.awl.com/cseng/titles/0-201-41972-6/

Regrettably, CD-ROM production is not perfect. If you believe the CD-ROM bound with this book is defective, the publisher will happily provide a replacement. Please refer to the previous page for details.